Austrian Historical MEMORY & National Identity

Contemporary Austrian Studies

Sponsored by the University of New Orleans and Universität Innsbruck

Publication of this volume has been made possible through a generous grant from the Austrian Ministry of Foreign Affairs and the Austrian Culture Institute in New York. The Bank Gutmann Nfg. AG in Vienna, the University of Innsbruck, and Metropolitan College of the University of New Orleans have also provided financial support.

Articles appearing in this journal are abstracted and indexed in HISTORICAL ABSTRACTS and AMERICA: HISTORY AND LIFE.

CONTEMPORARY
AUSTRIAN STUDIES,
VOLUME FIVE

Austrian Historical MEMORY & National Identity

Günter Bischof & Anton Pelinka
EDITORS

transaction publishers
New Brunswick (U.S.A.) and London (U.K.)

This book is printed on acid-free paper that meets the American National Standard for Permanence of Paper for Printed Library Materials.

Library of Congress Catalog Number: 96-24124
ISBN: 1-56000-902-0
Printed in the United States of America

Library of Congress Cataloging-in-Publication Data

Austrian historical memory and national identity / Günter Bischof, Anton Pelinka, editors.
p. cm. — (Contemporary Austrian studies ; v. 5)
Includes bibliographical references.
ISBN 1-56000-902-0 (alk. paper)
1. Historiography—Austria. 2. National socialism—Psychological aspects. 3. National characteristics, Austrian. 4. Fascism—Austria—Attitudes. 5. Holocaust, Jewish (1939–1945)—Psychological aspects. I. Bischof, Günter, 1953- . II. Pelinka, Anton, 1941- . III. Series.
DB99.2.A829 1996
943.605'22—dc20 96-24124
CIP

Table of Contents

Introduction 1

Topical Essays

Franz Mathis, *1,000 Years of Austria and Austrian Identity: Founding Myths* 20

Gunda Barth-Scalmani, Hermann J.W. Kuprian, Brigitte Mazohl-Wallnig, *National Identity or Regional Identity: Austria Versus Tyrol/Salzburg* 32

Heidemarie Uhl, *The Politics of Memory: Austria's Perception of the Second World War and the National Socialist Period* 64

Anton Pelinka, *Taboos and Self-Deception: The Second Republic's Reconstruction of History* 95

Brigitte Bailer, *They Were All Victims: The Selective Treatment of the Consequences of National Socialism* 103

Robert Edwin Herzstein, *The Present State of the Waldheim Affair: Second Thoughts and New Directions* 116

Wolfram Kaiser, *The Silent Revolution: Austria's Accession to the European Union* 135

Chad Berry, *Public, Private, and Popular: The United States Remembers World War II* 163

Proposals by the Advisory Commission on the Mauthausen Concentration Camp Memorial 183

FORUM: Toward a History of Austrian Intelligence Studies

Timothy Naftali, *Creating the Myth of the Alpenfestung: Allied Intelligence and the Collapse of the Nazi Police-State* 203

Siegfried Beer, *Early CIA Reports on Austria, 1947-1949* 247

Radomír Luža, *Research Note: My Files at the Czech Ministry of the Interior Archives, Prague, May 1995* 289

Research Note

Rüdiger Overmans, *German and Austrian Losses in World War II* 293

Review Essays

Günter Bischof, *Founding Myths and Compartmentalized Past: New Literature on the Construction, Hibernation, and Deconstruction of World War II Memory in Postwar Austria* 302

Günther Kronenbitter, *Austria-Hungary and World War I* 342

Book Reviews

Robert Knight: Gertrude Enderle-Burcel, Rudolph Jeřábek, Leopold Kammerhofer, eds., *Protokolle des Kabinettsrates der Provisorischen Regierung Karl Renner 1945*, vol. 1 357

Dieter Stiefel: Klaus Eisterer, *"Die Schweiz als Partner:" Zum eigenständigen Außenhandel der Bundesländer Vorarlberg und Tirol mit der Eidgenossenschaft 1945-1947* 364

Daniel E. Rogers: Rolf Steininger with Ingrid Böhler, eds., *Der Umgang mit dem Holocaust* 367

Matthew Paul Berg: Franz Olah, *Die Erinnerungen* 374

Andrei S. Markovits: Heinz Fischer, *Die Kreisky-Jahre: 1967-1983* 378

Kurt Richard Luther: Wolfgang C. Müller, Fritz Plasser, Peter A. Ulram, eds., *Wählerverhalten und Parteienwettbewerb. Analysen zur Nationalratswahl 1994* 384

Annual Review

Reinhold Gärtner 390

List of Authors 398

Introduction

"The historian does simply not come in to replenish the gaps of memory. He constantly challenges even those memories that have survived intact."[1]

The identities of national communities are imagined, historical memories are constructed.[2] While scholarship on Austrian identity has flourished, the investigation of Austrian historical memory has had a slow start in Austria.

The literature on Austrian identity is rich. Michael P. Steinberg has recently written a brilliant analysis of the pre-World War II history of the Salzburg Festival. He shows how the festival was a project grounded in the tradition of Austrian Baroque theatricality and was based on the urgent need for an Austrian identity vis-à-vis Germany. The organizers of the Salzburg festival artificially reconstituted an Austrian identity and became the principal spokesmen of its ideology. Mozart's Salzburg began to represent an Austrian counterproject to Wagner's Bayreuth. Delicate and refined Austrian Catholic baroque culture became the counterpoint to materialistic bourgeois Protestant Bayreuth.[3] Austrian identity built on the myth of "Austrians as the *better Germans*" became a focal point in the ideology of the Salzburg Festival.

One of Austria's greatest historians in the twentieth century, Friedrich Heer, also focussed on the culturally formative Baroque period. Shortly before his death he penned a complex portrait of Austria's difficult and often quixotic and paradoxical 1000-year search for an identity at the crossroads of Central Europe. In what amounts to a psychohistory of Austria, Heer avers that in its long struggle for a national identity Austria was unmatched by any other historical entity in Europe in the extent of its deeply rooted identity problems. Heer, the consummate Viennese intellectual, who knew Freud's *oeuvre* so well, in fact argues that throughout the nineteenth and twentieth century Austria lived in a never ending crisis, constantly threatened by a complete loss of identity.[4] In contrast, the émigré historian Felix Kreissler has rather narrowly grounded the origins of postwar Austrian identity in the Austrian resistance against

Hitler and the Nazis.[5] Empirically the soundest scholars on Austrian identity are the Vienna historians Ernst Bruckmüller and Gerald Stourzh. Bruckmüller approaches the Austrian nation from a broad social science perspective, tracing the deep historical and institutional roots of Austrian identity.[6] Gerald Stourzh has published a series of graceful essays, written specifically to refute the German historian Karl Dietrich Erdmann, whose attempts to reintegrate (*Vereinnahmung*) postwar Austrian history into the larger context of German history unleashed a rare Austrian *Historikerstreit*.[7]

Are the Austrians simply *Germans too*, as Erdmann asserted? Most Austrian historians almost violently disagreed. The Erdmann controversy[8] came somewhat as a surprise given the assertion of a firm and self-confident Austrian identity throughout the 1980s, manifested in the opinion polls and by the appearance of a whole slew of historical studies on Austrian identity in the same decade. The defensive reaction of some Austrian intellectuals to the Erdmann thesis may indicate that postwar Austrian identity may be more fragile than the chroniclers of Austrian consciousness had been led to believe by the polls. In their recent studies, Bruckmüller, Stourzh, and Anton Pelinka have tried to update transformations in Austrian identity by analyzing how Austria might be affected by the repercussions of the post-Cold War international arena and the challenges of European integration into the European Union.[9]

In spite of the ideology of the Salzburg Festival and the late attempts by conservative Catholic and communist intellectuals in the 1930s to construct an Austrian identity vis-à-vis Nazi Germany, the First Austrian Republic lacked a firm will to exist as a small state and never marshaled sufficient self-confidence as a nation. Its fateful attraction toward Germany finally ended in the Anschluß of 1938.[10] The *Ostmark*'s and Vienna's degradation in being banished to the provincial periphery of the Third Reich, as well as the experience of the people in the "Danube and Alpine *Gaus*" with Nazi repression of all expressions of Austrian identity, taught the Austrians valuable lessons.[11] There can be no question that the infatuation of numerous Austrian Nazi fanatics and sympathizers was paralleled by an Austrian identity that was grounded in opposition to and disgust with the oppressiveness of Nazi totalitarianism.[12]

The end of World War II was experienced as a complex mix of liberation, defeat, and occupation, and fifty years later the historical memory of the transformation from war to peace is still reflected along these lines. While the founding fathers of the Second Republic created the myth of the blank slate and a new beginning (*Stunde null*) to put National Socialism behind them, the continuities with the First Republic, the Austrofascist corporate state, and National Socialism prevailed. Most of the political system and its culture and institutions—the core constitutional and legal framework of the First Republic—were reinstated and reestablished.[13]

One of the most radical breaks with the past came with the invention of a new Austrian identity during the quadripartite occupation (1945-1955). Austria literally had to "discover herself" (*Selbstfindung*), as Emil Brix has aptly put it.[14] First, the political elites reimagined Austrian identity as radically *anti-German* in order to disconnect Austria from most of her World War II past and distance the new nation and her citizens from any responsibility for Nazi war crimes.[15] The myth of Austrians as *non-Germans* replaced the myth of the better Germans. We only have to recall the radical break Americans made with their British brethren during the American Revolution to understand this aspect of nation building (in the course of this distancing, Americans built on British opposition "country" Whig ideology and constructed a new identity of American exceptionalism).

Austrians' *Verstrickung* in the murderous Nazi regime and the Holocaust was *externalized*, thus shifting this burden onto the (West) Germans (the East Germans blamed the capitalist West Germans as well).[16] Austrians exorcized the calamities and *burdens* of their recent World War II past, heeding the words of the poet Robert Browning's dying Paracelsus:

> I saw no use in the past: only a scene
> Of degradation, ugliness and tears
> The record of disgraces best forgotten
> A sullen page in human chronicles
> Fit to erase.[17]

Second, historians of Austrian national identity have not paid sufficient attention to the importance of historical memory in Austria's postwar national identity. Along with exclusively blaming the Germans for the Nazi war crimes, the Austrian intellectual elites constructed the *founding myth* (some call it the "big lie") of postwar Austria as a nation of victims. In this postwar hyperinflation of "victims," rabid Nazis, sympathizers, bystanders, aryanizers, *Wehrmacht* soldiers, all were generously embraced and many soon received war-related welfare payments (*Opferfürsorge*) from the government. The horrendous suffering of Jews, gypsies, homosexuals, social misfits, forced laborers, even the resistance fighters was willfully purged from public memory and relegated to oblivion. Austrians did not want to be reminded that the option of *not* collaborating with the Nazi regime existed and that brave souls had opted to resist.

Historical memory is the raw material of history. In a volume on historical memory and national identity it needs to be stressed, then, that the political and intellectual elites' construction of the "victim mythology" became a core element of postwar Austrian identity. Individual Austrians reshaped their World War II recollections of themselves as "victims" to fit their present need of forgetting the chamber of horrors that was Nazi Germany. This *shared* Austrian identity of victimhood thus became the collective memory of the war and part of national identity. The highly selective public memories constructed by politicians and publicists resonated with the vast majority of Austrians who increasingly came to recognize their own past in the shared collective memory of Nazi war crimes committed *sans* Austrians. Individual selective memory increasingly struck Austrians as authentic as they gained distance from the war (Waldheim); the retouched public memory provided Austria with a usable past for forty years.[18] The former U.S. ambassador to Great Britain, Raymond Seitz, made a remark that might also apply to Austrians: "Americans are good at scraping the muck of the past from their boots and getting on with the job."[19]

Austria as the *Opfernation* became part and parcel of all World War II commemoration, at least until the 1980s. *Topographical* spaces such as war memorials commemorated the war as a dutiful and heroic struggle for the *Heimat*. *Symbolic* spaces such as emblems and official historical commemorations centered on Austria as victim. In the *functional* spaces of war memoirs soldiers and generals insisted on pure and simple *Pflichterfüllung*, only having done their duty.[20]

The French historian Jacques Le Goff has analyzed the intersection of historical memory and collective identity: "The relationship a nation has with its past, the traumas it has suffered, the idiosyncracies of its historiography, are all crucial parts of its collective identity. It is the duty of both nations and individuals to face their history squarely and without blinkers. Amnesia is tragic and voluntary amnesia is a serious disorder."[21] In other words, nations have a higher moral *duty* to historical truthfulness, not only vis-à-vis the international community but also to prevent identity crises. Friedrich Heer would have agreed.

Third, as all Austrian roots in German history became taboo, Austria's *very own and separate historical past* had to be utilized for identity formation. At this time the inventors of the new Austrian identity grabbed the "Ostarrichi myth" from the dustbin of history and celebrated it in the "950 years of Austria" festivities in 1946.[22] The Austrians utilized the *benefits* of their ancient past by instrumentalizing antiquity, rooting the credentials of the Austrian nation in a remote past. David Lowenthal has analyzed this aspect of historical memory: "Nations and individuals habitually trace back their ancestry, institutions, culture, ideals to validate claims to power, prestige, and property" and, one might add, national identity.[23]

Fourth, one constituent facet of postwar Austrian identity hitherto almost unexplored is Austria's deep-seated anti-communism. Going back to at least World War I, anti-Bolshevism became part of Austrian ideology. Given the deep roots of anti-communism in Austria, anti-Bolshevism as a core aspect of the Nazi ideology made National Socialism attractive to many Austrians not only because it easily dovetailed with their anti-Semitism. When the Nazi regime collapsed, anti-Bolshevism was one strain of the Nazi ideology that in the Cold War era survived untouched, not only in Austria but in other countries as well.[24] The intense anti-communism of people from both Austrian *Lager* like Foreign Minister Karl Gruber or Interior Minister Oskar Helmer in fact was as attractive to the Anglo-American powers, as their anti-German animus was to the French.[25] In fact, the curious combination of reliable Austrian anti-German and anti-communist sentiments[26] was a crucial step toward the Western Allies accepting the mythology of Austria as a victim of National Socialism. Austrian anti-communism did not even have to go through the tergiversations that U.S. anti-communism experienced after 1945. By 1947/48 Americans had completed reshaping their pro-Soviet and anti-Nazi wartime attitudes into the monster of "red fascism," a crucial prerequisite for the U.S. ideology of anti-communism.[27] Austrians had been fierce anti-communists all along and this ideological predisposition smoothed Austria's path toward becoming a "secret ally" of the West by the early 1950s.[28] Austria's reorientation to the West rather than her traditional bridge function to the East became part of her postwar identity.

Fifth, with the reestablishment of Austrian sovereignty based on the international status of permanent *neutrality* in 1955, Austrian identity came to rely on an existence vis-à-vis the rigid division of Cold War Europe into military blocs. In spite of having turned westward, by the 1960s Austria turned back to her traditional "manifest destiny" of providing a bridge between East and West, a meeting ground for and mediator between the superpowers. In the 1980s this took the form of a revival of the *Mitteleuropa* myth by Austrian intellectuals.[29] Austria's unique international status at the faultline of the Cold War in Central Europe—while almost oblivious to the harsh realities of Cold War confrontation and nuclear arms races—along with domestic factors such as growing prosperity, social peace, and stable democratic institutions led to the self-perception that Austria was an "island of the blessed." After 1955 the faith of Austrians in this postwar construct of their "nation" constantly increased, thus strengthening Austrian self-confidence and identity.[30]

Sixth, one more aspect is crucial in understanding postwar Austrian identity, namely the persistence of overbearing *regional and local* identities in Austria. In most instances regional pride has a much longer tradition than "national" identity. This should not come as a surprise given the many territorial transmutations and sudden historical breaks in what constitutes "Austria," from tiny *Ostarrichi* on the Danube in 996, via mighty Habsburg imperial Austria, to the small Republic of Austria.[31] Like the Texans in the United States and the Bavarians in Germany, the Vorarlbergers, Tyrolians, Salzburgers and Carinthians in Western and Southern Austria identify more strongly with their regions than with their respective nations; an obvious element of distance from and resentment against the central capital Vienna is mixed into this. Only the Lower Austrians, Viennese and the Burgenländer—the Eastern Austrian regions from whence the multinational Habsburg Monarchy was governed—feature a stronger sense of Austrian rather than regional identity.[32]

Present day Western historiography is full of urgent pleas for a more *diverse* understanding of national pasts. In the United States this means a rewriting of U.S. history to be more inclusive of the previously ignored such as black slaves or Amerindians and more mindful of the ethnic and social diversity so characteristic of the United States.[33] In Great Britain historians quarrel over how much local Irish or Scottish history should be taught next to "British" national and global history.[34] James Sheehan has suggested for German history what Fritz Fellner has championed for the Austrian lands within the historic "Germany," namely the study of the rich diversity of traditions within the German lands, before Bismark forced unification and his *kleindeutsch* solution on Germany and before nationalist German historians came to see Bismarck's Germany without the Habsburg Monarchy as the culmination of the course of German history.[35]

In a fine recent review article William D. Bowman has suggested treating the rich new historiography on Austrian regions and their particularism, as well as their *reluctant integration* into Austrian national history and historiography, as a new paradigm in approaching Austrian history and identity. Bowman suggests that the suppression of Austrian regionalism may have been necessary after the war to nourish a fragile Austrian identity, but with Austria's integration into the new Europe this diversity within Austria ought to be cherished.[36] It may take historians such as Bowmann and Ritter, without "anti-*Piefke*" chips on their shoulder and with the safe distance of the Atlantic between them and Austria, to remind Austrian historians to be less worried about crude German *Vereinnahmungstendenzen* and be more sensitive to the rich fabric of their regional variety and diversity.

Or does it take historians from Western Austria to rebel against traditional Viennese *Vereinnahmungstendenzen* to define what constitutes Austrian identity? The two lead essays in this volume, written before Bowmann's essay was published, happen to stress the crucial importance of regional identities within Austria and their potential to offer Austria a more permanent solution to her identity problems. In his lead essay to this volume, *Franz Mathis* argues that all the attempts (emanating largely from Vienna) to build an identity on Austria's long and grand imperial history[37] were misconceived and have failed. He then asks poignantly, "How should the constant recollection of the glorious past of a much larger empire help to support the identification with a small republic?" Mathis suggests that the small Republic of Austria ought to take Switzerland as a model and build a viable identity on the richness of her *diverse* regional identities.[38] Mathis, a Vorarlberger himself, and his Tyrolese and Salzburg born University of Innsbruck colleagues *Brigitte Mazohl-Wallnig*, *Hermann Kuprian*, and *Gunda Barth-Scalmani* concur. In fact the trio backs up Mathis' claim with rich empirical research on the strong regional identities of Tyrol and Salzburg, which next to Vorarlberg are the states with the weakest national identity. In the politics of Austrian identity, historians born and socialized in Western Austria primarily challenge Austrian identity politics centralized in Vienna.

Heidemarie Uhl, *Anton Pelinka*, and *Brigitte Bailer* show how much postwar Austrian identity was structured around a highly selective historical memory of World War II. Uhl presents the strange career of the postwar Austrian "victim mythology." In the 1943 Moscow Declaration the Allies conceded Austria the status of "Hitler's first victim." The founding fathers of the Second Republic utilized this Allied statement to free Austria of any responsibility for Nazi war crimes and *externalize* all war related guilt. Austria became a "nation of victims." By 1949 most of the more than half a million Austrian Nazis and sympathizers were reintegrated into the body politic and the dark side of World War II history was purged from private and public memory. The controversy about Kurt Waldheim's World War II record in the 1986 presidential election became the turning point in Austrian World War II historical memory. Waldheim elucidated the paradoxes of naive *Pflichterfüllung* in a murderous regime. After Waldheim a complex picture, more truthful to the past, is emerging and portrays Austrians as *both* victims and perpetrators.

Pelinka analyzes the foreign and domestic political functions of Austria's postwar historical distortions and taboos (Austria's *Lebenslüge*). He argues that the opportunism of the Founding Fathers becomes understandable when viewed from the perspective of those building a political consensus in a fragile democracy by integrating the former Nazis and their families, who constituted 25 percent of the Austrian electorate. In Pelinka's analysis, the taboos, self-deceptions, and selective historical memory served a "protective function" by building a usable past. It allowed for time to heal the wounds of a contentious and violent past. The pleas and critiques of a younger generation of historians, demanding the acknowledgment of complex past, no longer risk tearing the nation apart. Bailer shows how

Austria's founding fathers instrumentalized the *Opferdoktrin* to universalize Austrian victimhood. By 1950 the inflated Austrian catchall notion of "victimhood" came to *include* Austrian Nazis, aryanizers, and soldiers returning late from the war and provided the basis for all war-related welfare payments. Cynical politicians from all political camps, hungry for Nazi voters did everything in their power to *exclude* the true victims of the war (Jews, gypsies, etc.) in order to minimize restitution payments demanded by the occupation powers and Jewish organizations. Bailer's essay on the failure of domestic *Wiedergutmachung* adumbrates one of the darkest, most immoral, and least known chapters of Austrian postwar history.

The centrality of the 1986 "Waldheim affair" as a turning point in postwar Austrian historical memory is not only stressed by Uhl but also in the essay of the distinguished American historian *Robert Herzstein.* Waldheim's wartime biographer[39] has come to interpret his wartime career as an innocuous *Plichterfüller* and his distinguished postwar career built on selective memory and denial, as a quintessentially representative Austrian tale. Based on the "as if" (*als ob*) theory of the Viennese émigré psychoanalyst Helene Deutsch, Herzstein now enriches his earlier work with suggestions for a psychobiographical access to the Waldheims as representative Austrians. Herzstein concludes by citing Vaclav Havel: "Falsifiers of history do not safeguard freedom but imperil it."

The young German historian *Wolfram Kaiser* lends his rich expertise in European integration history for updating Austria's most recent chapter on the road to Europe.[40] With a refreshing and critical eye from his broader perspective of German, British, and Scandinavian integration history, Kaiser traces the Austrian struggle with integration into the institutions in Brussels as well as in the political, social, and economic fallout in Austrian politics since the referendum in June of 1993. He is particularly searing in his critique of Vienna's political elites and their inability to mentally adapt to a large political community. He detects provinciality and even xenophobia in the smug centers of power in Vienna, avers failures in educating the public about the costs and responsibilities of being part of the new Europe, and unmasks the contradictions of trying to salvage Austrian neutrality in a Europe without rigid blocs. According to Kaiser's analysis one may have to add a new isolationist attitude vis-à-vis European integration, a distancing harking back to a Cold War golden age of "the island of the blessed" mentality, to present-day Austrian identity (trans)formations.

In order to allow for a comparative view of national cultures of historical memory, we add *Chad Berry*'s essay on U.S. memory of "the good war." Berry's finely tuned analysis distinguishes between *public*, *private*, and *popular* memories. While pressure from U.S. World War II veterans has forced an uncritically heroic and bland public memory upon Americans (as witnessed in the affair around the Smithsonian's historical exhibit on the dropping of the atomic bomb in the summer of 1995), the private memory of veterans is much more truthful about the horror and senselessness of war. Hollywood's popular memory has to straddle both these public and private memories. Even though the Austrian experience of World War II, ending for many in defeat, was very different from the victorious American "good war" experience, Berry's analytical categories may offer new insights into Austrian historical World War II memory.

The dramatic transformation of the Austrian memory of the war is best exemplified by the report of an international commission on the meaningful construction of an adequate historical memory of Austria's only concentration camp at Mauthausen.[41] We present an English translation of this report since it carefully outlines a model of an open, sophisticated and multi-layered new culture of memory mindful of the complexities of Austria's World War II past. One can only hope that the Austrian government will take the lead in allowing future generations of Austrians to live with a complex past by providing the funds for the many activities suggested in this report. Clearly, such a report could only have been written in post-Waldheim Austria by a younger generation of Austrian historians inspired by Mauthausen survivors and distinguished historians from abroad.

With our FORUM on "intelligence studies" we introduce a vigorous new branch of historical scholarship in the Anglo-American world, which should also have much to offer to Austrian historians. It seems clear that the study of modern great power politics will always be incomplete without a serious investigation of the role played by secret intelligence services. The recent sensation about the CIA admitting to having buried some ninety secret arms caches in the Austrian Alps in the early 1950s for the benefit of a prospective Austrian guerilla force in case of a Soviet invasion should have taught Austrians a lesson. Most of the historical profession appeared as innocent about U.S. Cold War defense plans for Austria as the political class and the public at large were, yet all pleaded ignorance.[42]

With *Timothy Naftali* and *Siegfried Beer* we present two leading younger practitioners of this innovative branch in historical scholarship. Naftali possesses an impressive command of World War II Anglo-American counterintelligence records. This allows him to construct a plausible scenario as to why the British and the Americans came to believe that Hitler was building an "Alpine fortress" (*Alpenfestung*) in the Austrian and Bavarian Alps for the final reckoning with the Allies. By early 1945, the German *Abwehr*, which had been thoroughly penetrated by the Allies, collapsed. In the final weeks the SS's *Reichssicherheitshauptamt* emerged as the principal agency to plan "werewolf" guerilla activities against the Allied occupiers and build a putative *Alpenfestung*. Allied counterintelligence never penetrated RSHA and therefore had to base its analysis on very spotty and unreliable intelligence; consequently it came to vastly exaggerate German preparations for the final struggle. Allied strategy was in part based on such faulty intelligence and the mirage of the *Alpenfestung*.

Austria's foremost practitioner of intelligence history, Beer provides a very useful institutional history of the wartime Office of Strategic Services and the early Central Intelligence Agency and their respective involvement in Austrian affairs. He also attaches four early CIA reports on Austria which are published here for the first time and provide a valuable insight into the kind of analysis U.S. intelligence provided to American policy makers regarding Austria. *Radomir Luza*'s research note provides a fascinating insight into postwar Austria as a haven for Cold War spying. Similar to the many Germans who gained access to the files the East German secret service "Stasi" accumulated on them, Luza has requested and been granted access to Czech intelligence files collected on him while he worked in Vienna during part of the 1960s. Luza's terse report opens up another dark hole of postwar Austrian history, namely what one might modestly call the "collaboration" of numerous Austrians (some with dual loyalties) with foreign intelligence services (incidentally also suggested in Herztein's essay).

One has to remember that in the early Cold War the Vienna of *The Third Man* and Salzburg were situated on top of the Cold War faultlines in Central Europe and constituted valuable "windows" to look behind the iron curtain; they figured among the world's spy capitals. The top U.S. diplomat in Vienna, Coburn Kidd, argued that "the intelligence saturation of Austria is fantastic" and speculated that every fourth inhabitant in the city of Salzburg spied for some domestic or foreign intelligence service. Kidd argued tongue-in-cheek that spying was Austria's "main invisible export," correcting the country's otherwise unfavorable balance of payments. Here is an interesting field of investigation for economic historians: when did tourism replace spying as the main invisible export to balance Austrian budget deficits?[43]

Rüdiger Overmans's research note provides another fascinating glimpse into Austrian World War II history. His recently completed vast statistical analysis of World War II death rates suggests that Austrian soldiers in the German Army died in significantly lower numbers than German soldiers.

Two longer historiographical review essays by *Günther Kronenbitter* on recent literature of Austria-Hungary's role in the origins of World War I and in the war, as well as my own essay on a number of recent studies on Austrian historical memory of World War II, book reviews, and the annual review of Austrian politics complete this volume.

Some of the lead essays in this volume (Mathis, Mazohl-Wallnig et al., Uhl, and Berry) were written and first delivered as part of the annual UNO-Innsbruck symposium "Historical Memory and the Creation of National Identity in a Comparative Perspective: Austria and the United States," which gathered 12/13 June 1995, in Innsbruck, Austria. We regret that Professor Fritz Fellner did not submit his fine lecture on Austrian manifest destiny and memory of the Habsburg Empire for publication in this volume since it created a lacuna for this volume that we could not fill. We would like to thank Professor Jorge Klor de Alva of the University of California at Berkeley, Professor David Blight of Amherst College in Massachusetts, and Dr. Jon Kukla, the Director of the Historic New Orleans collection, for their valuable contributions to the symposium and its discussions and regret that we could not publish their papers in this volume. Professor Franz Mathis deserves our gratitude for his invaluable contribution in conceptualizing and organizing the Innsbruck symposium and his help in raising the funds. We are grateful to the University of Innsbruck and its *Rektor* Professor Hans Moser and the University of New Orleans and its Dean of Metro College Robert Dupont for financially supporting the symposium and thus ultimately making this volume possible.

This volume was again produced in New Orleans. Our production editor Judy Nides and our new copy editor Jennifer Shimek did a fantastic job for a timely and efficient production of this volume. Gerald Steinacher in New Orleans and Ellen Palli in Innsbruck helped with the daily details of shepherding along the manuscripts. Joseph Autin of the UNO Computing and Communications division helped with accessing recalcitrant discs. We are most grateful to Dr. Heidemarie Uhl of Graz for helping us secure the photographs for this volume and Branko Lenart for granting us permission to reproduce some of his fine photographs of Styrian war memorials.[44] Professor David Herrmann of Tulane University graciously agreed very late in the production of this volume to translate the Mauthausen Report for us. We would also like to thank our colleagues at the *Institut für Zeitgeschichte* in Vienna for granting us permission to publish an English translation of this report. Dean Dupont as always was instrumental in keeping our finances straight.

We are most grateful once again to *Sektionschef* Dr. Peter Marboe in the Cultural Section of the Austrian Foreign Ministry and Dr. Wolfgang Waldner, the Director of the Austrian Cultural Institute in New York, for helping us secure crucial financial support from the Austrian government without which *CAS* could not be published. Dr. Anton Fink, a Director of the Bank Gutmann Nfg. AG, was instrumental in getting us financial support from that institution, a role that Professor Mathis played with the University of Innsbruck and *Rektor* Moser.

Last, but not least, we would like to thank a number of anonymous readers for reviewing manuscripts and our advisory board for their ongoing support. We welcome a number of new members to our advisory board and would like to thank those who have completed their term for services beyond the call of duty.

Günter Bischof
New Orleans, April 1996

NOTES

1. Josef Hayim Yerushalami, *Zakhor: Jewish History and Jewish Memory* (Seattle: University of Washington Press, 1982), 94, quoted in David Lowenthal, *The Past is a Foreign Country* (Cambridge: Cambridge University Press, 1985), 210.

2. For an outstanding introduction on the interaction of historical memory and national identity from a broad comparative perspective, see John R. Gillis, ed., *Commemorations: The Politics of National Identity* (Princeton: Princeton University Press, 1994); on nationalism, see Eric J. Hobsbawm, *Nations and Nationalism: Programme, Myth, Reality* (New York: Cambridge University Press, 1990).

3. Michael Steinberg, *The Meaning of the Salzburg Festival: Austria as Theater and Ideology, 1890-1938* (Ithaca, NY: Cornell University Press, 1990).

4. A second unrevised edition has been released in time for Austria's 1996 millennium commemorations, see Friedrich Heer, *Der Kampf um Österreichs Identität* (Vienna: Böhlau, 1996), 10, 17, 86f, 92, 182; for a first massive intellectual biography of Heer, see Evelyn Adunka, *Friedrich Heer: Eine Intellektuelle Biographie* (Innsbruck: Tyrolia, 1995); her final chapter is on *Der Kampf um Österreichs Identität* and its reception, 587-607.

5. Felix Kreissler, *Der Östereicher und seine Nation: Ein Lernprozeß mit Hindernissen* (Vienna: Böhlau, 1984).

6. Ernst Bruckmüller, *Nation Österreich: Sozialhistorische Aspekte ihrer Entwicklung* (Vienna: Böhlau, 1984).

7. Gerald Stourzh's essays were conveniently published in *Vom Reich zur Republik: Studien zum Österreichbewußtsein im 20. Jahrhundert* (Vienna: Edition Atelier, 1990); for a critique of Stourzh's book see Michael P. Steinberg's review in *Contemporary Austrian Studies* 2 (1994): 249-51. Karl Dietrich Erdmann's contested 1985 essay "Drei Staaten - zwei Nationen - ein Volk?" was published along with a second essay that gave the book its title in *Die Spur Österreichs in der deutschen Geschichte* (Zurich: Manesse, 1989).

8. For the interested English-speaking reader the "Erdmann controversy" is conveniently summarized with all the appropriate references by Harry Ritter, "Austria and the Struggle for German Identity," *German Studies Review*, Special Issue on German Identity (Winter 1992): 111-29.

9. Ernst Bruckmüller, *Östrerreichbewußtsein im Wandel: Identität und Selbstverständnis in den 90er Jahren*, in *Schriftenreihe des Zentrums für angewandte Politikforschung*, vol. 4 (Vienna: Signum, 1994); Stourzh, *Vom Reich zur Republik*, 99-113; Anton Pelinka, *Zur Österreichischen Identität: Zwischen deutscher Vereinigung und Mitteleuropa* (Vienna: Ueberreuther, 1990).

10. Gernot Heiss, "Pan-Germans, Better Germans, Austrians: Austrian Historians on National Identity from the First to the Second Republic." *German Studies Review* 16 (1993): 411-33.

11. On the complexity of Austrian feelings during this time, the best work is still Radomir Luza, *Austro-German Relations in the Anschluss Era* (Princeton: Princeton University Press, 1975).

12. For a sketchy yet subtle summary, see Ernst Hanisch, "Der lange Schatten des Staates: Österreichische Gesellschaftsgeschichte im 20. Jahrhundert," in *Österreichische Geschichte*, ed. Herwig Wolfram (Vienna: Ueberreuter, 1994), 380-98.

13. Many of the essays in Wolfgang Mantl, ed., *Politik in Österreich. Die Zweite Republik: Bestand und Wandel* (Vienna: Böhlau, 1992) deal with the questions of change and continuity in and after 1945, as does the essay by Gerhard Botz and Albert Müller, "'1945': 'Stunde Null', Historischer Bruch oder Kontinuität mit der NS-Zeit und der Ersten Republik?", in *Jahrbuch 1995* ed. Dokumentationsarchiv des Österreichischen Widerstandes (Vienna, 1995), 6-27.

14. For an introduction to the pragmatic invention of the Austrian "*Staatsnation*" (reflecting Western European traditions), replacing the ancient "*Kulturnation Österreich*" (reflecting Central European traditions) after World War II, see the tightly argued essay by Emil Brix, "Zur Frage der österreichischen Identität am Beginn der Zweiten Republik," in *Die bevormundete Nation: Österreich und die Allierten, 1945-1949*, ed. Günter Bischof and Josef Leidenfrost (Innsbruck: Haymon, 1988), 93-104.

15. For a brisk recent introduction to postwar Austro-German relations, see Andrei S. Markovits, "Austrian-German Relations in the New Europe: Predicaments of Political and National Identity Formation," *German Studies Review* 19 (February 1996): 91-111; see also Gabriele Holzer, *Verfreundete Nachbarn: Österreich - Deutschland. Ein Verhältnis* (Vienna: Kremayr & Scheriau, 1995).

16. Hermann Weber, "'Weiße Flecken' in der DDR-Geschichtsschreibung," *Aus Politik und Zeitgeschichte* B 11/90 (9 March 1990): 3-15; see also the references in my review essay in this volume.

17. Robert Browning, *Paracelsus*, pt. 5, lines 814-16, quoted in Lowenthal, *The Past Is a Foreign Country*, 64.

18. This paragraph is heavily indebted to David Thelen's outstanding introduction "Memory and American History" in a special feature on U.S. historical memory in the *Journal of American History* 75 (March 1989): 1117-29. On the intimate interaction and constant reinforcement of private and public memory, see my review essay on postwar Austrian historical memory in this volume.

19. Quoted in *The Economist*, 27 May 1995.

20. For a theoretical approach to historical memory see Jacques Le Goff, *Geschichte und Gedächtnis*, trans. Elisabeth Hartfelder (Frankfurt am Main: Campus, 1992); on the memory and denial of National Socialism and the Holocaust, see also *Erinnern oder Verweigern: Das Schwierige Thema Nationalsozialismus*, in *Dachauer Hefte*, vol. 6 (Munich: DTV, 1994).

21. Preface to the German edition (1991), *Geschichte und Gedächtnis*, 7 (my translation).

22. An outstanding contribution on the creation of the Ostarrichi myth as a constituent part of postwar Austrian national identity is Walter Pohl's "Ostarrichi Revisited: The 1946 Anniversary, the Millennium, and the Medieval Roots of Austrian Identity," *Austrian History Yearbook* 27 (1996): 21-39.

23. See Lowenthal's impressively learned analysis of the utilization of the "benefits and burdens of the past" in *The Past Is a Foreign Country*, 35-73, (quote on "antiquity" 52f).

24. Apart from a brief summary of the roots of Austrian anti-communism in Margarete Hannl's essay "Mit den 'Russen' leben: Besatzungszeit im Mühlviertel 1945-1955," *Zeitgeschichte* 16 (February 1989): 147-66, there is no serious investigation of Austrian anti-communism. From the U.S. perspective this may be surprising, given the rich literature on U.S. anti-communism, see Ellen Schrecker, *The Age of McCarthyism: A Brief History with Documents* (Boston: Bedford Books, 1994), and André Kaenel, ed., *Anti-Communism and McCarthyism in the United States (1946-1954): Essays on the Politics and Culture of the Cold War* (Paris: Editions Messene, 1995), including an essay by this author on the politics of anti-communism in the executive branch.

25. Gruber's "gut" anti-communism comes alive in his speeches, see Michael Gehler, ed., *Karl Gruber: Reden und Dokumente 1945-1953* (Vienna: Böhlau, 1994); see also my essay "The Making of a Cold Warrior: Karl Gruber and Austrian Foreign Policy, 1945-1953," *Austrian History Yearbook* 26 (1995): 99-127; on Helmer, see Wilhelm Svoboda, *Die Partei, die Republik und der Mann mit den vielen Gesichtern: Oskar Helmer und Österreich II. Eine Korrektur* (Vienna: Böhlau, 1993); on the importance to the French of postwar Austrian distancing from Germany, see Thomas Angerer, "Besatzung, Entfernung...Integration? Grundlagen der politischen Beziehungen zwischen Frankreich uind Österreich seit 1938/45," in *Frankreich - Österreich: Wechselseitige Wahrnehmung und wechselseitiger Einfluß seit 1918, ed.* Friedrich Koja and Otto Pfersmann (Vienna: Böhlau, 1994), 82-102.

26. An interesting parallel to explore in this adaptation of "enemy images" might be a comparison with the post-World War I U.S. anti-communist "red scare," and the U.S. wartime anti-German hysteria neatly dovetailed into whipping up postwar anti-communist hysteria. On the important topic of *Feindbilder*, see the outstanding collection of essays by Ragnhild Fiebig-von Hase and Ursula Lehmkuhl, eds., *Enemy Images in American History* (Providence, RI: Berghahn Books, forthcoming 1997), in particular Mark Ellis' fine essay on German Americans in World War I.

27. See Thomas G. Paterson and Les K. Adler, "Red Fascism: The American Image of Aggressive Totalitarianism," *American Historical Review* 85 (April 1970): 1046-64, reprinted in Paterson, *Meeting the Communist Threat: Truman to Reagan* (New York: Oxford University Press, 1988), 3-17.

28. Günter Bischof, "Österreich - ein 'geheimer Verbündeter' des Westens?", in *Österreich und die europäische Integration 1945-1993*, ed. Michael Gehler and Rolf Steininger (Vienna: Böhlau, 1993), 425-50, and idem, "'Austria Looks to the West': Kommunistische Putschgefahr, geheime Wiederbewaffnung und Westorientierung am Anfang der fünfziger Jahre," in *Österreich in den Fünfzigern*, Thomas Albrich et al. (Innsbruck: Österreichischer Studien Verlag, 1995), 183-209.

29. See Charles S. Maier, "Whose Mitteleuropa? Central Europe Between Memory and Obsolescence." *Contemporary Austrian Studies*, vol. 1 (New Brunswick: Transaction, 1993), 8-18.

30. Bruckmüller, *Österreichbewußtsein im Wandel*; idem, "Das Österreichbewußtsein," in: *Politik in Österreich*, 261-78; see also the subtle essays by Wolfgang Kos, *Eigenheim Österreich: Zu Politik, Kultur und Alltag nach 1945* (Vienna: Sonderzahl, 1994).

31. Fine analyses of these numerous and intricate transmutations are provided by Erich Zöllner, *Der Österreichsbegriff: Formen und Wandlungen in der Geschichte* (Vienna, 1988), and Richard G. Plaschka, Gerald Stourzh, Jan Paul Niederkorn, eds., *Was heißt Österreich? Inhalt und Umfang des Österreichbegriffs vom 10. Jahrhundert bis heute* (Vienna: Österreichische Akademie der Wissenschaften, 1995).

32. Bruckmüller, *Östereichbewußtsein im Wandel*, 18-25.

33. See for example the thoughtful presidential address to the Organization of American Historians by Joyce Appleby, "Recovering America's Historic Diversity: Beyond Exceptionalism," *Journal of American History* 79 (September 1992): 419-31.

34. Keith Robbins, "National Identity and History: Past, Present and Future," *History* 75 (October 1990): 366-87.

35. Of Fritz Fellner's numerous statements along this line, the most accessible article is "The Problem of the Austrian Nation after 1945," *Journal of Modern History* 60 (June 1988): 264-89; see James J. Sheehan, "What is German History? Reflections on the Role of the Nation in German History and Historiography," *Journal of Modern History* 53 (march 1981): 1-23; and idem *German History, 1770-1866* (Oxford: Oxford University Press, 1990); see also Günter Bischof, "The Historical Roots of a Special Relationship: Austro-German Relations between Hegemony and Equality," in *Unequal Partners: A Comparative Analysis of Relations between Austria and the Federal Republic of Germany and Between Canada and the United States*, ed. Harald von Riekhoff and Hanspeter Neuhold (Boulder: Westview Press, 1993), 57-92.

36. William D. Bowman, "Regional History and Austrian Identity," *Journal of Modern History* 67 (December 1995): 873-97.

37. Fritz Fellner has pointed out more than once that Austria's claiming all of Habsburg history for herself constituted a gross appropriation (*Vereinnahmung*) of Czech, Hungarian, Polish, etc. history that these peoples surely have resented.

38. Gerald Stourzh was the first prominent scholars to suggest the "Swiss model" for Austrian identity formation, see his 1986 essay "Wandlungen des Östereichbewußtseins im 20. Jahrhundert und das Modell der Schweiz," reprinted in *Vom Reich zur Republik*, 71-98. In a similar vein, Anton Pelinka also pushes the "Swiss model" for viable and modern Austrian small-state identity in the post-Cold War world in his chapter "Small Is Beautiful," *zur Österreichischen Identität*, 146-151.

39. Robert Edwin Herzstein, *Waldheim: The Missing Years* (New York: Arbor House/William Morow, 1988); on his valiant but frustrating struggle to have more CIA documents released that might shed light on the U.S. government's postwar treatment of Waldheim with kid gloves, see also his "The Pending Reform of the FOIA: A Researcher's Report," *The Society for Historians of American Foreign Relations Newsletter* 27 (March 1996): 31-42.

40. *Contemporary Austrian Studies* has made the Austrian path towards European integration one of its main foci from the very beginning of its existence, see our first volume *Austria in the New Europe* (New Brunswick: Transaction, 1993).

41. Austria's hesitation in coming to grips with the Mauthausen concentration camp system in her public and private memories is representative of the much larger failure of acknowledging the prominent participation of Austrians in the Holocaust. On this problem see Rolf Steininger and Ingrid Böhler, eds., *Der Umgang mit dem Holocaust: Europe - USA - Israel* (Vienna: Böhlau, 1994), and the review by Daniel Rogers in this volume. On the larger moral and philosophical issues involved, see Omer Bartov's pathbreaking essay "Intellectuals on Auschwitz: Memory, History and Truth," *History & Memory* 5 (Spring/Summer 1993): 87-129.

42. For background see Herbert Lackner, "Kalter Krieg beim Wurstelprater," *profil*, 29 January 1996, 38-42; Günter Bischof, "US-Waffen und Eichhörnchen-Käfig: Österreich als 'geheimer Verbündeter'," *Die Presse*, 24 January 1996, 3, and idem, "Österreichs Scheu vor Machtpolitik," *Die Presse*, 7 February 1996, 2.

43. See the "secret and personal" letter from Coburn Kidd to Francis Williamson, 7 October 1950, Box 7, Lot M-88, Record Group 43, National Archives, Washington, D.C.

44. Branko Lenart initially shot these pictures for his outstanding photo essay in Stefan Riesenfellner and Heidemarie Uhl, *Todeszeichen* (Vienna: Böhlau, 1994), 218-258, a book that I extensively review in this volume.

1,000 Years of Austria and Austrian Identity: Founding Myths

Franz Mathis

The central question of the following contribution runs as follows: Have 1,000 years of Austrian history been a source of Austrian identity or have they been a myth that has done more harm than good to the creation of a solid Austrian identity? I am well aware that such a question—at least to some—may sound somewhat provocative. But before I try to explain what I mean and in order to avoid any misunderstanding from the very beginning, I should like to stress that I am a strong believer in an Austrian identity. My conception of an Austrian identity, however, differs from that of others.

My main argument is that 1,000 years of Austrian history have not only contributed extremely little to creating an Austrian identity, but have even tended to hinder such an identity from being created. Such a statement challenges the notion cherished by so many that Austria's identity is firmly rooted in her long history. Let me examine the first part of the statement which states that Austria's long history has not been able to create a solid Austrian identity.

When the term "Austria" in the form of *Ostarrichi* was used in a document in 996, it referred to a certain area in today's Lower Austria, which the people used to call *Ostarrichi*, a land in the east. At that time this land was ruled by the house of Babenberg.[1] Later on, the name was gradually applied to all the lands that the Babenbergs acquired on both sides of the Danube before the end of their rule in 1246. It was not, however, applied to Styria, which had been added in 1192.[2] The same policy was pursued by the Habsburgs, who finally followed the Babenbergs after 1278. The name of Austria remained restricted to the core territories in today's Lower and Upper Austria,[3] that is, it was not extended over the lands that the Habsburgs acquired during the following centuries; these retained their former names such as Carinthia, Tyrol and—much later—Salzburg. The representatives of the lands—the nobility, the clergy, the citizens, and sometimes even the peasants—felt much more attached to their lands than to the total of the Habsburg territories, and any attempts to have them convene together were to fail.[4] On the other hand, *Österreich*, or Austria, as the name of the original Babenberg territories, did undergo a transformation insofar as it was gradually adopted as the name of the ruling family and was substituted for the old name of Habsburg.[5] Thus, it was finally used to designate both the ruling family and the original territories.

Although, in the sixteenth and seventeenth centuries there were some attempts to extend the name to other parts of the Habsburg lands such as to *Vorderösterreich* in the west, or to *Innerösterreich* in the south, these—in the end—did not prevail. Instead of using the name of Austria for all the Habsburg territories, people—at most—referred to them as Austrian lands, indicating that they belonged to the house of Austria.[6] Even as late as in the nineteenth century—after the formerly Roman Emperor Franz in 1804 had called himself Emperor of Austria and after the Austrian-Hungarian dual monarchy had been established in 1867—there was still no official name of "Austria" for the western half of the empire;[7] instead, it was referred to as "the kingdoms and the lands represented in the imperial council."[8]

Yet, the fact that the name "Austria" was at least used in everyday life might suggest that something like an Austrian identity had been created during all these centuries of common leadership by the house of Austria. A closer look, however, shows that this was only partially the case. If people felt as Austrians, this feeling was almost exclusively directed towards the monarch. It was the monarch that held the highly heterogeneous parts together.[9] A more general feeling of belonging together, of sharing a common spirit of citizenship, of being a national entity like the French, the British or—later on—the Germans and even the Italians, was still lacking. Even the bureaucracy and the army, which have been said to have developed an Austrian identity,[10] felt—at least in my opinion—more attached to the emperor than to the state as such; it was not before the 1880s that they were called *Staatsdiener* instead of *Fürstendiener*, servants of the state instead of servants of the prince.[11] All this was quite different from the Hungarian half of the empire where the Hungarian memory also dated back to the year 1001, when a Hungarian kingdom had been established. In this case, however, from the very beginning the Hungarian identity referred much more to a certain land and its population and much less to a ruling dynasty. On the other hand, in Austria the name was less and less identified with the original territories of today's Lower and Upper Austria, but instead with a group of regions joined together in the course of the centuries and with little more in common than being ruled by the same family. And this, in my view, also explains the different development that Austria and Hungary took after World War I.

Although Hungary, too, lost a great deal of the territories that it had dominated within the dual monarchy, it was much easier for the Hungarians to identify with the new and, at the same time, traditional Hungary, since the core of their land remained more or less untouched by the new borders. The opposite was the case in Austria: the end of the Habsburg empire was not so much seen as a reduction to the core lands or as a breaking away of the periphery from the center, but rather as the collapse of a whole into its parts. The monarchy had ceased to exist; the main figure of identification—the emperor—had resigned. A new Austria had to be built just as a new Czechoslovakia, a new Poland, and a new Yugoslavia were called into being. And just as these other successor states were erected upon certain parts of the former empire, the new Austria was established on the part where the German language was spoken, and consequently it was called *Deutschösterreich*. This again is proof enough that a genuine Austrian identity strong enough to outlive the monarchy had only marginally developed. It was so weak that Austria's new leaders acted in the same way as the Italian Austrians, the Polish Austrians, and the Slovenian Austrians did: they opted for an integration into the larger country of the same language and declared the new state a part of Germany. This, however, was rejected by the victorious Allies in the peace treaty of St. Germain in 1919.[12] The following inter-war period was too short and too turbulent to give rise to a new Austrian identity. Austria somehow got stuck—as Anton Pelinka puts it—half way between a second Bavaria and a second Switzerland.[13]

All this, I think, may amply show that despite almost 1,000 years of "Austrian" history no real and well-founded Austrian identity had been established. Yet today no one will doubt that an Austrian identity does exist, an identity which according to public opinion polls is constantly on the rise.[14]

What is it that meanwhile has created such an identity? It is certainly not Austria's 1,000 year old history, but a history which—as I see it—is much younger. It is the history of the last fifty years and especially that of the first years after World War II.[15]

In 1945, Austria experienced something which seems so vital for the creation of national identity, but which the country had never experienced before:[16] the liberation from a suppressive regime that it had finally learned to hate. The Austria of former centuries had been imposed from above; moreover, any democratic movements that could have been channeled into a wider Austrian identity were suppressed rather than encouraged.[17] Unlike in Germany or Italy, the liberal-democratic movements of the nineteenth century did not coincide with a national Austrian movement, since the term "Austria" had already been occupied by the monarchs, that is, by the opponents of democratization.

But if, after 1945, the opposition against and the liberation from Nazi Germany was at the basis of a genuine and broader Austrian identity, there may be doubts about whether this will be sufficient for the future. This takes me to the second half of my initial argument: that recurrent allusions to Austria's long history, regularly made at the various anniversaries and intended to foster Austrian identity, actually hinder it.[18] Since today's Austria is quite different from the Austria of the Habsburgs, I cannot see how such allusions should contribute more to the creation of an Austrian identity than they did in the more than 900 years before. In addition, I consider them not only futile but even dangerous and counterproductive.

How should the constant recollection of the glorious past of a much larger empire help to support the identification with a small republic? Is one not tempted to feel a kind of minority complex and try to reestablish at least part of the former glory?[19] "The central position in the heart of Europe"—I quote from a book published by the former minister of finance Hannes Androsch in 1988—"provides the country with a geopolitical position and an importance reaching far beyond the possibilities of a small country."[20] Although I would not have any objections against a foreign policy that aims at mingling in world politics, I do suspect, however, that the constant conflict between aspirations and reality will harm rather than support a positive identification with today's Austria.[21] The allusions to Austria's long history make it difficult to identify with a small country, something with which the Swiss, for example, have no problems at all. Is it not characteristic that in Austria the small Switzerland is hardly ever seen as a model?[22] If we favor a strong Austrian identity—and I emphasized at the beginning that I do—we should much rather look for strengths and even weaknesses of today's Austria instead of being carried away by nostalgic dreams.[23]

But how can a historian—you may object—argue along such unhistorical lines, stressing the present instead of the past as should be his business? I do not think that such an attitude must necessarily be unhistorical. Quite to the contrary, when we look at today's Austria as the result of developments that occurred more than 1,000 years ago, we are more historical than if we simply recall and attempt to find pride in deeds and events that were performed or happened in former times. Austria's population, her economy, her society, her culture, and even her landscape are the results of many centuries dating at least as far back as the early Middle Ages. Such a thoroughly historical approach would view Austria from a different angle: not from the center of a dynasty whose Austria contained a different set of regions each time it expanded or reduced the sphere of its rule, but rather from the various parts that form today's Austria no matter when and for how long they were ruled by this dynasty. Today's Austria is not what the Habsburgs made of her regions, but the result of countless developments on a regional and local scale. And it is these results—good as well as bad—that we should identify with when we think of Austria.

With regard to the ethnic structure of Austria's population—to give you only a few examples—Günter Hödl has recently shown how many different origins the Austrians have:[24] they are the descendants of Celtic, Roman, various Germanic, Slavic, and several other peoples that at some time settled in today's Austria; place names, dialects, and folklore are concrete, present-day proofs of this diversity. Economic structures developed as a consequence of regional conditions: early and dense industrialization in Vorarlberg, a longer persistence of agriculture in Burgenland, raw material processing in upper Styria as well as in parts of Lower and Upper Austria, diversified manufacturing, trade, and services in large cities like Vienna and Graz, summer and winter tourism in the mountainous regions of Salzburg, Carinthia, and the Tyrol. Less diversification may be found—and in this case it is the Habsburg rulers who are to blame—in the Austrians' religious creeds, which thanks to the counter-reformation are overwhelmingly Catholic even if they do not live up to it all the time. Regional diversity, however, again characterizes the voting behavior of the people in Austria, which is the result, in part, of historical conditions. In cultural affairs, one may—as an Austrian—identify with the classical and light classical music of Vienna and Salzburg, with the architecture of the large number of medieval castles, churches, and market places in the old towns, with regional and local literature as well as with the manifold forms of popular culture. Even the ways in which Austria's landscape, her mountains and her plains, her rivers and lakes are presented to the eyes of visitors and natives alike, are the results of many centuries of human cultivation.

All these examples—and many more might be cited—may serve to underscore that it is the diversity and not the nonexistent homogeneity of the country and her population that may constitute a lasting Austrian identity, an identity that would draw its elements from all spheres of life and would be wide enough to include everyone and exclude no one.[25] Besides, such an identity would have at least two more advantages.

First, it would no longer be necessary to search for the typical Austrian because there simply is no such specimen. But again, scholars, politicians, and others have repeatedly tried to describe such a typical Austrian by suggesting and even believing that the characteristics of such a typical Austrian may be found in Austria's 1,000 year old history, which is thought to have shaped *the* Austrian.[26] In doing this, they have even distorted and misinterpreted historical facts. In his already mentioned booklet about Austrian identity, Androsch writes

> that the origins of Austrian identity are deeply rooted in the about 1,000 year old history of that conglomerate of lands grown together through conquest, marriage, treaties and hereditary divisions, a state which—often as a reaction to threats from outside—had become a unity the core of which is the republic of today.[27]

The very opposite was the case, one is tempted to say. The same also applies to another of his statements that "the contact, although hostile, with the highly developed culture of the East has no doubt left its traces in the Austrian identity, as well as the Thirty Years War and the conflicts with France, Italy and Prussia."[28]

Like the constant references to Austria's long history, the attempts to define the typical Austrian have had at least two negative consequences. First, they have preoccupied our minds to the extent that we have too little time for reflecting about other, more reasonable and more promising possibilities for defining Austrian identity. Second, since such attempts are bound to fail and are always open to debate, they have aroused and kept alive the discussion about the existence of such an identity and, by doing this, have been as counterproductive as the recollection of Austria's "glorious" past.

The second advantage of stressing diversity instead of nonexistent homogeneity is that it allows us to refrain from a false and unjustified feeling of being different from the people in other countries. As soon as one tries to describe a group of people as a homogeneous entity, there is the danger and the temptation of drawing some kind of dividing line between oneself and others, which is the first step towards feeling superior to others.[29] Especially in the decades after World War I, attempts have been made to distinguish the "typical" Austrian from the "typical" German, depicting him as the more sympathetic or better type of German speaker. He is less straightforward and not so rough, more tolerant, more cosmopolitan, and more European than the German, having preserved his humane heart and soul—to quote from Anton Wildgans' "Rede über Österreich."[30] Thus, it is only logical to call the brutal counter-reformation of the sixteenth and seventeenth centuries "a very un-Austrian solution."[31] Accepting diversity, however, includes the awareness that similar characteristics, good as well as bad, may be found in other countries, too, so that there is no reason for feeling superior or inferior towards others.

The same is true for the term "national," which—as you may have noticed—I have stubbornly tried to avoid. Although I am well aware of the different connotations that the term may have in western as opposed to central and eastern European countries, in our understanding it again implies a kind of cultural homogeneity, which in most countries simply does not exist.[32] If the term "national" were understood in the western European sense as implying a "political nation" and referring exclusively to the population living within an area defined by borders and not by a common language, culture, or other such characteristics, I would not object to it at all.[33] But since in the Austrian debate "nation" has very often been conceived of as "cultural nation," the existence of an Austrian nation has repeatedly been a bone of contention, questioning rather than strengthening Austria's identity. This is why I suggest we not use the term "national" in this context.[34]

After presenting what I have to offer with regard to 1,000 years of "Austria" and the creation of an Austrian identity, be it national or not, I should like to add that I am rather confident about the chances of maintaining and even strengthening the kind of identity that I have suggested so far. For if we look at the so-called opinion leaders, that is, the newspapers as well as the electronic mass media, we will find that at least after World War II—consciously or unconsciously—they have contributed a great deal to creating and promoting an Austrian identity. It is not so much the editorials dealing with the question of national identity that I am alluding to,[35] but the indirect impact they have by using Austria as a frame for their coverage reporting about Austrian politics, Austrian culture, Austrian economy, Austrian society, Austrian sports, and so on.[36] It is true that similar tendencies may be observed on a regional level, but there seems to be a healthy balance between regional and statewide coverage, with the consequence that, for example, outstanding personalities are claimed as Tyrolians or Styrians by regional media and, at the same time, as Austrians by the state-wide newspapers, radio, and television. Thus, it has become natural to have a regional and a local as well as an Austrian identity. And since such a "natural" Austrianism—as William Bluhm calls it in his "Building an Austrian Nation"[37]—has almost automatically developed over these last five decades, I would suggest that we should not hinder its further growth by referring too often and too much to Austria's 1,000 years of history, which for such a long time have failed to create a truly Austrian identity.

NOTES

1. Erich Zöllner, *Der Österreichbegriff: Formen und Wandlungen in der Geschichte* (Vienna: Geschichte und Politik, 1988), 9f; Ernst Bruckmüller, "Millennium!—Millennium? Das Ostarrichi-Anniversarium und die österreichische Länderausstellung 1996," *Österreich in Geschichte und Literatur* 39 (1995): 142ff.

2. Zöllner, *Österreichbegriff*, 15.

3. Reinhard Rudolf Heinisch, "Patriotismus und Nationalismus in den österreichischen Ländern im konfessionellen Zeitalter und im Hochbarock (1521-1713)," in *Volk, Land und Staat: Landesbewußtsein, Staatsidee und nationale Fragen in der Geschichte Österreichs* (Schriften des Instituts für

Österreichkunde 43), ed. Erich Zöllner (Vienna: Österreichischer Bundesverlag, 1984), 38f.

4. Ibid., 24f.

5. Zöllner, *Österreichbegriff*, 35ff.

6. Erich Zöllner, "Österreichbegriff und Österreichbewußtsein im Mittelalter," in *Volk, Land und Staat*, 12; Heinisch, "Patriotismus und Nationalismus," 31.

7. Zöllner, *Österreichbegriff*, 58ff.

8. Heinisch, "Patriotismus und Nationalismus," 31. It was not before 1915 that in an imperial decree the two parts of the monarchy were officially called "States of Austria and Hungary." Ernst Hoor, "Wandlungen der österreichischen Staatsidee: Vom Heiligen Römischen Reich zur Österreichischen Nation," in *Österreich. Von der Staatsidee zum Nationalbewußtsein: Studien und Ansprachen mit einem Bildteil zur Geschichte Österreichs*, ed. Georg Wagner (Vienna: Österreichische Staatsdruckerei, 1982), 443.

9. Manfried Rauchensteiner, "Österreichbewußtsein und österreichische Staatsidee im Zeitalter des aufgeklärten Absolutismus und im Vormärz," in *Volk, Land und Staat*, 45, 52.

10. Heinisch, "Patriotismus und Nationalismus," 28, 41. Cf. Ernst Bruckmüller, *Nation Österreich. Sozialhistorische Aspekte ihrer Entwicklung* (Vienna: Böhlau, 1984), 66f.

11. Waltraud Heindl, "Die österreichische Bürokratie. Zwischen deutscher Vorherrschaft und österreichischer Staatsidee (Vormärz und Neoabsolutismus)," in *Österreich und die deutsche Frage im 19. und 20. Jahrhundert: Probleme der politisch-staatlichen und soziokulturellen Differenzierung im deutschen Mitteleuropa (Wiener Beiträge zur Geschichte der Neuzeit 9)*, ed. Heinrich Lutz and Helmut Rumpler (Vienna: Geschichte und Politik, 1982), 81.

12. Gerald Stourzh, *Vom Reich zur Republik: Studien zum Österreichbewußtsein im 20. Jahrhundert* (Vienna: Wiener Journal Zeitschriftenverlag, 1990), 31ff.

13. Anton Pelinka, *Zur österreichischen Identität. Zwischen deutscher Vereinigung und Mitteleuropa* (Vienna: Ueberreuter, 1990), 15, 19.

14. Anton Staudinger, "Die nationale Frage im Österreich der Ersten und Zweiten Republik," in *Volk, Land und Staat*, 177; Georg Wagner, "Von der Staatsidee zum Nationalbewußtsein," in *Österreich: Von der Staatsidee zum*

Nationalbewußtsein, 124ff; Peter Gerlich, "Nationalbewußtsein und nationale Identität in Österreich: Ein Beitrag zur politischen Kultur des Parteiensystems," in *Das österreichische Parteiensystem (Studien zur Politik und Verwaltung 22)*, ed. Anton Pelinka and Fritz Plasser (Vienna: Böhlau, 1988), 251ff; Ernst Bruckmüller, *Österreichbewußtsein im Wandel: Identität und Selbstverständnis in den 90er Jahren* (Vienna: Signum, 1994); Stourzh, *Reich*, 100ff.

15. Felix Kreissler, *Der Österreicher und seine Nation: Ein Lernprozeß mit Hindernissen* (Vienna: Böhlau, 1984); cf. Staudinger, "Nationale Frage," 177, Stourzh, *Reich*, 49ff., and Bruckmüller, "Millennium," 137ff.

16. Pelinka, *Identität*, 24. He rightly stresses that unlike other countries the Austrian democracy was not the result of a revolutionary process from the inside but the result of outside pressure.

17. Rauchensteiner, "Österreichbewußtsein," 52; William T. Bluhm, *Building an Austrian Nation: The Political Integration of a Western State* (New Haven: Yale University Press, 1973), 14ff.

18. See also Fritz Fellner, "Das Problem der österreichischen Nation nach 1945," in *Die Rolle der Nation in der deutschen Geschichte und Gegenwart (Einzelveröffentlichungen der Historischen Kommission zu Berlin 50)*, ed. Otto Büsch and James J. Sheehan (Berlin: Colloquium, 1985), 198f.

19. See Pelinka, *Identität*, 30.

20. Hannes Androsch, *Auf der Suche nach Identität. Österreich, Vergangenheit, Gegenwart und Zukunft. Eine Synthese der Widersprüche* (Vienna: Christian Brandstätter, 1988), 19.

21. Stourzh, *Reich*, 26f.

22. Pelinka, *Identität*, 148. For exceptions see Stourzh, *Reich*, 72ff., 86ff.

23. Pelinka, *Identität*.

24. Günther Hödl, "Von der Vielfalt der Geschichte Österreichs," in *Kärntner Jahrbuch für Politik 1994* (Klagenfurt: Kärntner Druck- und Verlagsgesellschaft, 1994), 65-83.

25. Kreissler, *Der Österreicher*, 542.

26. A typical and very recent example of such a point of view may be seen in Androsch, *Identität.* Cf. also Anton Wildgans, *Rede über Österreich* (Vienna: F. Speidel'sche Verlagsbuchhandlung, 1947), 20ff, where he says that "*im Laufe der Jahrhunderte sich ein Typus herausbildete, den ich am liebsten bezeichnen möchte als den österreichischen Menschen.*" Wildgans then goes on to describe the typical Austrian, who as a consequence of having lived together with other nationalities is supposed to have become "*Völkerkenner, Menschenkenner, Seelenkenner, mit einem Wort: Psychologe,*" although it is well known that it was the very lack of good cooperation between the nations within the Habsburg monarchy that finally made it collapse.

27. "*daß auch die Ursprünge der österreichischen Identität tief verwurzelt in der rund tausendjährigen Geschichte jenes durch Eroberung, Heirats- und Vertragspolitik sowie Erbteilung zusammengewachsenen Länderkonglomerates liegen, in jenem vielfach als Reaktion auf die Bedrohung von außen erst zu einer Einheit zusammengewachsenen Staatsgebiet, dessen Kern die heutige Republik Österreich darstellt.*" Androsch, *Identität*, 14.

28. "*der, wenn auch kriegerische Kontakt mit der hochentwickelten Kultur des Orients zweifellos in der österreichischen Identität seine Spuren hinterließ ebenso wie der Dreißigjährige Krieg und die Auseinandersetzungen mit Frankreich, Italien und Preußen.*" Ibid., 19.

29. To see how absurd such attempts may become, see Wildgans, *Rede über Österreich*, 25, when he maintains that the Austrian has a "*besondere Fähigkeit zum Dienen an einer Idee,*" since the monarchy had been an idea rather than a real fatherland for all.

30. Ibid., 26f; Pelinka, *Identität*, 127; Zöllner, *Österreichbegriff*, 88; Staudinger, "Nationale Frage," 174; cf. Fritz Fellner, "Die Historiographie zur österreichisch-deutschen Problematik als Spiegel der nationalpolitischen Diskussion," in *Österreich und die deutsche Frage im 19. und 20. Jahrhundert*, 48ff.

31. Androsch, *Identität*, 22.

32. Gerlich, "Nationalbewußtsein," 237.

33. Stourzh, *Reich*, 21, and Karl Dietrich Erdmann, "Drei Staaten—zwei Nationen—ein Volk. Überlegungen zu einer deutschen Geschichte seit der Teilung," *Geschichte in Wissenschaft und Unterricht* 36 (Oktober 1985): 677. Erdmann also distinguishes between *Staatsnation* and *Kulturnation.*

34. Bluhm, *Austrian Nation*, 8ff ; Fellner, "Problem," 196ff; Günther Berka, *Gibt es eine österreichische Nation?* (Vienna: Österreichische Landsmannschaft, 1961).

35. Bluhm, *Austrian Nation*, 158 ff.

36. Gerlich, "Nationalbewußtsein," 244f.

37. Bluhm, *Austrian Nation*, 207, 240.

National Identity or Regional Identity: Austria Versus Tyrol/Salzburg

Gunda Barth-Scalmani
Hermann J.W. Kuprian
Brigitte Mazohl-Wallnig

Introduction
(Mazohl-Wallnig)

It is no coincidence that the topic of "National Identity or Regional Identity" is presented by three speakers instead of one. There is indeed an important reason for doing so. Regional identity in general can only be adequately considered within the framework of a state infrastructure which comprises a plurality of regions. In the case of Austria this pluralistic approach is especially evident. When considering a plurality of regional identities in juxtaposition to a singular national Austrian identity it is necessary to move from merely theoretical to concrete methods. Representing this diversity of regional identities in Austria, we have chosen to appear as a trio instead of offering individual solo performances.

In our introductory comments we will deal with two general considerations concerning the topic of regional and national identity in the context of history and historiography. Offering this perspective from Innsbruck we will then present more tangible evidence using the example of Tyrol as an Austrian core territory which can look back upon a tradition of over 600 years of membership within Austria. The question of regional as opposed to national identity takes a completely different character when dealing with an Austrian region whose short period of membership began as late as the beginning of the nineteenth century. Finally, using Salzburg province as an example, we will demonstrate the distinct differences of the identity of this new region, in comparison with the core region Tyrol.

It could be a great research assignment to expand exemplary studies on identity development to neighboring non-German regions outside the borders of modern Austria. This kind of survey cannot be presented in this paper, but these cursory considerations make it evident that especially in the case of Austria, a clear separation of regional and national identity development is indeed questionable.

Was it regional or national consciousness that led Bohemia, or should we say the Czechs, Hungary, or should we say the Hungarians, Trentino, or should we say the Italians, to demand secession from the Austrian Empire (*Österreichischer Gesamtstaat*), a state which was unable to awaken feelings of a distinct Austrian identity? Prejudiced by the nationalist traditions of nineteenth century historiography, we have generally lent credence to nationally oriented historical explanations, thereby overlooking the fact that in many cases pre-modern structures remained active behind and under the surface of modern national identity. This feeling of identity often grew within the confines of traditional or historical rights, which were not yet overlapped by the more recent dynamics of ethnic and national identity developments.

The concept of the "regional" can be of great value in tracing these older historical structures. Today the concept and term "region" has regained significance. The vision of a future Europe, whose traditional nation-state borders have become obsolete has permitted the rediscovery of the historical traditions of regions transcending current nation-state borders. The "*Europa Region Tirol*" (European region of Tyrol), for example, was recently introduced as a model of transnational cooperation. "Regions" as a concept has also gained new relevance in scholarly historiographic debate mainly because this term implies reflection about the prerequisites of defining regional development within a given geographical area. This sets it apart from traditional *Landesgeschichte* which restricted itself to merely describing local historical situations. Current research on regional history has set itself the goal of "localizing and interpreting its own sphere of research where certain political prerequisites, social cultural factors and historical experiences create a social internal sphere within a territorial foundation."[1] In summary this leads us to see the drawing of political borders as arbitrary and to search out common denominators beyond the confines of such demarcations. A concept of the "region" thus understood supplies us with a useful heuristic instrument for future social historical comparative research.

In addition to the above mentioned considerations, our deliberations will be based primarily on the regional concept of historical rights as opposed to subsequent nation-state interpretations. We will deal with the following questions: By what means have regional identities based on historical rights survived, or have they originated within the framework of a larger Austrian national state? Were said regional identities congruent or incongruent with national identities? What role did historiography play within this set of variables?

Considering the interdependency of actual historical developments and historiographic discourse, on the one hand, and the function that history as a discipline plays in creating identities, on the other, it is important, when studying Austria, to observe the following point. In Austria, state formation and accompanying historical writing lacked any semblance of national coherence, national in this case understood in the *ethnic* sense of the term. At the same time, when Prussia and Italy were experiencing the professionalization of historiography based on and supportive of the creation of national unification, Austria's national historiography was national merely in the western sense of the word, in the sense of the *Gesamtstaat*, when all countries under Habsburg rule were united in 1804 by the creation of the *Kaisertum Österreich*.

Fifty years after the founding of the Austrian state, the *Institut für österreichische Geschichtsforschung* was founded in 1854 for the specific purpose of supplying this young political entity with the history of several hundred years, a history on which the modern Austrian state could base its historical legitimacy and future identity.[2] This relatively new Austrian state lacked those traditional and long lasting qualities that its politicians and historians of the second half of the nineteenth century tried to ascribe to it. After all, it had been institutionalized just fifty years previous in 1804 through the one-sided imperial decree of the then Emperor of the Holy Roman Empire, the Habsburg Francis II. Francis II then tried to turn his feudal mandate of rule into a sovereign state in the modern sense of the word.

About one hundred years earlier in 1713 a similar attempt to weld the areas of Habsburg rule into one indivisible unit had required the approval of the estates of the respective lands and regions (*Stände*). But the entity that was declared indivisible by the Pragmatic Sanction of

1713 was indeed far removed from an integrated nation-state in the modern sense of the word. This "monarchistic union of estates"[3] retained its character of regional plurality up to the end of the eighteenth century. This plurality is apparent also in the diverse legal qualities of the respective provincial rulers, termed *Landesfürsten.* In the eighteenth century a hereditary Austrian crown or Austrian kingdom had not yet been established. This situation was similar to that of the Bohemian and Hungarian crown which the Habsburgs had arrogated in the seventeenth century against the bitter opposition of the respective estates.[4] It should be noted that Charles V had already entertained visions of establishing a hereditary kingdom in Austria, and he was aware of the fact that monarchist absolutism can be enforced only on the basis of inheritance but not on elective procedure (*Erbmonarchie contra Wahlmonarchie*).

Austria therefore was and is not only difficult to define as an object of historical research because of its territorial plurality (around the beginning of the eighteenth century the Habsburg monarchy stretched from the Netherlands to southern Italy), but above all because of the legal plurality of its individual parts. Austria was, according to the public law sense of the word, *inexistent de jure* until 1804.

The real and essential common legal bracket which encompassed the various domains of Habsburg rule was indeed the Holy Roman Empire, an Empire which existed up to 1806. This Holy Roman Empire was in the hands of the Habsburgs whose nearly uninterrupted rule began in the second half of the fifteenth century.[5] The Habsburgs, like the other powerful territorial rulers within the Empire, did not refrain from hollowing the feudal legal basis of the Empire through well-directed attempts to transform their own inherited lands into modern territorial state structures.

Due to their double function the Habsburgs tried to reconcile two contradictory positions: to protect the federal and regional aspects of imperial plurality and to set up a centralist unified state. This ambivalent situation was made even more complicated by the fact that the kingdom of Bohemia was part of the Holy Roman Empire whereas the kingdom of Hungary was not.

The consequences of this concrete historical situation can be clearly traced in the Austrian historiography. Because of the paralyzing coexistence of the Empire and the inherited Austrian lands under Habsburg rule, neither the one nor the other could develop into a modern nation-state, and it is not a coincidence that the Holy Roman Empire broke up in 1806 immediately after the founding of the Austrian Empire in 1804. Analogous to this political coexistence one can discover the lack of an *imperial* as well as a specifically *Austrian* state historiography. Instead we find a distinct tendency to accentuate the regional history of the estates, that is, the history of the former lands on the one hand and the history of the ruling house as a dynasty on the other.[6] This historiographic development also facilitated the formation of a number of regional identities and prevented the emergence of a specific Austrian consciousness held together by the bracket of a nation-state. The long tradition of separateness enjoyed by the different *Länder* produced their own historiographic tradition and their own identity; the lack of state structure at the imperial level prohibited the institutionalization of corresponding imperial historiography and identity.[7]

In the short period of approximately one hundred years in which an Austrian *Kaisertum* existed on a political and legal claim to be a unified Austrian state, an Austrian national identity could not develop because the centrifugal influences of the respective national, that is, regional, traditions were stronger. Because of this situation neither the Holy Roman Empire nor Austria was able to generate a process of historiography which would have been able to accompany and support the creation of a nation-state as was the case in Italy. The Austrian state saw itself confronted instead by a political as well as a historiographic process of establishing national identities in the respective heterogeneous parts. This happened at the very moment when the Austrian *Gesamtstaat* tried to legitimize its own historical traditions. Ironically, the very longevity of the historical and legal independence of its parts proved a prerequisite to the regional, and thereby in many cases the national, collective consciousness of the ethnic parts of Habsburg Austria. This linking of historical rights to national identification began in the nineteenth century and can be well demonstrated in the case of Bohemia. Palackys history of Bohemia, for example, was commissioned by the Bohemian estates in the 1820s and only later in the second half on the nineteenth century was it reinterpreted as a national history of Bohemia. Neither the Holy Roman Empire nor Austria were able—for historical as well as historiographic reasons—to generate a collective identity based on a nation state concept. Therefore regional identities were able to offer a much more durable base structure for national identity within the framework of the Austro-Hungarian monarchy.

For the Germans in Austria this interlinking of *Reichsgeschichte*, that is, history of the Holy Roman Empire and Austrian history, had a distinct effect after the break-up of the Habsburg Empire. The identification with a *Reichsgeschichte*, that is, imperial history, turned into an ethnically defined German national identity. This inheritance effects even the present. This identification can neither live up to the historical *diversity* nor the *common* history of both, the German Reich and the *Österreich*. It is therefore understandable why Austria today is continuously confronted with the topic of its identity; why the question of a specific Austrian as opposed to a German identity leads to heated political and historiographic debate; why professors of Austrian history seem to be forced to continuously define the dimensions and legal definitions of their research field.[8]

We hope it has become clear why even within the limits of present-day Austria regional particularities appear more important than in many other countries, and why until today an Austrian from Tyrol is first and foremost a Tyrolean, and why an Austrian from Salzburg for the Tyrolean is almost as foreign as a Bavarian.

The Example of Tyrol

(Kuprian*)

Considering from a historical perspective the development of regional identities using the example of Tyrol, two quotations seem to capture the essential characteristics of the position. The first quotation reads,

> Tyrol's intellectual, social and political foundations are: Loyalty to God and to the heritage of her fathers, the intellectual and cultural Unity of the Land of Tyrol, the freedom and dignity of the individual, the orderly family unit as the basis of people and state...to uphold and protect these fundamentals is the supreme duty of the legislature and executive of the Land.[9]

* I would like to thank Mrs. Howard and Gisela Chase (Cobham, Surrey) for translating my part of this essay.

But although this seems to be a categorical statement of eighteenth or nineteenth century values, it does not originate from a *Landesordnung* regulation of that time. It is in fact the preamble to the 1959 constitution of Tyrol which is still valid today. The Tyrolean *Landtag* (diet) adopted this on the occasion of the 150th anniversary of the events of 1809.[10]

Just a few years earlier in 1953, this same regional government had only with great difficulty reached an agreement to do away with the passage, adopted from the constitution of 1921, referring to the *provisional* incorporation of Tyrol in the democratic Republic of Austria. Up to this moment, Tyrol's claim for substantive constitutional sovereignty was seen to be the decisive and historically based character of its political self-understanding. This brings us to the second question. In the words of the 1921 Constitution of the Land of Tyrol, "Tyrol is an independent, autonomous sovereign land which *presently* constitutes a part of the democratic Republic of Austria. As an independent land it exercises all sovereign rights which have not been or will not be specifically assigned to the state."[11]

In those two quotations we can find a number of features and socio-cultural factors, which have in the past and still do characterize both the official *Landesbewußtsein* (regional consciousness) as well as Tyrol's relationship with Austria.[12] It is productive at this stage to look at the collective concepts embodied in this term such as loyalty, God, unity, and freedom, in an attempt to briefly demonstrate a few aspects of the historical development of the strained relationship between regional and national state identity using the example of Tyrol.

Loyalty to God, Emperor, and fatherland—but also the will to defend this unity and freedom of the land—are essential factors of a clichéd evaluation which has and continues to be seen both internally and from the outside, as fundamental to the Tyrolean identity. However, on closer consideration these turn out to be not so much old, traditional values as ideas that emerged during the last century in the course of national discussions on a political and cultural level within the Habsburg monarchy.

Prior to this, Tyrol's union with the Habsburg Dynasty as the sovereign authority of the land—which in 1363 resulted from the renunciation by the then *Landesfürstin* (Duchess) Margarethe Maultasch of her rights in favor of her relations, the Dukes Rudolf, Albrecht, and Leopold[13]—has not always been free from conflict, although the relationship was founded on mutual demands of loyalty between the *Stände* (estates) and the *Landesherrn* (sovereign). In the first instance, however, this historical process was only about the securing or extension of privileges enjoyed by the nobility vis-à-vis the sovereign. To a lesser extent this was also a conscious attempt to form a supraregional state consciousness, which would encourage a territorial feeling of belonging to the Reich or to the Habsburg *Österreichischen Erbländern* to the East.[14]

It is the geopolitical location of the Alpine area which in the Middle Ages and thereafter has determined the economic, cultural, and therefore also the political north-south orientation of the Alpine region between Bavaria and the upper Italian area. Apart from that, the territorial process of unification of the land in this period did not come about in a uniform manner. Furthermore, any identity-promoting effect was, on the whole, restricted—if at all—to the elite of the governing aristocracy and also to the common religion. This feeling of identity seemed to penetrate into the consciousness of the greater parts of the population only in instances when a "threat to the living space" by military intervention from the outside appeared imminent. (Key events here are the Thirty-Year War, the Austrian War of Succession etc.)[15] In contrast to later periods, the ethnic-language feeling of belonging to the German or Italian "nation" did not play an important role.

All these statements and conclusions, however, rest largely on the current state of research into the history of our land which until now has been based on the hypothesis that the union with the Habsburg Dynasty since 1363 helped to accelerate the political and judicial emergence of a Tyrolean regional identity in the Maximilian epoch at the beginning of the sixteenth century. We still require, however, an analysis of those philosophical and cultural factors of identity which may have played a role in the lower, collective demographic stratum. Such an analysis poses a huge problem due to a lack of sources, but it is based on the admittedly compelling logic that such a regional identity could only have developed with the aid of permanent confrontation over established political privileges between the *Landesfürsten* (sovereigns) and the *herrschenden Adel* (ruling aristocracy).

A new dimension to the question of regional identity emerged—not only for the Tyrol of Habsburg times—at the beginning of the sixteenth century, with the first assembly in 1518 of the *Stände* (estates) of all the Habsburg regions in Innsbruck under the chair of Emperor

Maximilian I. It was then that initial tendencies towards the emergence of a dynastic *Gesamtstaat* (nation) became identifiable. Even if no predominantly centralized administrative institutions had been formed, Tyrol appeared to become for some time the center of the Reich (empire).

Very soon, however, a new focal point emerged as a result of the simultaneous enlargement of Habsburg rule eastwards into Bohemia and Hungary, a development that was once again to push the land of Tyrol towards the outer edge of political interest. Regional identity was consequently allowed to develop without a break into the middle of the seventeenth century under its own dynastic branch of the House of Austria, until the line of Tyrol died out in 1665, after which a step-by-step centralization of governmental structure based in Vienna occurred.[16]

Entirely in line with the values of the age of *aufgeklärter Absolutismus* (enlightened absolutism), it was Maria Theresia who attempted to signal the integration of Tyrol into the *Gesamtstaat* by subordinating Tyrol's regional administration directly to the central authorities in Vienna, and by creating a common system of criminal law. Her son Joseph II continued this strict corporate policy which evoked a strong reaction from the Tyroleans, with protest no longer concentrated only in the ruling aristocratic elite. Self-consciousness had in the meantime found a much wider basis.[17]

Furthermore, the reference to the special historical position of the land of Tyrol had in that context reached an even greater importance, as interference in daily events became more extensive. For the first time it became evident that a regional feeling of identity could be used visibly and successfully against *zentralstaatliche* (corporate) endeavors. Kaiser Joseph's heirs were forced to repeal a number of unpopular administrative reforms. Furthermore, his heirs had to acknowledge that the successful setting up of the desired nation-state was only going to be possible by taking into consideration regional identities. Tyrol still looked upon itself as an independent land or region with her own constitution, her own legal system, and a sovereign who, by accident, also ruled over other *Länder*.

A new kind of understanding and evaluation of the different regions and *Länder* of the Habsburg monarchy evolved in the wake of the Napoleonic wars. This is the period around the year 1809 of the so-called *Heldenzeitalter* (era of national heroes),[18] about whom Madame de Stael said that Tyrol had developed a feeling of special consciousness evolving from the seclusion of the mountains and the obligation of self-defense.[19]

As mentioned earlier, it was Kaiser Franz II (First) who in 1804 proclaimed a *Kaisertum Österreich* (Austrian Empire) in an eventually unsuccessful attempt to create a modern nation-state (along the lines of the French model) from the cultural, social, religious, economic, and national variety of the Habsburg dominions.[20] Thus, the Tyroleans—and this term also encompasses the Italian and Ladinic population of the then southerly part of the country called the Trentino—in their resistance to French and Bavarian occupation, did not aim at restoration under *Austrian* rule but under the reign of the Emperor and with the preservation of their long-established privileges.[21]

As it turned out, they were bitterly disappointed as many of the modern and much-hated administrative reforms enacted during the Bavarian occupation were not revoked under the *Neuordnung Europas* (new structure of Europe)[22] that emerged at the Congress of Vienna in 1815. Tyrol, like every other region, was made part of the new Austria without any special administrative rights.[23]

This "epoch of heroes" had extensive repercussions for the Tyrolean people and for regional identity. First, Tyrol was seen in the eyes of the Habsburgs as a dependable Austrian-minded bulwark loyal to the Emperor and on which the dynasty could rely in times of crisis. It was from the outside, therefore, that the land of Tyrol was subsequently bestowed with the role of a care region in the new Austrian identity—a situation that Tyrol had not sought for itself. Second, Tyrol characterized itself by accepting this image of a conservative alpine region which had remained backward in regard to economic, cultural, and social structure due to the stubborn revolt and resistance against an enemy described as having been corrupted by ideas of enlightenment. This self-consciousness was made stronger by the growing tendency to mythologize the heroes of the struggle for freedom as tragic. Andreas Hofer, the most famous of these heroes, was taken to symbolize all the traditional and moral values of the land of Tyrol, values such as loyalty, religion, courage, and love of freedom. By no means are all these values specific only to Tyrol but, in the course of the nineteenth century, they had increasingly become an integral part of the Tyrolean identity. Regular celebrations of commemoration, numerous and unfactual literary and artistic interpretations, as well as the economic exploitation of this material conspired to distort the true historic facts that led to the events of 1809.[24]

Another important development must be considered in this context: the relationship between regional and state identities intensified during the second half of the last century through the growing assertion of a new self-image defined largely on the basis of the ethnic languages of the diverse nationalities within the Habsburg monarchy. This type of national movement resulted from the revolutionary and liberal demands surrounding the events of 1848 and threatened to undo all previous efforts to achieve territorial and regional integration. This resulted from the aspirations of the diverse language-defined nations who gradually extended beyond their borders in search of new cultural and political options and identities outside the national union of the Danube monarchy.[25] At the same time they began internally to reposition their national demands in terms of cultural disputes as well as socio-political competition across the whole social spectrum.[26] In other words, the national movements manifested themselves through different aspects of identity and hence represented a far more pivotal role than just the simple voice of political opposition vis-à-vis a modern state.

Laurence Cole has analyzed this phenomenon in his recently completed study on German national identity in Tyrol in the years 1850 to 1914.[27] He concluded, amongst other findings, that region and nation do not necessarily represent areas which preclude each other, but must be viewed as integral parts of any process of social and cultural construction which strengthen each other. Cole warns us, however, against overemphasis on the disintegrative power of nationalism as it has found its way into the Austrian historiography via the American School of, for example, Oscar Jaszi or Robert A. Kann.[28]

Returning to the land of Tyrol and referring to the model proposed by Cole, it is evident that there have been new factors in the relationship between Innsbruck and Vienna since the 1860s in as much as regional development did not always conform to that of the supraregional state. This was due to the fact that in Tyrol there has always been a political predominance of Catholic-conservative circles as opposed to the liberal government in Vienna, leading to countless ideological tensions. The growing national conflict within the land also contributed to this feeling of tension.[29]

With the growing demands for explicit national rights—which were granted to the Italian-speaking population of the previously mentioned Trentino region under the Austrian Constitution of 1867—the German Tyroleans feared for the unity of their land. Consequently, they saw themselves as the sole and legitimate guardian of the identity of Tyrol vis-à-vis the fight against Vienna and also the Italians, and they reclaimed a great number of cultural and commemorative festivities centered around the year 1809 for themselves. In other words, the German Tyroleans located within the land of Tyrol their own national identity and endeavored both to monopolize and to justify this the outside world. The Italian-speaking Tyroleans were categorically not included in this definition.[30]

Other festivities commemorating a common tradition of the land of Tyrol and the region often revealed disagreement. Another illustration of this is the dispute over the anniversary year of 1863, in which the dominant Catholic conservatives sought to address the question of religious unity on the occasion of the tercentenary of the Council of Trent, whereas the liberal minority intended to celebrate the 500th anniversary of the unification of Tyrol with Austria. Similar tensions were seen at the time of the great *Landes-Gedenkjahr* (centenary) of 1909, during the course of which the center of attention was the elderly Kaiser Franz Josef, and loyalty to Austria was hardly an issue.[31] The list of examples could easily be extended with a catalogue of nationally motivated riots and revolts (a key event is the Italian faculty question of 1904).[32]

It is instructive to recognize that such commemorative celebrations—which were ostensibly intended to deepen national identity—simultaneously showed a character of national division, and therefore proved to be unsuitable for fostering regional as well as supraregional co-operation.

The argument can be seen to have returned to its starting point. History shows that the political and judicial union of the land of Tyrol with Austria over the course of centuries resulted in large degree from the personal entanglement with the Habsburg dynasty. Given the hierarchical social and government structure on the one hand and the time taken to finalize the territory of the *Habsburgerreich* (empire) on the other, there seemed little need for further socio-cultural or emotional ties to a supranational state. The feeling of identity among the broad population at least was restricted to its own visible horizons.

This also holds true for the era of the Tyrolean freedom fighters, whose aims were expressed in terms of God and the defense of the Catholic faith, the Kaiser and the return to sovereignty under the umbrella of Habsburg Rule, and the fatherland (Tyrolean home). This fundamental state of affairs did not significantly alter in the course of the "politicization and nationalization of the masses"[33] during the second half of the nineteenth century. On the contrary, the associated demands for national and territorial demarcation had a strengthening effect on the search for regional and ethnic patterns of identification, whereas the House of Habsburg was unsuccessful in offering the concept of a nation on the basis of national identities. Bureaucratic centralization and political disputes did their bit to sharpen the fields of conflict between center and periphery.[34]

Given this perspective, it may not be surprising to find that Tyrolean policy followed a separatist path after the collapse of the Habsburg Monarchy in November 1918. The House of Habsburg had, after all, relinquished all powers to govern, and as a consequence, the traditional legal and historical ties with the Austrian state were declared void. This was not, after all, just a question of a new orientation in policy by the land of Tyrol but also a crisis of *Landesbewußtsein* (regional consciousness) following the loss of the southerly part of the land. The German Tyroleans continued to hope for preservation of the unity of the land in often desperate and politically unrealistic balancing acts between the threat or refusal of Anschluß (annexation) to the German Reich—or to Italy—and stubborn diplomatic interventions with the Allied victors and with the U.S. President Woodrow Wilson.[35] The independence and neutrality of what was meant to be a united state that would cover north and south Tyrol—including the Ladinic area—was under consideration until 1919 when the Paris Treaties (St. Germain, Versailles) created a political pact by which the rest of the former Crown dominions remained part of the Republic of Austria.[36]

In the wake of this decision, a further change in the relationship between regional and national identities with regard to Tyrol became apparent. As the hoped-for departure from Austria by constitutional means had been unsuccessful, any political or administrative reforms originating from Vienna were henceforth received with even greater skepticism. There were reservations about the new state, which also found itself in a collective crisis of identity.

By way of illustration it is valuable to recall the initial quotation about the provisional nature of the incorporation of Tyrol into Austria from the year 1921. The main characteristic of Tyrolean interests has been the loss of the region's unity, which has repeatedly been made an issue across all social and political strata north and south of the Brenner Pass. One reaction to this was the intensification of the *Schützenmythos* (home defense myths)[37] surrounding Andreas Hofer [38] and also the *Herz-Jesu* (Sacred Heart)[39] Catholic festivities: Another reaction was the founding of commemorative festivities as well as *Heimat* and *Trachtenvereinen* (folklore institutions), all of which are intended to strengthen a common feeling of regional identity and to keep alive the cultural heritage of the Tyrol region.[40] The day when *Deutsch-SüdTirol* (German-South Tyrol) was officially and lawfully incorporated into the Kingdom of Italy, 10 October 1920, was declared a *Landestrauertag* (Regional Day of Mourning). It happens that—by irony of fate—this same date has become the *Landesfeiertag* (Regional Day of Celebration) for the Carinthian region in the wake of a referendum which secured the unity of that land.[41]

Finally it can be noted with just a touch of irony that the historical identity of the Tyrolean region has of course sought out its equivalent during the Second Republic, and this remains an ongoing process. Whether in the shape of regional exhibitions, or contributions to Austria's thousand year anniversary celebrations, or in academic conferences or political speeches on special occasions, it seems that any future repositioning of the land of Tyrol north and south of the Brenner Pass cannot, in the context of a common European development, rely exclusively on the interchange and commercialization of its intellectual and cultural foundations—or indeed its peculiarities. As far as the political dimensions of regional identity and nationhood since the Second World War are concerned, it is not least the experience between 1938 and 1945 that has finally turned the "loyal Tyroleans" into "good Austrians."[42]

The Case of Salzburg
(Barth-Scalmani)

Nearly all the U.S. college undergraduates who frequent programs in Salzburg will probably assume that the geographical shape of the Republic of Austria is the result of a common history. Austrians of the same age explain their local identity by stressing their differences from neighboring provinces (Upper Austria, Tyrol) and, most prominently, the capital Vienna. But can this be called deeply rooted regional identity?

For the historian things are not that easy. The historian is required to answer questions like: What are the historical elements of regionalism? How can we link present day regionalism with traces of the historical past? These questions reveal that we are already constructing the past and the memory of the past without going into a more complex and self-aware analysis of who is constructing what past for what kind of purpose. So instead of theoretically listing components of regional identity let's take a rather pragmatic approach.

It is important to remember that Austrian historiography was dominated for a very long time by a Viennese viewpoint; therefore, the question of various regional identities was not on the agenda or was hidden behind the more important question of national identity. In connection with the referendum regarding joining the European Community in 1994, slogans of "growing regionalism" were used more frequently. This type of rhetoric has been used in Salzburg for years by some politicians who liked to instrumentalize regional identity or celebrate it on historical anniversaries.

Salzburg has a very short history as a part of Austria; in fact, it is the second youngest of all the Austrian provinces. The Burgenland became a part of Austria after World War I, having been the westernmost part of the Hungarian half of the double monarchy Austro-Hungary. Salzburg is a relatively old part of Austria; it was made a part of Austria in 1816.[43] Even though it shares 179 years of common history with Austria, Salzburg still feels itself to be separate from Austria. A former provincial governor liked to point out that Salzburg was already a center of Christianity and culture when Vienna was still an area of pagan beliefs, and that the first church built there, Rupert's chapel, was initiated by missionaries sent from Salzburg.[44] Evidence of that kind of feeling, that Salzburg is different from Vienna, and subconsciously maybe even superior to it can still be found today. I will give only one example which is taken from an economic-financial viewpoint: In the financial adjustment between the federal state, the provinces, and the communities (the so-called *Finanzausgleich*), Salzburg is a province that raises more money in taxes than it gets back from the common funds.[45] This fact is a matter of regular discussion between representatives of the ministry of finance and their local counterparts. However, historians might claim that this is a relatively young phenomenon originating in Austria's postwar economic development. Thus, historians are forced to search for their examples in a far more remote past.

With few exceptions many Austrian provinces had the experience of losing parts of their lands in the course of the twentieth century. These losses shaped the provincial and the Austrian mind because they felt that an injustice had been done to them (Carinthian, Styrian, Tyrolean for example). But this feeling of not having been treated fairly by the international community was a good breeding ground for sentiments of "unity as underdogs."

Salzburg can trace its geographical shape back to the times of the Holy Roman Empire. Of all the clerical/ecclesiastical states within the Empire it is the only one that could more or less preserve its territorial integrity (with a few minor losses).[46] Events that occurred between 1803 and 1816 allowed Salzburg to do so. But it is important to analyze Salzburg's history not just in light of these events, but in light of its greater history, before it lost its status as an independent state of its own.

From the Middle Ages onwards, Salzburg had been an independent clerical/ecclesiastical state within the framework of the Holy Roman Empire. The process of territorial adjustment had been finished approximately around 1410 (apart from slight changes 100 years later).[47] The prince-archbishops were both spiritual and worldly sovereigns of their country. Salzburg for the next two-and-a-half centuries initiated a rather clever seesaw policy in the politics of power between two stronger neighbors who embraced small Salzburg: Bavaria, or the dynasty of the Wittelsbach family, and Austria, or the Habsburg family. The prince-archbishops successfully maintained an equilibrium by ensuring that the *Domkapitel* (board of clergymen) was filled not only with sons of noble families from these spheres of power. Yet after the Thirty Years War the archbishop was quite obviously leaning more and more towards the Austrian side, and around the year 1700 Salzburg was already seen from a Bavarian viewpoint as a "political branch office of Vienna."[48]

Traditional political arguments regarding Salzburg's relative independence are numerous. But they won't tell us much about the feeling of the inhabitants of that specific region. When studying the eighteenth century, modern terms like "political identification" or "emotional identification" do not explain an individual's relationship to the territory in which he lived, nor are they appropriate for discussing national consciousness. People in the eighteenth century lived in bonds of social ranks/strata. The inhabitants of Salzburg were first of all subjects of the prince-archbishop; they existed in relation to him and to God. The tightness of this bondage, this legal relation, depended on their individual social position within the *ständische Gesellschaft* (order of the estates). For example, only the craftsmen and tradesmen who were exercising a profession (limited in numbers by self-regulation) were *burghers*, or citizens, and thus enjoyed a certain amount of freedom, for example, in administrating their town.[49] But the servants of their household fell under the juridical responsibility of their masters; they all were subject to the ruling sovereign, the prince-archbishop.

A more prominent example will make this point clearer: like his father, Wolfgang Amadeus Mozart served as musician at the court of the prince-archbishop, thus he was part of the court-folk. Technically he belonged to the household of an absolute sovereign and at the same time was a subject of this sovereign because he was living on his territory. Under this viewpoint he was a Salzburger, somebody living on service rendered to the sovereign of this archbishopric. When he left Salzburg in 1781 he was not a Salzburg subject any more, but did he become an Austrian subject in Vienna? He neither had been a Salzburg citizen nor had he become an Austrian citizen.

Salzburg lacked one important element on which modern identification with one's territory was to be based. This *Landesbewußtsein* did not develop in relation to the figure of a sovereign but was built on the existence of other important social ranks/strata. Normally the three traditional estates, the prelates, the knights, the towns and rural communities, *die Landstände*, represented the *Landschaft*, the diet.[50] In contrast to the Tyrol, in Salzburg after the sixteenth century, the farmers were not included in the assembly of the Salzburg estates.

In other contemporary Austrian provinces (Lower Austria, Styria, Carinthia) these *Landstände* were a rather strong counterpoint to the sovereign and played an important role in politics, especially during the sixteenth and seventeenth centuries. Their strength and importance derived mainly from their approval of taxes and tariffs, their responsibility for the military and defense, a medical agenda, and some parts of schooling. They developed their own staff of civil servants. On a visual level one still can see their importance as nearly all Austrian provincial capitals have a *Landhaus*, a building of their estates.

Salzburg lacked such a representational building of her estates because they never were as strong as those in the Habsburg areas.[51] Furthermore, no strong nobility existed in Salzburg in pre-absolutist times that could function as a nucleus for identification with one's territory via representation through these *Stände*. But the institution of the diet as such was to become important in the nineteenth century.

Between 1803 and 1816 Salzburg saw several changes of rulers and reigns. The year 1803 marks the end of the ecclesiastical rule and of Salzburg's independence as a state; for the next two years Salzburg was the electorate of a Habsburg archduke who had to give up Tuscany. His loss was compensated with the reign over four previous ecclesiastical states: Salzburg, Berchtesgaden, Eichstätt, and Passau. De jure it was an independent state still within the Holy Roman Empire, de facto it was a satellite of Austria, the new Austria of 1804. In retrospect, it was important that Salzburg remained undivided even after the end of the ecclesiastical reign, that the city of Salzburg continued to be a capital and residential city, that the administration, the civil servants remained. The electorate prince even tried to initiate modern reforms. The country legally was still a *Reichsstand* (Imperial Estate) within the Holy Roman Empire.

But this lasted only for two years, and as a result of the Peace Treaty of Preßburg, in December 1805, the electorate was dissolved. Austria was to be compensated for the loss of Tyrol; therefore Salzburg and Berchtesgaden were made part of Austria. The city and big parts of the country had already been hit by the war, French occupation, and enforced contributions. In this moment Salzburg feared for its autonomous statehood, because the bigger framework, the Holy Roman Empire, was being dissolved in August 1806.

But who in Salzburg shared those fears in December 1805 and January 1806? The feelings of the majority of the inhabitants are not documented; the statements that are referred to come mainly from the urban and intellectual middle class, by numbers a small group. Many feared that Salzburg would be subordinated under other decentralized centers of Habsburg administration such as Linz in Upper Austria or Graz in Styria. The reality of the situation proved to be worse than the feared subordination, because Salzburg was administered directly by the central authorities in Vienna. As a Salzburg eye witness observed, "Austria does not present herself to be liked in the newly acquired territories. Everywhere the Habsburgs lay foot to, bureaucratic leveling starts: these narrow-minded heads are only able to understand unity as uniformity: all economic, public and private circumstances have to be changed according to their opinion."[52] Certainly a historian can read this statement from the other viewpoint too: Salzburg had to be integrated into the Austrian administration by all means to render the acquisition profitable.

What really triggered an anti-Austrian, or should I say anti-Habsburg, mood was the fact that a lot of money raised as taxes or customs duty in Salzburg was used in Vienna in a series of unsuccessful attempts to balance the budget.[53] Symbolically Vienna took even more. During this era there was a growing interest in the past. All the newly excavated Roman artifacts around Salzburg were shipped from the westernmost province to the capital; likewise the oldest manuscripts and precious books of the monasteries and archives were transported to the museums, archives, and libraries of Vienna. They have remained there ever since.

Everyday life was also profoundly affected. By springtime 1809 French troops occupied the pre-alpine part of the country again, and heavy financial contributions were demanded. The country was split, because in the southern alpine regions the farmers supported the uprising of the Tyrolean Andreas Hofer in words and actions; the *Pinzgau* (southwesternmost district) declared her wish for union with the Tyrol, the *Pongau* and the *Lungau* were to follow.[54]

Other historians see the origin of a new territorial identity in these fights against a foreign enemy.[55] Anton Wallner, one of the local Salzburg guerillas fighting against the French, declared to fight "for our monarch and the fatherland."[56] Statements like this are difficult to deconstruct. Why should Wallner—a modest innkeeper—orient himself towards the Habsburg monarch in 1809? Was he still thinking in terms of the Holy Roman Empire? Or was it just propaganda? The statement does seem to suggest that there was no longer a representational figure in Salzburg who could symbolize a new territorial identity.

The statement of the abbot of St. Peter's monastery in 1810 characterizes the mood of the people much more clearly, “All are sighing for a new ruler, might he come from Paris or Petersburg, in order to have a center toward which to turn. But unhappy the prince who might get Salzburg, he receives a bled country of poor subjects.”[57] At the first anniversary of the French occupation, in April 1810, a chronicler reported with regards to the economic situation in Salzburg, “misery is growing every day.”[58] For most of the inhabitants the fight for material survival was more essential than the question of political/regional identity.

When the inhabitants of the city of Salzburg heard the first rumors in 1810 that Napoleon would hand Salzburg to his Bavarian allies, happy expectations, even pro-Bavarian sentiments, were rising. But the feelings of the urban population were not typical of those in the country. In contrast to the city dwellers, the farmers in the alpine parts remained skeptical because they remembered the Bavarians as enemies in the fights of 1809.[59]

From October 1810 to 1816 Salzburg operated under five years of Bavarian rule. At the beginning nearly everybody was sympathetic to the Bavarians. Salzburg was made the ninth district in Bavaria and was quickly and forcefully integrated in the centralist Bavarian administration, which by Salzburg standards meant modernization. But many Salzburg civil servants were stripped of their rank, whereas Bavarian civil servants were offered career options in the newly acquired district. The pro-Bavarian mood dwindled gradually, and the male farming population escaped the enforced military draft by going abroad.

Salzburg remained a pawn in matters of international diplomacy. At the Congress of Vienna in 1814 Salzburg was considered to be a bargaining chip. Against the intention of Prince Clemens Metternich it was finally made Austrian. But one fifth of its area, the pre-alpine and fertile agrarian land west of the rivers Salzach and Saalach, remained Bavarian territory.

After the second Anschluß and final unification with Austria in April 1816, the Emperor of Austria visited the country to accept the tribute of inheritance, *Erbhuldigung*. He was welcomed by crowds. The most important group among the citizens of the city of Salzburg, the merchants, saw the negative economic consequences for them quite clearly though, and their potential pro-Austrian feelings were limited by hard-boiled facts. By 1811 Austria was a bankrupt country with extremely high customs, and the supraregional trading business from which they had profited would soon end.

Salzburg was made a sub-district of Upper Austria. The university had already been abolished by the Bavarians, and the archbishop, the highest clergymen of the Catholic Church, was still living outside the country. With no ruler in residence, and no center of higher bureaucracy or learning, Salzburg was deprived of important functions. Salzburg's darkest time, the period after 1816, is termed "provincial," a negative way of describing her status. At the same time Munich and Vienna were booming cultural centers of the Biedermeier era and its leading social group, the *Bürgertum*. But in Salzburg grass was growing on the main squares of the city.

The Salzburgers did not see themselves as Austrian. Joseph Ph. Felner (1769-1850), a Salzburg born high civil servant, observed in 1817, "the Salzburger ceases to be a Salzburger, but he is not yet Austrian because they differ from him in remarkable nuances in ways of eating, habits, needs, likings, even in character."[60]

The contrast between Salzburg's insignificant present and its glorious past created a need for a new identity. But among what people was this new mood shared? The answer is the middle class, the traditional *altständische Bürgertum*, and its new members, the civil servants, teachers, free-professionals (lawyers, medical doctors), and priests.

In a time of romantic orientation towards the past and under the circumstances of Metternich's political rule, culture became the sphere of new local identity. In 1833 Salzburgers started to collect and preserve their own antique excavations to prevent them from being incorporated into the museum in Upper Austria; clubs which by law had to pretend to be unpolitical (like the *museum*) functioned as forums for the public opinions of the middle class whose self-confidence was rising. The foundation of a music academy, the *Mozarteum* in 1842, an arts club, the *Kunstverein* in 1844, singing choirs, the Salzburger *Liedertafel* in 1847, federations to promote agriculture, the *k k. Landwirtschaftsgesellschaft* in 1848, and a society for research into the local past, the *Landeskunde* in 1860,[61] must be interpreted in two ways. First, these activities must be understood as reflecting the growing self-confidence of the middle class in public life, *Verbürgerlichung*.

Second, these activities made it possible for individuals to feel pride in their own environment (they no longer envied Linz or Innsbruck's similar institutions), and integrated a lot of middle class people, who did not originate from the area, into Salzburg society. It was thus that the bonds of identification were shaped.

In the political sphere, the mere existence of the old diet and estates helped to initiate political representation. Although the Upper Austrian authorities tried very strongly to fully incorporate Salzburg into their administration, even the district commissioner of Salzburg—the highest civil servant sent from Linz—opposed his Upper Austrian colleagues. Some Salzburg deputies and the abbot of St. Peter urged the emperor not to merge the Salzburg estates with the Upper Austrian estates. Finally in 1827 he allowed the Salzburg estates to assemble again, and they issued a strong statement detailing their resentment about legal unification with Upper Austria. Although they were not allowed to call the diet into action, it had been important that the estates had met.[62]

In the course of the first half of the nineteenth century, the idea of representation had changed. People no longer wanted representation via the estates; they wanted representation that was somehow more direct. Democratic representation was the new aim. In the course of the 1848 revolution, the Catholic Church and the nobility deliberately resigned all privileges in a new provincial constitution.[63] In the Austrian constitution of March 1849, Salzburg was already mentioned as an independent *Kronland*; one year later it received the administrative organization of a *Kronland*, personified in the highest office of a *Statthalter* of its own. Even as the constitutional debate in Austria continued, Salzburg's legal and constitutional status could not be rescinded. However, during the period of neoabsolutism the goal of democratization via representation shifted to the old idea of representation via privileged estates.

In order to save money after the wars of 1859, Emperor Franz Joseph placed Salzburg de facto under Upper Austrian administration in April 1860, whereas de jure the title of *Kronland* remained. This action was not appreciated by members of the urban economic establishment or by civil servants. Secret reports by the director of the police, who was the highest civil servant, observed that "the growing attachment to Austria and the self-sacrificing devotion of patriotic attitudes might freeze and be replaced by pro-Bavarian sympathies."[64]

The final implementation of constitutionalism with the *Februarpatent* of 1861 had consequences for Salzburg. In February 1861 the provincial constitution was issued; already in March 1861 the first election (based on taxes, voters organized in four curias) to the new diet took place. From then until the end of the monarchy, Salzburg had its own provincial government with a governor appointed by the Emperor. One might assume that all these political developments strengthened regional identity for those who formed the political elite of the time. This was further backed by economic development. The last three decades of the nineteenth century were characterized by an upswing based on tourism and trade and to some extent on old mining activities.[65] Salzburg enjoyed a happy existence as one of the smallest crown lands in Cisleithania. Local patriotism in the first half of the nineteenth century could especially be traced among the urban middle class and the clergy. The more schooling provided, the more the elements of an Austrian nationalism intensified (for example, schools held annual celebration of the emperor's anniversary, and textbooks contained Habsburg mythology). Although historians observed less federal tendencies than in Tyrol, Carinthia, or Bohemia, Salzburg's patriotism—to use a contemporary equivalent to regional identity—easily harmonized two orientations: an Austrian, Habsburg identification for the day-to-day reality, and a German, partly even Pan-German, self-awareness for cultural settings. As Hanns Haas brilliantly stated, "German was the sentiment, Austrian the social reality."[66]

After World War I the shock over the monarchy's end was as traumatic in Salzburg as in other German parts of the Habsburg territory, although in the beginning Salzburg took comfort in the fact that it did not have to face a loss of territory. On 7 November 1918 a provisional provincial constitution was issued, the first one given without the consent of Vienna.[67] The political structure of the next two decades showed consensus among the political parties, was dominated by Christian Socials, and was integrated by the Social Democrats. The referendum for the Anschluß in May 1921 was supported by all parties. The society was more or less segmented according to the three political camps because political parties had a vital role beyond that of politics (in sports and leisure activities for example), but Salzburg never became a hotbed of ideological combat.

One melody that was played from the beginning with growing success certainly constituted the regional identity of the time, backing the old theme of anti-Viennese feeling with new tunes. Vienna was governed for the first time by Social Democrats; the Christian Socials dominated the Alpine countries, where the Catholic Church still had more impact on culture, society and politics. Thus "black" Salzburg stood in an opposition to "red" Vienna. Vienna with its huge administrative infrastructure, derived from the imperial days, needed economic support from the provinces, in the hard days of inflation and struggle, to organize the basic support of food. This further aggravated the split between Salzburg and the "waterhead" ("*Wasserkopf*") in the east. Furthermore, in political discourse and everyday conversations, Vienna—with its traditionally higher number of Jewish people and after World War I housing a high percentage of Jewish refugees from Eastern Europe[68]—was depicted as the urban metropolis controlled by Jewish politicians and as morally undermined by the Jewish cultural establishment. The opposite slogans of "*das verjudete Wien*" and the "clean" Catholic countryside constituted the perception of many inhabitants of Salzburg.

After the Anschluß of March 1938,[69] the regional identity defined by its old name and territorial integrity was not erased. Unlike other Austrian provinces, Salzburg maintained its name and was not attached to neighboring "*Länder*."[70] Regional pride in the smallest *Reichsgau* was nourished by new elements: being close to Hitler's seat in Obersalzberg and housing the main artists and Nazi party and state representatives during the time of the summer festival. Thus Salzburg's regional identity was not interrupted though covered until the first years of the war by a thick layer of *großdeutsch* patriotism.

In April/May 1945 the war ended with the four-power Allied occupation of Austria. Salzburg's democratic politics restarted on the local level. Under the tutelage of the U.S. occupation power, local communal and provincial authorities were formed. The political elite decided in May 1945 to contact the government in Vienna and to support it whole-heartedly.[71] This decision concerning the reconstitution of political life in the other western provinces also rejuvenated national Austrian politics; an Austrian identity started to flourish again in the western provinces. It was not easy to carry out these goals. Vienna was situated in the Soviet zone, and in the beginning, the Western Allies did not know how to judge the government of Renner, who some early cold-warriors considered to be a puppet on the Soviet string. Consequently, the U.S. occupation forces in Salzburg were ordered not to follow directions from Vienna. But this changed by the end of 1945.

But the fact that Austria remained occupied by four Allies until 1955—Lower Austria, Burgenland and some parts of Vienna being Soviet occupied falling economically more and more behind—influenced the general orientation. The postwar geopolitical development created a blend of identities. Under the layer of the Austrian consciousness was the pragmatic day-to-day western-oriented Salzburg identity. This could be easily linked with Salzburg's past.

The western orientation was not only a result of better economic conditions in Salzburg after World War II. This became clear from the late 1970s and early 1980s onwards when intellectual debate favored the concept of *Mitteleuropa*. It stressed a cultural link between Austria and its neighboring countries Czechoslovakia and Hungary—then still behind the Iron Curtain of communist rule—by referring to the old ties of the imperial days. This *Mitteleuropa* movement never flourished as strongly in Salzburg as in Vienna where personal memories, family relations, and traces of the past were much more present. Not even after the dramatic political changes in the fall of 1989 did it assert a new importance for the average Salzburg inhabitant. The Salzburgers lacked the experience of the Viennese who traveled easily across open borders to Bohemia, Moravia, Slovakia and Hungary on a daily basis and felt the common heritage everywhere. From a Salzburg point of view these borders were still a five-hour car ride away, whereas for the Viennese they were only an hour away at most.

Since World War II the province of Salzburg, especially the area around the city of Salzburg has been growing through internal migration within Austria. That means that many who are settling in Salzburg have socialized with the prevailing regional self-confidence and pride. Apart from politicians and the mass media who stress this point at every opportunity,[72] other factors come into play to create that special Salzburg feeling, due to geography possibilities for winter and summer sports are abundant; a society oriented towards leisure activities gains value from this. Although not every Salzburger attends the summer festival, the attention of the world press makes many think that Salzburg is the *secret cultural capital* of Austria, at least during the summertime. Thus the blend of memories of a great historical past and the self-fulfilling prophecies of the modern agenda produce the feeling of being a unique part of Austria.

It was Thomas Bernhard, the writer born in Salzburg, who showed in his autobiographical writing the other side of this mental disposition, namely the provincial narrowness, the petty bourgeois pride against outsiders. Both sides of the coin constitute Salzburg.

NOTES

1. *Geschichte und Region* 1 (1992): 8.

2. Alphons Lhotsky, *Geschichte des Instituts für österreichische Geschichtsforschung (1854-1954). Festgabe zur Hundertjahrfeier des Insituts* MIÖG Studies 17 (Vienna: Böhlau, 1954).

3. Wilhelm Brauneder and Friedrich Lachmayer, *Österreichische Verfassungsgeschichte* (Vienna: Rohrer Manz, 1992). The term "monarchistic union of estates" ("*Monarchische Union von Ständestaaten*") was first used by Otto Brunner, *Land und Herrschaft* (Vienna: Rohrer, 1939).

4. The Bohemian crown with the "*verneuerte Landesordnung*" of 1627, and the Hungarian crown since the Peace of Frieden von Karlowitz in 1699.

5. With Emperor Friedrich III (1452-1493).

6. See also Alphons Lhotsky, *Österreichische Historiographie* (Vienna: Verlag für Geschichte und Politik, 1961).

7. At the end of the nineteenth century we notice few attempts in Austrian historiography to see and study this connection between Austria and the Empire. See Alphons Huber, *Österreichische Reichsgeschichte* (Vienna: Tempsky und Freytag, 1895); see also Arnold Luschin von Ebengreuth, *Österreichische Reichsgeschichte* (Vienna: Buchner, 1896).

8. On this topic see Herwig Wolfram and Walter Pohl, eds., *Probleme der Geschichte Österreichs und ihrer Darstellung* (Vienna: Verlag der Österreichischen Akademie der Wissenschaften, 1991).

9. Präambel der Neufassung der Tiroler Landesordnung 1959; Wolfgang Pfaundler, *Tiroler Jungbürgerbuch* (Innsbruck: Inn-Verlag, 1967), 689.

10. Helmut Alexander, "Technik und Landesbewußtsein in Tirol," *Technik, Politik, Identität: Funktionalisierung von Technik für die Ausbildung regionaler, sozialer und nationaler Selbstbilder in Österreich* (Stuttgart, 1996).

11. "Landesgesetzblatt für Tirol, Nr. 145 ex 1921; Josef Riedmann," Verfassungsentwicklung und Demokratisierung in Tirol 1918 - 1920. Beiträge zur inneren Geschichte des Landes in den ersten Jahren nach dem Ende des Ersten Weltkrieges," *Tiroler Heimat* 45 (1981): 77-103.

12. Josef Riedmann, "Bemerkungen zu neueren Darstellungen der Landesgeschichte von Tirol," in *Probleme der Geschichte Österreichs und ihrer Darstellung*, ed. Herwig Wolfram and Walter Pohl (Vienna: Verlag d. Österreichischen Akademie d. Wissenschaften, 1991), 179-184; idem., "Geschichtsschreibung und Geschichtsbewußtsein in Tirol vornehmlich in der ersten Hälfte des 20. Jahrhunderts. Ein Versuch," *Tiroler Heimat* 57 (1993): 291-304.

13. Franz Huter, "Der Eintritt Tirols in die 'Herrschaft zur Österreich (1363),'" in *Beiträge zur Geschichte Tirols. Festgabe des Landes Tirol zum Elften Österreichischen Historikertag in Innsbruck 1971* (Innsbruck, 1971), 179-196.

14. Josef Fontana , ed., *Geschichte des Landes Tirol*, 4 vols. (Bozen: Tirolia-Verlag, 1985-1988).

15. Josef Riedmann, *Geschichte Tirols* in *Geschichte der österreichischen Bundesländer*, ed. Johann Rainer, 2nd ed., (Vienna: Geschichte und Politik, 1988), 141-64.

16. Ibid.

17. Helmut Reinalter, *Aufklärung—Absolutismus—Reaktion: Die Geschichte Tirols in der 2. Hälfte des 18. Jahrhunderts* (Vienna: Schendl, 1974).

18. Erich Egg, "Die Tirolische Nation," in *Die Tirolische Nation 1790-1820. Ausstellungskatalog zur Landesausstellung im Auftrag des Landes Tirol zum Gedenkjahr 1809-1984*, 2nd ed., (Innsbruck: Rauchdruck, 1984), 6-7.

19. Karl Ilg, "Die Anfänge der volkskundlichen Studien in Tirol," in *Tirol im Jahrhundert nach Anno Neun*, ed. Egon Kühebacher, Schlern-Schriften 279 (Innsbruck: Universitätsverlag Wagner, 1986), 153-162.

20. Wilhelm Brauneder, ed., *Heiliges Römisches Reich und moderne Staatlichkeit* (Frankfurt: Lang, 1993).

21. Michael Forcher, "Tirol im 19. Jahrhundert: Zwischen Irredentismus, Deutscher Frage und Verfassungskämpfen," in *Tirol im Jahrhundert nach Anno Neun*, ed. Egon Kühebacher, Schlern-Schriften 279 (Innsbruck: Universitätsverlag Wagner, 1986), 9-29, hier 9-12.

22. Klaus Günzel, *Der Wiener Kongreß: Geschichte und Geschichten eines Welttheaters* (Munich: Koehler & Amelang, 1995).

23. Johann Rainer, "Tirol unter bayerischer Herrschaft," in *Tirol im Jahrhundert nach Anno Neun*, 31-36.

24. Johann Holzner, "Andreas Hofer im Spiegel der Literatur," in *Tirol im Jahrhundert nach Anno Neun*, 37-50; Meinrad Pizzinini, "Zur Entstehung des Andreas-Hofer-Bildes," in ibid., 57-66; ders., *Andreas Hofer: seine Zeit—sein Leben—sein Mythos* (Vienna: Kremayr & Scheriau, 1984).

25. Robert A. Kann, *Das Nationalitätenproblem der Habsburgermonarchie*, 2 vols. (Graz-Köln: 1964); Gerald Stourzh, *Die Gleichberechtigung der Nationalitäten in der Verfassung und Verwaltung Österreichs 1848-1918* (Vienna: 1985).

26. Hermann J.W. Kuprian, "Spannungsfeld Staat und Gesellschaft in Österreich in der zweiten Hälfte des 19. Jahrhunderts. Mit einem kurzen Ausblick auf Tirol," in *Rerum novarum, Geschichte und Region/Storia e regione* (1993): 21-42.

27. Laurence Cole, "Province and Patriotism: German National Identity in Tyrol in the Years 1850-1914," (Ph.D. diss., European University Institute Florence, 1995).

28. Ibid., 524.

29. Josef Fontana, *Der Kulturkampf in Tirol, 1861-1892* (Bozen: Athesia, 1978).

30. Cole, "Province and Patriotism," 514-516.

31. Ibid., 12-175.

32. Elisabeth Dietrich, "Im Namen seiner Majestät des Kaisers von Österreich! Revolutionäre, italienische Nationalisten und Irredentisten vor österreichischen Gerichten zwischen 1848 und dem Ersten Weltkrieg," *Innsbrucker Historische Studien* 10/11 (1988): 305-324; Hedda Leeb, "Geschichte der Universität Innsbruck von 1898 bis 1908" (Ph.D. diss., University of Innsbruck, 1967), 85-159.

33. Peter Urbanitsch, "Die Nationalisierung der Massen," in *Das Zeitalter Kaiser Franz Josephs*, vol. 2, *1880-1916: Glanz und Elend* (Horn, 1987), 119-124; idem., "Politisierung der Massen," in ibid., 106-118.

34. Hanisch Ernst, *Der lange Schatten des Staates. Österreichische Gesellschaftsgeschichte im 20. Jahrhundert. Österreichische Geschichte 1890 - 1990* (Vienna: Ueberreuter, 1994), 209-241.

35. Thomas Albrich, Klaus Eisterer, and Rolf Steininger, eds., *Tirol und der Anschluß: Voraussetzungen, Entwicklungen, Rahmenbedingungen 1918-1938* (Innsbruck: Haymon, 1988); Hermann J.W. Kuprian, "Aspekte zum deutsch-österreichischen Verhältnis in den ersten Jahren nach dem Zusammenbruch der Habsburgermonarchie," *Österreich in Geschichte und Literatur* 37 (1993): 1-18.

36. Richard Schober, *Die Tiroler Frage auf der Friedenskonferenz von Saint Germain* (Innsbruck: Wagnerische Universitätsbuchdruckerei, 1982), 155-167, 202-317; idem., "Die österreichische Anschlußbewegung an Deutschland im Spiegel der italienischen Diplomatie (1918-1921)," in *Historische Blickpunkte. Festschrift für Johann Rainer*, ed. Ulrike Kemmerling-Unterthurner, Hermann J.W. Kuprian, and Sabine Weiss (Innsbruck: Institut für Sprachwissenschaft, 1988), 613-627.

37. Christoph von Hartungen, "Die Tiroler und Vorarlberger Standschützen—Mythos und Realität," in *Tirol und der Erste Weltkrieg*, ed. Klaus Eisterer and Rolf Steininger (Innsbruck: Österreichischer Studienverlag, 1995), 61-104; Klaus Eisterer, "'Der Heldentod muß würdig geschildert werden.' Der Umgang mit der Vergangenheit am Beispiel Kaiserjäger und Kaiserjägertradition," in ibid., 105-137.

38. Laurence Cole, "Andreas Hofer: The Social and Cultural Construction of a National Myth in Tyrol, 1809-1909," in *European Forum Working Paper* 1994/3 (Florence: European University Institute 1995).

39. About the *Herz-Jesu* cult see R.J. Dessl, "Herz-Jesu-Verehrung im 18. und 19. Jahrhundert," *Jahrbuch des Oberösterreichischen Musealvereines. Gesellschaft für Landeskunde* 132 (1987): 81-136; Bildungswerk der Diözese Bozen-Brixen, ed. (Bozen: Athesia-Verlag, 1995); Franz X. Schädle, "Das Herz-Jesu-Gelöbnis Tirols. Seine dogmatisch-pastoralen Auswirkungen," (M.A. thesis Vienna: 1990).

40. Wolfgang Meixner, "Mythos Tirol: Zur Tiroler Ethnizitätsbildung und Heimatschutzbewegung im 19. Jahrhundert," in *Geschichte und Region/Storia e regione* 1 (1992): 88-106; Michael Gehler, "'Regionale' Zeitgeschichte als 'Geschichte überschaubarer Räume': Von Grenzen, Möglichkeiten, Aufgaben und Fragen einer Forschungsrichtung," in *Geschichte und Region/Storia e regione* 1 (1992): 85-120.

41. Josef Riedmann, "Der 'Tiroler Landestrauertag' am 10. Oktober im jährlichen Gedenken an die Annexion SüdTirols durch Italien," in *Tirol im 20. Jahrhundert: Festschrift für Viktoria Stadlmayer* (Innsbruck: 1989), 191-202; Hermann J.W. Kuprian, "Der Tiroler Separatismus der Ersten Republik," in *1918/1919—Die Bundesländer und die Republik. Protokollband des Symposiums zum 75. Jahrestag der Ausrufung der 1. Republik am 12. und 13. November 1993 im Grazer Stadtmuseum*, ed. Gerhard M. Dienes and Markus Jaroschka (Graz: Grazer Stadtmuseum, 1994), 49-66, 89-93; Helmut Rumpler, ed., *Kärntens Volksabstimmung 1920. Wissenschaftliche Kontroversen und historisch-politische Diskussionen anläßlich des internationalen Symposions Klagenfurt 1980* (Klagenfurt: 1981).

42. Gerald Stourzh, *Vom Reich zur Republik: Studien zum Österreichbewußtsein im 20. Jahrhundert*, (Vienna: Edition Atelier, 1990).

43. *175 Jahre Salzburg bei Österreich* (Salzburg: Schriftenreihe des Landespressebüros, 1991).

44. Today it can be easily visited by exiting the Stephansplatz at the subway station.

45. Gunda Barth, "Das Wirtschaftssystem im Bundesland Salzburg," in *Das politische, soziale und wirtschaftliche System im Bundesland Salzburg. Festschrift zum Jubiläum '40 Jahre Salzburger Landtag in der Zweiten Republik,'* ed. Herbert Dachs (Salzburg: Schriftenreihe des Landespressebüros), 434.

46. Peter Putzer, *Kursalzburg: Ein Beitrag zur territorialen Verfassungs- und Verwaltungsgeschichte zu Ende des Alten Reiches* (Salzburg: 1969).

47. Heinz Dopsch, "Salzburg im Hochmittelalter," in *Geschichte Salzburgs*, Vol. I/1, ed. Heinz Dopsch and Hans Spatzenegger (Salzburg: Anton Pustet 1981), 346.

48. Reinhard R. Heinisch, "Salzburgs Beziehungen zu Bayern und Österreich in der Frühen Neuzeit," in *Österreich in Geschichte und Literatur* 23 (1979): 275.

49. Gunda Barth-Scalmani, "Der Handelsstand der Stadt Salzburg am Ende des 18. Jahrhunderts: Altständisches Bürgerrtum in Politik, Wirtschaft und Kultur" (Ph.D. diss., University of Salzburg, 1992).

50. Lorenz Hübner, *Beschreibung der hochfürstlich-erzbischöflichen Haupt- und Residenzstadt Salzburg und ihrer Gegenden verbunden mit ihrer ältesten Geschichte* (Salzburg: F.X. Oberer), 256-262.

51. Heinz Dopsch, "Landschaft, Landstände und Landtag," in *Der Landtag* (Salzburg: Schriftenreihe des Landespressebüros, 1990), 22.

52. Peter Putzer, "Staatlichkeit und Recht nach der Säkularisation," in *Geschichte Salzburgs. Neuzeit und Zeitgeschichte*, Vol. II/2, ed. Heinz Dopsch and Hans Spatzenegger (Salzburg: Anton Pustet, 1988), 646.

53. Franz Ortner, "Zwischen Habsburg und Wittelsbach—Säkularisation und Franzosenkriege: Vom Kurfürstentum zum Wiener Kongreß—Salzburg 1803-1816," in *Geschichte Salzburgs. Neuzeit und Zeitgeschichte*, Vol. II/2, 600.

54. Hanns Haas, "Landesbewußtsein und Gruppenidentität," in *175 Jahre Salzburg bei Österreich*, 44.

55. Peter Putzer, "Vom Reichsstand zum Bundesland," *175 Jahre Salzburg bei Österreich*, 21.

56. Ibid.

57. Ortner, "Salzburg 1803-16," 611.

58. Putzer, "Staatlichkeit," 648.

59. Ortner, "Salzburg 1803-16," 614.

60. Haas, "Landesbewußtsein," 47.

61. Hanns Haas, "Salzburg in der Habsburgermonarchie: Vormärz, Revolution und Neoabsolutismus," in *Geschichte Salzburgs: Neuzeit und Zeitgescheichte*, Vol. II/2, 686.

62. Haas, "Vormärz," 671.

63. Franz Spatenka, "Salzburg im Revolutionsjahr 1848," *Salzburg Archiv* 11 (1991): 105.

64. Hanns Haas, "Salzburg in der Habsburgermonarchie: 2. Das liberale Zeitalter," in *Geschichte Salzburgs Neuzeit und Zeitgeschichte*, Vol. II/2, 721.

65. Fritz Gruber and Karl-Heinz Ludwig, "Der Metallbergbau," in *Geschichte Salzburgs: Neuzeit und Zeitgeschichte,* Vol. II/4, 2595-2631; Johann F. Schatteiner, "Der Salzbergbau Dürrnberg und die Saline Hallein," in ibid., 2631-2712; Josef Wysocki, "Die Wirtschaft Salzburgs im 19. Jahrhundert," in ibid., 2713-2742.

66. Hanns Haas, "Nationalbewußtsein, Patriotismus und Krieg," in *Geschichte Salzburgs: Neuzeit und Zeitgeschichte,* Vol. II/4, 992-93.

67. Ernst Hanisch, "Die Erste Republik," in *Geschichte Salzburgs: Neuzeit und Zeitgeschichte,* Vol. II/2, 1060.

68. Beatrix Hoffmann-Holter, *Abreisendmachung: Jüdische Kriegsflüchtlinge in Wien 1914-1923.* (Vienna: Böhlau, 1995).

69. Ernst Hanisch, *März 1938: Eine Salzburger Perspektive* (Salzburg: Schriftenreihe des Landespressebüros. Salzburg Diskussionen Nr. 10, 1988), 20-29.

70. Ernst Hanisch, "Die nationalsozialistische Herrschaft 1938-1945, in *Geschichte Salzgurgs*, Vol. II/2, 1145.

71. Ernst Hanisch, "Salzburg in der Zweiten Republik: Der politische Wiederaufbau," in *Geschichte Salzburgs*, Vol. II/2, 1180.

72. Every historical commemoration of Salzburg's past serves that purpose, the most recent example being the "millennium." When official Austria is celebrating 1,000 years of "*Ostarrichi*" as regional name mentioned in a document, Salzburg is already celebrating 1,000 years of the city's right to mint coins and points out that she had been a flourishing economic center in 996 and that the bishopric exercised influence far beyond the current borderlines of today's Austria.

The Politics of Memory: Austria's Perception of the Second World War and the National Socialist Period

*Heidemarie Uhl**

Fifty years after the end of the Second World War, the rule of the National Socialists in Austria has become a "past that refuses to be forgotten." Austria's perception of itself as the first free country to have fallen victim to Hitlerite aggression and its consequent refusal to acknowledge any responsibility for participating in the Nazi regime went unchallenged for many years. In fact, it remained unchallenged until the controversies surrounding Kurt Waldheim's candidacy for the presidency finally sparked off a wider public debate. Austria is, of course, not the only country currently trying to cope with its highly controversial past. Its recent efforts to reassess the war and National Socialism largely mirror similar debates in many European countries since the 1980s, when the political myths that were cultivated during the postwar period were finally shattered. These debates took on diverse forms and were carried out under a variety of headings, from the controversy among German historians over the question of whether or not a historicist and relativizing approach to Nazi crimes was permissible,[1] to the debate in France over the relative impact of the Resistance and Nazi collaborators during the Vichy regime.[2] Along with Austria's attempts to reinterpret its role in the Second World War, another point that clearly emerges in these debates is that these controversies must be viewed against the background of the prevailing historical memory of each nation, since the arguments used in historic

* I am grateful to Ursula Stachl-Peier for translating this essay from German into English.

reappraisal efforts are essentially aimed at revealing the repression, taboos, and common interpretations of the past.

In this respect, even critical evaluations of the Second World War and Austria's years under National Socialism tend to be colored by a specifically Austrian policy on history. Since 1945, "Austrian historical memory"[3] has been dominated by Austria's view of itself as the first victim of Hitlerite aggression. This article will discuss the pervading impact of this theory on the country's construction of a historical identity. It will also cover Austria's political attempts to come to terms with its Nazi legacy through 1986 when the debate over Kurt Waldheim's alleged membership in the *Sturm Abteilung* (SA) finally provoked a wider debate and a reappraisal of Austria's Nazi past.

The Theory of Victimization in Austrian Historical Consciousness

Even before the end of the war, on 27 April 1945, a provisional government, comprised of members of the Socialist Party (SPÖ), the newly constituted People's Party (ÖVP, the successors of the former Christian-Socials), and the Communist Party (KPÖ), issued a joint Declaration of Independence to the effect that "the democratic Republic of Austria" would be reestablished. The Constitution of the Second Republic included attempts to clearly define Austria's responsibility for participation in the Nazi regime. Quoting the Moscow Declaration issued at the meeting of the Allied foreign ministers on 30 October 1943, Austria adopted the label of "first free country to fall a victim to Hitlerite aggression," and the annexation of March 1938 was pictured as military occupation which was "imposed on the country."

The Declaration of Independence from the Third Reich also contains an extensive discussion of the involvement of Austrian nationals in the German *Wehrmacht*. This was a highly controversial issue as the Moscow Declaration had unambiguously stated that Austria had a responsibility for participation in the war on the side of Hitlerite Germany. Such imputations were denied by the provisional government, however, which justified its dismissal by pointing to the "fact that Adolf Hitler's National Socialist government, having totally subdued the Austrian people and rendered it powerless, led it into a pointless and hopeless war of conquest which no Austrian had ever wanted." Anticipating the line of argumentation that was later to be adopted in the negotiations for the State Treaty, they argued that the country's "own contribution to her liberation" as demanded by the Moscow Declaration presumed the existence of an independent Austrian state or government and could thus not apply as long as no such state or government existed. While the provisional government promised to "immediately seize all available measures in its power in order to contribute to her liberation," it also pointed out that "this could only be a modest contribution given the exhaustion of our people and depletion of the country's resources."[4]

This "Austria-as-Hitler's-first-victim" theory which dominated Austria's perception of itself in the years between 1945 and the 1980s can be summed up as follows: In March 1938 Austria was occupied and annexed by Germany against its will; it was liberated in April/May 1945 by Austrian resistance fighters and the Allies. The years between 1938 and 1945 were described as a period of foreign rule and, as far as Austria's role and participation in the war was concerned, these were portrayed as a period of resistance and persecution, of the nation's fight for its liberation. This perception of its past is also visible in Austria's national emblem. The eagle, which had also been used during the First Republic, was now additionally adorned with broken chains to symbolize Austria's liberation from foreign domination.[5] Efforts to promote and reinforce this perception of history included the erection of monuments commemorating the death of those who had lost their lives in the struggle for Austria's liberation in Vienna and the provinces,[6] an officious anti-fascist exhibition in 1946 in the *Vienna Künstlerhaus* with the title of "We'll Never Forget,"[7] and the publication of the "Red-White-Red Book" by the Austrian government in 1946, whose aim was to highlight the important role played by the Austrian resistance movement during the war years.[8]

All these activities promoted a view of history which had little to do with the historic reality of Nazi rule in Austria and could only be upheld as long as central aspects of the Third Reich were completely ignored. One of the first to adopt a more critical stance was Gerhard Botz, who pointed out that not only was Hitler an "Austrian export article," but that in Austria a higher percentage of the population were members of the National Socialist Party than in Germany (in 1942, approximately 688,000 persons, that is 8.2 percent of the total population, were NSDAP members; if their families are included in the count ca. 25 percent of the population can be said to have been sympathizers of the Nazi party). Botz further pointed out that anti-Semitism in Austria was at least as virulent as in Germany. As regards Austrian attitudes to the war, evidence would suggest that a large majority of the Austrian people joined in the "blitzkrieg euphoria." War weariness, the consequent anti-German feeling, and increased emphasis on Austria's independent status emerged only after the defeat of the German *Wehrmacht* at Stalingrad, the promulgation of the Moscow Declaration, and the abortive assassination attempt on Hitler on 20 July 1944.[9] However, resistance operations remained restricted to small-scale and localized efforts, and no nationwide Austrian Freedom Movement was ever organized.[10]

For the founding fathers of the Second Republic, the official view of the Nazi era was less a matter of revealing historical truth than of following the "dictates of political reason,"[11] and accepting the status of victim offered by the Moscow Declaration. Although this interpretation only partially reflected the experiences of the majority of Austrians, it provided the country with a welcome opportunity to distance itself from National Socialism, at least *ex post facto*, and to obtain "moral absolution"[12] at a time when the Third Reich was heading for defeat and the full extent of Nazi crimes was gradually becoming obvious. It was therefore not only at the level of the official state policy that this picture of Austrians fighting against National Socialism and for the country's liberation was enthusiastically espoused and made the central point of reference. The story of the Austrian anti-fascist struggle was shared by all three parties and used as an integrating factor. Nor, indeed, was it a view exclusively promulgated by the political elites. In May 1945 over 10,000 people participated in a memorial ceremony held at the Central Cemetery in Graz to commemorate the death of 142 victims of the Nazi regime and thus to express their "revulsion at the execrable crimes" and objection to a "system which has for ever inscribed itself in blood into world history."[13] For the Styrian Governor, the Socialist Reinhold Machhold, the death of the 142 victims "testified to Austria's struggle against the despots of the Third Reich," but he also stressed the "grave guilt that the Austrian people had heaped upon itself by tolerating the Nazi yoke and participating in the war."[14] Similar professions came from the Socialist and Communist Parties as well as from representatives of the conservative People's Party, among them Alfons Gorbach, who on the eve of the first general elections in November 1945 declared that the new democratic Austria was based on the "legacy left by the martyrs from amongst the ranks of all three parties," and demanded "justice for the victims of the Nazi regime which implies punishment for the guilty."[15] Soon after, Gorbach was to become a vociferous proponent of a policy of reconciliation towards former members of the National Socialist party.[16]

However, the integrative force of the Austria-as-Hitler's-first-victim theory was short-lived. First signs that the discourse of "double speak"[17] would become the characteristic feature of the Austrian view of history emerged as early as 1945. The integration of former members of the National Socialist Party became the main topic of domestic political debate—partly motivated by party-political interests—while the controversy over Austria's responsibility for the war was increasingly repressed and eventually restricted to periodic statements issued by societies representing the victims and the Communist Party, which by then no longer held any political sway.[18] In foreign politics, the theory of Austria as Hitler's first victim had an even greater significance. It was used as a legal instrument to fend off any compensation and reparation claims against the Austrian state for its participation in the war and in Nazi crimes.

Ironically, the official version of events promoted by the "Red-White-Red Book" gives an indication of the extent to which the official story of the Nazi era was guided by political opportunism and the gap between this interpretation and the collective experience of the Austrian people, which was often diametrically opposed to what was officially promulgated. The book's stated aim was to provide justification for Austrian "demands to be accepted and treated as a 'liberated state' in line with the Moscow Declaration." In a chapter entitled "The Austrians and the War" it claimed that

> the Austrian population had from the start been opposed to the "Hitlerite war" except by those for whom the end of the war was the only possibility to shake off the Nazi yoke. ...Every Austrian soldier can confirm that the treatment of Austrian soldiers in the German *Wehrmacht* was particularly unfair and humiliating. ...Anyone seeking to give a correct and fair appraisal of the situation Austria found itself in right from the beginning of the occupation will have to admit that the blood tribute exacted from Austria in this war was nothing but an additional terrible burden on a country which was already suffering under the heavy burden of occupation, and thus worse than in other occupied countries.[19]

We shall not go into a detailed discussion of the contradiction between the official view and historic reality, especially the denial that the Anschluß had been enthusiastically welcomed by a large majority of the population and that Austrian soldiers readily identified with the German *Wehrmacht* in the Second World War. Even the Moscow Declaration was primarily a means to an end, with the statements issued by the Allied foreign ministers being used less as a framework for the construction of postwar Austria than as a propaganda instrument to strengthen the Austrian resistance movement, as Günter Bischof recently showed.[20] Still, insistence on Austria's status as first victim, sanctified by international law, became the central strategy during the negotiations for the State Treaty, with the emphasis placed on the "Austrians, but no Austria" argument which essentially said that, because no Austrian state and no Austrian government existed at the time, Austria could not be held responsible for the crimes committed by the Nazi regime. Regarding the involvement of Austrian nationals in military actions, it was argued that, like the residents of other occupied regions, Austrians had been forced to "serve in a despised war machinery."[21] It was also this line of argument that was successfully employed by the Austrian government in the last round of negotiations when, on 14 May 1955, they persuaded the Allies to omit the "share of the responsibility clause."[22]

Although this "historic fiction" had lost its pragmatic justification[23] with the signing of the State Treaty, national self-portrayals continued to hinge upon the myth of Austria-as-Hitler's-first-victim, which, until the Waldheim controversy, was also responsible for Austria's positive image abroad. International attention initially focussed on the Federal Republic of Germany which, as the successor state of the Third Reich, was held liable for the Holocaust and had to prove to a critical public that it was capable of implementing a democratization process.[24] Austria, in contrast, chose to present itself as an occupied state, and to ignore the large number of Austrians who had been members of the NSDAP and held leading positions in the Nazi apparatus of terror and oppression. Ernst Kaltenbrunner, who after 1943 was the highest ranking SS officer after Heinrich Himmler, Adolf Eichmann and a considerable number of other Austrians who were in charge of organizing the "final solution," including Odilo Globocnik who masterminded "Operation Reinhard" in which between 1.9 and 2.2 million Jews lost their lives, as well as the commander of the extermination camps of Sobibor and Treblinka, Franz Stangl,[25] were all perceived as Germans and never as Austrians. The arrest and execution of Adolf Eichmann in 1961 represented a key event in Germany's efforts to come to grips with its past, and was followed by a much-publicized series of trials (the "Auschwitz trials") at which several former SS officials were convicted of war crimes.[26] Similar trials in Austria usually ended in outrageous "not guilty" verdicts for the defendants, often pronounced after witnesses of the prosecution had been crassly mocked and ridiculed.[27] Austria preferred to view the war from the perspective of the victim, for example, at the national memorial exhibition which was opened on 13 March 1978 at Auschwitz, the symbolic location of Nazi crimes, where leading politicians have consistently stressed that "Austrians need feel no remorse when they come to Auschwitz-Birkenau. ...The Austrian president, its chancellor and foreign minister only mention Austria's victims and strong involvement in the resistance." Responsibility for the war and the admission of guilt was obviously the prerogative of West Germany, while GDR politicians traditionally invoked memories of Communist resistance.[28]

Even Austria's foremost memorial to the Holocaust, the Mauthausen concentration camp, did not escape reinterpretation and appropriation by official bodies for legitimization purposes. After heated debates (which included the discussion of a proposal to demolish the camp) Mauthausen was finally established as a commemoration center following initiatives by international associations of former prisoners. In 1970, a museum was added by the Austrian government. Its didactic educational approach, however, continues to focus on the portrayal of Austria as Hitler's victim (which also underlies the design of a further exhibition installed in 1982 which presents Austrians in other Nazi concentration camps and ghettos), despite the fact that the history of Mauthausen provides much clearer evidence of Austria's participation in the oppression of Europe than proof of its role of victim. Only 1 percent of the prisoners in Mauthausen were Austrian nationals, while the guards and warders were mainly Austrians and Germans.[29]

In Austria, as in the other two successor states of the Third Reich, the ideology espoused by the country's founding fathers after 1945 not only determined the choice of political symbols but it also left its mark on the strategies and measures underlying efforts to come to terms with the legacy of Austria's Nazi past. A comparative study by Agnes Blänsdorf clearly showed that the denazification, compensation, and reparation policies adopted by the three successor states were closely linked to how the countries perceived their role in the war, to what extent they felt liable for events, which claims were accepted and which rejected, and which issues were considered controversial and which fit for discussion.[30] Immediately after the war, far-reaching denazification measures were implemented in the occupied territories in Germany and Austria which reflected the desire of the victorious powers and the new political elites, who were mostly former opponents of the Nazi regime, to punish those who were responsible for the war and Nazi crimes and to remove all former members of the National Socialist Party who had held positions in the state apparatus from public life. After a few years, however, the rigorous moral approach of the early period was replaced by a more lenient policy of integration which aimed at bringing political stability and pacification to the postwar societies. This meant that the denazification program was never fully implemented, and, given its idealistic sociopolitical aims, must be judged a failure. In Austria, these difficulties were compounded by the fact that national and party political interests played a major role right from the beginning. Registration procedures, for examples, included exemption clauses for those Nazis who had "never abused" their positions and "proved through their behavior even before Austria was liberated that they viewed the establishment of an independent Republic of Austria positively." Between 85 and 90 percent of the 550,000 registered NSDAP members and applicants for membership thus pleaded mitigating circumstances. Another important factor was that responsibility for the denazification measures in Austria was assumed by the provisional government, whereas in Germany these were controlled by the Allies. In Austria, the treatment of former Nazis was thus open to exploitation for partisan ends, as was soon to become apparent when in the to the elections of 1945 all parties, vying for the votes of the large number of people who felt threatened by the denazification program, issued statements officially exonerating Nazi sympathizers.[31] The State President, Dr. Karl Renner, declared that only a small percentage of the NSDAP members had been ardent and steadfast supporters of the party, while "the majority had given in to economic, social or even personal pressures."[32]

Consequently, even in 1946 around 90 percent of former NSDAP members and applicants for membership were judged to be "less incriminated" (42,129 persons, mostly Nazi officials and members of the SS, were still considered guilty) and subsequently amnestied. Following their reinstatement in their jobs they also received compensation for losses suffered after 1945.[33] While denazification in Austria was characterized by efforts to exonerate and reintegrate former Nazis, the official policy adopted with regard to compensations for Jewish victims was marked by attempts to ward off claims. Claims for compensation and reparation payments were rejected, and the "Austrians, but no Austria" line of argumentation was rigidly applied. When the Jewish Claims Conference, having successfully completed negotiations with West Germany which led to the adoption of the Federal Compensation Payment Act in 1953, filed similar claims for compensation against Austria, these were rejected by the Austrian Government that argued that when these crimes against the Jewish community were committed, Austria had been occupied by Germany and could therefore not be held legally responsible; similarly, no moral responsibility could be inferred as the crimes against the Jewish people were perpetrated by the Germans. The members of the Committee for Jewish Claims on Austria were informed that "all the suffering to which the Jews were subjected during this period was inflicted on them by the Germans and not by Austrians; Austria could not be held responsible for any of these evil doings, and where there is no responsibility there can be no claims for compensation."[34] Only after protests from the international community and the Allied Council did the Austrian government bow to pressure and make compensation payments, insisting all the time, however, that no responsibility for the crimes could be inferred from this.[35]

In fact, this persistent portrayal of itself as a victim so as to dismiss claims brought against the state by the victims of Nazi persecution (Austrian Jews, Sintis and Romanis, and homosexuals) has provoked the sharpest criticism. Today, there is general agreement in Austria that the Austria-as-Hitler's-first-victim theory is derived from a dubious, or at least very one-sided, perception of its Nazi past. Critics such as Robert Menasse have even argued that "this Republic was founded on an historic lie, on the lie that Austria was exclusively the victim of Nazi aggression."[36]

Still, this interpretation—despite, or perhaps precisely because of the fact that it had so little to do with historic truth and people's experiences—informed official interpretations of the country's Nazi past and colored its historical memory of the Second Republic, both official perceptions and individual and collective recollections. In the discussions of Austrian memory it was less a matter of what could be publicly pronounced than what was covered by the official cloak of silence. Taboo topics included the wide-spread approval of the Anschluß in 1938 and—at least initially—enthusiastic espousal of National Socialism, the crimes against political opponents, Jews, and other discriminated minorities which were perpetrated in Austria or by Austrians, as well as Austria's participation in war crimes.[37]

M. Rainer Lepsius, the German sociologist, coined the term "externalization" to describe Austria's way of coping with its past. While for the Germans their National Socialist past represents an extremely negative phase and thus a central point of reference which has been "normatively internalized" as a constant reminder, warning, and yardstick for political action, Austrians tended to see this period as belonging to Germany's but not their own history. National Socialism was thus seen as something imposed by external forces for which Austria could not be held responsible.[38] The same applies to Austria's perception of its role in the Second World War. In a standard textbook, *Geschichte Österreichs*, the two authors Ernst Görlich and Felix Romanik wrote in 1970, "The Second World War belongs to world history, but not to Austrian history. It was not an Austrian war. Austria did not participate in it."[39]

The Politics of "Double Speak"

The line of argument that depicts Austria as a victim represents only one side of efforts to interpret the past, namely the one used in official presentations of the country, especially in foreign politics, schoolbooks, and other official publications. In domestic politics, opposing views could be heard soon after the end of the war as the political situation became increasingly more stabilized. This was partly due to a relaxation in tense relations, especially with the western occupation powers, and partly due to the escalation of the Cold War, as even former Nazis were able to identify with anti-Communism and the concept of the Soviet enemy. However, the main impetus for a reorientation in Austria's historical policy was provided by the stabilization of the political scene and power relations in Austria after the general elections in November 1945. The outcome was an overwhelming victory for the Socialists and People's Party, while the

Communist Party, whose campaign had focussed on its resistance record, gained only 5 percent of the vote.[40] This surprising result seemed to suggest that legitimization efforts based on references to the Austrian liberation struggle would henceforth carry little weight in domestic politics and could thus be abandoned. Interest subsequently focussed on the integration and social rehabilitation of former Nazis, in particular in the elections of 1949 when the "less incriminated" former NSDAP members were again allowed to vote, and the "undignified vying for the votes of former Nazis" reached its climax.[41] As the two bigger parties concentrated more and more on wooing the Nazi vote, they increasingly distanced themselves from the resistance fighters and victims of fascism—even those in their own ranks. A few years ago the Socialist Josef Hindels recalled how concentration camp survivors were admonished by prominent politicians to "stop talking of the atrocities in the concentration camps because people don't want to hear about it any more."[42]

While the parties contended for the Nazi vote, there were also first indications that official policy on portrayals of the past were gradually changing, most significantly in the area of war memorials. The change was restricted to local and regional initiatives, and thus stood in stark contrast with concurrent trends in Vienna where political culture differed markedly from the conservative rural attitudes which prevailed in the provinces. By 1948/49, rural areas gradually began to abandon the anti-fascist perspective of the Austria as Hitler's victim theory which had informed the country's perception of the past as well as its conception of memorials. In an effort to provide legitimization for the state, by the end of the 1950s, references to the Austrian struggle for liberation had been replaced by a politically labeled view of history which was largely confined to associations of former resistance fighters and the Communist Party. Whereas proposals for the erection of monuments to the memory of resistance fighters met with outright rejection,[43] after 1950, more and more people called for the erection of war memorials. At first, these changes in commemorative culture were seen as a paradigm shift in popular attitudes to military service by Austrians in the *Wehrmacht*. A commentary on the memorial services of 1949 put it as follows: "From now on all those Austrians who were killed in action in the Second World War will also be afforded a place of honor in the memory of our people," and not only commemorated as victims because " [I]t is not true that it was solely the clever workings of the system that drove all these hundreds of thousands of soldiers to their deaths. There were heroes in all the ranks of the *Wehrmacht* who conscientiously fulfilled their duty and showed great courage."[44] The war memorials which were subsequently erected not only served to preserve the memory of the dead soldiers but also visible signals that "the fatherland again paid tribute to its sons who were killed in the worst fight."[45]

In the years that followed, war memorials assumed a normative status in determining collective memory. While few monuments were erected that aimed at preserving the memory of resistance fighters and victims of the regime, almost every local authority erected a monument to its dead soldiers. Often, the planning and erection of the memorials coincided with the establishment of local *Kameradschaftsbund* associations.[46] The *Kameradschaftsbund*, as the umbrella organization of all the veterans' associations in Austria, thus assumed a monopoly position, and henceforth dominated the interpretation of the Second World War. The political parties, at whose initiative the majority of monuments to the memory of the freedom fighters had been erected, increasingly withdrew, not without first assuring the *Kameradschaftsbund* of its support. Leading politicians from all parties (except the Communist Party), publicly called for a "full rehabilitation of the soldiers, also of those who fought on the side of Germany." These appeals may well have been motivated by the promise of election gains. In 1952, for example, the Styrian *Kameradschaftsbund* was comprised of 60,000 members organized in 300 local associations, and thus represented a powerful force.[47]

Not only local politicians bestowed public praise on the dead for being "soldiers who protected our fatherland in battle," and who were prepared "to fulfill their duty by risking their own lives" (as the Styrian Governor Josef Krainer put it in 1961), but similar comments at dedication ceremonies came also from members of the federal government.[48] Such public recognition by leading politicians was precisely what the generation of soldiers needed to give the years they had wasted in the *Wehrmacht* some meaning.[49] Above all, it furthered the *Kameradschaftsbund's* declared aim of rehabilitating the *Wehrmacht* soldiers, who were suddenly no longer the victims of Nazi war policies but heroes who had given their lives in fulfillment of their duties at the altar of their fatherland.[50]

The *Feliferhof* memorial in *Graz*'s central cemetery, commemorating the Nazi-murder of 142 people. Initially built in 1947, the Graz artist August Raid crafted the glass mosaics seen here on the theme of "mankind defiled" in 1967. (Branko Lenart Art Photographs, Graz)

August Raid's realistic frescoes of the suffering soldier painted for the *Kriegermahnmal* on the sacral ground of the village cemetery of *St. Georgen/Murnau* in Styria (1957). (August Raid collection, photo by Fürböck, Graz)

Wilhelm Gösser's unheroic *guter Kamerad*, the archetypical dying soldier who "did his duty," in the *Langenwang* war memorial in Styria (1952). (Branko Lenart Art Photographs, Graz)

The contested *internationales Mahnmal* in the central cemetery in *Graz* financed and built by Yugoslavia and the Austro-Yugoslav society (1961), commemorating Yugoslav Nazi victims (partisans, women and children). Local Styrian politicians distanced themselves from singling out Nazi victims and wanted to see *all* victims of war memorialized, including the postwar German refugees from Yugoslavia.
(Branko Lenart Art Photographs, Graz)

In short, the 1950s witness the emergence of a policy of "double speak," an ambiguous perception of history which was to prove the most pervasive influence on Austria's specific construction of the past. In international politics, Austria emphasized its role as Hitler's first victim, and—by pointing to the Austrian resistance movement as proof—as anti-Nazi state, whereas at the national level, the memories of the resistance and Nazi crimes were marginalized. While the Austrian negotiators in the negotiations for the State Treaty insisted on the deletion of the "share of responsibility clause," Austrian politicians were paying public tribute to the former *Wehrmacht* soldiers, praising them for so conscientiously fulfilling their duties and for their willingness to make sacrifices for their homeland. Yet, as soon as Austria's share in the responsibility for the Nazi crimes was queried—for example with respect to claims brought against the state by Jewish victims—all charges were rejected and justified by Austria's legally acknowledged status as Hitler's first victim and the fact that after March 1938 the Austrian state and Austrian government had ceased to exist.

The Waldheim Debate and its Consequences

The first time Austria saw itself seriously confronted with its Nazi past was during the Waldheim debate. Waldheim's comment that he "had only done exactly what hundreds of thousands of Austrians had done, namely fulfill my duty as a soldier," all of a sudden revealed the contradictions inherent in the country's official version of the past, especially its assessment of military service in the *Wehrmacht*. This crucial comment formed the focus of a highly charged emotional debate over appraisals of the war and postwar period, over incriminating behavior or perhaps only unwanted involvement in the Nazi regime, and above all—and this was the crux of the conflict—over the question of how the war generation viewed the period from the contemporary perspective. It was precisely because Kurt Waldheim was no war criminal and, for all intents and purposes, not even a member of the Nazi party that the "Waldheim affair" was able to trigger the "great awakening" and thus the most profound identity crisis in the history of postwar Austria. Waldheim's biography showed that he was an average Austrian *Mitläufer* who had neither been a fervent National Socialist nor an outspoken opponent of the Nazi regime but rather someone that "always tried to conform."[51] Waldheim was no exception; he was the archetype. The majority of Austrians had acted in a similar fashion and—after the war—tried to fit the years spent under Nazi rule smoothly into their life histories. For this war generation, Waldheim was a symbolic figure. Every criticism of the presidential candidate's past was interpreted as a critique of their own past and thus a threat to their own identity which had been so painfully constructed. Their justifications and excuses were challenged by the postwar generation who, from the vantage point of someone not handicapped by personal involvement, could view the Nazi era from a greater distance and thus more critically.

As an exhaustive treatment of the conflict would go beyond the scope of this paper,[52] this discussion will focus on the long-term effects of the Waldheim debate. Essentially it prompted the overthrow of the traditional version of events and made way for a new perception of Austria's Nazi past. Commemoration ceremonies to mark the fiftieth anniversary of the Anschluß offered a fit opportunity to respond to the delegitimization of the traditional view of history and to formulate a new normative vision of the Nazi past. During the anniversary year, institutions at all levels of political life—from the government, parties, the media, universities, schools, churches, to small local groups—organized commemoration ceremonies, historical projects, exhibitions, lecture series, discussions, and produced publications and erected monuments to publicly manifest their position which was mainly informed by a new "basic agreement on Austrians' shared responsibility."[53] The Waldheim affair of 1986 and its antithesis, the anniversary year of 1938, 1988, have provided the momentum needed to bring about a change in Austria's historical memory, and have also initiated a paradigmatic shift in history studies. For the first time the focus was on the "role of Austria in the creation and functioning of National Socialism."[54] Previously, research in contemporary history and on the period between 1938 and 1945 had concentrated on the aspect of "resistance and persecution."[55] Although these studies documented the crimes which were perpetrated by the Nazi regime (for example, in the publications by the Documentation Archives of the Austrian resistance movement), responsibility for them was attributed to the Nazi regime, and they were never perceived as a problem that should concern Austrian society. Since 1986, "the coordinates of analysis"[56] have changed and interest now essentially focusses on new issues, including:

* the ambivalence of the Anschluß which cannot be seen merely in terms of military occupation by a foreign power but as a "kind of take-over of power by National Socialism from within;"[57]
* the complex reality of Austria under Nazi rule, characterized by the ambivalent processes of enthusiastic support and conformism, of resistance and destruction.[58] The anthology entitled *Nazi Rule in Austria* was the first attempt to provide a comprehensive picture of the period 1938-45.[59] A more differentiated view was also applied in a reevaluation of the role of the resistance movement in Austria. Research on the resistance was reassessed in terms of its impact on the legitimization process,[60] and resistance itself underwent reinterpretation, for example to be defined as an "Austrian Civil War" between supporters and opponents of National Socialism;[61]
* Austria's participation in Nazi crimes,[62] Austrians as high-ranking officials responsible for the extermination of the Jewish people,[63] as well as everyday anti-Semitism in the attacks on the Jewish community in March 1938 and during the 1938 November pogroms, further the "Aryanizations,"[64] the treatment of Jewish victims and the masked survival of anti-Semitic feelings after 1945.[65] Other topics addressed included the most controversial point of contention, the role of the *Wehrmacht* and especially the "war of destruction" waged against the Soviet Union and in the Balkans.[66]

These topics show that research in history increasingly concentrated on what had previously been the blind spot of Austrian historical memory. The upcoming generation of Austrian historians sees its task as educating the nation, and aims to make sure that an "acknowledgement of Austria's responsibility" will be a central point of the discussion[67] and thus provide a counterbalance to the misrepresentation of historical events which pervaded prior accounts of the past. However, recently this position has come under considerable criticism. Anton Pelinka, for example, argued that the myth of Austria as victim was being replaced by another myth, that of Austria as perpetrator of crimes, which undoubtedly could be morally justified but also fell short of the whole truth, as it did not take into consideration the constraints under which decisions in the postwar period had to be taken. He pointed out that the turning of a painful past into a taboo provided essential protection for the social integration process.[68]

Has the deconstruction of the victim myth, of the "lie underlying Austrian life," achieved the aim envisioned by the politicians, leading to the adoption of a more critical attitude toward the past? An answer to the question of how National Socialism and the Second World War are viewed today, fifty years after the end of the war and nearly ten years after the Waldheim affair, is far from clear cut. There is general agreement that the Nazi period cannot be denied and must be seen as an integral part of Austria's history and that the Second Republic must take on a moral responsibility for its participation in the Nazi crimes and the murder and expulsion of Austrian Jews. The first official apology by the Republic of Austria "for crimes of National Socialism perpetrated by Austrians" (from a speech by Present Waldheim)[69] was made during the memorial year of 1988. Since then, the Austrian nation has on numerous occasions been admonished "to live in truth before our history, with its bright and dark hours" (as President Klestil put it in his inaugural address),[70] most recently by President Klestil and Chancellor Vranitzky during their official visits to Israel. Surveys show that such public admissions of guilt are approved of by the majority of the population. When Chancellor Vranitzky pronounced in Jerusalem in 1993 that Austrians bore collective responsibility for the crimes of the Nazi regime, 81 percent of the population agreed fully or partly, and only 17 percent felt such a statement unacceptable.[71] The ceremonies to commemorate the fiftieth anniversary of the end of the war in the Mauthausen concentration camp and in the Austrian Parliament offered another occasion for politicians to pay official tribute to the victims of Nazi crimes.

In many areas, a much more differentiated perception of the past has taken hold. Much of what would have passed unnoticed or unchallenged before 1986 is today likely to meet with vociferous protests. In 1992 the Styrian governor and his deputies accepted patronage for a meeting of an SS veterans' association, yet were later forced to withdraw the offer after vehement public criticism.[72] The numerous local initiatives to erect monuments to the memory of

The *Synagogendenkmal* in *Graz* (1988). The Jewish synagogue was burned down in the November progrom 1938; its original floor plan is indicated by the layout of the tiles in the foreground. This memorial was dedicated on the occasion of the fiftieth anniversary of the November progrom on November 11, 1988, and has become a symbol of post-Waldheim memorial culture in which the dark chapters of World War II become an integral part of Austrian history.
(Branko Lenart Art Photographs, Graz)

One of two locally inspired 1988 memorials reminding the people of *Aflenz* near Leibnitz in Styria that their village housed a subcamp of the Mauthausen concentration camp in which 350 to 400 people perished in 1944/45. The text reads: *"Mahnmal zum Gedenken aller Toten des KZ-Nebenlagers Aflenz von 1944 bis 1945. Mahnend der Leibnitzer Bildungs - und Jugendclub der Gewerkschaft."* (Branko Lenart Art Photographs, Graz)

victims of the Nazi regime in recent years would suggest that the "shared responsibility view" is not confined to national Austrian politics but has become politically acceptable at the local level as well.[73]

However, public discourse has also been informed by a reverse trend which has sought to play down or at least partially justify certain aspects of National Socialism. Since Jörg Haider was elected chairman of the Freedom Party in 1986, the FPÖ has increasingly assumed the role of mouthpiece for this interpretation of history. In their polemic they have resuscitated a line of argumentation from which the other parties dissociated themselves after the Waldheim debate, that is explicit support for former *Wehrmacht* soldiers. At a meeting of veterans' associations at the Ulrichsberg in Carinthia in 1990, Jörg Haider, then governor of Carinthia, declared in his address to World War II soldiers, "In the near future, your sacrifice will be shown in its true light because the history of Europe has clearly proved that the foundations for peace and freedom have been laid by you." Through such pronouncements, Jörg Haider "deliberately refuses to join in the consensus of opinion of the Second Republic, and adopts a position of fundamental opposition,"[74] as is also evidenced by public responses to his most recent speech at a meeting of Waffen SS veterans at Krumpendorf in Carinthia in which he described them as respectable citizens who were intellectually superior. For the majority of commentators in the media, the FPÖ chairman has "moved away so far from the basic democratic consensus of the Second Republic that there is no turning back."[75]

The replacement of the Austria-as-victim thesis by the public admission of Austrian responsibility, and attempts to play down and gloss over the impact of National Socialism on the one hand, and an Austria-as-perpetrator view of the Nazi period on the other hand, have produced a more pluralistic, contradictory, and controversial view of the past. However, it is precisely these conflicting perceptions of the past in which the contrasting *Weltanschauungen* that inform them are clearly still manifest.

NOTES

1. See Charles S. Maier, *The Unmasterable Past: History, Holocaust, and German National Identity* (Cambridge: Harvard University Press, 1988); *"Historikerstreit:" Die Dokumentation der Kontroverse um die Einzigartigkeit der nationalsozialistischen Judenvernichtung* (Munich: Piper, 1987).

2. See Tony Judt, "Die Vergangenheit ist ein anderes Land: Politische Mythen im Nachkriegseuropa," *Transit* 6 (August 1993): 87-120.

3. Waltraud Kannonier-Finster and Meinrad Ziegler, *Österreichisches Gedächtnis: Über Erinnern und Vergessen der NS-Vergangenheit* (Vienna: Böhlau, 1993). General discussions of Austria's Nazi past and Austrian attempts to define its identity include: Gerhard Botz and Gerald Sprengnagel, eds., *Kontroversen um Österreichs Zeitgeschichte: Verdrängte Vergangenheit, Österreich-Identität, Waldheim und die Historiker* (Frankfurt: Campus, 1994); F. Parkinson, ed., *Conquering the Past: Austrian Nazism Yesterday and Today* (Detroit: Wayne State University Press, 1989); Ernst Bruckmüller, *Österreichbewußtsein im Wandel: Identität und Selbstverständnis in den 90er Jahren* (Vienna: Signum Verlag, 1994); Susanne Breuss, Karin Liebhart, and Andreas Pribersky, *Inszenierungen: Stichwörter zu Österreich* (Vienna: Sonderzahl, 1995); and Erika Weinzierl, "Österreichische Nation und österreichisches Nationalbewußtsein," *Zeitgeschichte* 17 (October 1989): 44-62.

4. *Staatsgesetzblatt für die Republik Österreich*, 1 May 1945.

5. Gustav Spann, "Zur Geschichte von Flagge und Wappen der Republik Österreich," in *Österreichs politische Symbole: Historisch, ästhetisch und ideologiekritisch beleuchtet*, ed. Norbert Leser and Manfred Wagner (Vienna: Böhlau, 1994), 59; Peter Diem, *Die Symbole Österreichs: Zeit und Geschichte in Zeichen* (Vienna: Kremayr & Scheriau, 1995), 124f.

6. Wolfgang Lauber, *Wien: Ein Stadtführer durch den Widerstand 1934-1945* (Vienna: 1987); Heidemarie Uhl, "Erinnern und Vergessen. Denkmäler zur Erinnerung an die Opfer der nationalsozialistischen Gewaltherrschaft und an die Gefallenen des Zweiten Weltkriegs in Graz und in der Steiermark," in *Todeszeichen. Zeitgeschichtliche Denkmalkultur in Graz und in der Steiermark vom Ende des 19. Jahrhunderts bis zur Gegenwart*, ed. Stefan Riesenfellner and Heidemarie Uhl (Vienna: Böhlau 1994), 130ff. As the only overview of Austrian monuments to the memory of the resistance, still useful is Erich Fein, *Die Steine reden: Gedenkstätten des österreichischen Freiheitskampfes. Mahnmale für die Opfer des Faschismus. Eine Dokumentation* (Vienna: Europaverlag, 1975).

7. Wolfgang Kos, "Die Schau mit dem Hammer: Zur Planung, Ideologie und Gestaltung der antifaschistischen Ausstellung 'Niemals Vergessen!,'" in *Eigenheim Österreich: Zu Politik, Kultur und Alltag nach 1945* (Vienna: Sonderzahl, 1994), 7-58.

8. *Rot-Weiß-Rot-Buch: Gerechtigkeit für Österreich! Darstellungen, Dokumente und Nachweise zur Vorgeschichte und Geschichte der Okkupation Österreichs.* Nach amtlichen Quellen. Erster Teil (Vienna: 1946). A second volume was planned but never published.

9. Gerhard Botz, "Eine deutsche Geschichte 1938 bis 1945?," *Zeitgeschichte* 14 (October 1986): 19-38; Hans Safrian, "Österreicher in der Wehrmacht," in *Österreicher und der Zweite Weltkrieg*, ed. Dokumentationsarchiv des österreichischen Widerstandes, Bundesministerium für Unterricht, Kunst und Sport (Vienna: Österreichischer Bundesverlag, 1989), 47ff.

10. Radomír Luža, *Der Widerstand in Österreich 1938-1945* (Vienna: Österreichischer Bundesverlag, 1985), 315 ff.; Hans Mommsen, *Widerstand und politische Kultur in Deutschland und Österreich* (Vienna: Picus, 1994).

11. Lonnie R. Johnson, "Die österreichische Nation, die Moskauer Deklaration und die völkerrechtliche Argumentation: Bemerkungen zur Problematik der Interpretation der NS-Zeit in Österreich," *Jahrbuch 1988,* ed. Dokumentationsarchiv des österreichischen Widerstandes (Vienna: Österreichischer Bundesverlag, 1988), 47.

12. Ibid., 48.

13. Ibid.

14. "Wir geloben, die Schuld zu tilgen," *Neue Steirische Zeitung*, 29 May 1945.

15. Alfons Gorbach, "Gedenkt der Blutzeugen für Österreichs Freiheit," *Steirerblatt*, 2 November 1945.

16. Dieter A. Binder, "Steirische oder Österreichische Volkspartei," in *Volkspartei - Anspruch und Realität: Zur Geschichte der ÖVP seit 1945*, ed. Robert Kriechbaumer and Franz Schausberger (Vienna: Böhlau, 1995), 579ff.; Robert Kriechbaumer, "Alfons Gorbach," in *Die Politiker: Karrieren und Wirken bedeutender Repräsentanten der Zweiten Republik*, ed. Herbert Dachs, Peter Gerlich, and Wolfgang C. Müller (Vienna: Manzsche Verlags- und Universitätsbuchhandlung, 1995), 166f.

17. Anton Pelinka, "Von der Funktionalität von Tabus," *Informationen der Gesellschaft für politische Aufklärung 45* (June 1995): 2; see also Pelinka's essay in this volume.

18. Margit Reiter, "Zwischen Antifaschismus und Patriotismus: Die Haltung der KPÖ zum Nationalsozialismus, Antisemitismus und Holocaust," in *Schwieriges Erbe: Der Umgang mit Nationalsozialismus und Antisemitismus in Österreich, der DDR und der Bundesrepublik Deutschland*, ed. Werner Bergmann, Rainer Erb, Albert Lichtblau (Frankfurt: Campus, 1995), 180.

19. *Rot-Weiß-Rot-Buch,* 94f.

20. Günter Bischof, "Die Instrumentalisierung der Moskauer Erklärung nach dem 2. Weltkrieg," *Zeitgeschichte* 29 (November/December 1993): 345-66; see also Robert H. Keyserlingk, *Austria in World War II: An Anglo-American Dilemma* (Kingston: McGill-Queen's University Press, 1988).

21. Eva-Marie Csáky, ed., *Der Weg zu Freiheit und Neutralität: Dokumentation zur österreichischen Außenpolitik 1945-1955* (Vienna: 1980), 130 (Dokument 52).

22. Gerald Stourzh, *Geschichte des Staatsvertrages 1945-1955: Österreichs Weg zur Neutralität*, 3rd. ed. (Graz: Styria, 1985), 167.

23. Johnson, "Österreichische Nation," 50.

24. Werner Bergmann, Rainer Erb, and Albert Lichtblau, "Die Aufarbeitung der NS-Zeit im Vergleich: Österreich, die DDR und die Bundesrepublik Deutschland," in *Schwieriges Erbe*, 16.

25. Botz, "Eine deutsche Geschichte," 28; Peter R. Black, *Ernst Kaltenbrunner: Ideological Soldier of the Third Reich* (Princeton N.J.: Princeton University Press, 1984).

26. Hans Lamm, ed., *Der Eichmann-Prozeß in der deutschen öffentlichen Meinung: Eine Dokumentensammlung* (Frankfurt: Ner Tamid Verlag, 1961); Peter Steinbach, *Nationalsozialistische Gewaltverbrechen. Die Diskussion in der deutschen Öffentlichkeit nach 1945* (Berlin: Colloquium Verlag, 1981), 52f.

27. Reinhard Tramontana, "Spruch heil: NS-Prozesse in der Zweiten Republik," *profil,* 18 April 1979, 25-28; Simon Wiesenthal, *Doch die Mörder leben*, ed. Joseph Wechsberg (Munich: Droemer Knaur, 1967), 77ff.; Helge Grabitz, "Die Verfolgung von NS-Verbrechen in der Bundesrepublik Deutschland, der DDR und Österreich," in *Umgang mit dem Holocaust: Europa—USA—Israel*, ed.

Rolf Steininger (Vienna: Böhlau, 1994), 198-220.

28. Andreas Maislinger, "'Vergangenheitsbewältigung' in der BRD, der DDR und Österreich. Vergleich psychologisch-pädagogischer Maßnahmen," *Zukunft* (June 1990): 48-54.

29. Gottfried Fliedl, et al, *Gutachten über die zukünftige Entwicklung der Gedenkstätte Mauthausen.* Im Auftrag des Bundeskanzleramtes (Vienna: 1991), 22-42. Florian Freund, Bertrand Perz, and Karl Stuhlpfarrer, "Historische Überreste von Tötungseinrichtungen im KZ Mauthausen," *Zeitgeschichte* 22 (September/October 1995): 297-317.

30. Bergmann, Erb, Lichtblau, "Aufarbeitung der NS-Zeit," 17.

31. Agnes Blänsdorf, "Zur Konfrontation mit der NS-Vergangenheit in der Bundesrepublik, der DDR und Österreich: Entnazifizierung und Wiedergutmachungsleistungen," *Aus Politik und Zeitgeschichte* B.16/17 (1987): 9ff.

32. Quoted in ibid., 11.

33. Ibid.; Oliver Rathkolb, "NS-Problem und politische Restauration: Vorgeschichte und Etablierung des VdU," in *Verdrängte Schuld, verfehlte Sühne: Entnazifizierung in Österreich 1945-1955*, ed. Sebastian Meissl, Klaus-Dieter Mulley, and Oliver Rathkolb (Vienna: Verlag für Geschichte und Politik, 1986), 73-99.

34. Quoted in Hans Safrian and Hans Witek, *Und keiner war dabei: Dokumente des alltäglichen Antisemitismus in Wien 1938* (Vienna: Picus, 1988), 12.See Gustav Jellinek, "Die Geschichte der österreichischen Wiedergutmachung," in *The Jews of Austria*, ed. Josef Fraenkel (London 1967), 398.

35. Brigitte Bailer, *Wiedergutmachung kein Thema: Österreich und die Opfer des Nationalsozialismus* (Vienna: Löcker, 1993), 77-98.

36. Robert Menasse, *Das Land ohne Eigenschaften: Essay zur österreichischen Identität*, 3rd. ed. (Vienna: Sonderzahl, 1993), 15. Further respected publications on Austria's treatment of its Nazi past include Josef Haslinger, *Politik der Gefühle: Ein Essay über Österreich*, 1988, re-edit (Frankfurt: Fischer, 1995), and Ruth Beckermann, *Unzugehörig: Österreicher und Juden nach 1945* (Vienna: Löcker, 1989).

37. Heidemarie Uhl, "Österreichs späte Konfrontation mit der NS-Vergangenheit: Die Zweite Republik in der Diskussion um 'Anschluß' oder 'Überfall,'" *Das Parlament*. Sonderausgabe zur Frankfurter Buchmesse. Bonn, 8/15 October 1993,

18f.

38. M. Rainer Lepsius, "Das Erbe des Nationalsozialismus und die politische Kultur der Nachfolgestaaten des 'Großdeutschen Reiches,'" in *Kultur und Gesellschaft: Verhandlungen des 24. Deutschen Soziologentags, des 11. Österreichischen Soziologentags und des 8. Kongresses der Schweizerischen Gesellschaft für Soziologie in Zürich 1988*, ed Max Haller, Hans-Joachim Hoffmann-Nowotny, and Wolfgang Zapf (Frankfurt: Campus, 1989), 247-264.

39. Ernst Josef Görlich and Felix Romanik, *Geschichte Österreichs* (Innsbruck: Tyrolia, 1970), 551.

40. Manfried Rauchensteiner, *Die Zwei: Die Große Koalition in Österreich 1945 - 1966* (Vienna: Österreichischer Bundesverlag, 1987), 62-67.

41. Rudolph Neck quoted in Blänsdorf, "Konfrontation," 11.

42. Josef Hindels, "Nazivergangenheit und Gegenwart," *Zukunft* 9 (1987): 22.

43. Heidemarie Uhl, "Denkmalkultur und Zeitgeschichte: Veränderungsprozesse und Konflikte in der regionalen Denkmallandschaft seit 1945," in *Lebenszeichen: 10 Jahre Abteilung Zeitgeschichte an der Karl-Franzens-Universität Graz,* ed. Abteilung Zeitgeschichte (Graz: ADEVA, 1994), 169-195.

44. "Helden und Opfer: Totengedenken im vierten Jahr nach Kriegsende," *Murtaler Zeitung*, 29 October 1949.

45. "Dem Andenken der Gefallenen," *Kleine Zeitung*, 5 June 1951.

46. Heidemarie Uhl, "Gedächtnisraum Graz. Zeitgeschichtliche Erinnerungszeichen im öffentlichen Raum nach 1945," *Graz 1945: Historisches Jahrbuch der Stadt Graz* 25 (1994): 630; and, by the same author, "Erinnern und Vergessen," 146ff.

47. "Ehrenrettung der Soldaten," *Sonntagspost*, 30 November 1952.

48. "Zehntausend auf dem Karmeliterplatz bei der Enthüllung des Grazer Ehren- und Mahnmales," *Tagespost,* 24 October 1961. Cf. Uhl, "Gedächtnisraum Graz," 630f.

49. Friedrich Altenburg, *Das Kriegsbild ehemaliger Soldaten am Beispiel der Veteranenverbände.* (M.A. thesis, University of Salzburg, 1989).

50. Reinhold Gärtner and Sieglinde Rosenberger, *Kriegerdenkmäler: Vergangenheit in der Gegenwart* (Innsbruck: Östereichischer Studienverlag, 1991); Anton Pelinka, "Kameradschaftsbünde als Männerbünde. Ein Versuch in 10 Thesen," in *Handbuch des österreichischen Rechtsextremismus*, ed. Dokumentationsarchiv des österreichischen Widerstandes (Vienna: Deuticke, 1993), 283-288.

51. Anton Pelinka, "Der verdrängte Bürgerkrieg," in *Das große Tabu: Österreichs Umgang mit seiner Vergangenheit*, ed. Anton Pelinka and Erika Weinzierl (Vienna: Edition S, 1987), 150.

52. Cf. Hanspeter Born, *Für die Richtigkeit Kurt Waldheim* (Munich: Herbig, 1987); Richard Mitten, *The Politics of Prejudice: The Waldheim Phenomenon in Austria* (Boulder: Westview, 1992); Ruth Wodak, et al. *"Wir sind alle unschuldige Täter:" Diskurshistorische Studien zum Nachkriegsantisemitismus* (Frankfurt: Suhrkamp, 1990).

53. See Heidemarie Uhl, *Zwischen Versöhnung und Verstörung: Eine Kontroverse um Österreichs historische Identität fünfzig Jahre nach dem "Anschluß"* (Vienna: Böhlau, 1992); Ruth Wodak, et al., *Die Sprachen der Vergangenheiten: Öffentliches Gedenken in österreichischen und deutschen Medien* (Frankfurt: Suhrkamp, 1994).

54. Gerhard Botz, "Österreich und die NS-Vergangenheit: Verdrängung, Pflichterfüllung, Geschichtsklitterung," in *Ist der Nationalsozialismus Geschichte? Zu Historisierung und Historikerstreit*, ed. Dan Diner (Frankfurt / Main: Fischer, 1987), 146.

55. Gerhard Botz, "'Eine neue Welt, warum nicht eine neue Geschichte?'" *Österreichische Zeitschrift für Geschichtswissenschaften* 1 (1990): 50ff.; Agnes Blänsdorf, "Die Einordnung der NS-Zeit in das Bild der eigenen Geschichte: Österreich, die DDR und die Bundesrepublik Deutschland im Vergleich," in *Schwieriges Erbe: Der Umgang mit Nationalsozialismus und Antisemitus in Österreich, der DDR and der Bundesrepublik Deutschland* (Frankfurt: Campus. 1995), 22ff. The most comprehensive bibliography of research on the Nazi period in Austria is Karl Stubenvoll, *Bibliographie zum Nationalsozialismus in Österreich. Eine Auswahl* (Vienna: Kammer für Arbeiter und Angestellte, 1992).

56. Ernst Hanisch, "Die Präsenz des Dritten Reiches in der Zweiten Republik" (unpublished manuscript, 1995), 1.

57. Gerhard Botz. "War der 'Anschluß' erzwungen?," in *Fünfzig Jahre danach: Der "Anschluß" von innen und außen gesehen*, ed. Felix Kreissler (Vienna: Europaverlag, 1989), 108f.

58. Anton Pelinka, "Österreich unter nationalsozialistischer Herrschaft: Zulauf, Anpassung, Widerstand, Vernichtung," in *Politik in Österreich. Die Zweite Republik: Bestand und Wandel*, ed. Wolfgang Mantl (Vienna: Böhlau 1992), 35-48; Ernst Hanisch, *Der lange Schatten des Staates: Österreichische Gesellschaftsgeschichte im 20. Jahrhundert* (Vienna: Ueberreuter, 1994), 337-394.

59. Emmerich Tálos, Ernst Hanisch, Wolfgang Neugebauer , eds., *NS-Herrschaft in Österreich 1938 - 1945* (Vienna: Verlag für Gesellschaftskritik, 1988).

60. Hans Mommsen, "Widerstandsforschung und politische Kultur in Deutschland und Österreich," *Jahrbuch 1994,* ed. Dokumentationsarchiv des österreichischen Widerstandes (Vienna: 1994), 8-13.

61. Pelinka, "Der verdrängte Bürgerkrieg, " 144f.

62. Florian Freund and Bertrand Perz, *Das KZ in der "Serbenhalle:" Zur Kriegsindustrie in Wiener Neustadt* (Vienna: Verlag für Gesellschaftskritik, 1988); Florian Freund, *Arbeitslager Zement: Das Konzentrationslager in Ebensee und die Raketenrüstung* (Vienna: Verlag für Gesellschaftskritik, 1989).

63. Hans Safrian, *Eichmann und seine Gehilfen* (Frankfurt: Fischer, 1995).

64. Safrian and Witek, *Und keiner war dabei;* Kurt Schmid and Robert Streibel, eds., *Der Pogrom 1938: Judenverfolgung in Österreich und Deutschland* (Vienna: Picus, 1990); Irene Etzersdorfer, *Arisiert:Eine Spurensicherung im gesellschaftlichen Untergrund der Republik* (Vienna: Kremayr & Scheriau, 1995).

65. Robert Knight, ed., *"Ich bin dafür, die Sache in die Länge zu ziehen:" Wortprotokolle der österreichischen Bundesregierung von 1945-52 über die Entschädigung der Juden* (Frankfurt: Athenäum, 1988); Helga Embacher, *Neubeginn ohne Illusionen: Juden in Österreich nach 1945* (Vienna: Picus, 1995).

66. Safrian, "Österreicher in der Wehrmacht," 53ff. The public discussion of this last "taboo" was sparked by an exhibition entitled "War of Annihilation—Crimes Perpetrated by the *Wehrmacht* between 1941 and 1944" which was organized by the Hamburg-based *Institut für Sozialforschung* and went on show in Vienna in October/November 1995. Cf. Hubertus Czernin, "Das letzte Tabu," *profil,* 23 October 1995, 19. An anthology to accompany the exhibition was published: Hannes Heer and Klaus Naumann, eds.,*Vernichtungskrieg: Verbrechen der Wehrmacht 1941 bis 1944* (Hamburg: Hamburger Edition, 1995).

67. Anton Pelinka, "Unterdrückung, Befreiung, Bewältigung: Zum Umgang mit Österreichs widersprüchlicher Vergangenheit," in *Totenbuch Theresienstadt: Damit sie nicht vergessen werden*, 2nd ed., ed. Mary Steinhauser, and Dokumentationsarchiv des österreichischen Widerstands (Vienna, 1987), 25.

68. Pelinka, "Von der Funktionalität von Tabus," 1-3; and by the same author, "Die Erfindung Österreichs: Zur dialektischen Entdeckung von Wirklichkeit," in *Reden über Österreich*, ed. Manfred Jochum (Salzburg: Residenz, 1995), 9-21. Similar rejections were raised by Ernst Hanisch with respect to what he called an "accusatory-moralizing portrayal of history," "Präsenz des Dritten Reiches," 1f.

69. "Fernsehansprache des Bundespräsidenten Dr. Kurt Waldheim am 10. März 1988 anläßlich der 50. Wiederkehr der Besetzung Österreichs," *Jahrbuch der österreichischen Außenpolitik. Außenpolitischer Bericht 1988* (Vienna: Manz, 1989), 459-462.

70. "Ohne Geschichte auch keine Zukunft. Ansprache von Bundespräsident Thomas Klestil nach der Vereidigung," *Wiener Zeitung*, 9 July 1992.

71. "Hohe Zustimmung für Vranitzky-Worte in Israel," *Der Standard*, 16 June 1993; " Last der Geschichte, Chancen der Zukunft," *Der Standard*, 19 November 1994. The second article quotes from the speech of Thomas Klestil in the Knesset.

72. Reinhold Gärtner, "Der Umgang mit Gedenkstätten und Gedenktagen in Österreich," in *Schwieriges Erbe,* 271ff.

73. Ibid, 268ff.; Uhl, "Erinnern und Vergessen," 171ff.

74. Hans Rauscher, "Haider ist anders," *Wirtschaftswoche,* 20 February 1992, 2.

75. Hubertus Czernin, "Die Folgen von Krumpendorf," *profil,* 30 December 1995, 11.

Taboos and Self-Deception: The Second Republic's Reconstruction of History

*Anton Pelinka**

Fifty years after the founding of the Austrian Republic, scholars must begin to analyze the opportunism of the founding fathers. They must not legitimize it, nor make excuses for it, but they should try to understand it. Fifty years after the beginning of a period marked by growing stability, this republic, which is the result of its own success, must be able to face critical analysis. Scholars and critics must be willing to provide this analysis.

The Second Austrian Republic is built on a one-sided, and therefore distorted, view of historical reality. According to this point of view, Austria was the victim of National Socialist Germany because of the military occupation. The victim hypothesis of the Moscow Declaration, isolated from the hypothesis of joint responsibility, has become the basis for Austria's identity as a victim. What has been forgotten more or less is the second part of the Moscow Declaration which holds Austria responsible for National Socialism and its crimes. This process of forgetting started as early as 27 April 1945, when in the preface of the Declaration of Independence only the victim hypothesis was formulated, while the hypothesis of joint responsibility was almost hidden at the end of the document. Another part of this forgetfulness was that the State Treaty no longer included any reference to the concept of joint responsibility.

* This paper was presented in May 1995 at the Vienna conference "*Inventur 45/55*"; we are grateful to the conference organizers Wolfgang Kos and Georg Rigele for permission to reprint it in English.

The value in the concept of joint responsibility is its insistence on remembrance. It asks Austrians to remember that there were approximately 600,000 members of the German National Socialist Party in Austria. It asks them to remember the remarkably high proportion of Austrians among the direct participants in the Nazis' machinery of destruction.

It is important to determine upon whose shoulders the burden of responsibility rests. By defining National Socialism as the alliance of Austrian foolishness and the Prussian sword, August Maria Knoll suggests that responsibility belongs on the shoulders of a particular segment of Austrians. Out of the neurotic conflicts among the different nationalities at the end of the Austrian monarchy a specific brand of Austrian National Socialism arose. It was exemplified by people like Odilo Globocnik and Arthur Seyss-Inquart. They were Austrians from multilingual regions who adamantly insisted on being more German than the Germans; Austrians who had to suppress their own unique non-German past, their non-German origin.

Today, Austrians still opine that they are specifically qualified for functions in the east and southeast of Europe—as if the figure of Alexander Löhr (executed in Belgrade for his war crimes) constituted a special recommendation for Austria's extraordinary competence.

The Logic of Opportunism

The falsification of reality was the consequence of opportunist foreign policy considerations. In 1945 and later, not being German had its advantage. Austria attempted to uncouple itself from the fate of Germany. There is a direct path from the Declaration of Independence to the State Treaty and neutrality, a path marked by emphasizing the unique character of Austria versus that of Germany.

However, opportunist domestic policy considerations followed an entirely different logic, namely that of a free political market of democracy. Before 1949, political parties tried to attract the votes of home-comers ("*Heimkehrer*"), a code word for former Nazis. In 1949 campaigning for the votes of former Nazis was fierce. The consequences of this are well known: the foundation of the VDU (Association of Independents), the "rehabilitation" of former Nazis, the protectionism practiced by the coalition parties along lines of proportional representation, the fact that both the SPÖ and ÖVP had *their* "Nazis" whom they protected, and, finally, a number of ex-

Nazis fully aware of the fact that one or the other party would protect them. The precedent for this behavior was set much earlier. Directly following the period of denazification, the committees founded by the three anti-fascist parties were united in a common principle, namely the unspoken rule of "if you 'de-Nazify' my Nazi, I will 'de-Nazify' your Nazi." Later, in the 1950s, the Reder case became the epitome of this attitude. Heinrich Gleißner, who had been imprisoned in Dachau, and Ernst Koref, politically prosecuted by the Nazis, competed with and against each other to see who was better able to protect the mass murderer of Mazzabotto, who had been without nationality but then became Austrian.

Foreign and domestic policy opportunism formed a diametrically opposed antagonism. This contradiction was bridged by a policy of double speak: Oskar Helmer and Karl Gruber were the most important representatives of an Austro-Orwellian language culture, a "tongue-in-cheek" regulation language. The policy expressed vis-à-vis the Allied Forces was different from the one employed internally.

The result was pragmatic cynicism and primitive naiveté. The Slovenes in Carinthia were to feel this kind of pragmatic cynicism. Before 1945, the bilingual educational system in Carinthia was seen as proof of the tolerant, even generous Austrian attitude towards its minorities, and this proof helped thwart Yugoslavian claims. After 1945, the Slovenes in Carinthia had done their duty, and Austria no longer needed to emphasize its friendliness towards minorities. The bilingual school system was sacrificed.

An example of primitive naiveté can be found in the attitude of Leopard Figl and other founding fathers who compared their own roles as victims with the fate of (mostly Jewish) exiles. They came to the conclusion that once more the Jews had managed an easy way out of the problem.

The Construction of History

From the beginning, the hypothesis of Austria's innocence was strongly contradicted not only by historical reality but also by developments in domestic politics. Thus, this hypothesis created a need for constructing history.

History was recounted, written, recorded, and made by the political camps. Catholic-conservative historians were responsible for Ignaz Seipel and Leopold Kunschak, while Karl Renner and Otto

Bauer relied on social-democratic historians. As a consequence, this distorted representation of history formed the point of departure for the committee of historians created by Bruno Kreisky.

Slowly, historians, social scientists, and writers belonging to a younger generation not directly affected by the war began to challenge the hypothesis of Austrian innocence as well as a type of historiography controlled by coalition parties and political camps. An excellent example of this is Robert Knight's edition of the Council of Ministers protocols. The distortions and falsifications of the postwar period were dragged into the sharp and unmerciful light of research. All of a sudden, Renner turned out to be an opportunist trying to ingratiate himself with Hitler and Stalin. Kunschak's image was dismantled, and he was revealed to be a violent anti-Semite. Suddenly the bishops were exposed as persons adept at submitting to the wishes of whomever was in power.

One must ask the following question: who in 1945 could have written and analyzed history outside of the political camps? There was no one outside these political camps. There was no one who could have written historical accounts free from *Lager*-specific distortions.

It was a part of the logic of postwar circumstances that in the times of consociational democracy with its elite consensus, the fragmentation of society was paralleled by a similar development in the field of historiography. The perception of past and present became fragmented as well. If the one camp was in control of bourgeois university historiography, the other camp had Charles Gulick as its historian, who in turn was countered by Gordon Shepherd from the other camp. Exposing the lies of the Second Republic is good and correct, but it is not enough. Exposing lies alone is, although morally convincing, not analytical enough. People exposing the lies of the postwar years often countered the unbearable cynicism of the founding fathers like Gruber or Helmer with a kind of moralism that is sometimes equally hard to tolerate.

The Meaning and Function of Taboos

What remains is the question of how these self-deceptions function. This question can be formulated as a synthesis, as answer to thesis (victim) and antithesis (lifelong lie). Historical perceptions are never free of values and, most of all, never free of functions.

Historical perceptions fulfill certain tasks. In relation to self-deceptions two primary functions can be recognized.

The first function is that of taking taboos hostage. In 1945 and later, all politically relevant traditions, the camps, had their sore spots from the most recent past. Even if these spots were not equally intense, they still existed among all the camps. These sore spots (for example, Renner's approval of the Munich Agreement, including his explicit praise of the wisdom of Hitler's policy, dated 1 November 1939, or the competitive anti-Semitism of the Christian Socialists versus the National Socialist brand of anti-Semitism) were something of which the political elite was well aware. These skeletons in the closet were, however, officially not used against each other for fear that the other party might reciprocate and violate the taboo. Thus, a process of trust formation was initiated through the *mutual respect of taboos*.

The second function is that of integration through renunciation of the truth. The entanglement of the victim hypothesis as expressed in foreign policy and the domestic appeasement of former Nazis made it possible to gradually integrate a large portion of these former Nazis into the basic consensus of the Second Republic. This double strategy of integration is expressed by the intellectually inconsistent parallelism of the two liberation acts of 27 April 1945 and 15 May 1955. For a large number of Austrians who had not experienced 1945 as liberation, the State Treaty meant a second, one could say subsidiary, liberation. The cheers in front of the Belvedere swept over all contradictions—not intellectually, certainly not morally, but politically. Followers of the Nazi party and the National Front (who had experienced 1938 and 1945 from different perspectives, the former as winners, the latter as losers), the Social Democrats and the Catholics, the Communists and the monarchists, they all could find themselves in the "Austria is free" dictum of 15 May 1955.

People who want to expose self-deceptions also have to ask themselves to identify which alternative courses of action the founding fathers could have taken in the spring and summer of 1945:

* More democracy? Possibly along the lines of the Julius Raab, former leader of the Austrian militia movement, or those of the Stalinist Ernst Fischer?

* More anti-fascism? In a land which could not have known what the outcome of a fair plebiscite in the spring of 1938 would have been?
* Less opportunism? In a world political situation in which it was clear that the fate of the country was primarily in the hands of the Allied Forces?

In view of the real options in 1945, it seems necessary to understand the reasons why the taboos of not mentioning Austrian co-responsibility or the Austrian roots of National Socialism were created. Renner and Schärf and Helmer, Raab and Gruber, they were people interested less in truth than in practical politics. This does not have to be a contradiction. They do, however, represent two types of logic principally different from each other.

Taboos and other self-deceptions have an ambivalent protective function. They cover painful wounds and make healing possible through a ritualized banning of contact, especially a banning of discussion. However, this function of taboos is—if it follows the analysis above—effective only for a limited time. There is a point when the healing process must be completed.

The Generation Conflict

The termination of this healing process occurs in the course of a generation change. This was the case in Austria. People exposing these self-deceptions belong to a younger generation; resistance to them is expressed mostly by the older generation.

The revolution of those exposing lies and dismantling myths signifies the emancipation of a generation that is turning against coalition historiography, against the instrumentalization of the victim hypothesis, and against the covering up of Nazi continuities. However, if the standards used by critical historiography and social sciences to evaluate Kurt Waldheim in 1986 had determined or even only codetermined thinking in 1945, who could have survived? Certainly not Karl Renner and definitely not the political inventor of Kurt Waldheim, Karl Gruber, the resistance fighter whose anti-Semitism is openly expressed in all documents and is the prototype of this kind of self-deception.

The generation conflict is also the conflict of the postwar period. The political culture of the postwar period was characterized by the fact that instead of a political market a permanent power monopoly was created. Instead of the willingness to take risks, securing and stabilizing existing conditions became Austria's goal. This included bans on being outspoken (Renner's "Commemorative Paper," Kunschak's anti-Semitism) and on risking change (leaving the coalition, alternative concepts of democracy).

Now, in the post-postwar period, it has become possible to be outspoken and take risks. Exposing lies is the order of the day. This has been evolving concurrently with the speedy development of the "Third Camp" in the Kreisky era, which was bound to lead to an ambivalent kind of openness, both full of potential and dangerous at the same time. As to whether or not the taboos created around the many Austrian wounds and weaknesses were successful, the answer is both yes and no.

Unfortunately, the simplistic slogans of the chairman of the movement have characterized the debate of the 1990s. The fact that the banal Carinthian populist determines what is considered a political issue shows that full stabilization, that true healing has not been accomplished. However, a broad constitutional basis unites the political positions of traditional parties with the political positions of new parties, thereby also uniting different generations. Indeed, the post-postwar period has come, whether we like it or not, and just as no society can do without taboos, the post-postwar period will not be an exception.

FURTHER LITERATURE

Ernst Bruckmüller, *Österreichbewußtsein im Wandel: Identität und Selbstverständnis in den 90er Jahren* (Vienna: Signum, 1994).

Gabriele Holzer, *Verfreundete Nachbarn: Österreich—Deutschland, Ein Verhältnis.* (Vienna: Kremayr & Scheriaun, 1995).

Robert Knight ed., *"Ich bin dafür, die Sache in die Länge zu ziehen": Die Wortprotokolle der österreichischen Bundesregierung von 1945-1952 über die Entschädigung der Juden* (Frankfurt am Main: Athenäum, 1988).

Anton Pelinka, *Karl Renner zur Einführung* (Hamburg: Junius, 1989).

Heidemarie Uhl, *Zwischen Versöhnung und Verstörung: Eine Kontroverse um Österreichs historische Identität 50 Jahre nach dem "Anschluß"* (Vienna: Böhlau, 1992).

William Wright, ed., *Austria, 1938-1988; Anschluß and Fifty Years* (Riverside, 1995).

Meinrad Ziegler and Waltraud Kannonier-Finster, *Österreichisches Gedächtnis: Über Erinnern und Vergessen der NS-Vergangenheit* (Vienna: Böhlau, 1993).

They Were All Victims: The Selective Treatment of the Consequences of National Socialism[1]

*Brigitte Bailer**

The Initial Situation and Political Climate

The constitution of the Austrian Republic by the Provisional State Government happened wholly under the shadow of the Moscow Declaration of 1 November 1943.

The Declaration of Independence of 27 April 1945 expressly points out that the Austrian people were rendered powerless with no will of their own. This clearly implies that Austria was entirely a victim of the National Socialist (NS) regime and could not be held responsible for the crimes of National Socialism. This argument, especially in matters of the so-called "*Wiedergutmachung*" (restitution), was the predominant theme in all the attempts of justification by the Republic.

The final clause of the Moscow Declaration also proved essential for the situation of the victims. In it, Austria's attention is drawn to the fact that "it bears responsibility for taking part in the war on the side of Hitler Germany, which it cannot escape, and that its own contribution to its liberation unavoidably be taken in consideration in the final settlement." In 1945 there was a distinct emphasis on this contribution, and there was an attempt to portray the Austrian resistance and those men and women who had been a part of it as heroes. The semi-official newspaper *Neues Österreich* stressed in countless articles the fight for liberty as an example for the recreated

* This paper was presented in May 1995 at the Vienna conference "*Inventur 45/55*"; we are grateful to the conference organizers Wolfgang Kos and Georg Rigele for permission to reprint this essay in English.

republic. In the beginning of 1946 the federal government ordered the collection of reports from the resistance for the preparation of the official *Rot-Weiß-Rot Buch*. Apart from foreign policy considerations, the politicians of the young republic were confronted with the task of creating a new Austrian consciousness, independent of the seven years of National Socialist propaganda. Here, the resistance fighters offered themselves as role models with whom Austrians could identify. They had symbolically raised the Austrian banner through the years of German occupation, even though the "broad masses of the people" certainly did not follow their example as a commentary in *Neues Österreich* postulated on 24 April 1945.

Relatively soon this attempt to make heroes of the members of the anti-fascist resistance disappeared from the media. Presumably, it did not achieve the admiration of the population which it had sought.

Consistent with the rejection of resistance members as heroes was the belief that the victims of National Socialism were only those who came to harm or lost their lives for their political engagement. The largest group of victims, the Austrian Jews, appeared in public only marginally or were not mentioned at all. The newspapers did publish reports on National Socialist crimes with regard to the European Jewry. Surviving Jewish victims played no role at all in those reports, and found no attention in the media. Unlike the resistance fighters, the Jewish victims could not be politically instrumentalized. Acknowledgment of the crimes perpetrated against the Jews by Austrians put the theory of Austrian victimization in question. The tendency to ignore surviving Jews also corresponded with Austrian anti-Semitism.

Reflecting these tendencies, the Provisional State Government created the first measures of the republic to redress the victims of National Socialism. The first law for the social welfare of victims, passed by the cabinet on 17 July 1945, took into consideration only the victims of political resistance, and planned measures to support only this group of persons. Concerning the Jewish victims, the edict for the observation of the law for the social welfare of the victims of National Socialism stipulated at the end of October 1945:

> The racially persecuted, who cannot prove such an active engagement, are like all other Austrians who passively suffered damage, not taken into account in this law and must

> wait until a settlement of the indemnification, and reparation claims of all those Austrian citizens takes place, who suffered damage by National Socialism.

But victims had to wait for this settlement. The returning former Jewish prisoners as well as the returning refugees (especially those from Shanghai and Karaganda) had to rely on the social welfare support from the Jewish community, itself impoverished, and dependent on donations from overseas. It was mostly American Jews who, by the means of the Joint, helped in this difficult task. Without help from abroad, the Jewish community in Vienna would not have been able to carry on with this urgently needed welfare. Due to the years of privations and mistreatments, a great number of the homecomers were sick, undernourished, and unable to work. Their families had either been murdered or lived scattered throughout the world. Most of their former apartments were still occupied by the National Socialists, or "Aryanizers" (*Ariseur*). Their shops had either been looted after the occupation (Anschluß) and then liquidated by force, or were likewise still in possession of the Aryanizers. Only in 1946-47 were the most important laws for restitution agreed upon. They called for the restoration of property which had been seized from 1938 onward to the former owners. But not all cases of property seizure were dealt with in these laws. Though a legal resolution with regard to the obligatory return of Aryanized apartments to the former owners existed, it was never agreed upon by the National Council. In 1950 the Minister of Justice, Otto Tschadek, called such a law "an absolute danger," as it would cause "an absolute disturbance among the population." Although in 1945 the Austrian Federal Government was conscious of the fact that Austrians were guilty of the persecution, robbing, and murdering of the Jews, it was trying at the same time, as can be seen from a memorandum of the Chancellory of State, to push responsibility for the crimes of National Socialism towards the German Reich and its citizens: "The persecution of Jews took place during the occupation of Austria by German troops. The persecutions were ordered by German authorities and carried out with their help." In 1953 Federal Chancellor Julius Raab responded to the claims by the Committee for Jewish Claims on Austria:

> The Federal Government of Austria regrets that after the occupation of Austria persecution took place and that it was

> not possible for the Federal Government to protect their citizens against the aggression of the overpowering occupiers at the time: it could not do anything else but call for help to the powers of the time; it could not do anything else but call for help to the powers of the League of Nations, of which Austria was also a member. Its appeal remained unheard. What happened to Austria in the following years had the same effect as a natural catastrophe; Austria is not able by its own strength to make good the damages or even only soothe the want that originated in these years.

With this line of argument, the whole of Austria became a victim. Eventually, this term "victim" experienced an inflationary widening. Within a short while, everybody was a victim. In 1949, the socialist member of Parliament, Rosa Jochmann, herself an inmate of the women's concentration camp of Ravensbrück for many years and a staunch spokeswoman for the victims of National Socialism, said in a radio lecture:

> We were all victims of fascism. Victim was the soldier, who experienced the war at the front in its most terrible form. Victim was the population who was waiting in the hinterland full of horror for the call of the cuckoo in order to flee to their shelters and who, with longing, wished for the day which would take this fright from them. Victims were those who had to leave their native country to carry the mostly sad lot of the emigrant. Finally, we were victims, who in prisons, penitentiaries and concentration camps were defenseless prey of the SS.

Later on, even the former National Socialists reached a kind of status as victim; they were seen as victims of the denazification demanded by the Allies, said to be very rigid; in the eyes of some members of Parliament, they were seen as victims of the people they had previously harmed, namely the victims of persecution.

During the course of this metamorphosis, the actual victims of National Socialism were pushed to the background and ignored. They, who would have reminded Austria of its guilt, were erased from the collective memory. This process of forgetting, facilitated and occasioned by the victim theory, required that the Austrians minimize the crimes that they perpetrated. Together with fellow travelers, sympathizers, and simple participants in the National

Socialist regime, these criminals could be re-integrated into Austrian society without any problems.

This re-integration had practical benefits for politicians. Socialists (SPÖ), conservatives (ÖVP), and Communists (KPÖ) with pragmatic considerations regarding their election to the National Council in 1949 fervently courted the potential votes of the former Nazis ("*Ehemalige*") (relations and friends included) of more than a million people.

Opposite this considerable reservoir of voters stood a comparatively small number of victims living in Austria, who had no homogenous lobby. The parties represented in Parliament determined, based upon their day-to-day politics, whose concerns should be heard. It was through elected politicians that these people could air their concerns.

In addition, a number of prejudices effective even after 1945 influenced the controversy about National Socialism's victims and culprits. Anti-Semitism, virulent in Austria since the nineteenth century, impeded and aggravated the success of Jewish demands, as can be seen, for instance, in the protocols of the cabinet and ministers' council published by the British historian Robert Knight.

The Concrete Political Action

According to the above mentioned rejection of any Austrian co-responsibility with regard to the National Socialist war crimes, the most influential Austrian politicians had always denied any obligation for the payment of restitution. In answering a parliamentary question from SPÖ members, the Minister of Finance, Reinhard Kamitz, said:

> The payment of any kind of restitution is out of the question, because Austria did no damage to anyone and therefore is not obliged to pay any kind of reparation. If Austrian citizens took part in inflicting such damages, they did not do so as Austrian citizens but either as individuals or as ordered by the people in power at the time.

In accordance with this principal position Austria only paid welfare for victims of National Socialism. This can be seen in the term referring to the victims' welfare law (*Opferfürsorgegesetz* or OFG) which has been amended thirty times since it was first agreed upon in 1947. This law separates the victims of National Socialism into two categories with different claims:

1. Victims of the political resistance could claim pensions if they were not able to earn their living themselves because of damages to their health dating back to National Socialist persecution;
2. Victims of persecution for racist, nationalist, or religious reasons, most of them survivors of the Holocaust, could not claim any pensions. These groups received little support with which to re-establish themselves. Only as a result of long negotiations and Allied pressure was it possible to include particularly hard hit victims of persecution into the circle of those entitled to claim pensions. But, according to the OFG, you had to be an Austrian citizen when claiming restitution. Former Austrians who fled in 1938 and afterwards, and who, in the meantime, had accepted the citizenship of their new home country were and still are excluded from pensions under that law.[2]

Only in the 1950s were the first measures of restitution included in the OFG. The Seventh Amendment, decided by the National Council on 18 July 1952, granted restitution in lump sums for each month spent in custody. The Eighth Amendment, decided a year later after intervention by the Allies, extended this compensation to persecuted people who were no longer Austrians citizens. Only Allied efforts, by the United States and Great Britain in particular, where numerous former Austrians had found refuge, and the negotiations by the Committee for Jewish Claims on Austria, which began in 1953 and concluded in 1961, succeeded. The persecuted were granted lump sum payments from two national aid funds, and were compensated not only for time spent in custody but also in internment (Twelfth Amendment of the OFG).

The demands of the victims' organizations were always met by descriptions of the tight financial situation of the state, which was supposed to make more generous help for the victims impossible. But at the same time the federal government, and in particular, the VdU[3] and ÖVP members of Parliament, did everything to end the denazification and refund the "*Ehemalige*" for damages suffered by denazification, for which considerable sums were spent and more still would have been necessary. The U.S. occupation force estimated the cost of the 1952 laws in favor of the denazified at ös 36 million According to these laws, the cost for the city of Vienna would have been ös 16 million. Several initiatives and laws already passed by the National Council in favor of the former National Socialists failed because of the Allied Council's veto and could only be realized after the conclusion of the *Staatsvertrag* (State Treaty) in 1955.

In the 1950s the measures in favor of the former National Socialists in most cases ran parallel with measures in favor of the NS victims or were even intermingled as in the 1950 case of the "Fund for the Compensation of Hardships."

Since 1948-49 the ÖVP (and later the VdU) pressed for an amendment of the Third Restitution Law, (which was valid in cases where seized properties were in private hands after 1945), in favor of the Aryanizers. Immediately before and after election to the National Council in 1949, ÖVP members raised motions for the amendment of the Third Restitution Law, and were met with resistance by the SPÖ faction and the Allied Council. Instead, the SPÖ suggested a general Compensation of Hardships Fund, which would serve to eliminate all hardship caused by Hitler and the Nazis.

During the last session of the National Council before the summer break in 1950, members of the SPÖ and ÖVP coalition government filed a motion "concerning a federal law about the compensation of hardship in cases of restitution and the creation of a hardship compensation fund." This motion mixed up the interests of different groups of victims with those of the Aryanizers. While there were, in parts I and II of the draft, obvious contradictions to the Third Restitution Law and its treatment of the formerly persecuted, in part III there was a suggestion for a Compensation for Hardships, which included the Aryanizers. The document stated that the acquirers of former Jewish property, among others, "should be fed from the heirless Jewish property, a tax from the proceeds of restituted property, the sale of which will be carried out within a period of five years after the restitution." This fund was created to compensate those who could not file claims under the Third or Seventh Restitution Law (the latter dealt with claims resulting from working agreements in the private economy). "Honest acquirers" (*redliche Erwerber*)[4] who were obliged to restitute former Jewish property and presumably suffered unjust hardships as a result of restitution were also eligible for compensation. These owners of former Jewish property already had better conditions according to the Third Restitution Law. The net effect of this hardship fund would mean that so-called "honest acquirers" of Aryanized property should be compensated from the property of Jews who had been murdered by the National Socialists! The draft also proposed the payment of compensation for times of imprisonment; this would have satisfied the victims' organization which had been seeking this type of restitution for a year. Protests of the U.S. occupiers against the deterioration of benefits for the formerly persecuted caused the federal government to withdraw this draft.

On 18 July 1952, the National Council passed in the same session the already mentioned Seventh OFG Amendment (introduction of a compensation for imprisonment), and a law for the compensation of civil servants who had been reprimanded by the NS regime. It also included three laws in favor of former National Socialists: (1) an amnesty concerning the forfeit of property; (2) an amnesty for charged National Socialists; and (3) a law in favor of the civil servants who had been persecuted under the "National Socialist Law"[5] in 1945 and thereafter.

From today's point of view the attitude in the 1950s regarding the equitable compensation of all parties seems rather cynical. In 1951, ÖVP member Lujo Toncic-Sorinj formulated the principle like this: "At least at the same time with the pacification in the National Socialist sector, we must achieve pacification in the sector of restitution, in the sector of the politically persecuted. A general settlement is the only possible way." This point of view resulted in an *equalization* of victims and National Socialists which cannot be justified. This equalization was also expressed by the appropriation of pensions after OFG, which has been in effect since 1 January 1950 in accordance with the "war victims welfare law" (*Kriegsopferversorgungsgesetz*).[6] This means that the pension of a former KZ prisoner is appropriated according to the same allocations that the pension of a former member of the Waffen-SS is.

To some extent these parallel measures of compensation for the victims and perpetrators were indirectly caused by the Allies, who often combined their agreement or rejection regarding improvement for the former National Socialists with a demand of further improvement for the victims of National Socialism. After the end of the war competition for former National Socialists or other perpetrators arose. There were, for example, after 1945, many former resistance fighters, especially people who had fought in Spain on the side of the Spanish republic, who had entered the Austrian police force. In the course of the Cold War, the Austrian government, in particular the minister responsible for internal affairs, Oskar Helmer, saw to it that these men—mostly communists—were removed from the police and replaced by former National Socialists. Also, those who were not too heavily incriminated were left in their positions; those, as Josef Hindels writes in his unpublished memoirs, who were estimated by Helmer as "reliable anti-communists...were also accepted by the Americans."

After 1945 the shortage of living space caused by the war constituted a central problem for a long time. Politically persecuted and Jewish victims were particularly affected. Up to the end of 1938, approximately 44,000 of the 70,000 apartments with Jewish occupants were forcibly seized from their owners to accommodate "Aryan fellow countrymen." (*Volksgenossen*). After the end of the war, the victims organizations and the Jewish community demanded the restitution of those apartments. Those who had returned from prison, concentration camps, and countries of refuge found no apartments and had to rely on the help of friends and relatives or had to live in mass quarters, while the Aryanizers were still living in their former apartments. As mentioned, a law that would have regulated the restitution of these apartments never came about.

It was possible to expropriate apartments from National Socialists under a law for claiming apartments which was connected to the National Socialists Law. These apartments were to be redistributed by the housing office. At the end of the war many Nazis had fled from Vienna to the west, so their empty apartments were assigned to Nazi victims by Vienna's housing office. Only a short time later many of these assignments had to be canceled as Nazis—aided by law courts which did not accept these preliminary assignments—managed to expel the victims once more. In a number of cases wives of Nazis, who were able to prove that they themselves had never been members of the Nazi party, claimed their former apartments and received eviction notices for the victims who had been assigned to these apartments. In 1950, Minister of Justice Tschadek felt obliged to call upon the courts to stop the dislodging of victims.

A number of special difficulties arose from the termination of denazification in 1957. The National Socialists Law, passed only one day after the Eleventh Amendment to the OFG, included a general amnesty and entitled those who had been denazified to reclaim their properties, allotments, and furniture which had been forfeited.

Some of these allotments had been passed over to Nazi victims by the city of Vienna, and furniture had been given to victims by the Soviet forces as a *Lebedenko*-donation: a "donation" for which they had to pay rent. Now the victims had to either return the furniture to the former Nazis (some had previously done this) or pay a discharge. In order to do so they were granted an interest-free loan by the city of Vienna.

The position of some politicians on this issue can be illustrated by the statement of ÖVP member of Parliament Fritz Polcar concerning owners of allotments who had been affected by denazification:

> These provisions of the NS law have affected some 6,000 Viennese families, mostly workers, clerks, government officials, and small business owners. By the NS law these families were stripped of their property and their rights which they had accomplished in years of hard work—rights and property which had been earned in a regular way—an acquisition which did cost them years of hard work, enormous sacrifices, and renunciation of the joys of life.

One should ask if this statement also applied to most of Vienna's Jewry who had been robbed in 1938 and thereafter.

During the second half of the 1950s the negotiations between the Austrian federal government, the Committee for Jewish Claims on Austria, and the Austrian victims organizations showed only slow progress. Simultaneously there was much concern about the so called *Spätheimkehrer* (late returnees), the former soldiers who had spent quite a long time in captivity mostly in the Soviet Union, and were now returning home. According to a statement by the member of Parliament Felix Slavik, the Republic felt obliged to care for them regardless of cost because "they had suffered enormous economic losses by returning to economic life so much later." Among these *Spätheimkehrer* there were men weighed down by guilt like the Gestapo officers Auinger and Sanitzer. On 25 June 1958 the Austrian Parliament passed a "Federal law...concerning financial aid for late returnees" (*Bundesgesetz...über finanzielle Hilfeleistungen an Spätheimkehrer*). All returnees who had come home after 30 April

1949 and whose behavior had not been "irreconcilable with the aims of a free democratic Austria" were put in the same category with those who had been

> forced to leave Austria for political reasons or for their descent, their religion, or their nationality in order to escape persecution and who had been arrested and interned for political or military reasons by a foreign power between 6 March 1938 and 9 May 1945. This under the condition that this internment lasted on after 30 April 1949 for the same reasons.

This regulation concerning the victims affected only one small group of the people driven out by National Socialism, people who had fled to the Soviet Union and had been interned by Stalinist repression. Those who had fled from Austria after 1938 and had been interned as enemy aliens in countries at war with the Reich were granted a compensation only when the 12th *Opferfürsorgegesetznovelle* came into effect four years later in 1962. However all the *Spätheimkehrer* mentioned above gained redress of ös 300 for each month of captivity after 1 May 1949. By means of this law the Austrian Parliament had produced a legal identification of National Socialist persecution and Allied measures. In doing so the politicians broke the logic of the victim theory; there was certainly less reason for Austria to feel responsible for the captivity of *Wehrmacht* soldiers than for the crimes against NS victims which had been committed by Austrian offenders.

Conclusion

The reintegration of former National Socialists had far-reaching social and psychological consequences. It prevented an analysis of the content of the National Socialist system and its ideology. The condemnation of the NS regime remained on the surface; it concentrated on NS crimes, but it lacked an analysis of the social preconditions and the authoritarian roots of the regime. Thus prejudices which had been utilized by the NS regime persisted after 1945. These prejudices particularly affected those groups of victims who were discriminated against and forced to live on the fringe of our society: Roma and Sinti gypsies, homosexuals, social misfits, and the physically and mentally handicapped. With the exception of Roma and Sinti, these groups have been ignored by the OFG up to now. A June 1995 amendment counts the handicapped as victims, but still disregards homosexuals and social misfits. The *Nationalfonds* (National Fund) which passed Parliament at the same time for the first time accepts those persecuted for sexual orientation or being social misfits or being handicapped as victims of National Socialist violence.

The shrouding of victims from public conscience on a linguistic level, which had affected the Jewish victims immediately after the end of war when they were defined as victims of political persecution, was extended to all kinds of victims only a few years later. The linguistic denial of victims continues to this day as evidenced by the historians Siegfried Mattl and Karl Stuhlpfarrer:

> If one is talking about *Heimkehrer* (returnees) he is not talking about those who returned from exile, if one is talking about victims of war he is not talking about those who fell victim to Hitler's aggression, and if one is talking about the victims of expulsion he does not mean those who were forced to leave Austria for political reason or because they were Jews.

This development created a kind of tacit understanding with the "*Ehemaligen*" (former Nazis) whose deeds were excused or even denied.

A complex interplay of historical, psychological, and social mechanisms seriously interfered with the confession of guilt. Austria has assimilated its victims quietly but has never accepted them as an important part of its history.

NOTES

1. This essay is based on my larger study *Wiedergutmachung Kein Thema: Österreich und die Opfer des Nationalsozialismus* (Vienna: Löcker, 1993); all specific references in this essay can be found therein.

2. These are not to be mixed up with old age pensions as part of the social insurance system (*Allgemeines Sozialversicherungsgesetz*). Since the 1950s those pensions are paid to former insured persons abroad, but only on certain conditions which cannot be explained here due to their staggering complexity.

3. *Verband der Unabhängigen*, the League of Independents, a party, founded in 1949, in which mostly former National Socialists found a new political home. In 1956 the Freedom Party succeeded the VdU.

4. That is a term of the *Allgemeines Bürgerliches Gesetzbuch*—Civil Law Code—implying that the acquirer acted in good faith and was entitled to the acquisition.

5. That law enforced the registration and punishment of former National Socialists according to the extent that they had been involved in the National Socialist regime and the crimes it committed. That law regulated denazification; today it is the main law for the persecution of Neo-Nazis.

6. This law takes care for former soldiers who are not able to earn their living anymore because of damages to their health suffered during their service in the war. Former members of the Waffen-SS are also taken care of by the same law.

The Present State of the Waldheim Affair: Second Thoughts and New Directions

Robert Edwin Herzstein

I first became involved in the Waldheim matter in the middle of March 1986 when the World Jewish Congress asked me to research the presidential candidate's wartime past. Two years later, I published a book entitled *Waldheim: The Missing Years.** The work engendered some discussion and controversy, but judging by the comments made by a younger generation of Austrian historians, *Waldheim* has apparently contributed to the ongoing Austrian debate about the recent past. Yet why did a U.S. scholar have to perform this difficult task? What elements in Austrian culture prevented a local historian from investigating and revealing Kurt Waldheim's wartime past, say in 1956 or 1976? True, Viennese journalists contributed to Waldheim's exposure—but only some forty years after the war had ended. Was there some kind of national compact that mandated discretion, even concealment, as the price of personal advancement? Perhaps so: I recall that when I was in Vienna, I once or twice received the assistance of serious scholars who cautioned me against acknowledging their help. Presumably, their careers might suffer.

The Waldheim affair sowed a lush harvest. Today, a new generation of Austrian (and non-Austrian) historians seems to be making up for lost time. Investigations into Austrian anti-Semitism, the Austrian victim myth, and the *Ostmark*'s contribution to the Nazi war machine have yielded rich if painful truths. In this essay I concentrate on the Austrian environment in which Waldheim emerged after the

* (New York: Arbor House/William Morrow, 1988); all unattributed quotes in this essay can be found in the book.

war, the persona which his peers enabled him to adopt, the debate over his deceit and discovery, and the imminent disclosure of further documentation.

Foreigners should avoid self-righteousness—much less threats—or the temptation to relish Austrian discomfort. Analogies with two other countries may be helpful. Japanese society has not been diligent in its collective examination of past wrongs. Japanese statesmen rarely acknowledge these facts; school books tend to avoid words that condemn Japan for its militarism, aggression, and atrocities. Nor have Americans found it easy to contemplate all of their nation's activities during the Second World War. The shameful relocation and expropriation of Japanese-Americans, and the atomic bombing of two Japanese cities remain sources of consternation to many (but not all) among us. And as we Americans learned once again, in the wake of Vietnam, confronting our own past is often difficult. The same is true of the French, who, like the Austrians, fabricated their own postwar mythos. Where the Austrians eagerly wrapped their nation in the "first victim" banner of the Moscow Declaration, French of all persuasions embraced the myth of the *resistance*. While exaggerating the numbers and exploits of the heroic *resistants* and *maquis*, France discouraged serious investigation of the collaborationist phenomenon. After the rush to vengeance in 1944-45, former *collaborateurs* quietly resumed their lives, sometimes at high levels. The archives remained locked. Often, foreign scholars such as Stanley Hoffmann, Robert O. Paxton, and Michael Marrus had to reveal the truths which French public life seemed to shun. The late President Mitterand, who served both Vichy and the resistance, was a perfect symbol of French national discretion, of Gallic *Verdrängung*. But without repentance, one cannot face history, and without understanding history, we go forward blindly, chained to prejudices inherited from an unjust past.

Postwar Austrians concocted their own mythos, one which served to unite the country and banish thoughts of a painful and shameful past. Politicians of all stripes seized upon the Moscow Declaration's "first victim" language, and used it to good effect. The deputy Rosa Jochmann, for example, declared in 1949 that "We were all victims of fascism." Even less implicated Nazis could be viewed as victims—of the tepid Allied denazification process. In this new Austrian world, anyone who bore witness to the truth was an embarrassment—and a threat to the new politics and old prejudices. In his powerful book *From*

Prejudice to Persecution, Bruce F. Pauley has effectively investigated these pernicious resentments.[1] Again, it is revealing that an American, rather than an Austrian, had to carry out this difficult task.

As both Pauley and Thomas Albrich have skillfully shown, Austrian anti-Semitism survived the Holocaust.[2] In 1945 only 28 percent of Austrians questioned favored the return of emigrants. They need not have worried; by 1949, only about 11,000 Jews lived in Austria. If 65,000 Austrian Jews had fallen victim to Hitler's death machine, then the German Nazis had committed this crime, unaided. The fact that Austria had nurtured Adolf Hitler, that Austrian anti-Semitism had contributed to his strength in Austria long before the Anschluß, were inconvenient facts. After all, since anti-Semitism rarely surfaced as a political weapon after 1945, why bother with such annoying hangovers from the past?[3] So there was little public discussion of the Austrians who ran concentration camps, or assisted Adolf Eichmann in his work of deportation and murder. Most Austrians were content to maintain their silence about the huge number of Nazis in the *Ostmark*. As for the equally large throng of veterans of Hitler's war machine, they had been, in Kurt Waldheim's words, "doing their duty;" they were only guilty of *Pflichterfüllung*. Of course, Jörg Haider, who is a major figure in Austrian politics, once described the wartime killer and SS officer Walter Reder as man who "did his duty."[4] But an irony emerges here: If Austrians had not celebrated the memory of General Alexander Löhr—executed by the Yugoslavs as a war criminal in 1947—would the process of uncovering Kurt Waldheim's past have begun in 1985-86?

Apologists for Austrian innocence, like longtime foreign minister (ÖVP) Karl Gruber, had a clever response to the mention of the murder of 65,000 Austrian Jews: "So long as Austria was left alone, no Jew suffered harm." Following this political line, elites of both non-communist parties pandered to the will of the majority. In their world, the remaining Jews, and Jewish organizations which made claims against Austria, were embarrassments. Any reference to the culpability of Austrians could only impede the big parties in their rush to win the votes of "less implicated" former Nazis. And rush they did, in their ruthless quest for the votes of "less implicated independents." One grotesque measure, cited by Brigitte Bailer in an important article, merits mention.[5] A failed bill introduced in 1950 would have compensated former Nazi claimants for any losses by endowing them with property once owned by Jewish victims of Hitler's Reich. Thanks to Allied pressure, the bill failed. More typical was the housing situation in Vienna. At the end of the war, victims of the greater German Reich sometimes took control of apartments vacated by fleeing Nazis. Later, many of these Nazis went to courts in Vienna, which often returned their apartments to them. In other cases, the non-Nazi widows of former Nazi renters could evict victims. In 1950, the justice minister belatedly called upon the courts to stop this process, but this measure was awfully late.

All postwar Austrian governments successfully refused all pleas for restitution and reparations, and only reluctantly agreed to provide victims with *Fürsorgemaßnahmen.* After all, how could a "victim" be held responsible for any horrors inflicted upon other victims? In the words of a Foreign Ministry official involved in delicate negotiations with Israel, the "events of the recent past" occurred under Nazi occupation, so Austria "has nothing to do with these things." In the State Treaty of 1955 Austria won four-power approval for its insistence that language about responsibility for recent events be stricken from the document. "After the war," Albrich writes, "the Austrian Jews thereby became—either here or as emigrants—the first victims of the Austrian interpretation of the Moscow Declaration."[6] But as Bailer shows, the reintegration of former Nazis, and the disinterest in their victims, came at a price. The process "impeded a meaningful confrontation with the National Socialist system and its ideology." She concludes that the "condemnation of the NS regime remained stuck at a superficial level."[7] For example, *Versunkene Welt*, the powerful Vienna exhibition, did not appear until 1984. In this marvelous work of prose, photography, and art, one sees the once living face of Austrian Jewry. Forty years after the destruction of this community, Austrians were permitted to gaze upon it as a relic.[8] Presumably, the country would not have ready for the exhibition ten or thirty years before.

In the selectively amnesiac national consensus, Vice-Chancellor Adolf Schärf could equate returning prisoners of war with the survivors of Hitler's concentration camps. The Western Allies, increasingly wary of Soviet designs, virtually abandoned denazification in favor of militant anti-communism. Endorsing an amnesty for former Nazis, a state secretary (Ferdinand Graf, ÖVP) praised the measure for "strengthening the will of the Austrian people to defend itself against Bolshevism." In fact, many members of the resistance, some of whom had fought for the Spanish Republic, had joined the police force in 1945. During the early Cold War, with U.S. support, Interior Minister Oskar Helmer purged the leftists from the police force. Often, former Nazis, now seen as reliable anti-communists, took their places.

The consensus forged in 1945-50 set the stage for the emergence of a man like Kurt Waldheim. Waldheim was never "Austria," as his belated critics later alleged; that was too simplistic. Rather, Waldheim was a typical product of a certain Austrian political culture. He was average, rather than striking; a facilitator, but probably not a war criminal; married to an ardent Nazi, but not a party member; enrolled in minor Nazi organizations, but possessed of an anti-Nazi father; an opportunist and a dissembler, not a ranting hater; adept at retouching the past, but ever so cleverly. Like Bruno Kreisky, Waldheim was anxious to "overcome" the past, not confront it. Both men succeeded for a long time, but both ultimately paid a heavy emotional price for the effort.

Kurt Waldheim's career, writings, and behavior serve as marvelous examples of the self-serving national compact. So does his fate in 1985-86. After all, Socialists anxious to prevent Waldheim's election worked in tandem with agents of the World Jewish Congress (WJC). What is fascinating is their logic: if Austrians thought that the SPÖ was using his war record against Waldheim, they would rally around the conservative candidate. But if they were led to believe that the foreign press was attacking Waldheim, they would reject the "great Austrian," not for moral reasons, but because tourism and the Austrian economy would suffer! That was the strategy. Waldheim's enemies could have cared less about confronting his past—or theirs. The strategy exploded in their faces, but its genesis reflected the national mythos. What was the relationship between the Waldheim persona and the broader public culture? Working with historians and psychoanalysts attending a meeting in San Francisco in May 1989, I addressed this difficult issue.[9] How could someone live an alternative life, without collapsing under the pressure of a false identity? I concluded that the delusional use of language, encouraged by peer cohorts in the surrounding culture, contributed mightily to the construction of the Waldheim persona. I summarize and update some of my hypotheses.

To Kurt Waldheim, World War II was an immense and dangerous detour, one which deflected and almost destroyed his career possibilities. The career, for which his father had sacrificed and suffered, had taken on a life of its own. Interestingly, the only time Waldheim used the word *Trauma* with me occurred in reference to the Russian campaign. Badly wounded, Waldheim feared he would die. "That for me was the trauma," he said, and "after that everything else was not so interesting." (Hence, we are to believe that Waldheim omitted the Balkans from his memoirs, not out of guilt, but due to ennui.) Waldheim's language only became passionate when he confronted some form of his own death. His mother is mentioned because she feared that her son might die; Waldheim recalled World War II as an incident that almost resulted in Kurt's death. The uproar over his concealment was, he seemed to believe, an attempt to kill him, politically, morally, and above all, career-wise (*Rufmord*). The reality was his own survival, vindicated by the subsequent career itself. In this world, the career becomes life, while its termination foreshadows annihilation.

Kurt Waldheim could not very well attack the National Socialist regime with conviction. In an emergency, he could dredge up his father and say, "He hated the Nazis," but Waldheim could not very well allude to his wife, and say, "She joined the party at the tender age of eighteen." Silence was better. The résumé, which is supposed to be a history, is in the Waldheim instance divorced from the past, by necessity; it has evolved into an eternal present, an *anti-history*, a guarantee of survival, the negation of death. Hence resignation was out of the question. As his wife said in 1986, if Kurt weakened or resigned in the face of the charges against him, then and only then would he be "guilty."

If Kurt Waldheim weakened or collapsed in the face of the attack, then many of his peers would, at least morally, share his shame and thereby acknowledge some form of guilt. This could not be allowed to happen. "I am you," said Waldheim to his fellow citizens, so do not turn your backs on me and your fathers. Waldheim strengthened the ties between himself and a majority of his countrymen. He received support from some of his old wartime comrades. Waldheim knew nothing, they said, and we knew nothing with him. So he clung to power (actually, to prominence rather than power), and most of the press proclaimed the nation's purity and innocence. The World Jewish Congress, or the U.S. media, or me (an "*Oberwaldheimjäger*") were guilty.

Whatever Waldheim consciously believed about his own activities, he did retain some degree of ethical autonomy. This residue forced him to deal with the Holocaust, albeit indirectly. In his own writings, Waldheim had ignored the Jewish presence in, and contribution to, Austrian history, culture, and economy before 1938. But writing in the late 1970s, the U.N. chief painted a grim picture of a family odyssey. During the summer of 1945, the Waldheim family (wife Cissy and daughter Liselotte) traveled from Upper Austria back to the capital. "We made the journey," wrote Waldheim,

> in a cattle car chock-a-block with produce, poultry, freight of every kind, and as many other passengers as could be squeezed aboard. We were crammed against the baby's cradle, and her carriage sat atop the trunks and baggage that held everything we owned. Elisabeth, who was not well, rested on a pile of straw. I…perched on an apple crate. Every now and then she and I exchanged places to keep our limbs from getting cramped…. It was impossible to sleep and there was no room to stretch our legs…. The trip, which ordinarily took three hours, lasted two-and-a-half days…. We stopped for hours at interminable places…, whose names we couldn't even ascertain because our cattle car had no windows, and they seldom let us leave the train. We were hungry and, above all, thirsty. Liselotte never stopped crying. By the third and final night all the passengers were showing signs of strain. One of them, vexed beyond endurance, threatened to smash the baby's cradle to give himself more room.[10]

Waldheim survives, however, as he always has, and the next paragraph takes us from the train nightmare to the inauguration of a brilliant career. The conclusion is inescapable: Kurt Waldheim saw himself as a kind of Jew, even as a Holocaust survivor. This was the Austrian *Opfermythos* refined to its ultimate degree.

In 1989 and 1990, at the urging of the historian Peter Loewenberg, I applied Helene Deutsch's theory of the "*als ob* personality" to Kurt Waldheim. The analyst Helene Deutsch wrote about the "as if" (*als ob*) personality, a marginal type of individual whose main characteristics are outward adaptability and inner emotional hollowness.[11] Such people, Deutsch notes, accommodate themselves to new ideologies and situations with "striking ease and speed," but the outcome is "always a spasmodic, if skilled, repetition of a prototype without the slightest trace of originality." She adds, "It is like the performance of an actor who is technically well trained but who lacks the necessary spark to make his impersonations true to life." As if she knew Waldheim, Deutsch concluded that the "as if" personality combines

> a completely passive attitude to the environment with a highly plastic readiness to pick up signals from the outer world and to mold oneself and one's behavior accordingly. The identification with what other people are thinking and feeling is the expression of this passive plasticity and thus renders the person capable of the greatest fidelity and the basest perfidy.[12]

Of such a type, Deutsch wrote nearly fifty years ago that "aggressive tendencies are almost completely masked by passivity, lending an air of negative goodness, of mild amiability which, however, is readily convertible to evil." As Deutsch observes, "Thus it can come about that the individual can be seduced into asocial or criminal acts by a change in his identifications, and it may well be that some of the asocial are recruited from the group of 'as if' personalities who are adapted to reality in this restricted way." Such personalities, Deutsch believes, are narcissistic, lack deep personal ties to others, identify with the authority of the moment, and evade conflict with a submerged or underdeveloped conscience. Kurt Waldheim, the Austrian patriot, turned German soldier, turned diplomat, turned democratic leader, turned crusader for world peace, turned Austrian patriot fighting the evil world is seen in Deutsch's theoretical model.

Waldheim is interesting because ultimately, he is so ordinary. Waldheim, the "as if" person, can turn himself into a German officer, and, when the source of authority changes, into a victim of the Nazi regime. Through his own words we learn of Waldheim's "Holocaust" experience—not enough air, a cramped cattle car, screaming children, asocial behavior, a sick young mother, an endless ride, guards preventing one from leaving the train. So Waldheim becomes the Holocaust victim, and forty years later who will dare to question the victim about his role as a perpetrator?

Just as the Moscow Declaration seemed to depict Austria as a victim of macrohistory, so Waldheim rewrote his microhistory along lines calculated to obliterate the truth and expunge any sense of guilt.[13] If Austria was a victim—and by 1945 Waldheim assumed this to be true—then who was to blame for the rise of Nazism in Austrian history? The culprit, said Waldheim and his friends, must be sought in general historical forces, such as the break-up of the Habsburg Empire in 1918, or the economic conditions preceding the Anschluß. These distortions had to be defended at all costs. The alternative would be a collapse of the moral and personal microcosm constructed so carefully, and with so much collusion since 1945.[14]

The Waldheim case became a public scandal in the winter of 1986. The often venomous reaction of the candidate and his defenders was more shocking than most of the evidence against Waldheim. The appeal, overt and covert, to anti-Semitic feelings must be put in context. By the spring of 1986 public opinion was turning against Israel in much of the West. Lebanon, the Palestinian issue, and relentless "anti-Zionist" propaganda (often anti-Semitism without the swastika) had changed many minds. If Israel was no longer the victim, then maybe the Jews had *never* been victims. Pseudo-historians gained audiences for obscene theories about the phony nature of the Holocaust. Many people had tired of the hunt for alleged war criminals, feeling that decent old men were being hounded by vengeful, Jewish-supported bureaucrats. And in Central Europe, newly prosperous West Germans and Austrians, fearful of more economic turmoil, asked how long they would have to apologize for sins (possibly) committed by other people, in a time long past? To much of Austria, the World Jewish Congress was the evil-doer, and Waldheim was its victim. Holocaust denial, reverse victimization, and Waldheim's political survival merged in the Austrian presidential election.

Kurt Waldheim—the eternal follower become world leader—was the product and guarantor of a political culture trapped by its unwillingness to engage in a healthy though painful process, called by Germans "mastering the past," of facing the past bravely, honestly, and with civil courage. Free of the Nazi albatross, and cleansed of the Holocaust (which he experienced in that boxcar), the official Waldheim draped himself in the garb of higher necessity (help to build a democracy, raise a family, serve the cause of world peace). Waldheim showed an uncanny ability to merge his own psychic and political needs with those of his cohorts. Personal supporters (especially family and peers among Austrian elites), made complicit by their acquiescence or their silence over a long period of time, reacted supportively in a time of crisis. The Waldheim affair, however, cast a wide net in Austria. It also damaged the reputation of Simon Wiesenthal, and later resulted in an indictment of him by a Jewish author.

In the late spring of 1987, I met in Vienna with the two men who were the subjects of Eli M. Rosenbaum's 1993 book, *Betrayal*.[15] After a lengthy interview of Kurt Waldheim in his official residence, the Hofburg Palace, I remained convinced that the Austrian President and former two-term Secretary-General of the UN had acted as an accessory in the commission of war crimes and crimes against humanity during World War II. Simon Wiesenthal, with whom I also conferred, did not concur in this judgment. Nevertheless, he responded honestly to my questions. It was Wiesenthal who called to my attention documents on Waldheim stored in two Berlin repositories. During subsequent conferences in Washington and New York, Wiesenthal acknowledged that Kurt Waldheim had lied, and probably knew about atrocities committed by German forces in the Balkans. He suggested that Waldheim resign as president of Austria. Further than this Wiesenthal would not go.

This reticence provided Eli Rosenbaum with his target. Originally, Rosenbaum planned to write a book about his own role in the Waldheim case. For reasons that are unclear, delay followed delay, and a new publisher needed to be found. Clearly, Rosenbaum hoped to profit from the notoriety which an attack on Wiesenthal would engender. He doubtless convinced himself that Wiesenthal was the culprit, blocking the investigation of Waldheim at every turn. Rosenbaum, an attorney and principal deputy director of the Nazi-hunting Office of Special Investigations in the U.S. Justice Department, was instrumental in uncovering Waldheim's past. But at times he was painfully unfamiliar with German army organizations and procedures. Rosenbaum, for example, seemed to think that officers in the field depended upon staff lieutenant Waldheim's reports to his superiors at headquarters before they could carry out reprisals against alleged partisans and their helpers. This was not the case. And throughout the book, the author mixed the sins of Waldheim's units with accusations against Waldheim the individual.

Elsewhere, where he was more comfortable with the facts, Eli Rosenbaum was especially effective in unmasking the anti-Semitic innuendo that infected so many Austrian newspaper correspondents, politicians, and ordinary citizens. Richard Mitten, of course, had already done this in greater detail.[16] But Rosenbaum's book was not really about Kurt Waldheim. It is about two protagonists, Eli Rosenbaum and Simon Wiesenthal. The author portrays himself as the idealistic, determined young avenger of the truth. One does not know how much of the book presents the whole story, since the author has "re-created" quotations and changed "minor circumstances in a few passages." In breathless prose, he purports to tear aside the veil of deception and criminality covering the wartime years of Kurt Waldheim. Blocking his path in 1986 is the villain of the piece, an old man named Simon Wiesenthal, director of the Documentation Center in Vienna. A figure respected throughout the world, the seventy-eight year-old former concentration camp inmate had kept the "murderers among us"—Eichmann and many others—in the public eye for almost forty years. Wiesenthal, Rosenbaum tells us, was allied with the People's Party candidate Kurt Waldheim during his 1986 presidential campaign, thanks to the murky and unpleasant vagaries of Austrian politics. According to *Betrayal*, Wiesenthal, who hated the former socialist chancellor Bruno Kreisky, had allegedly been protecting Waldheim. For a more dispassionate dissection of the Kreisky/Wiesenthal relationship, readers would be well advised to consult the recent work of Helga Embacher.[17]

As much as anyone, Kreisky made himself the symbol of the postwar Austrian consensus, and in this he was a kind of Waldheim of domestic politics. A Jew with conflicted feelings about his heritage and Israel, Kreisky found himself the defender of a myth which turned former Nazis and Jewish survivors into honorary and equal victims.[18] When attacked by Wiesenthal, Kreisky exploded in rage. Perhaps the tensions were too much for him. Like Waldheim in 1986, Kreisky reacted badly to anyone who questioned his interpretation of the victim mythos. But let's return to Rosenbaum.

Eli Rosenbaum asserts that Wiesenthal failed to make anything of a French-held document showing that Waldheim, contrary to his published statements, had served in the bloody Balkan theater during the war. Wiesenthal's mistake—and it was a serious error—occurred in 1979. Satisfied that investigation proved that Waldheim was neither a Nazi or an SS man, Wiesenthal made nothing of the fact that Waldheim had served in the *Wehrmacht* in former Yugoslavia. But he if he was so dishonest, why would Wiesenthal share this embarrassing document with me in 1986? It would have been in his interest to cover it up. But Rosenbaum, in a consistently uncharitable tone, concocts a conspiracy. True, Wiesenthal was in no rush to embarrass Waldheim and his ÖVP. Yet Rosenbaum is as impassioned in his hunt for Wiesenthal as he is when indicting Waldheim. He never gives the old Nazi-hunter the benefit of the doubt, and every mistake made by

Wiesenthal becomes one more tool in *Betrayal*'s destruction of one man's work. Rosenbaum's savage attack reminded me of some of the Austrian comments about my own work, like the one made by an author who repeated the absurd charge that I had turned Kurt Waldheim into a "major figure in the context of the Holocaust."[19]

Wiesenthal's reluctance to attack Waldheim owed something to his loathing for the World Jewish Congress.[20] The WJC's heated rhetoric, laced with threats, bothered Wiesenthal, who was active in the small and vulnerable Jewish community in Vienna.[21] Wiesenthal let himself be drawn into an unseemly war of words with the WJC, which on the Waldheim issue was, and is, far closer to the truth than he was. Wiesenthal, who has a big ego but also a marvelous sense of humor, becomes, in Rosenbaum's hands, a self-promoting fraud who built his reputation on the work of real Nazi-hunters. But the cover-up of Waldheim's wartime past did not begin with Wiesenthal's failure in 1979. The search for the complete truth has taken us from Vienna to San Francisco to New York and back to Vienna in the early 1950s, long before Wiesenthal labored to block Rosenbaum's heroic efforts. Now, the final act may be written in Langley, Virginia.

I hope that a legislative proposal which I drafted for the U.S. House of Representatives will lead to the accessibility of important, hitherto concealed records. This bill (H.R. 1281), which I describe below, is slowly making its way through the Congressional labyrinth.[22] I began with a question: How could someone so prominent as Dr. Waldheim bury his wartime past? Austrian political culture helped, but Austria was an occupied country for ten years. Did more powerful forces assist Waldheim in his concealment? In an op-ed piece I wrote for the *New York Times* back in 1986, I suggested that the concealment of Waldheim's exploits in the Balkans during World War II could not have been the work of one man, acting alone. Indeed, early in 1948, persons representing the Department of State received information—forwarded to the United Nations War Crimes Commission—implicating Waldheim in alleged war crimes. I believe that this Yugoslav case was a political fabrication, and have proven that in *Waldheim: The Missing Years*, but more important is this central truth: State Department files showed that *Kurt Waldheim had served in the Balkans.*

In 1952 the State Department noted that Waldheim received his law degree from the University of Vienna in 1940, married in 1944, and entered the reborn Austrian Foreign Service in November 1945. What else was he doing during the war? According to the State Department, Waldheim was *working in the legal system, assisting judges* and the like. The information in question was supplied by the Personnel Office of the Austrian Foreign Ministry. At that time the head of this agency was none other than the thirty-three year-old Kurt Waldheim. The State Department's recording clerk in Washington added an interesting comment: Waldheim had little contact with U.S. diplomatic personnel, but more information would be forthcoming. This proved to be a false prophecy. The incomplete biography went forward to Ambassador George Bush, when he voted to make Kurt Waldheim Secretary-General of the United Nations in 1971. What was so marvelous about the future "*großer Österreicher*"?

Kurt Waldheim, according to the State Department, understood U.S. thinking, and was especially "receptive to our way of approaching problems," more so than anyone else in the Foreign Ministry. Later, Waldheim's service apparently improved, for one cable, released to me in 1990, observes that "[Waldheim] has proven most cooperative and helpful in promoting U.S. interests." Other phrases fell into the same mold: "cooperative and receptive to U.S. interests," and "has an understanding of American thinking and foreign policy objectives," which by 1970 has been upgraded to "an excellent understanding of American thinking and foreign policy objectives." What prevented me from finding more?

Under Title VII, Section 701 (b) of the CIA Information Act,[23] "operational files" of the agency are exempted from the Freedom of Information Act. The much used and abused Executive Order 12356 enables an agency to exempt certain materials from disclosure. The CIA can conceal materials which "document the conduct of foreign intelligence or counterintelligence operations of intelligence or security liaison arrangements or information exchanges with foreign governments or their intelligence or security services," and as "files of the Office of Security which document investigations conducted to determine the suitability of potential foreign intelligence or counterintelligence sources." In other words, Austrian intelligence contacts with U.S. assets remain barred to historians, forty years after the fact. By the end of 1990, I was stymied.

A few articles about my dilemma, by columnist A.M. Rosenthal in the *New York Times*, helped matters. The CIA has begun to disgorge some of its vast documentation on Kurt Waldheim, and in my book on the subject, I will publish some of them. But it is already apparent from these confidential statements that Kurt Waldheim served U.S. foreign policy interests. This is not surprising. Waldheim owed his early career to Karl Gruber, an informant for the U.S. Army's Counter-Intelligence Corps' 430th Detachment. As Günter Bischof has shown with great clarity, Gruber was an early and ardent ally of the Americans as he worked to free his country of its occupiers. Gruber as also an effective salesman, convincing Henry R. Luce and other powerful Americans of the need to support an independent, anti-communist Austria.[24] To his Cold War enemies, however, Gruber was an "American agent in the Austrian government." This was an exaggeration, for Gruber was an Austrian patriot who found it convenient to work with the West. Convenient, but also dangerous. Waldheim learned this lesson in 1947-48, when the Yugoslav government accused him of war crimes in order to destroy Gruber. Belgrade did so in order to block the signing of a state treaty that would ignore Yugoslav claims.

Placed in sensitive centers of cold war intrigue, Waldheim informed U.S. contacts about difficult diplomatic negotiations, and provided them with information about Austrian personnel stationed in places like Moscow. Senior U.S. diplomats at the United Nations assumed that Waldheim was working for the CIA, that he was cooperative and a good source of information. On one occasion, Waldheim unwillingly undertook a dangerous mission, one that nearly cost him his life. The CIA was particularly concerned about the vast and potentially embarrassing trove of intelligence data stored in the embassy's safes in Tehran, Iran. Pressured by the United States, the Secretary-General, who was campaigning for a third term, flew to Tehran in a vain attempt to secure the release of the American hostages. Soon after the Tehran fiasco faded from the headlines, the CIA reciprocated, and its efforts proved to be more successful than Kurt Waldheim's.

In 1980, a suspicious Congressman, Rep. Stephen Solarz of New York, asked Waldheim about allegations charging him with concealed Nazi ties. In its letter to Solarz, the CIA subsequently allayed the Congressman's suspicions. When I inquired about this matter seven years later, the agency noted that its biographical data on Mr. Waldheim were based upon "open source materials." When I asked about the identity of those sources, I learned from David D. Gries,

Director of Congressional Affairs for the CIA, that "we are not able to identify open source materials the researcher may have used to prepare his 1980 response [to Solarz]." In fact, the CIA's 1980 report to Solarz, which cleared Waldheim, contained inaccurate information which to my knowledge did not then or now exist in "open source materials." Waldheim was safe for almost six more years.

The State Department and the CIA helped to fabricate and disseminate the false biography that enabled Kurt Waldheim to deceive the world and lead the United Nations. In return, Waldheim provided the U.S. with sensitive information, undertook one dangerous mission, and kept the Americans informed about attempted Soviet penetration of the Secretariat. In the summer of 1980 Waldheim bragged to a CIA informant that he had the Western powers "in his pocket," but was "less certain of the support of the Soviet Union and China." Indeed, in 1981 Waldheim's famous luck took a permanent turn for the worse. The Secretary-General, who yearned for a Nobel Peace Prize, desperately campaigned for a third term. Finally, the Russians also turned against the incumbent. After supporting Waldheim on the first ballot (13 October 1981), the Russians abstained, as did their German Democratic Republic. Britain and France deserted him at the same time. On the second ballot, which destroyed Waldheim's chances, only four powers remained loyal to him: the United States, the Philippines, Spain, and Japan. This information, provided by the mission of a power friendly to the United States, completely contradicts the wild rumors regarding a Soviet connection.

After reading one of A.M. Rosenthal's article, Rep. Carolyn Maloney contacted me. The congresswoman, who represents New York's 14th District, is now the ranking member of the Subcommittee on Government Management, Information and Technology. Her legislation, H.R. 1281, which awaits hearings in the House, is based upon my draft proposal. The bill now enjoys the support of twelve co-sponsors. This proposed amendment to the 1947 National Security Act, called the "War Crimes Disclosure Act," would apply to anyone excludable from the U.S. under the "Holtzman Amendment." According to H.R. 1281, researchers could no longer be denied access to documentation concerning such persons. Perhaps Austrian historians, who have been so productive in examining their nation's recent history, will call for release of state documents relevant to the Waldheim affair. One would like to see the material prepared by the

Intelligence Service of the *Bundesheer* in 1971, when Waldheim was seeking the Secretary-Generalship of the United Nations. At that time, Ambassador Karl Gruber and others anticipated attacks on Waldheim's wartime record. Apparently, they received useful documentation. Where is it?

H.R. 1281 should be of interest to Austrian historians, as well as their American colleagues. Documentation on Waldheim will teach a lot about Cold War collaboration between Austrians and Americans, both before and after 1955. And if we gain access to all the material controlled by Austrian and official U.S. agencies, our historical memory will no longer fall victim to misused concepts of national security (in the United States) or the "victim mythos" (in Austria). Perhaps the best advice to all us comes from a different kind of *Mitteleuropäer*. On 26 July 1990, in Salzburg, President Vaclav Havel of Czechoslovakia met briefly with Kurt Waldheim. Havel, much criticized for visiting the Austrian leader, offered profound insights into the process of denial. Havel knew whereof he spoke:

> Fear of history in these parts is not only fear of the future but also fear of the past. He who fears what is to come usually also fears facing what has already been. And he who fears facing his own past must necessarily fear what lies before him.
>
> Too often in this corner of the world, fear of one lie leads only to another lie, in the vain hope that it will cover up not only the first but also the very practice of lying. But lying can never save us from the lie. Falsifiers of history do not safeguard freedom but imperil it.
>
> The assumption that one can with impunity navigate through history and rewrite one's own biography belongs to the traditional Central European delusions.
>
> If someone tries to do this, he harms himself and his fellow citizens. For there is no full freedom there where freedom is not given to the full truth. In this or other ways, many here have made themselves guilty. Yet we cannot be forgiven, and in our souls peace cannot reign, as long as we do not at least admit our guilt. Confession liberates.
>
> I have many reasons for the statement that the truth liberates man from fear....
>
> Let us try then to free this sorely tested region not only from its fear of the lie but also of its fear of the truth. Let us at

> last look sincerely, calmly and attentively into our own faces, into our past, present and future. We will reach beyond its ambiguity only when we understand it.[25]

NOTES

1. Bruce F. Pauley, *From Prejudice to Persecution: A History of Austrian Anti-Semitism* (Chapel Hill: University of North Carolina Press, 1992).

2. Thomas Albrich, "Es gibt keine jüdische Frage. Zur Aufrechterhaltung des österreichischen Opfermythos," in *Der Umgang mit dem Holocaust, Europa-USA-Israel*, ed. Rolf Steininger (Vienna: Böhlau Verlag, 1994), 147-66.

3. Robert Knight, "'Neutrality' Not Sympathy: Jews in Post-War Austria," in *Austrians and Jews in the Twentieth Century: From Franz Joseph to Waldheim*, ed. Robert S. Wistrich (New York: St. Martin's Press, 1992), 220-29.

4. Tony Judt, "Austria & the Ghost of the New Europe," *The New York Review of Books*, 15 February 1996, 23.

5. Brigitte Bailer, "Gleiches Recht für alle? Die Behandlung von Opfern und Tätern des Nationalsozialismus durch die Republik Osterreich," in *Der Umgang mit dem Holocaust, Europa-USA-Israel*, ed. Rolf Steininger (Vienna: Böhlau Verlag, 1994), 183-97.

6. Albrich, "'Es gibt keine jüdische Frage,'" 152.

7. Bailer, "Gleiches Recht," 196.

8. Joachim Riedl, ed., *Versunkene Welt* (Vienna: Katalog zur Veranstaltungsreihe Versunkene Welt, 1984).

9. "Accommodation to the Present as Prelude to Rewriting History: The Example of Dr. Kurt Waldheim, 1938-1980," a paper read at the meeting "The Rise of Adolf Hitler and Other Genocidal Leaders: Psychoanalytic and Historical Symposium," sponsored by the San Francisco Psychoanalytic Institute and the Northern California Psychiatric Society, San Francisco, CA, 21-22 April 1989. Readers interested in the complete revised paper may wish to consult "The Psychology and Politics of Holocaust Denial: Kurt Waldheim and the 'As If' Personality,'" in the *Journal of Preventive Psychiatry and Allied Disciplines*, 4 (1990): 199-218.

10. Kurt Waldheim, "Coming of Age," in *The Challenge of Peace* (New York: Rawson, Wade Publishers, Inc, 1980), 25-26.

11. Helene Deutsch, "Some Forms of Emotional Disturbance and Their Relationship to Schizophrenia," in *Neuroses and Character Types: Clinical Psychoanalytic Studies* (New York: International Universities Press, 1965), 262-78.

12. Ibid., 2.

13. On the political manipulation of the Moscow Declaration, see Günter Bischof, "Die Instrumentalisierung der Moskauer Erklärung nach dem 2. Weltkrieg," *Zeitgeschichte* 20 (November/December 1993): 345-66.

14. I recall a one-sided conversation with a top aide to the president, at some point early in 1987. The gentleman regaled me with a long, overbearing, condescending mini-lecture on Austrian history, in which the key event was the Nazi execution of the rightist Chancellor Engelbert Dollfuss in July 1934. I heard nothing about Dollfuss' persecution of the socialists, nothing about the regime's rapprochement with Hitler from the summer of 1936, not a word regarding the fate of the Jews or the collaboration with the Nazis by men like Kurt Waldheim.

15. I base these comments on "The Waldheim Quagmire," a review of Eli M. Rosenbaum's *Betrayal* in *New York Newsday*, 19 December 1993.

16. Richard Mitten, *The Politics of Antisemitic Prejudice: The Waldheim Phenomenon in Austria* (Boulder: Westview Press, 1992). Unfortunately, the book tries to deliver more than its title promises, and winds up with far less. This is too bad, since the material on the Austrian press is enlightening and useful. What could have been a solid investigation of the Austrian scene becomes a superficial overview of the entire Waldheim affair—in 260 turgid pages. Mitten rehashes the work done by others, including the WJC, the U.S. press, and the researchers who examined military documents relevant to the Waldheim matter. The result—for instance, in comments made about my work and interpretations, or the intentions of the WJC—is often inaccurate or confused. The book, poorly edited with endnotes awkwardly placed between chapters, thus becomes a series of essays, or a hodge-podge that fails to focus upon its central theme. Incredibly, a book that purports to be serious scholarship even lacks an index.

17. Helga Embacher, "Die innenpolitische Partizipation der Israelitischen Kultusgemeinde in Österreich," in *Schwieriges Erbe: Der Umgang mit Nationalsozialismus und Antisemitismus in Österreich, der DDR und der*

Bundesrepublik Deutschland, ed. Werner Bergmann, Rainer Erb, and Albert Lichtblau (Frankfurt: Campus Verlag, 1995), 321-38.

18. On Kreisky and Jewishness, see the informative article by Herbert Pierre Secher, "Kreisky and the Jews," in *The Kreisky Era in Austria*, vol. 3 of *Contemporary Austrian Studies*, ed. Günter Bischof and Anton Pelinka (New Brunswick, NJ: Transaction Publishers, 1994), 10-31. For a different approach, see Robert S. Wistrich, "The Kreisky Phenomenon: A Reassessment," in *Austrians and Jews in the Twentieth Century: From Franz Joseph to Waldheim*, ed. Robert S. Wistrich (New York: St. Martin's Press, 1992), 234-46.

19. A. Khol, Th. Faulhaber, and G. Ofner, *Die Kampagne: Kurt Waldheim—Opfer oder Täter? Hintergründe und Szenen eines Falles von Medienjustiz* (Munich: Herbig, 1987), 195.

20. Richard A. Stein, *Documents Against Words: Simon Wiesenthal's Conflict with the World Jewish Congress* (Rotterdam: STIBA, 1992) makes Wiesenthal's case.

21. For Wiesenthal's version, see his *Justice not Vengeance* (New York: Grove Weidenfeld, 1989), 310-22.

22. Readers interested in a more detailed look at this legislation may consult "The Pending Revision of the FOIA: A Researcher's Comment," in the *Newsletter of the Society for Historians of American Foreign Relations*, forthcoming in 1996.

23. Passed by the Congress in 1984, see 50 U.S.C. 431, "Protection of Operational Files of the Central Intelligence Agency."

24. Günter Bischof, "The Making of a Cold Warrior: Karl Gruber and Austrian Foreign Policy, 1945-1953," *Austrian History Yearbook* 23 (1995): 99-127. Strangely enough, Bischof ignores Yugoslavia's attack on Waldheim, which had Gruber as its object. See my *Waldheim: The Missing Years* (New York: Morrow, 1988), chapters 12-14.

25. "2 Heads of State Call on Waldheim," *New York Times*, 27 July 1990, 1.

The Silent Revolution: Austria's Accession to the European Union

*Wolfram Kaiser**

Introduction

The statement "Austria has always belonged to Europe"[1] is banal in its reference to a common geographical space, but problematic, when made about Austria's policy towards West European integration since 1945.[2] In this latter, political context it implies that Austria's accession to the European Union (EU) on 1 January 1995 was but a marginal adjustment of traditional, Austrian European policy to the changing international circumstances since 1989. It appears as if membership in the European Free Trade Association (EFTA), founded in 1959-60, as well as the bilateral free trade agreement with the European Community of 1972-73 and membership in the European Economic Area (EEA), which enlarged the internal market and came into force on 1 January 1994, were natural steps on a straight road to full EU membership, a view that may well become fashionable among contemporary historians and political scientists.[3] It is sometimes linked to the idea that at least in the early postwar period—although formally neutral—Austria was in fact a "secret ally" of the West.[4] To stress continuity in Austrian European policy from membership in the Organization for European Economic Cooperation (OEEC) and EFTA to EU entry suggests the need for only very modest domestic economic and political adjustments. This also suited the government in connection with the 1989 application

* The author would like to express his gratitude to Thomas Angerer, Peter Cullen, Michael Gehler, and Josef Melchior for their helpful comments and suggestions.

and during the 1994 referendum campaign as it appeared the most effective policy to secure the greatest possible public support for EU membership.[5]

The continuity thesis is, however, flawed in at least three respects. First, it fails to appreciate the qualitative differences between the EEC/EC and EFTA. The Community method of integration involves common policies, in trade for example, some of which are decided by qualified majority voting. Moreover, it has always implied the long-term objective of closer political integration. In contrast, the alternative concept of intergovernmental cooperation within loose institutional structures was exclusively designed to safeguard trade interests. Second, the continuity thesis tends to ignore that from the early 1960s onwards, EFTA membership, particularly in the view of Bruno Kreisky and others in the Social Democratic Party (SPÖ), who so successfully formed the self-perception of Austrians in the 1970s and 1980s, acquired significant secondary functions. Austria avoided close political association with West Germany, thus sustaining the process of Austrian nation-building. In fact, Austria avoided close political association with the West generally, thus supporting its emerging self-image as a peace-loving nation and essential bridge in the East-West and North-South conflicts, an illusion which, in the 1990s, has come back to haunt Austrian foreign policy-makers. Third, the idea that EU membership necessitates only marginal changes grossly underestimates the impact of EU membership on Austria. Affected areas include economic policy, institutions and political culture, and Austrian identity which rests on Austrians' and Austrian politicians' perception of themselves and the wider world since 1945, particularly since the Kreisky era.

Only one year after Austria's accession to the EU, the far-reaching consequences of EU membership, which even indirectly contributed to the breakdown of the grand coalition on 12 October 1995, are slowly becoming more apparent. At a time of a domestic crisis of orientation, the change amounts to a silent revolution.

The 1994 EU Referendum

After the EU entry negotiations were concluded on 1 March 1994, the Austrian government decided to hold a referendum on EU membership on 12 June 1994. This date was well in advance of the referenda in the Scandinavian applicant countries, and it was chosen to prevent the referendum debate from getting mixed up with the campaign for the federal election due on 9 October 1994.[6] Opponents of EU membership alleged that the government wanted to bulldoze Austrians into voting "yes" by trying to prevent a thorough public debate of the advantages and disadvantages of membership. In Austria, unlike the Scandinavian countries, the referendum was obligatory under the constitution. EU membership was considered to fundamentally affect central constitutional principles, such as the democratic and the federal principles, amounting to a total revision, or *Gesamtänderung*, of the constitution which, according to Article 44, requires a referendum in addition to a two-thirds majority in parliament.[7]

The referendum debate was characterized by a very marked and stable elite consensus on the desirability of EU membership.[8] This consensus encompassed the two governing political parties, the Social Democrats and the Christian Democrats (ÖVP), as well as the small opposition Liberal Forum Party (LIF). LIF support was crucial insofar as it precluded the opponents from presenting the question of EU membership as a partisan issue of government versus opposition. The elite consensus also encompassed all major interest groups other than environmental organizations, as well as the four institutions of Austrian organized corporatism, or *Sozialpartnerschaft*. In general, the media also advocated EU membership. At the national level, the tabloid newspaper *Täglich Alles*, with its aggressive anti-EU propaganda,[9] was the only significant member of the media to campaign against membership. Some regional newspapers also opposed EU membership. On the political party level, the Green Party and the right-wing populist Freedom Party (FPÖ) opposed EU entry. In the mid-1980s the FPÖ leader Jörg Haider had been among the first to demand EC membership. The party line, however, was progressively reversed from 1992 onwards in the hope that it would be possible to exploit the widespread dissatisfaction with the grand coalition in the run-up to the 1994 election.

In comparison with the Scandinavian countries, opinion polls in Austria since the application had indicated a volatile majority in favor of membership which dwindled temporarily during the critical phase of the entry negotiations in the winter of 1993-94. Nonetheless, the final result of the referendum surpassed considerably the expectations of the "yes" camp. On voting day turnout was 82.4

percent; 66.6 percent voted in favor and 33.4 percent against.[10] The analysis of voting patterns shows that the pro-EU parties managed more successfully than the anti-EU parties to unite their supporters behind the official party line. According to one exit poll, 66 percent of ÖVP supporters, 73 percent of SPÖ supporters and 75 percent of LIF supporters voted in favor of EU membership, while only 62 percent of Green Party supporters and 59 percent of FPÖ supporters voted against it.[11]

Regional variations in Austria were much less marked than in Finland, Sweden, or Norway.[12] Without exception, all voting districts returned a "yes" vote. In terms of the *Länder*, at 74.7 percent, support for membership was highest in the Burgenland in the east. During the negotiations the Burgenland had been awarded objective 1 status in the EU Structural Funds, promising substantial financial support for infrastructural improvements and private investment in that region. Support for membership was lowest in Tyrol in the west, at 56.7 percent, where the referendum debate was dominated by the controversial transit and real estate issues.[13] There was no significant urban/rural cleavage. The "yes" vote was, however, significantly lower among women and younger age-groups, a phenomenon that has been attributed to a more pronounced fear of job losses among low-skilled, low-paid, female blue-collar workers[14] and a general skepticism towards "growth logic" and "big institutions."[15]

When voters were asked for their main motive for voting in favor of EU membership, 39 percent mentioned the expectation of general economic advantages, 19 percent the avoidance of isolation of Austria, 17 percent a positive personal attitude towards European integration, and 13 percent the hope for higher external security. Among those who voted against membership, agriculture and environmental concerns featured prominently. Significantly, only 15 percent mentioned neutrality, an argument frequently raised in the period up to the referendum by opponents on the political Left, primarily the Greens.[16] No "mega factor" can be identified which decided the outcome of the referendum.[17] Instead, a cumulation of different motives and reasons was responsible. It seems that abstract interests were generally more influential than personal expectations or worries.

According to exit polls, few voters registered a protest vote against the government, as Haider had hoped. They did, however, in the subsequent federal election on 9 October when the two government parties combined lost more than 12 percent of the total vote and, consequently, their previous two-thirds majority in parliament. As a result, the smaller opposition parties were in a position to negotiate a strict system of parliamentary scrutiny of government policy within the EU in return for their approval of EU entry, which was ratified by the *Nationalrat*, the Austrian parliament, on 11 November 1994 and shortly afterwards by the *Bundesrat*, the federal council.

During the referendum campaign, leading SPÖ and ÖVP politicians largely presented EU entry as a pragmatic economic policy measure designed to safeguard Austrian industrial exports, to provide general economic benefits by way of greater foreign direct investment in Austria, and to lead to a significant decrease in the level of consumer prices, particularly of foodstuffs, as a result of the significantly lower subsidy levels of the Common Agricultural Policy (CAP).[18] To join the EU, or so it seemed, was the best method to get even wealthier even faster. Not surprisingly, after EU entry this one-sided and distorted representation of the effects of EU membership caused the grand coalition considerable political embarrassment. The general long-term economic advantages of membership, which undoubtedly exist, are not easily noticeable for the majority of the population, and the immediate positive effects are not visible enough. By April 1995 Austrian prices for foodstuffs had in fact fallen by 7.6 percent in comparison with the previous year, but without affecting the overall living costs because of significant price increases in other sectors during the same period, particularly public services.[19] The resulting—unjustified—disappointment with the economic benefits of EU membership, which the government had stretched out of proportion during the referendum campaign, has contributed significantly to a substantial decline in public support for EU membership. According to one opinion poll in May 1995, only 44 percent of Austrians saw "only advantages" or "more advantages" in EU membership, while 53 percent saw more disadvantages.[20]

During the referendum campaign the governing parties largely failed to explain and to stress the non-economic advantages of EU membership, particularly the security dividend from membership in the EU and—initially—observer status in the Western European Union (WEU) which, in the long-term, is likely to develop into the defense wing of the EU. The reason for this failure was Austrian neutrality which formally still exists despite EU entry. Since the Kreisky era, the concept of neutrality has been so closely linked with the Austrian national identity that before the 1994 referendum and federal election no leading government politician was keen to cross this political minefield and risk a deep domestic split over Austrian foreign policy.[21] The government also failed, after the referendum, to keep Europe in the public debate by continuously discussing the effects of membership, leaving real or fictitious adverse consequences open to exploitation by Haider. The State-Secretary in the Chancellor's Office, Brigitte Ederer, who became general secretary of the SPÖ in autumn 1995, has admitted that "non-communication" on the part of the government after the referendum certainly contributed to the European hangover in Austria,[22] a hangover whose long-term significance should not, however, be exaggerated. Most new member states have experienced difficulties in managing the domestic adjustment process, registering lower rates of support for membership or further integration in the process.

Domestic Adjustment: Policies

Accession to the EU has affected several policy areas, necessitating structural adjustments, most of all in economic policy. The financial costs of membership contributed significantly to the budget crisis in September/October 1995, and thus even supplied the occasion for the breakdown of the grand coalition on 12 October 1995 and the subsequent early election on 17 December 1995.

The process of domestic economic adaptation to EU membership, in the form of privatization, deregulation, and the formation of transnational alliances, began before the preparations for the EEA, which eventually came into force one year later than was planned, on 1 January 1994. It is widely hoped that full EU membership will further the diversification and internationalization of the Austrian economy which, unlike the Swiss economy, trades mainly with the neighboring countries, particularly Germany, but also Italy, Switzerland, and, increasingly, the new Central European democracies. Supporters of EU membership also expect a positive effect in terms of growth and employment. According to one report, which was commissioned by the Austrian economics ministry before the referendum, EU membership could result in accumulated extra growth of about 3.4 percent by the year 2000. Unemployment is predicted to be 1.4 percent lower than if Austria had remained outside the EU.[23] However, based on the Cecchini report, which made much too optimistic predictions about the effects of the internal market program on economic growth within the EU,[24] this study very probably exaggerates the economic benefits of membership.

While export-oriented business and consumers will undoubtedly benefit from EU membership, the general long-term economic advantages have to be set against the short- and medium-term problem that EU membership has put an additional burden on the Austrian budget, estimated at 0.7 percent of GDP for 1995 and rising in later years.[25] In absolute terms, in 1995 the Austrian contribution to the EU budget was ös 28.1 billion, to which have to be added some ös 14 billion for extra costs, such as legal and administrative adaptations, and ös 8.4 billion compensatory payments to Austrian farmers. Such payments will be made for four years, amounting to ös 28.5 billion overall. At the same time, EU payments to the regions through the Structural Funds and to farmers through the CAP, amounting to some ös 14 billion in 1995, do not—with the exception of ös 2 billion—benefit the Austrian budget. As a result, according to one estimate, in 1995 the financial costs of EU membership led to an increase in the Austrian budget deficit of nearly ös 50 billion.[26] This deficit increase was clearly predictable given the terms of the Austrian accession. It was, however, largely ignored in the 1994 budget by both the SPÖ and ÖVP who did not want to antagonize their respective electoral clients with more drastic cuts in public spending or tax increases.

At the same time, the Maastricht convergence criteria for participation in monetary union have added considerable external pressure for short- and medium-term budgetary consolidation, if the Austrian government does not want to risk the stability of the schilling which has been attached to the Deutschmark since 1983 with exchange rate variations below 0.3 percent. Whatever the party political reasons for the breakdown of the grand coalition in October 1995, the sky-rocketing budget deficit in combination with the external pressure for budgetary consolidation produced a severe crisis in Austrian distributional politics. It remained to be seen at the time of writing, how the inevitable reforms of the civil service and of the pension and health systems, for example, would be managed. In any case, the breakdown of the grand coalition greatly accelerated the search for alternative coalitions which in itself marks a momentous change from postwar Austrian political traditions.

Apart from economic policy, EU membership has also affected several other policy areas, agriculture, for example, where participation in the CAP is accelerating the inevitable restructuring process. It is not, however, only the policies themselves that undergo change. The established corporatist, consensus-oriented domestic policy-making structures also need to be adapted to supranational and transnational decision-making. To optimize its influence within the EU, the Austrian government will be forced to develop a more anticipatory policy-making style and swifter decision-making procedures in EU-related policy matters than are compatible with the traditional long, drawn-out consultations with the social partnership institutions and with interest groups.[27] The social partnership institutions could increasingly be sandwiched between greater executive autonomy in EU-related matters, a general phenomenon within the EU, and competing demands for a greater role in the EU policy-making process by the *Länder* and the *Nationalrat*.

The intragovernmental decision-making structures have also had to be adapted to EU membership. The distribution of ministerial competences in EU matters had all along been disputed between the partners of the grand coalition. When temporarily renewed after the 1994 election, the SPÖ-ÖVP coalition eventually decided on a system of complete formal equality in the EU policy-making process. The Austrian position on the 1996 Intergovernmental Conference (IGC), for example, was for the foreign ministry and the chancellor's office to prepare jointly. As a general rule, for common working groups, those preparing EU Council meetings, for example, a system of rotation in the chairmanship was fixed.

Domestic Adjustment: Institutions

Change as a result of EU membership is not confined to policies and the policy-making process. The institutions themselves and the institutional balance within the Austrian political system are also affected. Further integration with the international environment has for some time been predicted to accelerate the process of disintegration of the formerly archetypical consociational patterns of the postwar political system in Austria.[28] These patterns include close connections between the SPÖ and ÖVP and the respective major economic interest groups, that is, the trade unions and the employers' and farmers' organizations. The general crisis of Austrian consociationalism is reflected, for example, in the long-term decline of the SPÖ and the ÖVP as well as in the credibility crisis of the social partnership institutions, which have been shaken as a result of widespread party nepotism. Generally, EU membership is likely to reinforce the existing trend towards much greater competition and confrontation in the political system.

At least temporarily, EU membership and the related question of Austrian representation in EU institutions also stimulated the domestic political debate about the proper constitutional role of the Austrian President. Chancellor Franz Vranitzky and President Thomas Klestil, a former career diplomat and member of the ÖVP until his election in 1992, disagreed initially as to who should represent Austria at European Council meetings. According to the Austrian constitution, the formal powers of the president, who is elected by universal suffrage, are significantly greater than those, for example, of the German president. While throughout the postwar period these powers were interpreted restrictively by the SPÖ and ÖVP, Klestil has been looking for a greater political role in domestic and foreign affairs. Vranitzky eventually clarified in Parliament that the president's role within the EU would in future be limited to representative functions, and that he would represent Austria at European Council meetings. However, this issue could well continue to prove controversial, as it is now part of the wider constitutional debate, initiated by Haider, about the possible introduction of a presidential political system.

EU membership has also had a significant impact on the center-periphery relationship in Austria. For a long time, accession to the EU seemed bound to result in a restructuring of the federal system of Austria which, because of the limited powers of the *Länder*, should appropriately be described as a decentralized unitary state.[29] Early on, the *Landeshauptleute* had established a linkage between EU membership and constitutional reform. On 8 October 1992 a "Political Agreement on the Reform of the Federal State" was signed by the *Länder* and the federal government. It included a general commitment to a redistribution of competences in accordance with the principle of subsidiarity, a reform of the financial system, and the establishment of the *Bundesrat* as the representation of the *Länder* governments similar to the German model. A joint commission was to develop concrete proposals.[30]

It soon became clear, however, that there was no agreement either on the interpretation of the joint declaration or even on the necessity, in principle, of any such reform which has been debated since the early 1960s. Toward the end of 1993, the federal government, led by the more centralist SPÖ, and the *Landeshauptleute*, put forward widely differing proposals. After protracted negotiations, the referendum date passed without an agreement being reached. Eventually, the *Landeshauptleute* removed the linkage. After the overwhelming result of the referendum, they did not want to be seen as responsible for the demise of the EU accession laws. As a result, it seemed likely in late 1995 that there would be no reform of the federal system at all for the foreseeable future. The relationship between the national and subnational levels in Austria will undoubtedly remain a contentious issue between the federal and the state levels and among the parties, as it is in several other EU member states with strong regional traditions.[31]

Greater political frictions between the *Länder* and the government in Vienna after the failure of the reform of the federal system were only avoided because the question of the involvement of the *Länder* in the policy-making process in EU matters had actually been solved, on the insistence of the *Landeshauptleute*, even before the entry negotiations began. Since 1992 the federal government has been constitutionally bound to inform the *Länder* about all EU questions "which affect their independent sphere of action or may otherwise be of interest to them." The *Länder* can issue a simple or a qualified opinion. The latter has to be supported by at least five out of the nine *Länder* with no dissenting votes. In EU negotiations the federal government may still deviate from such a qualified opinion, but subsequently this has to be justified within eight weeks. In order to coordinate their EU policies, the *Länder* founded the Integration Conference of the *Länder* (IKL) in 1991, comprised of the *Landeshauptleute*, and the Permanent Integration Committee of the *Länder* (SIL).[32] How cooperation between them and the federal government will evolve remains to be seen. At least the new formal powers of the *Länder*, even though they do not go nearly as far as those of the German Länder according to the new Article 23 of the

Grundgesetz,[33] provide some compensation for the loss of influence in the domestic political arena as a result of EU entry.

Finally, EU membership, in connection with the temporary loss on the part of the grand coalition of its previous two-thirds majority, has also affected the role of the *Nationalrat*. In comparison with most North European and North American parliaments, the *Nationalrat* used to be weak, having been marginalized as a result of the tradition of a grand coalition government with comfortable two-thirds majorities. Its domestic role is potentially enhanced by the constitutional formula for parliamentary scrutiny of the EU policy-making process, effectively agreed upon between the governing parties and the two smaller opposition parties, the Greens and the LIF. According to this formula,[34] the government is obliged to inform Parliament, in the form of the main committee, or *Hauptausschuß*, of the *Nationalrat*, about "any initiatives" within the EU. This scrutiny includes not just legislative but also political initiatives and encompasses all three pillars of the European Union, that is, also Common Foreign and Security Policy (CFSP) and interior policy matters. Positions taken by the *Hauptausschuß* bind the government. The government can invoke an escape clause when there are "compelling reasons of integration policy," but advance agreement of the *Hauptausschuß* is indispensable in those cases where EU decisions necessitate constitutional changes for which a two-thirds majority is subsequently needed in Parliament. It was further agreed that the parliamentary rules of procedure would be amended so as to provide for a new EU subcommittee of the *Hauptausschuß* to deliberate during major negotiations such as EU Council meetings. The government would have to consult this subcommittee before changing a previously agreed upon negotiating position. In late 1995 the necessary rule changes were delayed, however, because of the domestic political crisis. As the SPÖ and ÖVP regained their previously held two-thirds majority in the December election, it seemed doubtful in early 1996 whether both parties would still support these rule changes in their entirety.

The agreed formula can be seen as representing an attempt to tackle the increased democratic deficit in the domestic political context by replacing ex post parliamentary scrutiny with what amounts to a co-decision procedure.[35] What use Parliament makes of its new formal powers largely depends on the line taken by the parliamentary groups of the governing parties and by the government itself. There are, however, two compelling reasons why any government may wish to be seen as cooperative. First, no party can now afford to unnecessarily antagonize other potential coalition partners. Second, after their dramatic losses in recent elections, which have only partly been made up for by gains in the election in December 1995, the SPÖ and ÖVP have developed a keen interest in being perceived as deciding government policy based on the will of the people.

In addition to these domestic political motives, any Austrian government may also find it useful to employ real or fictitious domestic pressure from Parliament in the EU bargaining process. At the same time, positions taken by the *Hauptausschuß* may make it more difficult for the Austrian government to participate in the preparation of compromises or package deals within the EU. This effect could be observed in the spring of 1995 in the case of the debate about the Community directive for the transport of livestock. The Austrian negotiator was bound not to deviate under any circumstances from the demand, which proved non-negotiable, that the EU adopt existing Austrian legislation for itself.[36] In any case, it will be interesting to see how the Austrian system of parliamentary scrutiny will in practice compare, for example, with the strict Danish model, and whether and to what extent it will further the process of a parliamentarization of the Austrian political system.[37]

Domestic Adjustment: Political Mentality

The actual and potential effects of EU membership on policies, the policy-making process, and institutions are much greater than the continuity thesis supposes. But EU membership exerts perhaps the greatest pressure on the established political identity in which Austrians have learned to perceive themselves and the wider world since at least the Kreisky era, and in which Austrian politicians are accustomed to contemplate politics, articulate interests, and pursue policies.[38] After accession to the EU, Austria—"the island of the blessed"—is an island no longer. Unlike Switzerland, where a narrow majority of the population rejected even EEA membership in the 1992 referendum, Austrians—by joining the EU—have somewhat reluctantly embarked upon an open-ended process of societal change.

The political class, socialized in the cozy pre-1989 era, has displayed a pronounced unwillingness, born of political weakness in times of domestic and party political crisis, to fulfill their educative function and properly address, in public, the need for fundamental change. Reluctance to do so is often combined with honest surprise at how certain Austrian policies, particularly neutrality, are actually perceived in other EU states. The irritation is exacerbated by the difficulty of getting used to thinking and acting as part of a wider community of states with an enormous and long-established network of intersocietal and intergovernmental contacts and a certain degree of supranational decision-making. Three illusions of the pre-1989 postwar era, which over time became part of the belief system of all parties within what the *Klubobmann* of the ÖVP, Andreas Khol, has termed the Austrian constitutional arch, or *Verfassungsbogen*, cause Austrian politicians particular problems: the superficial internationalist rhetoric which stands in sharp contrast to societal reality, the idea of moral superiority of a neutral and peace-loving nation, and the somewhat immodest belief that the other EU states were only waiting for Austrian leadership, a slightly modernized political version of "Am österreichischen Wesen soll die Welt genesen."

In Austria's external relations, internationalist rhetoric, as well as actual involvement in diplomatic mediation and UN peace-keeping, concealed a distinctive lack of European or international orientation in the economy, in education, and other areas of Austrian society. Without recourse to the linguistic extremism of Peter Turrini or the late Thomas Bernhard, it is clear by now that the rhetoric also distracted from a distinctively xenophobic and inward-looking political culture which does not adapt easily, for example, to the idea of freedom of movement, not just of goods, but also of people, within the EU. At the political level, internationalism has often been confined to political rhetoric. In the 1990s Austria largely lacks a foreign policy elite with sufficient knowledge of the Union or interest in influencing its future development—more so, in fact, at the party political than at the official level or in the media. After the Eurocentric Alois Mock was forced out of office in early 1995, his successor as foreign minister, the new ÖVP leader Wolfgang Schüssel, showed very little interest in European matters, and on too many occasions allowed the State-Secretary Benita Ferrero-Waldner or senior officials to represent the Austrian government in EU institutions. It is also revealing that after Ederer moved from the chancellor's office, where she was Vranitzky's adviser in European matters, to become general secretary of the party, the SPÖ saw no need to quickly find a qualified replacement for the Austrian representative in the so-called reflection group of the EU, which was to prepare the 1996 IGC.[39]

For many Austrians, it is also part of their belief system that Austria's neutrality and its strictly anti-nuclear policy in particular are morally superior to policies of other member states, an attitude that tends to result in diplomacy which gives symbolism priority over results.[40] During the first year of EU membership it became clear in Austria's relationship with France that such an approach, while serving domestic interests nicely, is ineffective in a community of states with different traditions of policy and political style and with a high premium on mutual influence through long-standing contacts and informal exchanges.[41] The Austrian government first began a moral campaign against the renovation of the Slovakian nuclear power plant Mochovce, which the French nuclear industry wanted to turn into a pilot project in Eastern Europe.[42] Austria managed to prevent West European financial support for the project, but—ironically—the renovation is now being done to lower technical standards by a Czech-Russian consortium. Vranitzky subsequently also attacked the French government quite violently over its nuclear tests in the Pacific,[43] which merely provoked President Jacques Chirac into making a sarcastic remark about him in public.[44] Whatever the merits of the Austrian position, the symbolic political approach, which is preoccupied with consolidating a specific Austrian or political party self-image, could well continue to burden important bilateral relationships with other EU states, and thus minimize actual Austrian influence.

This moralism reflects the moral certainty that many Austrian politicians feel they possess in foreign policy matters. This is, however, largely based on the misperception, now increasingly shattered, that Austria's views, particularly its neutrality policy, are generally approved of, and that other EU states can learn from Austrian standards and benefit from an Austrian role as mediator, at least in relation to Central and Eastern Europe. On the contrary, the outside perception of the Austrian neutrality policy, in any case since 1989, varies from, at best, indifference to the sarcastic view that neutrality is a cheap policy of hanging on the coattails of WEU and

NATO.[45] In comparison with Sweden and Switzerland, which throughout the Cold War pursued credible defense policies, respect in other EU states for the neutrality policy of Austria, which spends only a slightly greater portion of its GDP on defense than Luxemburg or Iceland, is very limited. The official Austrian government assessment that the North Atlantic Treaty Organization (NATO) is, in the words of Andreas Khol, "a model of the past,"[46] is not shared widely in the rest of Europe. Demands that NATO should be replaced with a totally new and "cooperative" security system find very little echo indeed. Attempts by President Klestil in 1994-95 to confront the neutrality myth[47] proved largely unsuccessful: while more and more politicians tacitly agreed to the need for change in Austrian foreign and defense policy, no one was prepared to publicly take a lead in this domestically sensitive matter.

Overall, experience since Austria's accession to the EU has shown that the Austrian political class needs much more time to adapt to the Community culture than most expected or were previously prepared to admit. At the same time, they are required to develop policy priorities on a number of very important issues in the future development of the EU.

Policy Priorities in the European Union

A debate about Austria's future policy priorities within the EU effectively began only after the 1994 election. Initially, the government had announced the publication of a "White Paper" on EU policy in advance of the European Council in Essen in December 1994. But the fact that the 150 page draft contained no chapter on social policy caused such a disagreement within the coalition that, even though the document became public and was circulated to the other member states, publication was deferred for several months. The document is necessarily rather vague, but, analyzed in connection with other policy papers and public statements until late 1995, it does give some indication of the evolving policy priorities of the grand coalition within the EU with respect to such issues as institutional reform, eastern enlargement, the future of CFSP/WEU, and monetary union. The dominant overall impression is that, in the words of former Foreign Minister Mock, the government regards Austria as a "European core country" and will aim to belong to the integration core "wherever differentiated integration processes emerge,"[48] but particularly in regard to monetary union. The tacit consensus on this general line certainly encompasses the Liberal Forum Party, and to some extent even the Greens, who after the referendum immediately recognized the clear result and began to follow a new policy of reform of the EU from within.[49] Orthodox-fundamentalist opposition to membership or further integration had never been particularly pronounced. The term core Europe, or *Kerneuropa*, which was first used by the German Christian Democrat politicians Karl Lamers and Wolfgang Schäuble, is only used by the ÖVP and is otherwise disputed. However, to a large extent this merely reflects Austrian and EU political party faultlines as well as the determination, particularly on the part of the SPÖ, to avoid the impression of a Germanic bloc within the EU in order to retain good relations with the southern member states.

With respect to institutional reform, the grand coalition followed a moderately integrationist line. It did not take up far-reaching demands by the smaller opposition parties for a European constitution (LIF) or completely new forms of integration such as temporary divisions of competences between EU member states and regions (Greens). If obtainable, some strengthening of the European Parliament's powers of co-decision and control are welcome as would be the extension of majority voting in the Council, an upgrading of the Committee of the Regions (with regard to the supervision of the application of the principle of subsidiarity), for example, and enhanced transparency together with a simplification of the decision-making procedures.[50] In autumn 1995 it emerged that Austria would agree to a redistribution of votes in the Council of Ministers at the expense of the smaller states, which are considerably over-represented, but only if each member state retains one EU commissioner. Otherwise, the grand coalition had developed very little strong or specific views on any particular reform issue.[51]

The grand coalition took the view that the 1996 IGC should not be burdened with too many far-reaching demands for institutional reform. The coalition made this decision in an effort to prevent member states from using the lack of progress as an argument to delay eastern enlargement, which in the "White Paper" is described as a priority aim of Austria within the EU.[52] The Austrian government has supported the decision by the EU to treat each application separately and on its merits. However, it has emphasized that, if at all possible, a democratic Slovakia should not be left behind the other "Visegrad countries," and that the EU's relationships with Slovenia and, in the medium-term, with Croatia should be developed as quickly as possible. It is hoped that Slovenia will be in a position to join the EU in the first round of eastern enlargement. Apart from economic considerations, the shifting of the EU's external borders further east promises to yield a security dividend.[53]

As a result of the deepening budgetary and domestic political crisis, however, Austrian support for eastern enlargement appears to have cooled down somewhat since EU entry. While the German government's position is that the first round of eastern enlargement should take place by the year 2000, Khol of the ÖVP said in 1995 that he could not imagine this happening before 2005.[54] Since 1990 the Austrian economy has registered a massive positive net effect of the breakdown of the Iron Curtain in terms of both trade and employment, but enlargement, involving greater financial transfers to new member states, will be a mixed blessing in purely financial terms. According to one study commissioned by the chancellor's office, in the decade following a first round of eastern enlargement in the year 2000, the net financial effect for Austria, if Poland is included, would be negative.[55] Other potential domestic political repercussions of eastern enlargement include the likely adverse effects on Austrian agriculture. It is significant in this context that the Austrian EU Commissioner and former national agriculture minister Franz Fischler has been entrusted with the agriculture portfolio. Fischler, who is a member of the ÖVP, which has close political connections with the farming community, will be expected to develop a concept for the adaptation of the CAP in advance of eastern enlargement. In Austria it is hoped that his presence in Brussels may help to safeguard Austrian agricultural interests and to make the inevitable adjustments politically more acceptable.

Unlike on the enlargement question, the Austrian government did not, until late 1995, take any serious stance at all on the question of a strengthening of the CFSP and the development of a common EU defense identity. The latter would definitely necessitate the formal abandonment of neutrality.[56] Before 1989, Austrian neutrality had initially been re-interpreted to conform with the aim of EU membership, that is, as being restricted to the prohibition of membership in a military alliance.[57] Neutrality was still referred to in the application, but subsequently never mentioned in the entry negotiations. Instead, in June 1992 the Austrian government declared its preparedness "to participate in the CFSP and in its dynamic development actively and in a spirit of solidarity.... The Treaty of Maastricht has assigned to the WEU an important role in the development of the EU. On the occasion of its accession to the EU, Austria will draw the appropriate conclusions from this fact."[58] Accordingly, the government took up WEU observer status and also joined NATO's Partnership for Peace program in 1995. The 1994 coalition agreement also provided in general terms for full participation in any EU security arrangement which may emerge in the context of the 1996 IGC,[59] a formula which is wide open to conflicting interpretations. It seems that after the retirement of Mock, the ÖVP is now more concerned with the potential financial costs of a credible defense policy, which WEU and NATO membership would necessitate,[60] as well as with public opinion which is still attached to the neutrality concept. SPÖ moderates—like Vranitzky—advocated at least full WEU membership "in principle," if only in foreign newspapers,[61] but they did not seem prepared for the formal abandonment of neutrality in the near future, a step that would, according to one commentator, amount to "a break with the entire Austrian postwar history on which the ideological identity of the Second Republic is based."[62] Within the SPÖ, moreover, violent opposition of the pacifist wing to membership in any kind of defense community continues. It could well be strengthened if the SPÖ's long-term decline continued despite its unexpected success in the 1995 general election, and a new leadership resorted to populist exploitation of the issue to revive the party's fortunes.[63] In any case, the government's preoccupation with the domestic management of the neutrality issue made it seem unlikely at the time of writing that it would exert any influence at all on the EU reform debate in this particular field.

Finally, the Austrian government undoubtedly expects the schilling to be among the first currencies to enter the third stage of monetary union on 1 January 1999 or later.[64] Before the severe budget crisis of 1995, the conditions for this were generally quite good. The well-established Austrian hard currency policy enabled the schilling to join the European Monetary System (EMS) on 9 January 1995, only one week after Austrian EU entry. Inflation and interest rates are almost identical with those in Germany. Without substantial budgetary reform, however, it will be impossible for Austria to meet the convergence criteria of an annual budget deficit below 3 percent and a state deficit below 60 percent.[65]

Conclusion

Unlike Britain, Austria is at least geographically "at the heart of Europe." The analysis of Austria's accession to the EU suggests, however, that substantial domestic adjustments may still be needed before the Austrians can themselves make a significant contribution to the future development of the Union. These adjustments concern certain policy areas and institutions as well as the way in which Austrians in the postwar period have learned to perceive themselves and the wider world.

The grand coalition, renewed after the 1994 election and again in March 1996, was basically determined that Austria should belong to the integration core in Europe, if and when differentiated integration processes emerge. In principle, the solid "yes" vote in the 1994 membership referendum should allow any Austrian government to embark on an active integration policy, particularly as—unlike Sweden—there is currently no substantial organized opposition to EU membership or further integration in Austria. There are nonetheless several uncertainties in relation to domestic political developments in Austria, particularly after the breakdown of the grand coalition in October 1995, which may have an important bearing on Austrian EU policy.

One of these uncertainties relates to the greater possibility of alternative coalitions, particularly cooperation between the ÖVP and FPÖ, which renamed itself "Movement for Freedom" in January 1995. Haider is not opposed in principle to EU membership or further integration. However, any direct or indirect influence he may exert as a result of a formal coalition or the toleration by his party of an ÖVP minority government would introduce a populist element into government policy which might make Austrian EU policy less predictable and reliable. Equally, a center-left rainbow coalition, including the Greens, might also complicate the policy-making process in EU-matters. Finally, a general uncertainty exists, due to the possibility of another referendum on EU reform arising from the 1996 IGC. Such a referendum would not be constitutionally required, not even for the renunciation of neutrality, but it might nonetheless be called by the government particularly at times of a domestic political crisis in order to obtain public approval for its integration policy.

NOTES

1. Ludwig Steiner, "Österreich war schon immer in Europa," in *Österreichisches Jahrbuch für Politik 1994*, ed. Andreas Khol et al. (Vienna: Verlag für Geschichte und Politik, 1995), 455-69.

2. For an overview of Austrian foreign policy since 1945 see Helmut Kramer, "Strukturentwicklung der Außenpolitik (1945-1990)," in *Handbuch des politischen Systems Österreichs*, ed. Herbert Dachs et al. (Vienna: Manz, 1991), 637-57.

3. Among those studies that display a deeper understanding not just of Austrian postwar history, but also of the history of the Community and its member states, the degree of continuity appears somewhat exaggerated in Michael Gehler, "Zwischen Neutralität und Europäischer Integration: Österreich und die Einigungsbestrebungen in Westeuropa 1955-1994," *Geschichte in Wissenschaft und Unterricht* 45 (1994): 413-33. In contrast, EU entry is understood as a major break in Austrian postwar history in Thomas Angerer, "L'Autriche précurseur ou 'Geisterfahrer' de l'Europe intégrée? Réflexions dans la perspective des années 1950," *Revue d'Allemagne* 24 (1992): 553-61, and, by the same author, "Österreichische Souveränitätsvorstellungen und Europäische Integration: Mentalitätsgeschichtliche Grenzen der österreichischen Integrationspolitik," in *Österreichischer Zeitgeschichtetag Linz 1995*, ed. Rudolf Ardelt et al. (in press).

4. Gerald Stourzh, "The Origins of Austrian Neutrality," in *Neutrality: Changing Concepts and Practices*, ed. Alan T. Leonhard (Lanham: University Press of America, 1988), 35-57. See also Günter Bischof, "Österreich—ein "geheimer Verbündeter" des Westens? Wirtschafts—und sicherheitspolitische Fragen der Integration aus der Sicht der USA," in *Österreich und die europäische Integration 1945-1993*, ed. Michael Gehler and Rolf Steininger (Vienna: Böhlau, 1993), 425-50. For a short, critical overview of the "secret ally" debate see Michael Gehler, "Westorientierung oder Westintegration? Überlegungen zur politikgeschichtlichen Entwicklung Österreichs nach 1945 im wissenschaftlichen Diskurs," in *Österreichischer Zeitgeschichtetag Linz 1995*, ed. Rudolf Ardelt et al. (in press).

5. See, for example, the declaration by Foreign Minister Alois Mock when the Austrian application was lodged in 1989, quoted in Gerhard Kunnert, ed., *Spurensicherung auf dem österreichischen Weg nach Brüssel* (Vienna: Verlag Österreich, 1992), D 16. Since EU entry President Thomas Klestil has even described Austria as a "would-be founding member of the European Union."

6. An excellent overview of Austria's policy towards European integration since 1945 is Gehler, "Zwischen Neutralität und Europäischer Integration;" see also Oliver Rathkolb, "Austria and European Integration after World War II," in *Austria in the New Europe*, ed. Günter Bischof and Anton Pelinka (New Brunswick: Transaction, 1993), 42-61, and the collection of essays in Michael Gehler and Rolf Steininger, eds., *Österreich und die europäische Integration 1945-1993* (Vienna: Böhlau, 1993). For the history of the 1989 application see Heinrich Schneider, *Alleingang nach Brüssel: Österreichs EG-Politik* (Bonn: Europa Union Verlag, 1990), and—going up to 1993—Gerhard Kunnert, *Österreichs Weg in die Europäische Union: Ein Kleinstaat ringt um eine aktive Rolle im europäischen Einigungsprozeß* (Vienna: Verlag der Österreichischen Staatsdruckerei, 1993).

7. On the constitutional basis of the EU referendum see Wolfgang Mederer, "Österreich und die europäische Integration aus staatsrechtlicher Perspektive 1945-1992—unter Berücksichtigung des EWR-Abkommens," in *Österreich und die europäische Integration 1945-1993*, ed. Michael Gehler and Rolf Steininger (Vienna: Böhlau, 1993), 109-46.

8. For a comparative analysis of the referendum debates in Austria, Finland, Sweden, and Norway see Wolfram Kaiser et al., "Die EU-Volksabstimmungen in Österreich, Finnland, Schweden und Norwegen: Folgen für die Europäische Union," *Integration* 18 (1995): 76-87.

9. *Täglich Alles* even claimed that Austrian EU membership would allow the Spanish to seize Austrian tap water from the Alps. Other peculiarities of the referendum debate are collected in Doris Wöks-Kruschitz, "Absurditäten und Kuriositäten im Vorfeld der EU-Abstimmung," in *Österreichisches Jahrbuch für Politik 1994*, ed. Andreas Khol et al. (Vienna: Verlag für Geschichte und Politik, 1995), 363-77.

10. For the referendum results in each of the Austrian states see Anton Pelinka, ed., *EU-Referendum: Zur Praxis direkter Demokratie in Österreich* (Vienna: Signum, 1994), 197.

11. Fritz Plasser and Peter Ulram, "Meinungstrends, Mobilisierung und Motivlagen bei der Volksabstimmung über den EU-Beitritt," in *EU-Referendum. Zur Praxis direkter Demokratie in Österreich*, ed. Anton Pelinka (Vienna:

Signum, 1994), 87-119. The referendum result is also analyzed in detail in Fritz Plasser, Franz Sommer, and Peter A. Ulram, "Entscheidung für Europa: Analyse der Volksabstimmung über den EU-Beitritt Österreichs 1994," in *Österreichisches Jahrbuch für Politik 1994*, ed. Andreas Khol et al. (Vienna: Verlag für Geschichte und Politik, 1995), 325-54.

12. The EU debate is analyzed in a comparative *Länder* perspective in Christian Laireiter et al., "Die österreichische EG-Diskussion in den Ländern: Vergleichende Analyse von regionalen Konfliktpotentialen in sechs Bundesländern," *Österreichische Zeitschrift für Politikwissenschaft* 23 (1994): 67-88. For a historical perspective, which takes into account the EU debate in the *Länder* in the late 1980s and early 1990s, see the very detailed study by Christian Schaller, "Die innenpolitische EG-Diskussion seit den 80er Jahren," in *Ausweg EG? Innenpolitische Motive einer außenpolitischen Umorientierung*, ed. Anton Pelinka, Christian Schaller, and Paul Luif (Vienna: Böhlau, 1994), 27-269.

13. For the results of the entry negotiations in relation to Austria see Wolfram Kaiser, "Austria in the European Union," *Journal of Common Market Studies* 33 (1995): 411-25. In general, see F. Granell, "The European Union's Enlargement Negotiations with Austria, Finland, Norway and Sweden," *Journal of Common Market Studies* 33 (1995): 117-41.

14. Franz Birk et al., "Die Abstimmung. Die Märchen über die Volksabstimmung," *Zukunft—Zeitschrift für Politik, Wirtschaft und Kultur* 7 (1994): 5-8.

15. Plasser and Ulram, "Meinungstrends," 115.

16. Plasser and Ulram, "Meinungstrends," 111.

17. Günther Ogris, "Der Diskussionsprozess vor der EU-Abstimmung," *in EU-Referendum: Zur Praxis direkter Demokratie in Österreich*, ed. Anton Pelinka (Vienna: Signum, 1994), 121-48.

18. The economic benefits of EU membership had been the decisive motive behind the 1989 application. For the economic reasoning see Heinrich Schneider, "Gerader Weg zum klaren Ziel? Die Republik Österreich auf dem Weg in die Europäische Union," *Österreichische Zeitschrift für Politikwissenschaft* 23 (1994): 5-20.

19. "Der große Katzenjammer," *Profil*, 3 June 1995.

20. Ibid.; see also "Euro-Frust," *News*, 8 June 1995.

21. The secondary domestic functions of the neutrality status are still only beginning to be addressed properly. See Thomas Angerer, "Für eine Geschichte der österreichischen Neutralität," in *Die Neutralen und die europäische Integration 1945-1995*, ed. Michael Gehler and Rolf Steininger (Vienna: Böhlau, forthcoming 1996); Emil Brix, "The Position of Austria in the Architecture of Europe: The Quest for Identity," in *The Kreisky Era in Austria*, vol. 3 of *Contemporary Austrian Studies*, ed. Günter Bischof and Anton Pelinka (New Brunswick, NJ: Transaction, 1994), 175-82.

22. "Der große Katzenjammer," *profil*, 3 June 1995.

23. Bernhard Felderer et al., *Wirtschaftliche Folgen der Ausgrenzung Österreichs von der Europäischen Union* (Vienna: Institute of Advanced Studies Research Report, 1994).

24. For an introduction into the history of the internal market program and for the Cecchini report see Kristin Schreiber, "Binnenmarkt," in *Europa von A-Z: Taschenbuch der europäischen Integration*, ed. Werner Weidenfeld and Wolfgang Wessels (Bonn: Europa Union Verlag, 1991), 83-91.

25. Vereinigung Österreichischer Industrieller, *Wege aus der Budgetmisere. Vorschläge zur Gewinnung autonomer Handlungsspielräume im Hinblick auf den EU-Beitritt* (Vienna: unpublished source, 1994), 12.

26. "Ein teuerer Spaß. Die EU kostet den Staat heuer 48,5 Mrd.," *News*, 6 July 1995.

27. Peter Gerlich, "Regierungspolitik und Europäische Union," in *Europa als Herausforderung: Wandlungsimpulse für das politische System Österreichs*, ed. Peter Gerlich and Heinrich Neisser (Vienna: Signum, 1994), 19-41.

28. D. Mark Schultz, "Austria in the International Arena: Neutrality, European Integration and Consociationalism," *West European Politics* 15 (1992): 173-200. In general, for the debate about the decline of consociationalism in Austria see Richard Luther and Wolfgang C. Müller, eds., *Politics in Austria: Still a Case of Consociationalism?* (London: Frank Cass, 1992).

29. Andreas Kiefer, "Die Bundestaatsreform im Jahr 1993," in *Österreichisches Jahrbuch für Politik 1993*, ed. Andreas Khol et al. (Vienna: Verlag für Geschichte und Politik, 1994), 413-38.

30. Herbert Dachs, "EU-Beitritt und die Bundesländer," in *Europa als Herausforderung: Wandlungsimpulse für das politische System Österreichs*, ed. Peter Gerlich and Heinrich Neisser (Vienna: Signum, 1994), 185-208.

31. For the failure of the reform of the federal system in greater detail see Theo Öhlinger, "Das Scheitern der Bundesstaatsreform: Verfassungsrechtliche und verfassungspolitische Anmerkungen," in *Österreichisches Jahrbuch für Politik 1994*, ed. Andreas Khol et al. (Vienna: Verlag für Geschichte und Politik, 1995), 543-58 and Peter Pernthaler and Gert Schernthanner, "Bundesstaatsreform 1994," in *Österreichisches Jahrbuch für Politik 1994*, ed. Andreas Khol et al. (Vienna: Verlag für Geschichte und Politik, 1995), 559-84.

32. Dachs, "EU-Beitritt," 190.

33. For a comparative perspective, see Klaus Goetz, "National Governance and European Integration: Intergovernmental Relations in Germany," *Journal of Common Market Studies* 33 (1995): 91-116.

34. See Margit Körner, "Das EU-Begleit-Bundesverfassungsgesetz—die Mitwirkung der Parlamente von Bund und Ländern bei der Schaffung von neuem EU-Recht," in *Österreichisches Jahrbuch für Politik 1994*, ed. Andreas Khol et al. (Vienna: Verlag für Geschichte und Politik, 1995), 513-24.

35. Democratic aspects of EU membership are discussed in Gerda Falkner, "EU-Beitritt aus demokratiepolitischer Sicht," in *Europa als Herausforderung: Wandlungsimpulse fürs politische System Österreichs*, ed. Peter Gerlich and Heinrich Neisser (Vienna: Signum, 1994), 43-69.

36. "Fettnäpfchenhüpfen," *profil*, 10 April 1995.

37. For a comparative perspective see Peter Cullen, "Competing Legitimacy at the European and National Levels: The Ruling of the Constitutional Court and Parliamentary Scrutiny of European Union Affairs in Germany," in *The Changing Role of Parliaments in the EU*, ed. Finn Laursen and Spyros Pappas (Maastricht: EIPA, 1995), 61-93.

38. See the brief remarks in Gerald Stourzh, "Nach der deutschen Einheit: Österreichs Standort in Europa," *Europäische Rundschau* 18 (1990): 3-13. The question of the significance of EU membership for a progressive westernization, or *Verwestlichung*, of the Austrian political system and culture is discussed in Anton Pelinka, "Europäische Integration und politische Kultur," in *Ausweg EG? Innenpolitische Motive einer außenpolitischen Umorientierung*, ed. Anton Pelinka, Christian Schaller, and Paul Luif (Vienna: Böhlau, 1994), 11-26. For greater detail see the essays in Peter Gerlich and Heinrich Neisser, eds., *Europa als Herausforderung: Wandlungsimpulse für das politische System Österreichs* (Vienna: Signum, 1994).

39. After the breakdown of the grand coalition a senior official was eventually charged with the coordination of Austrian policy in the transitional period before the formation of a new government after the election in December 1995. Cf. "Stacher übernimmt Ederers EU-Agenden," *Der Standard*, 23 October 1995. For a critical discussion of the provincialism of Austrian politics and the lack of a qualified foreign policy elite at the political party level see also "Wien, Wien, nur du allein: Statt einer konzeptiven Außenpolitik dominieren Nabelschau und Opportunismus," *Der Standard*, 12 October 1995.

40. On the neutrality mythology see Andreas Unterberger, "Die außenpolitische Entwicklung," in *Die Zweite Republik: Bestand und Wandel*, ed. Wolfgang Mantl (Vienna: Böhlau, 1992), 204-39. Neutrality is seen as a symbol of the "mental reserve [of Austrians] against Western Europe's political culture" in Claus Leggewie, "Österreich in Europa oder: wie westlich ist die Zweite Republik?" *IWM Newsletter 50* (1995): 17-19.

41. The difficult relationship between Austria and France in the postwar period over matters of European integration is discussed in Thomas Angerer, "Besatzung, Entfernung.... Integration? Grundlagen der politischen Beziehungen zwischen Frankreich und Österreich seit 1938/45," in *Frankreich—Österreich. Wechselseitige Wahrnehmung und wechselseitiger Einfluß seit 1918*, ed. Friedrich Koja and Otto Pfersmann (Vienna: Böhlau, 1994), 82-102.

42. See "Heißsporne und Eisblumen," *Frankfurter Allgemeine Zeitung*, 22 September 1995.

43. Ibid.

44. "Am Ende sangen alle das Hohelied der Harmonie," *Frankfurter Allgemeine Sonntagszeitung*, 24 September 1995.

45. See, for example, the critical remarks by the German Christian Democrat Member of the *Bundestag* and foreign policy adviser of Chancellor Kohl, Karl Lamers, in an interview for the journal *profil*: "Wenn Neutralität, 'Europa à la Carte' also mangelnde Solidarität heißt, dann kann es das in der EU nicht geben." Lamers even went as far as to say that—as Austria was proving so difficult over the neutrality issue—the EU should have better developed its foreign and defense policy before allowing Austria to join. See "Der Beitritt kam zu früh," *profil*, 17 July 1995. The phenomenon that close partners of a neutral state may be disappointed by its neutrality policy is termed, somewhat euphemistically, the "affinity paradox" in Gerald Stourzh, "Some Reflections on Permanent Neutrality," in *Small States in International Relations*, ed. August Schou and Arne Olav Brundtland (Stockholm: Nobel Symposium 17, 1971), 93-8.

46. "Österreichische Sicherheitspolitik: Neutralität—WEU—NATO—OSZE. Dokumentation öffentlicher Stellungnahmen von Bundespräsident Dr. Thomas Klestil, Erster Präsident des Nationalrates Dr. Heinz Fischer und Klubobmann Dr. Andreas Khol," in *Österreichisches Jahrbuch für Politik 1994*, ed. Andreas Khol et al. (Vienna: Verlag für Geschichte und Politik, 1995), 471-85.

47. See, in particular, *Ansprache von Bundespräsident Dr. Thomas Klestil vor der österreichischen Gesellschaft für Außenpolitik und Internationale Beziehungen am 12 Oktober 1994 im Festsaal der Nationalbibliothek in Wien* (Vienna: unpublished source, 1994); "Deutliches Lob Klestils für Mock," *Der Standard,* 13 October 1994. For a semi-official exposition of the by now open-minded attitude of the *Aussenamt* towards Austrian participation in common European defense structures see Ernst Sucharipa, "Neutralität allein reicht nicht mehr," *Europäische Rundschau* 21 (1993): 15-24, and by the same author, "Von der Neutralität zur europäischen Sicherheitspolitik: Österreich und die europäische Union," *Integration* 16 (1993); 158-62.

48. Alois Mock, *Rede aus Anlaß der Entgegennahme des Europapreises Coudenhove-Kalergi 1994* (Vienna: unpublished source, 1994), 7.

49. For an exposition of the views of the Greens on EU reform see Johannes Voggenhuber, "Die EU reformieren!," in *Österreichisches Jahrbuch für Politik 1994*, ed. Andreas Khol et al. (Vienna: Verlag für Geschichte und Politik, 1995), 379-412. Before the referendum several leading Green Party politicians deviated from the official party line and advocated EU membership. See, in particular, Monika Langthaler, "Grüne und Europa: Plädoyer für eine neue Europapolitik der Grünen," in *Österreichisches Jahrbuch für Politik 1993*, ed. Andreas Khol et al. (Vienna: Verlag für Geschichte und Politik, 1994), 687-706.

50. See also Bundesregierung, *Weißbuch der Bundesregierung* (Vienna: unpublished source, 1995), 140-50.

51. The views of some academics, mostly constitutional lawyers, on institutional reform are collected in Anton Pelinka et al., eds., *Mitbestimmen, Menschenrechte und mehr Demokratie* (Vienna: Verlag Österreich, 1995).

52. Ibid., 124-30.

53. Hanspeter Neuhold, "EFTA-Erweiterung der Europäischen Union: Eine österreichische Sichtweise," *Integration* 17 (1994): 109-12.

54. "Österreichische Sicherheitspolitik," 485.

55. See Fritz Breuss's article in *Europa 96: Auswirkungen einer EU-Osterweiterung*, ed. WIFO/IHS/WIIW (Vienna: Verlag Österreich, 1995).

56. The implications of EU membership for Austrian neutrality are discussed in a constitutional perspective in Franz Cede, "Österreichs Neutralität und Sicherheitspolitik nach dem Beitritt zur Europäischen Union," *Zeitschrift für Rechtsvergleichung* 36 (1995): 142-8.

57. For the progressive reinterpretation of the neutrality status by the Austrian government to conform with EU membership see Paul Luif, "Austrian Neutrality and the Europe of 1992," in *Austria in the New Europe*, vol. 2 of *Contemporary Austrian Studies*, ed. Günter Bischof and Anton Pelinka (New Brunswick, NJ: Transaction, 1993), 19-41, and by the same author, "EFTA-Staaten und Europäische Union—Neutralität und GASP im Einklang," in *Die Gemeinsame Außen—und Sicherheitspolitik der Europäischen Union: Profilsuche mit Hindernissen*, ed. Elfriede Regelsberger (Bonn: Europa Union Verlag, 1993), 155-77.

58. Quoted in Peter Jankowitsch and Hannes Porias, "The Process of European Integration and Neutral Austria," in *Neutral States and the European Community*, ed. Sheila Harden (London: Brassey's, 1994), 35-62.

59. Bundesregierung, *Arbeitsübereinkommen zwischen der SPÖ und der ÖVP—Regierungsprogramm nach Abschluß der Koalitionsverhandlungen* (Vienna: unpublished source, 1994), 49.

60. NATO membership would make it necessary for the Austrian army to adopt NATO standards and would mean greater public spending on defense. Wild estimates of the extra budgetary costs of NATO membership range from ös 20 to 50 billion annually: "Rein in die NATO," *profil*, 19 June 1995; "NATO-Ticket um 20 Milliarden," *News*, 22 June 1995.

61. Vranitzky said this in an interview in the Spanish daily newspaper *El Pais*, quoted in "Nie wieder Korfu," *profil*, 22 May 1995.

62. Rudolf Burger, "Vae neutris!—Determinanten der europäischen Integration in österreichischer Perspektive," *Leviathan* 22 (1994): 353-66 is a brilliant, if somewhat sarcastic exposition of the roots of the neutrality "fetish."

63. In preparation of the 1996-97 IGC, Ederer, herself an ardent opponent of Austrian accession to WEU and NATO, charged a number of Austrian academics with analyzing the options for a reform of the CFSP and for a new European security system. A new Maginot Line over neutrality could easily be built around some of the results. See, in particular, the aggressive anti-NATO

propaganda in the article by Gerald Mader in *Europa 96: Sicherheit in Europa*, ed. Gerald Mader (Vienna: Verlag Österreich, 1995). Earlier suggestions for a post-1989 revitalization of the Austrian neutrality doctrine include the idea, not actually intended as an April fool hoax, that in the future Austria should be neutral "vis-à-vis the U.S. and...vis-à-vis Germany": Wolfgang Danspeckgruber, "Security in Europe 1992," in *Austria in the New Europe*, vol. 2 of *Contemporary Austrian Studies*, ed. Günter Bischof and Anton Pelinka (New Brunswick, NJ: Transaction, 1993), 107-36.

64. For one Austrian position on the question of the application of the Maastricht convergence criteria and on how monetary union should be run, see Beirat für Wirtschafts—und Sozialfragen, ed., *Europäische Wirtschafts—und Währungsunion—Neue Rahmenbedingungen für die österreichische Wirtschafts—und Finanzpolitik* (Vienna: Carl Ueberreuter, 1994).

65. As a result, in September 1995 the Austrian government was warned by the EU Commission, which oversees compliance with the convergence criteria, to reduce its budget deficit strictly according to the 1994 timetable for the period 1995-98. See "Wiener Koalitionsgespräche über Budget geplatzt," *Frankfurter Allgemeine Zeitung*, 13 October 1995. In an interview shortly after the breakdown of the grand coalition in October 1995, Helmut Kramer, Director of the *Wirtschaftsforschungsinstitut* in Vienna, calculated that to fulfil the convergence criteria on debt by 1 January 1999 the budget deficit would have to be cut back by at least ös 30 billion in 1996 and by the same amount in 1997. Cf. "Ohne Steuererhöhungen kein Budget 1996," *Der Standard*, 16 October 1995.

Public, Private, and Popular: The United States Remembers World War II

*Chad Berry**

One hundred years before fighting broke out in World War II, Carl von Clausewitz, the European military theorist, wrote that war was a "true chameleon" whose color changes to match its background. He continued,

> As a total phenomenon, its dominant tendencies always make war a paradoxical trinity—composed of primordial violence, hatred, and enmity, which are to be regarded as a blind natural force; of the play of chance and probability within which the creative spirit is free to roam; and of its elements of subordination, as an instrument of policy, which makes it subject to reason alone.[1]

Thus, according to Clausewitz, policy makers, soldiers, and artists all contribute to the paradoxical trinity that constitutes the totality of war. Put differently, Clausewitz speaks of public, private, and popular, and I would like to focus on the place where the elements of this trinity intersect—memory—as I describe the ways in which the people of the United States have remembered World War II, a memory that has been complex and at odds throughout much of the last fifty years.

A few words of clarification: World War II involved a mobilization such as the people of the United States had never experienced, and the mobilization, of course, involved not only getting soldiers and supply personnel across oceans but also countless changes within the country,

* I would like to thank John Bodnar, David Thelen, and Patrick Ettinger for their help in writing this essay.

particularly to produce the staggering amount of war matériel. Although I am concentrating on the memory of soldiers (or private memory) and how this memory compares with public and popular memory, I want to point out that during these past few years of commemoration of the fiftieth anniversary of the war, home front memories have often been ignored (especially publicly) in favor of GI commemoration, primarily, I believe, because women were so much a part of the home front, while men were so much a part of the battle front.[2] If World War II was "everybody's war," commemoration in the 1990s has seemed to be only for those who fought on the front lines.

Public Memory

I will begin with public memory, for no better reason other than this view of the war has been in many ways the most pervasive, or at least the one that many assume is the "true" memory of U.S. involvement in the war. According to public memory and accompanying public ideology, World War II was a *good war*, one in which the United States entered the conflict valiantly and heroically (and even arrogantly) to save the world from the evil associated with the Third Reich and Imperial Japan. The good war thesis became a powerfully seductive and intoxicating view of an idealized past and a golden age.[3]

According to the good war thesis, and in true cowboy-and-Indian fashion, the Allies, and particularly the Americans, were *good,* and the Axis, particularly the Japanese, who had embarrassed the country with the attack on Pearl Harbor, were *bad,* even to the point of being subhuman. The noted wartime correspondent Ernie Pyle described his thoughts of the Pacific enemy: "In Europe," he wrote, "we felt our enemies, horrible and deadly as they were, were still people. But out here I gathered that the Japanese were looked upon as something subhuman and repulsive; the way some people feel about cockroaches or mice." Seeing a group of prisoners, he wrote, "gave me the creeps, and I wanted to take a mental bath after looking at them." This is quite a justification of the good war.[4]

But historians have pointed out how specific myths and images of war, after being stripped of their context and molded into abstractions, have, in the words of Craig M. Cameron, "been appropriated to create a historical narrative...that has in turn served a variety of uses in...American society."[5] Throughout the last fifty years, veterans' groups, the military, and the federal government have shaped wartime memories to serve their own needs. For example, Cameron shows how heroic myths of "uncommon valor" among the United States Marine Corps in the Pacific War (liberation there was always seen as due primarily if not exclusively to the United States) were used repeatedly by the Marines in later years to protect their institution against government cuts and to solidify their past as an invaluable part of the country's defense arsenal. The myth of a good war and, by implication, good fighting, Cameron argues, not only perpetuated the uncritical acceptance of the good war thesis, it papered over questions about responsibility and ramifications of violence in the Pacific War, such as Marines so angry at the enemy that they tortured and killed prisoners of war and violated Japanese war dead, including shooting off the genitals of dead Japanese soldiers.[6]

For its part, the U.S. government had an enormous role in creating and sustaining the image of the good war and was aided greatly by a press that was expected to temper the violence. Because fighting never took place within the country, it was relatively easy for the government to create stories of the good war for the folks back home. And the press generally cooperated: *Life* magazine, for example, refrained from publishing graphic photographs that contained dead or injured soldiers. Because of the reporting of Ernie Pyle and other correspondents, soldiers were "boyish" and happy—indeed, eager—about marching off to fight. GIs were always kind to children, civilians, and prisoners of war abroad. The military, historian Michael C. C. Adams has argued, was a "surrogate father" that watched over its boys' morals.[7] But what the military as a surrogate father told American parents about their boys was sanitized. Paul Fussell, for example, disdains the "optimistic publicity" of public memory.[8] He says that soldiers knew that their experience was not only repeatedly "sanitized" but also "Norman Rockwellized" and even "Disneyfied."[9] A good example of sanitation was the GI phrase "snafu" (situation normal all fucked up), which became translated as "fouled up" here at home, because the *U.S. Infantry Journal* condemned profanity. Other examples from the war, including war crimes, rampant sexuality, alcohol abuse, homosexuality, and war psychoses, discount the image of the good war fostered by the government and the media.[10]

After the war, the government continued to perpetuate the good war in public commemoration. Valiant and "good" soldiers dominate the interpretation of two national war memorials, the United States Marine

Corps Memorial in Washington, D.C., and the memorial over the USS *Arizona* in Pearl Harbor, Hawaii. Indeed, interpretation at the two memorials has made them sacred U.S. Valhallas that house the souls of the brave and heroic. The Marine Corps memorial is taken from a staged photograph of Marines struggling to raise the American flag on Mount Surabachi on Iwo Jima in 1945. The image, which became emblazoned in the minds of most Americans, evokes the democratic ethos cultivated throughout U.S. involvement in the war: across an ocean brave soldiers were raising the flag together as citizens back home were doing their part: it was everybody's war.[11]

Unlike the interpretation at the Marine Corps memorial, the *Arizona* memorial does not completely mask the brutality of war. Because the memorial is built over the sunken wreckage of the battleship in which sailors are interred, the visitor is eerily able to watch air bubbles rise from the murky wreckage below the water. Any tinges of death, however, are eventually overwhelmed by the theme of a strong and ultimately triumphant United States rising from the Pearl Harbor attack: the monument is built of concrete and white marble in an elongated shape that sags in the middle, indicating that the country took a blow during the attack on Pearl Harbor but bounced back. Even in the *Arizona,* victory wins out over violence.[12]

Finally, it is easier to describe public memory by listening to voices trying to defend it. This was certainly true in 1995 as many voices clamored over a planned exhibition at the Smithsonian Institution's National Air and Space Museum that would include the *Enola Gay,* the B-29 bomber that dropped the first atomic bomb on Hiroshima. The experience of the *Enola Gay* exhibition shows the extent to which groups will fight to preserve public memory. Martin Harwit, then director of the museum, is reported to have wanted the exhibition to show an alternative to the good war, in his words, "a counterpoint to the World War II gallery we now have, which portrays the heroism of the airmen but neglects to mention in any real sense the misery of the war. I think we just can't afford to make war a heroic event where people could prove their manliness and then come home to woo the fair damsel."[13]

The Air Force Association (AFA) was one of the first groups to raise objections to the exhibition, arguing that instead of the heroic interpretation that was deserved, the "U.S. conduct of the war was depicted as brutal, vindictive, and racially motivated." Gen. Monroe W. Hatch, Jr., president of the AFA, said the plan "treats Japan and the

United States as if their participation in the war were morally equivalent."[14] Voices howled over casting doubt on the accepted justification of dropping the bomb, that close to a quarter of a million U.S. casualties would result (some said at least a million) by invading Japan. In reality, historians have obtained declassified estimates of 69,000.[15] Veterans were appalled. George R. Caron, a tail gunner on the *Enola Gay,* wrote, "We didn't start the war, and it had to be won by any possible means...Japan lost the war about a year before the atom bombs were dropped but wouldn't give up. I believe the Japanese would have fought on with the last man, woman, and child."[16]

Soon, the American Legion was involved in fighting the exhibition, and in May 1994 it passed a resolution that strongly objected to

> the use of the *Enola Gay* and the heroic men who flew her in an exhibit [that] questions the moral and political wisdom involved in the dropping of the atomic bomb and [implies] that America was somehow in the wrong and her loyal airmen somehow criminal in carrying out this last act of the war, which, in fact, hastened the war's end and preserved the lives of countless Americans and Japanese alike.[17]

Defenders of a heroic memory of World War II prevailed. On 30 January 1995, Smithsonian Secretary I. Michael Heyman announced that the original exhibition would be scrapped, as historians cried foul and leveled charges of historical cleansing and McCarthyism. It quickly became apparent that defenders of the good war would accept nothing but heroic victory. The pilot of the *Enola Gay,* Paul Tibbets, said that "those of us who gained that victory have nothing to be ashamed of.... The million of us remaining will die believing that we made the world a better place because of our efforts to secure peace that has held for almost fifty years." His is certainly a well-argued defense of the good war.[18]

Private Memory

The *Enola Gay* controversy proves that the effort to legitimize public memory can become a battle in and of itself. But what is not so clear until one begins exploring the *private* memories of actual soldiers is the often vast discord between public and private memory of World War II. Even though the Air Force Association and the American Legion would have one believe that every soldier who fought shares their heroic memory of World War II, private memories are much darker and more ambivalent. If public memory of World War II is highlighted by what some have called a conservative memory, including leitmotifs of valor, heroism, comradeship, release, and higher cause, private memory is often typified by a liberal experience, including themes of death, suffering, stupidity, and futility, themes that have never been easily communicable to the public.[19] According to Craig Cameron, private memory has been "preserved in quiet ways…in scrapbooks and personal memories," ways that have not captured much public attention.[20]

Reading the private memories of soldiers collected in oral histories quickly tempers the notion of a good war. The recollections of Dwayne Burns, then eighteen years old, on the eve of D-Day incorporate much of both the conservative and liberal experiences of war; he takes pride in comradeship but is also deeply fearful of imminent death. Dwayne Burns was ambivalent:

> We didn't know just what was ahead, but we were honed to a fine edge. We were as trained and ready as we'll ever be. We were tired of waiting and ready for the next step. Now here we sat, each man alone in the dark with his own thoughts and fears. These men around me were the best friends I will ever know. Four months is a long time when you live and work together, day and night. I wondered how many will die before the sun comes up tomorrow. "Lord," I pray, "please let me do everything right. Don't let me get anybody killed and don't let me get killed, either. I really think I'm too young for this. I should be home having a good time. Whoever told me I was a fighter anyway?"[21]

Other soldiers, however, were far less ambivalent, and their memories and opinions of their experience have little in common with the good war thesis. According to historian Michael Adams, combat was not glamorous for those engaged in it, nor were U.S. soldiers "happy warriors"; many soldiers, he argues, felt they put in more than their fair share of suffering and dying, and the memories of soldiers perfectly echo his point. Infantryman Charles Brummett, for example, remembered feeling like an animal while sleeping in the mud and snow and even resenting other soldiers who did not have to endure the harsh conditions. "It wasn't like some of the other service, you know," he said, "You didn't have a place to go inside to a good warm meal."[22] According to Adams,

> Some resented those who were home enjoying prosperity, and some have continued to suffer psychological or physical pain as a result of their wartime experience. Dealing with the experience of combat takes more than a parade. Death was normally not romantic, particularly when the victim was blown apart: many Americans fail to understand that most MIAs simply ceased to exist.[23]

Soldiers were often preoccupied with worry, as Dwayne Burns was; infrequently were they the proud, confident men marching forward in the good war. While on Okinawa, William Manchester remembered that his "throat was thick with fear."[24] According to Joe D. Reilly of the 501st Parachute Infantry Regiment, "Not much conversation took place in the plane. Each man had his own thoughts, anxiety, and fear. You wouldn't be human if you didn't. My thoughts were dominated by hoping the pilot would not get scared and would bring our plane into the drop zone area."[25] While in the plane over the English Channel, reality quickly dawned on Ken Cordry, a Screaming Eagle from the 101st Airborne. "After getting my seat in the plane," he said, "it finally struck me that this was it; that in a few minutes I'd be behind the German lines—that is, if we made it to our drop zone, and if I made the landing without being hit, and if I was able to find some of our men after landing. It was a terrible sinking feeling, realizing that within a few minutes I might not even be around on this old earth anymore."[26] Richard Scudder, from Oklahoma, remembers the tremendous anxiety he had as he was about to jump out of his plane and into the enemy territory of occupied France. "For the ride across the Channel," he said, "nothing seemed real. It seemed to me like the world was coming to an end. When our plane taxied down around on the runway, a real sick feeling came over us." Over France, he said, "all hell broke loose. The bullets hitting our planes sounded like someone was throwing gravel on a tin roof." His worry came to a head when it was his time to jump:

> As I got to the door, a burst of flak exploded right above my head. I don't know how this could ever happen but it did: A piece of that flak got under my helmet and hit me in the eyebrow, and the blood streamed down across my face, and I remember frantically feeling for a hole, thinking that I had been shot with one of those tracer bullets that I had witnessed coming up toward us. Thank God it was only a scratch in my

> eyebrow. That was a relief to find that I hadn't picked up a bullet.[27]

Ultimately, Ken Cordry's and Richard Scudder's fear and anxiety concerned death, and much of private memory is preoccupied with dying, either worrying that one's number might be up next or seeing the grotesque sight of bodies everywhere whose numbers had already been called. Harold Baumgarten knew what war was like, and before he shoved off for Europe he took steps to insure that things would be covered in the event that he died:

> I had a good background in American history and wartime battles and realized that it was not going to be easy, and I did not expect to come back alive, and wrote such to my sister—that she was to get the mail before my parents and break the news gently to them when she received the telegram that I was no longer alive.[28]

Elliott Johnson, who had landed in France on D-Day, 6 June 1944 and was able to take off his shoes and socks and change clothes on 4 July 1944 was later fighting in the Hürtgen Forest, and he recalled the horrific memory of a forward observer who had gone out with his crew. "White phosphorus was thrown at them," Johnson explained. "Two of the men burned before his eyes. He came running to where I was in another part of Hürtgen Forest. I went down the road to meet him. He was sobbing and falling into my arms. He kept saying, 'No more killing, no more killing, no more killing.'"[29] One soldier whose arm was blown off in Italy looked down on his injured self and cursed God and the United States because he suffered "for something I never did or know anything about."[30] Even somewhat ambivalent about his combat experience, William Manchester was obsessed with his dead comrades:

> Inside, though, I was still scared. I felt the growing reserve which is the veteran's shield against grief. I wondered, as I had wondered before, what had become of our dead, where they were now. And in a way which I cannot explain I felt responsible for the lost Raggedy Asses, guilty because I was here and they weren't, frustrated because I was unable to purge my shock by loathing the enemy...I was in the midst of satanic madness: I knew it. I wanted to return to sanity: I couldn't.[31]

Memories associated with D-Day in particular are peppered with haunting stories of death and the dead, and these memories impart a far different impression of a "good war's" invasion. Robert Flory, a paratrooper, remembered landing "in water up to my chest. I saw one plane take a direct hit and explode in mid-air. Every man in that plane died a quick and merciful death."[32] Others died far less mercifully. John Fitzgerald, another paratrooper, landed safely but soon began to see those who didn't:

> We passed the church where a trooper had landed direct on its steeple. His chute was still swaying slowly in the breeze with no one in it. Many of the troopers were killed before they hit the ground or shortly after they landed, and some were still hanging in trees looking like rag dolls shot full of holes. Their blood was dripping on this place they came to free. Seeing these first Americans dead and the way they had died had a chilling effect on us.[33]

On his way to fill his canteen at a well near a farmhouse, one sight in particular has never left John's mind:

> It was a picture story of the death of one 82nd Airborne trooper. He had occupied a German foxhole and made it his personal Alamo. In a half circle around the hole lay the bodies of nine German soldiers, the body closest to the hole only three feet away, a "potato masher" [German hand grenade] clutched in its fist. The other distorted forms lay where they fell, testimony to the ferocity of the fight. His ammunition bandoleers were still on his shoulders, but empty of all the M-1 clips. Cartridge cases littered the ground. His rifle stock was broken in two, its splinters adding to the debris. He had fought alone, and like many others that night, he had died alone. I looked at his dog tags. The name read Martin V. Hersh. I wrote the name down in a small prayer book I carried, hoping someday I would meet someone who knew him. I never did.[34]

Warner Hamlett, an infantryman with the 116th Regiment, remembered a moment when a fellow GI almost sensed that his death was imminent just as they landed on Omaha beach:

> While resting in between the obstacles, Private Gillingham fell beside me, white with fear. He seemed to be begging for help with his eyes. His look was that of a child asking what to do. I said, "Gillingham, let's stay separated as much as we can, because the Germans will fire at two quicker than one." He remained silent and then I heard a shell coming and dove into the sand facedown. Shrapnel rose over my head and hit all

> around me. It took Gillingham's chin off, including the bone, except for a small piece of flesh. He tried to hold his chin in place as he ran towards the seawall. He made it to the wall, where Will Hawks and I gave him his morphine shot. He stayed with me for approximately thirty minutes until he died. The entire time, he remained conscious and aware that he was dying.[35]

Finally, William R. Cubbins, a bomber pilot, always worried about dying in the night while in his plane. "To me," he has written in his memoirs, "death in the lonesomeness of night-blackened skies is so impersonal it violates the rules of dying. Death should never be without meaning or purpose, or dignity. To disappear suddenly in the faceless void of night is to lose one's very existence, to become as an incomplete sentence."[36]

Memories of war that included terrible death also include the bungling and botched plans of warfare, hardly a testimony to the theme of omnipotence of the good war. Harry Bare, a member of the 116th Infantry Regiment, found himself in charge of the remaining men in his squadron because so many had not made it from the landing craft:

> As ranking noncom I tried to get my men off the boat and make it somehow to the cliff, but it was horrible—men frozen in the sand, unable to move. My radio man had his head blown off three yards from me. The beach was covered with bodies—men with no legs, no arms—God, it was awful. It was absolutely terrible.[37]

Sims Gauthier, landing at Utah Beach, said there was mass confusion because so many officers were killed. "It was just like geese flying in the flock when the leader is killed," he recalled. Struggling to navigate the craft to its beach landing, Sims heard a tremendous explosion next to his craft that lifted it out of the water and sent a shock wave through it:

> Then I saw what had happened. An LCT with the four DD tanks had just been blown sky high and everything just disappeared in a matter of seconds. It was another mine, and I said, "Well Howard [Vander Beek], it looks like the stuff has hit the fan!" First wave, and still seven thousand yards from shore, and no control vessels for Red Beach, and four tanks and an LCT and crew on the bottom.[38]

Things were little better at Omaha Beach. Thomas Valence of the 116th infantry division quickly abandoned his instructions and, later, his equipment, as he struggled to stay alive while fighting the water and the German fire and trying to make it to the beach:

> It was then that he was first shot in the left hand: I floundered in the water and had my hand up in the air, trying to get my balance. I made my way forward as best I could. My rifle jammed, so I picked up a carbine and got off a couple of rounds. We were shooting at something that seemed inconsequential. There was no way I was going to knock out a German concrete emplacement with a .30-caliber rifle. I was hit again, once in the left thigh, which broke my hip bone, and a couple of times in my pack, and then my chin strap on my helmet was severed by a bullet. I worked my way up onto the beach, and staggered up against a wall, and collapsed there. The bodies of the other guys washed ashore, and I was one live body amongst many of my friends who were dead and, in many cases, blown to pieces.[39]

Other soldiers fifty years later still remembered the destruction of the war and could still see the human toll, particularly on children, who were fighting to remain alive even after their community had been liberated, as James Etter told me in an interview:

> I went to Fort Harrison, Indiana, and then from there to El Paso, Texas. And to basic training there. And then I went to Germany just outside of Nuremberg, the war was just over at that time. I got there in time to be a replacement troop and of course we landed in Le Havre, France. To see how, oh, the terrible destruction of war was unbelievable, really. I mean, Le Havre had been bombed both ways, you know. The Germans had took it from the French and the Germans had such a strong hold there then that the Allies had just bombed and bombed them then to get the Germans out. And to land there and see [the] destruction of Le Havre was not a pretty sight. And even though we had been real poor on the farm here and many times it was cornbread and beans or something like that, I don't think we ever went to bed hungry, not really. Not real hungry. I mean, we might have been hungry for something besides what we had or something but really not. And it was there that I [first] saw real poverty.

> Well, when we landed in Le Havre, you know, I saw children for the first time that, you know, they had given us stuff that I didn't think was very good to eat. It didn't look like it was anyway. And to throw that out and just see little kids running and grabbing it, dirt and all, and sticking it in their mouths, I had never saw that. You know, you flip a cigarette butt and three or four little fellows just diving for that. You know, and knocking the fire out and saving that butt. I had never saw that.[40]

Other soldiers, in elegant simplicity, remembered the war as among the most stupid of humankind's actions. Admiral Gene LaRocque, for example, was particularly virulent about World War II, and his memory and opinions would make one believe he was talking about the Vietnam War, not the supposedly "good war" of World War II:

> In that four years, I thought, what a hell of a waste of a man's life. I lost a lot of friends. I had the task of telling my roommate's parents about our last days together. You lose limbs, sight, part of your life—for what? Old men send young men to war. Flags, banners, and patriotic sayings.[41]

LaRocque was particularly critical of the consequences of the good war thesis, pointing out how he believed that the United States has been unique in its postwar legacy of always "fighting a war since 1940." "Count the wars—Korea, Vietnam—count the years. We have built up in our body politic," he continued, "a group of old men," mainly, he implies, those who served in World War II, "who look upon military service as a noble adventure. It was the big excitement of their lives and they'd like to see young people come along and share that excitement." The good war myth, he adds, is easy to sustain because "we've always gone somewhere else to fight our wars, so we've not really learned about its horror. Seventy percent of our military budget is to fight somewhere else."[42]

Overall, the hundreds of oral histories that have been collected of soldiers' memories of World War II impart quite a different viewpoint than the good war notion of public memory. The violence and stress associated with wartime combat made some ex-GIs unable to discuss their experience, which is quite different from the stereotypical veteran who is all too eager to discuss his heroic war stories. In 1993, for example, I interviewed Jesse Martin, who served with distinction in the Pacific War, earning a host of medals, including the Purple Heart and the Congressional Medal of Honor. But when his life history came to World War II, with tears in his eyes, he was absolutely unable to discuss his four years. The experience was too painful even fifty years later, and a significant part of his life history was left untold.[43]

Popular Memory

The third part of Clausewitz's trinity is artistic, or popular memory of war. Many have uncritically assumed that popular culture, particularly Hollywood movies, echoed the good war myth by sanitizing the experience for American viewers. Admiral LaRocque said that

> for about twenty years after the war, I couldn't look at any film on World War II. It brought back memories that I didn't want to keep around. I hated to see how they glorified war. In all those films, people get blown up with their clothes and fall gracefully to the ground. You don't see anybody blown apart. You don't see arms and legs and mutilated bodies. You see only an antiseptic, clean, neat way to die gloriously.[44]

Historian Craig Cameron has also been critical of Hollywood attempts to recreate the war experience for viewers, arguing that Hollywood, a major force in the sanitation of memory, has been interested first and foremost in profits, and the liberal view, he writes, would not be profitable until the 1970s.[45]

But a more critical viewing of Hollywood movies and even a reading of novels about the war leaves one to conclude that popular memory is not necessarily public memory, nor is it like private memory. In 1981, for example, Frank Capra, the famed director who produced *Why We Fight* for the government during World War II, a series designed to bolster support for the war, said that he lost interest in making optimistic movies about the war after directing *It's a Wonderful Life* in 1946, because he was demoralized by the incredible brutality witnessed on all sides in the war.[46]

What I want to suggest is that popular memory of the war, represented primarily in movies and novels, bridges the often discordant public and private memories. As historian John Bodnar notes, "Americans did most of their reflecting about the memory and meaning of the war...not when they viewed public memorials but when they went to the movies."[47] Popular memory of the war was a democratic middle ground that allowed debate between the public memory of victory and the private memory of violence.

I want to reconsider what has been hailed as one of the most "heroic" movies of World War II, *The Sands of Iwo Jima,* released in 1949 and starring John Wayne as Sergeant Stryker, a character, it is argued, responsible through the years for sending thousands of young men into military service. Sergeant Stryker is brave, good looking, tough, courageous, heroic, and even ruthless in his pursuit of victory in the Pacific. These traits were publicly cultivated in young men of fighting age during the war. Made with the help of the Marine Corps, the film shows actual footage of the fighting on the islands of Tarawa and Iwo Jima. Craig Cameron argues that *Sands* is the "single most important and lasting movie for the Marines' image."[48]

But one cannot watch the film without being amazed by the extent to which the valiant masculinity of the good war was challenged. Sergeant Stryker is criticized throughout the war for the man he has become, particularly by young Marine Pete Conway, played by John Agar, who hates Stryker because Stryker is just like Conway's own overly masculine father who has just been killed in action. "I'm a civilian, not a Marine," Conway barks to Stryker. The story line, then, becomes centered on the ability of war to unleash dangerously violent natures in men, represented in Stryker, versus the compassionate and sensitive man (presumably associated with peacetime), represented by Conway. Stryker's wife and ten-year-old son have abandoned him because he has chosen the Corps over his family, and when he gets no mail from his wife and son he gets "blind, staggering, stinking, falling down drunk" on liberty. Meanwhile, on his time off Conway meets the woman of his dreams; back on duty he begins talking about wanting to marry her, because maybe his number will come up on Tarawa Island. Stryker overhears Conway in the next tent and the following day warns him against getting serious with a woman under such circumstances. Eventually, Conway marries the woman, and they have a son nine months later. Conway tells Stryker he wants his son to read Shakespeare, not the Marine Manual. He wants his son "to be intelligent, considerate, cultured, and a gentleman," by implication, everything that Stryker is not. During the battle for Iwo Jima, Conway asks "Aren't you human at all?" when Stryker ignores a dying Marine's call for help because they might be spotted by the enemy. The conflict between Conway and Stryker is settled as the Marines are ascending Mount Surabachi, the last Japanese stronghold on Iwo Jima and, by the way, the setting for the photograph that became the Marine Corps

Memorial in Washington. Just as Stryker orders that the flag be raised on top of the volcano, he is fatally shot, and Conway finds a letter Stryker has written to his son, instructing him never to "hurt her [his mother] or anyone as I did" and asking him to be like him in some ways but not in others. The symbolic message cannot be ignored: men must abandon the overly masculine and violent behavior of war and return to loving relationships with women of peacetime.[49]

Other movies that have been criticized for cultivating the image of the good war are in fact, like *The Sands of Iwo Jima,* ambivalent about World II, particularly regarding male violence and male-female relationships. These include *The Best Years of Our Lives* and *To Hell and Back.* In the latter movie, Audie Murphy, hailed as the country's most decorated and heroic soldier, ultimately cares more about getting back home to care for his orphaned younger siblings. Although heroic publicly, privately he writes that "my eyeballs burn; my bones ache; and my muscles twitch from exhaustion. Oh, to sleep and never awaken. The war is without beginning, without end. It goes on forever."[50] He tells a woman he meets in Naples that he hopes his younger brother, who is boyishly obsessed with guns, never has to use them. *To Hell and Back* balances heroics with concerns about violence and responsibility.[51]

Even literature contained themes that reflected the dangerous tendency of men toward violence, as manifest in the war. Norman Mailer's *The Naked and the Dead,* published in 1949, is one such example. Sergeant Sam Croft, a significant character in the novel, is similar to Stryker: he lives for battle, he abhors weakness, and he has chosen fighting over women. Mailer also discusses the inequality of life in the military; his characters, like Charles Brummett, tire of the perquisites that officers have over GIs.[52]

These are only two examples of popular memory of World War II, but they reflect, according to John Bodnar, popular memory's enigmatic rather than doctrinaire character,[53] hence functioning as the borderland between the much different landscapes of public and private memories. As such, popular memory includes elements of victory from public memory and violence from the private, and popular memory seems to allow Americans themselves to arrive at their own conclusion about the war. Popular memory, as a part of popular culture, seems to sustain the cultural contradictions between public and private memory, and it is likely one of the reasons for the *Enola Gay* controversy.[54]

How, then, is the U.S. memory of World War II different from memory in other countries? One result of the good war thesis in the United States is that of declension; this thesis has often resulted in hopelessness in later decades because some Americans assume that the good war was part of a golden age and not a result of unique circumstances. Some Americans therefore believe that in order to reverse the postwar (particularly the post-Vietnam) decline, the country must return to that golden age. The problem, of course, as historians often point out, is that those who think things were better in the past or who want to return to the past know too little about it.[55]

This observation may suggest that such controversy over the *Enola Gay* is healthy, because it represents an attempt not only to challenge public memory but also to educate people about the past. Furthermore, it may indicate a key difference in U.S. memory of World War II, because unlike Austria, Germany, Japan, and perhaps even France, U.S. memory has been (at least until very recently) less forgetful. Adherents of the good war thesis were attracted to a past golden age, while in other countries, memory entailed escaping the past. But this attraction to the past should not be assumed to mean that U.S. memory of World War II is less complex or even one-sided. One haunting and troubling concern that many Americans have over the *Enola Gay* is the effort to censor memory (and particularly interpretation) about the past; if other countries are becoming more democratic in their memories of World War II, some Americans, particularly historians, believe the recent controversy indicates an undemocratic drift among the cultivators of United States public memory. Nevertheless, only by examining private and popular memory along with public memory can one come to terms with remembering the war in the United States and, by implication, other countries touched by the global conflict.[56]

NOTES

1. Carl von Clausewitz, *On War*, ed. and trans., Michael Howard and Peter Paret (Princeton: Princeton University Press, 1984), 89; cited in Craig M. Cameron, *American Samurai: Myth, Imagination, and the Conduct of Battle in the First Marine Division, 1941-1951* (New York: 1994), 2.

2. For a good collection of homefront oral histories, see Louis Fairchild, *They Called it the War Effort: Oral Histories from World War II Orange, Texas* (Austin: 1993).

3. The good war thesis is evident in such veterans' magazines as *American Legion* and *Air Force Magazine.* For use of the thesis by historians, see John Morton Blum, *V Was for Victory: Politics and Culture during World War II* (San Diego: 1976).

4. Ernie Pyle, *Last Chapter* (New York: 1945), 5.

5. Cameron, *American Samurai*, 20.

6. Ibid., 20; James J. Weingartner, "Trophies of War: U.S. Troops and the Mutilation of Japanese War Dead, 1941-1945," *Pacific Historical Review* 61 (Feb. 1992): 53-67.

7. Michael C. C. Adams, *The Best War Ever: America and World War II* (Baltimore: Johns Hopkins University Press, 1994), 12.

8. Paul Fussell, *Thank God for the Atom Bomb and Other Essays* (New York: 1989), 9.

9. Paul Fussell, *Wartime* (New York: Oxford University Press, 1989), 268.

10. Ibid.; Ernie Pyle, *Brave Men* (New York: 1944).

11. See Karal Ann Marling and John Wetenhall, *Iwo Jima: Monuments, Memories, and the American Hero* (Cambridge: 1991), 2-40.

12. Edward T. Linenthal, *Sacred Ground: Americans and Their Battlefields* (Urbana: 1991), 179-81.

13. Quoted in John T. Correll, "War Stories at Air and Space," *Air Force Magazine* 77 (April 1994): 26. For recent comments by historians on the controversy, see "History and the Public: What Can We Handle?" a special issue of the *Journal of American History* 82 (Dec. 1995): 1029-1144; see especially Martin Harwit, "Academic Freedom" in 'The Last Act,'" *Journal of American History* 82 (Dec. 1995): 1064-84.

14. See "Letters to the Editor," *Air Force Magazine* 77 (Nov. 1994): 6.

15. Martin J. Sherwin, "Hiroshima as Politics and History," *Journal of American History* 82 (Dec. 1995): 1085-93.

16. Letters to the Editor, *Air Force Magazine* 77 (Nov. 1994): 6.

17. Quoted in John T. Correll, "'The Last Act' at Air and Space," *Air Force Magazine* 77 (Sept. 1994): 64.

18. See John R. Dichtl, "A Chronology of the Smithsonian's Last Act," *OAH Newsletter* 22 (Nov. 1994): 1, 12; "Enola Gay Controversy Continues," *OAH Newsletter* 23 (Feb. 1995): 3; *Washington Post*, 30 Jan. 1995, D1, D8; *New York Times* 31 Jan. 1995; Brian D. Smith, *American Legion* (Nov. 1994): 26-29, 64-70; John Bodnar, "The Enola Gay and the Problem of Remembering World War II in America," unpub. ms. (in the author's possession); lecture by Martin Sherwin and Edward Linenthal, "Roundtable: Hiroshima and the Politics of History: The Enola Gay Controversy at the Smithsonian's National Air and Space Museum," OAH Annual Meeting, 30 March 1995, Washington, D.C.

19. See, for example, the very honest memoir by Leon C. Standifer, *Not in Vain: A Rifleman Remembers World War II* (Baton Rouge: Louisiana State University Press, 1992).

20. Cameron, *American Samurai*, 246; cf. James Jones, *WWII* (New York: 1975), 16. See also Eric J. Leed, *No Man's Land* (Cambridge: 1979).

21. Quoted in Ronald J. Drez, ed., *Voices of D-Day: The Story of the Allied Invasion Told by Those Who Were There* in *Eisenhower Center Studies of War and Peace*, ed. Stephen E. Ambrose and Günter Bischof (Baton Rouge: Louisiana State University Press, 1994), 131.

22. Tape-recorded interview with Charles Brummett by Chad Berry, Whiting, Ind., 9 April 1992 (Indiana University Oral History Research Center), 16.

23. Adams, *Best War Ever*, 157. See also Samuel A. Stouffer, *The American Soldier: Combat and its Aftermath* (Washington: 1949).

24. William Manchester, *Goodbye, Darkness: A Memoir of the Pacific War* (Boston: 1979), 358. Once combat grew more severe, Manchester noted that "a structured account of events is impossible. Continuity disappears; the timepiece in the attic of memory ticks erratically" (365).

25. Quoted in Drez, *Voices of D-Day*, 92.

26. Ibid., 71.

27. Ibid., 80.

28. Ibid., 29.

29. Quoted in Studs Terkel, *"The Good War": An Oral History of World War Two* (New York: 1984), 263.

30. Fussell, *Thank God for the Atom Bomb*, 33.

31. Manchester, *Goodbye, Darkness*, 374.

32. Quoted in Drez, *Voices of D-Day*, 87.

33. Ibid., 89.

34. Ibid., 89-90.

35. Ibid., 208-9.

36. William R. Cubbins, *The War of the Cottontails: Memoirs of a WWII Bomber Pilot* (Chapel Hill, NC: 1989), 189.

37. Quoted in Drez, *Voices of D-Day*, 207.

38. Ibid., 174.

39. Ibid., 202.

40. Tape-recorded interview with James and Sally Etter by Chad Berry, Hartford, Ky., 25 June 1992 (Indiana University Oral History Research Center), 15, 17.

41. Quoted in Terkel, "*The Good War*," 190.

42. Ibid., 190-91.

43. See also Fairchild, *They Called it the War Effort*. See tape-recorded interview with Jesse and Emma Martin by Chad Berry, Indianapolis, Ind., 7 Dec. 1993 (tape is in the author's possession).

44. Quoted in Terkel, *The Good War*, 193.

45. Cameron, *American Samurai*, 262.

46. Walter Karp, "The Patriotism of Frank Capra," *Esquire*, Feb. 1981, 32.

47. Bodnar, "Enola Gay and the Problem of Remembering," 5.

48. Cameron, *American Samurai*, 260.

49. Jeanine Basinger, *The World War II Combat Film: Anatomy of a Genre* (New York: 1986), 169-70.

50. Audie Murphy, *To Hell and Back* (New York: 1949), 46.

51. See Bodnar, "Enola Gay and the Problem of Remembering," 8.

52. Norman Mailer, *The Naked and the Dead* (New York: 1981); see Bodnar, "Enola Gay and the Problem of Remembering," 10.

53. Bodnar, "Enola Gay and the Problem of Remembering," 10.

54. See Richard H. Kohn, "History and the Culture Wars: The Case of the Smithsonian Institution's *Enola Gay* Exhibition," *Journal of American History* 82 (Dec. 1995): 1036-63.

55. See Adams, *The Best War Ever*, 158.

56. H. Taya Cook and Theodore Cook, *Japan at War: An Oral History* (New York: 1992); Henry Rousso, *The Vichy Syndrome: History and Memory in France Since 1944* (Cambridge: 1991).

Proposals by the Advisory Commission on the Mauthausen Concentration Camp Memorial*

Preamble

The Federal Ministry of Education and Art commissioned the Institute for Contemporary History at the University of Vienna on 23 July 1993 to convene an international scholarly commission "to make recommendations for a reassessment of the Mauthausen memorial, with particular reference to its educational purposes, and to carry out the organizational and administrative measures following from them." The Institute delegated this assignment to Florian Freund, Bertrand Perz and Karl Stuhlpfarrer.

The members of the Commission are:

Prof. Jacques Bariéty, Sorbonne University, Paris, *as Chairman*
Prof. Dr. Rudolf Ardelt, Institute for Modern and Contemporary History, University of Linz
Prof. Enzo Collotti, Department of History, University of Florence

* The editors would like to express their sincere gratitude to Dr. Florian Freund, Dr. Bertrand Perz, and Professor Karl Stuhlpfarrer of the Institute of Contemporary History in Vienna for granting permission to publish the "*Vorschläge der Sachverständigenkommission zur Gedenkstätte Mauthausen*" in English. We are equally indebted to Professor David Herrmann of Tulane University's History Department for agreeing to translate the report on very short notice. The report was first published in German in a superb special issue on the "KZ Mauthausen" in *Zeitgeschichte* 22 (1995): 357-71. Readers interested in Mauthausen and its subcamps should start with this *Zeitgeschichte* special issue and Gordon J. Horwitz's *In the Shadow of Death: Living Outside the Gates of Mauthausen* (New York: The Free Press, 1990), which Evan B. Bukey reviewed in *CAS*, I (1993): 175f.

Barbara Distel, Director of the Dachau Concentration Camp Memorial

Prof. Vaclav Długoborski, University of Katowice, Research Curator of the Auschwitz-Birkenau Concentration Camp Memorial

Dr. Florian Freund, Institute for Contemporary History, University of Vienna

Dr. Detlef Garge, Director of the Neuengamme Concentration Camp Memorial

Dr. Eva Grabherr, Director of the Jewish Museum, Hohenems

Dr. Ulrich Herbert, Director of the Research Office for the History of National Socialism, Hamburg

Dr. Sibyl Milton, U.S. Holocaust Memorial Museum, Senior Historian at the Holocaust Research Institute, Washington, D.C.

Dr. Wolfgang Neugebauer, Director of Research of the Archive for Documentation of the Austrian Resistance

Dr. Bertrand Perz, Institute for Contemporary History, University of Vienna

Dr. Frank Stern, Institute for German History, University of Tel Aviv

Dr. Karl Stuhlpfarrer, Institute for Contemporary History, University of Vienna

As representatives of the organizations of former inmates of the Mauthausen camp, the following participated in the work of the Commission:

Joseph Hammelmann, Luxemburg, President of the *Comité International de Mauthausen*

Kurt Hacker, Mauthausen Camp Association of Austria *(Österreichische Lagergemeinschaft Mauthausen)*

Dr. Hermann Lein, Mauthausen Camp Association of Austria

Dr. Ludwig Soswinski, Mauthausen Camp Association of Austria

Simon Wiesenthal, Jewish Documentation Center

Administrative Director: Sabine Schweitzer, Vienna

Dr. Irmgard Aschbauer and Wilhelm Gugig of the Mauthausen Camp Association of Austria placed themselves at the Commission's disposal for an informational conference.

The Commission began its work with a first session from 2 to 4 November 1993. This included an inspection of the Mauthausen memorial, the Melk memorial, and the former camp of Gusen. Dr. Peter Fischer, the Director of the Mauthausen Public Memorial and Museum under the Federal Ministry of the Interior, provided a tour of the Mauthausen site and a subsequent briefing on its operation.

From 20 to 22 March 1994 the Commission met in Vienna for a second working session. The concluding consultations for the present report took place there on 17 and 18 October.

The Mauthausen Concentration Camp and Its Subsidiary Camps

The Mauthausen concentration camp was set up in August 1938, and liberated by American troops on 5 May 1945. By the beginning of May 1945 a total of more than 190,000 inmates had been deported from all lands under Nazi control to Mauthausen, to the Gusen camp which was set up nearby in 1940, and to more than 40 subsidiary camps in the same complex. Systematic terror, executions, forced labor, and undernourishment killed approximately 100,000 inmates, or about one half of those sent to the camp.

This concentration camp in National Socialist Austria was initially set up to provide additional detention space for Austrian prisoners. In practice, however, the Austrian inmates constituted a minority of the prisoners held there. Mauthausen was chosen as the location for a concentration camp because of the granite quarries nearby, which the Vienna SS took over, and from which the inmates were to extract construction material for planned Nazi public architecture.

In spite of these practical considerations, the political function of the Mauthausen-Gusen concentration camp was paramount. Until 1942 the camp complex served primarily for the detention and execution of political and ideological opponents of the regime, a purpose which was expressed when Mauthausen-Gusen became the only concentration camp to be classified in 1941 as a "Stage III Camp," for the liquidation of dissidents.

The exploitation of the inmates as forced laborers in the German armaments industry led to the establishment of numerous subsidiary camps around the central Mauthausen site from 1942 onwards.

Mauthausen consequently took on the additional function of a central administrative unit for the outlying installations, while also serving as the site of death or execution for those exhausted and sick inmates from the subsidiary camps who could no longer endure the grueling labor there. The principal uses of the inmates were for construction, production work in the armaments industry, and the building of power plants. Starting in autumn of 1943, inmates were "lent" by the SS to construction firms, in return for compensation, to dig subterranean tunnels to shelter the most important armament works. In the final phase of the war, prisoners were also mobilized for clearing operations after bombing raids. At the end of 1944 there were approximately 10,000 inmates, and in Gusen and the subsidiary camps more than 60,000, which gives some measure of the extent to which the war economy relied upon forced labor from concentration camps toward the end of the Nazi regime.

On 5 and 6 May 1945 Mauthausen, Gusen and all the surviving subsidiary camps, with the exception of that at the Loibl Pass, were liberated by American troops.

The Public Museum and Memorial at Mauthausen

The Mauthausen concentration camp was largely intact at the time of its liberation by the US forces. For the prevention of epidemics, the Americans dismantled the tent camp and the huts of the so-called "Russian camp" shortly after the liberation. They took no measures for the erection of a memorial. Their primary concerns were to provide the former inmates with medical care and nutrition, to transfer the sick to public hospitals, and to return the deportees to their countries of origin as far as this was possible.

American commissions secured documentation for the legal prosecution of SS members. Numerous artifacts and documents were removed from the camp by the freed inmates, who brought them to their home countries.

Upon the final delineation of the occupation zones in Austria in the summer of 1945, Mauthausen fell within the Soviet sector. From late autumn 1945 until May 1946 the Soviet military used the former camp as housing for its soldiers. From May 1946 to June 1947 the site stood empty. During this period a great many of the camp's furnishings and structures disappeared.

In the early summer of 1947 the Soviet occupation authorities turned over the site to the Republic of Austria. In the transfer protocol the Federal Government pledged itself to preserve and maintain the buildings of the former concentration camp (five stone buildings and 39 huts) as a memorial to the victims. Thereafter, however, the majority of the huts were demolished or handed over to various parties which had an interest in using them.

Chiefly at the instigation of former inmates, at the beginning of 1949 the Austrian Federal Government declared the camp a public memorial and provided funds for the establishment and maintenance of the site as a monument. In May 1949 the *Landeshauptmann* of Upper Austria, Heinrich Gleissner, presided at the opening of the memorial.

In the following years monuments were erected by various nations on the site of the Mauthausen camp. In the early 1960s a memorial was also set up at Gusen on the initiative of former Belgian, French and Italian deportees, and shortly before that the former crematorium of the Melk camp was declared a public monument.

In July 1964 the Federal Government sanctioned the founding of a museum at the Mauthausen Public Memorial in collaboration with the Mauthausen camp association, with the intention of installing a permanent historical exhibit. The former inmate Hans Maršalék supervised the preparatory work. The Mauthausen museum was opened by Chancellor Bruno Kreisky on 3 May 1970, 25 years after the camp's liberation.

Thereafter various additions and remodelings were made to the exhibits. In 1982 the display was expanded to include an exhibition on Austrians in other National Socialist concentration camps and ghettos. Since the 1970s the Mauthausen camp memorial has recorded a massive increase in visitors, chiefly due to the influx of school classes as a result of the growing importance accorded to political education and contemporary history. Since the mid 1980s some 200,000 people have visited Mauthausen every year.

Fundamental Considerations for a Reorganization of the Memorial

Designation of the Memorial

The Commission proposes that the complex be renamed the **Mauthausen Concentration Camp Memorial** *(Gedenkstätte Konzentrationslager Mauthausen)*.

The International Character of the Memorial

The former concentration camp of Mauthausen is situated on Austrian territory. However, during the National Socialist regime it constituted one of the largest SS central camps within a camp system under the Third Reich that extended over the whole of Europe.

The inmates, who were overwhelmingly males of widely varying social origins, were deported to Mauthausen from all the lands which lay under Nazi domination. The resulting composition of the inmate population gave the camp an international character. The form and orientation of the memorial should reflect this.

The memorial must take account of this international character in all its activities, particularly with respect to its exhibitions, provision for visitors, and publicity.

This requires considering the needs of the descendants of the former inmates of the concentration camp, but also the interests of the growing stream of visitors from many countries, who must be offered access to a historical understanding of the memorial in their own languages. In particular the annual liberation celebrations and memorial ceremonies, in co-operation with the Austrian and international camp associations, must take account of this necessity.

The international character of the Mauthausen Concentration Camp Memorial, which is to be reorganized accordingly, should be perpetuated through close co-operation between the Austrian authority responsible for the memorial, and an international institution to be duly designated, in collaboration with the Austrian and foreign camp associations.

The Expansion of Scholarly Research

The objectives of the memorial have so far been construed as the upkeep of the site, its documentation, and visitor education. Scholarly research has been neglected. Certainly the testimony of survivors is irreplaceable, but a growing number of scholars have begun to work on sources scattered all over the world concerning the history of the camp and of its ideological, political and economic function within the Nazi system. This research cannot be ignored, and must instead be used and promoted by the memorial. The continuation of scholarly work and the public dissemination of its results will be all the more indispensable in the future, in order to counter the efforts of "revisionists" when the witnesses and survivors of the atrocities perpetrated in the camp are no longer living.

Renovation of the Forms of Presentation

The various Austrian authorities and persons who have been responsible for the Memorial have succeeded in making it into a significant place of remembrance. Proof of this lies in the sheer number of its visitors alone, which include over a million Austrians.

The increasing distance in time from the historical events, the inevitable change in the perspective of new generations, and the development of a body of historical research call for a renovation, which must also incorporate new techniques of museological and documentary presentation. Precisely to preserve its function, the memorial site must undergo a far-reaching transformation.

Since monuments to the victims of the Nazi regime throughout Europe are presently engaged in a process of reorganization, which in many instances has already been completed, the renovation of the Mauthausen Concentration Camp Memorial should incorporate and profit from experiences gained abroad.

Organizational Structure

The Republic of Austria should continue to be fully responsible for the memorial. In order to meet the requirements of continuous innovation and prompt response to the needs of research and education, however, the administrative structure of the memorial should be changed so as to afford it greater self-sufficiency and independence in these matters.

Configuration of the Historic Site

A substantial part of the historic architectural fabric of the Mauthausen concentration camp survives intact today. Special attention must be devoted to the preservation of these remains as a historical document and as an educational resource for the purposes of the memorial.

The superimposed elements on the site, which include the surviving installations and buildings of the concentration camp, the present administrative establishment, and the information office, should be completely disentangled. The memorial park should be more clearly distinguished from the original remains of the camp both architectonically and visually.

Interpretive Considerations

The renovation of the Mauthausen Concentration Camp Memorial requires a critical examination of the interpretations promulgated there in the past. Representations corresponding to the facts are to replace the creations of legend, in order to deprive "revisionists" of any points of attack.

The distance separating the present from the history of National Socialism and the concentration camps has increased. As a consequence, the chronological, spatial, political and economic context in which the history of the Mauthausen camp is represented should be substantially enlarged, and extended to cover the postwar period.

Changes of Function and the Subsidiary Camps

The broader connection between the establishment of the Mauthausen concentration camp and the extension of the camp system during the territorial expansion of National Socialist Germany should be more strongly emphasized. A proper representation of the changing function and expanding operations of the Mauthausen camp requires that the scope of the memorial include the so-called "Russian camp," the tent camp, the former camp at Gusen, and the former subsidiary camps. The majority of the inmates were detained at the auxiliary sites during the last years of the war. As a result the following steps are necessary:

a. Greater attention to the subsidiary camps in the Mauthausen Memorial itself (especially inclusion of the Gusen camp with the quarry, and the tunnel site at St. Georgen);
b. Activity at the sites of the former subsidiary camps (conservation, preservation of remains, research,

exhibitions, signs, memorial plaques etc.; connection with the facilities already existing or under construction at Melk and Ebensee). The clearer incorporation of the subsidiary camps and death marches into the collective memory does not require that individual memorials with exhibitions be set up in all of these places. These sites are, however, to be covered in the documentation and research work of the main memorial. To this end, the memorial should sponsor projects and activities that do not lie directly in the sphere of its authority and responsibility, but that relate to the overall purpose of its work. This requires that the memorial possess an infrastructure capable of meeting these needs.

Surroundings of the Camp

The complex network and circumstances in which the camp system in Austria was imbedded should be more strongly emphasized. Among other things, the connections and relationships should be stressed between the camp and:

a. its immediate surroundings (the city and its inhabitants, as well as contacts between the inhabitants, the SS personnel, and the inmates);
b. the labor sites and local businesses (quarrying, armaments production, tunnel construction etc., the hiring out of inmates to firms, the distribution, sale and use of the products manufactured by the inmates);
c. its infrastructure network (telephone, roads, water supply, electricity, construction materials, the provision of foodstuffs, of fuel for heating and for the crematorium, of *Zyklon B* for the gas chamber…);
d. the authorities (local administration, higher levels of administration, including municipalities, provincial councils, the *Gau,* the police, higher-ranking SS and police commanders, the NSDAP).

The Apparatus of Nazi Government and Extermination

The Mauthausen camp should be represented more firmly in the context of the Nazi apparatus of government and extermination, with particular attention to:

a. the role of Mauthausen and its subsidiary installations as a part of the Nazi camp system;
b. the importance of Mauthausen in the concentration camp system (its designation as a Stage III camp, the Mauthausen and Gusen camps as sites of mass murder);
c. the relationship of the Mauthausen-Gusen camp with the Hartheim "euthanasia institution"* (*Aktion 14 f 13*) as a site of the mass execution of camp inmates;
d. the development of the separate historical phases of the camp;
e. the evacuation marches to and from Mauthausen and the function of the Mauthausen camp as a collection point in the final phase of the National Socialist regime.

Inmates

At the outset the inmates of the Mauthausen camp were a more homogeneous group than in the later phases with respect to national origin and categories designated by the police and SS, but they never constituted a uniform body in simple juxtaposition to the guards. Their national and social origins, the various reasons for their deportation to the concentration camps, the racial and national distinctions made by the SS, and the consequent unequal treatment and their reactions to it divided the inmates into groups whose view of themselves and whose cohesion were extremely disparate. These differences in the attitudes of the inmates were reinforced by the assignment of functions within the so-called "inmates' self-administration" on the part of the SS. In view of this situation, the following problems must be considered in the memorial's work:

a. living conditions, suffering, the material situation, and the working conditions and death rates of the individual inmate populations;
b. the attitudes and behavior of the inmates, especially solidarity, resistance and obstruction by inmates and inmate groups in the context of the various types of

* On the Austrian "euthanasia institution" at Castle Hartheim in Upper Austria, see Gerhart Marckhgott, "'Euthanasie' in Oberdonau," *Zeitgeschichte* 21 (1994): 165-82, and the other essays in this special issue on "'Euthanasia' under National Socialism"; see also Horwitz, *In the Shadow of Death*, 55-82.

survival strategies, which must be represented and evaluated in a differentiated fashion to reflect the results of recent research. Self-interest on the part of particular groups and the conflict of different resistance efforts should not be glossed over, but rather analyzed in the general context of the camp system established by the SS;

c. the relative numerical proportions of the various inmate populations, with particular attention to changes over time;
d. the development of a racially differentiated structure of inmate society, the attitudes of the inmate groups, and change in these attitudes over time;
e. the relations of inmates and inmate groups with one another;
f. the unequal treatment of inmates and inmate groups by the SS and its consequences;
g. the survival strategies of inmates and inmate groups.

Guards

The guard functions of the SS, and from 1944 onwards also of Wehrmacht soldiers, as a component of the functional infrastructure must be covered in the work of the memorial, with special attention to be devoted to changes over time and in structure (recruitment, national origins, the division of labor, the behavior of guard personnel etc.). The camp administrators and guards who dealt with the inmates were formally divided into groups with specific functions. These groups were sharply divided internally and in their relationship to one another by opposing interests, conflicts and rivalries, which influenced their interaction with the inmates. As a consequence:

a. the camp command and the guards are to be accorded greater attention than in the past, in documentation as well as in research;
b. the biographical profile of the perpetrators should also be analyzed in order to show that they did not stand outside society or on its fringes, but rather in its midst;
c. the situation of the perpetrators in postwar society is to be discussed;
d. besides the inmates and guards, the local population, the laborers, workers and employees of assorted firms, and

the representatives of various authorities were involved in the events in a great variety of ways. Their wide range of attitudes must be considered, both in the National Socialist period and in the postwar era.

Liberation and the Postwar Period

The fate of the inmates after liberation, the foundation and development of associations of former inmates, the treatment of the perpetrators and victims in society, the history of the memorial, and the historiography of the Mauthausen camp should be taken into account in the work of the memorial. This should include:

a. representation of the liberation, incorporating the point of view of the liberators as well as of the inmates.
b. the fate of the liberated, sojourns in Displaced Persons camps, emigration or return to other countries, the new lives of the survivors, and methods of organization and assimilation;
c. the treatment of the Mauthausen camp and its subsidiary installations in the Second Republic and in other countries, the situation of the Mauthausen camp in the collective memory, and the history of the memorial;
d. the various mechanisms for internalizing the experience employed by the former inmates and inmates' associations, by the former guards, and by the population, the juridical issues in the postwar trials, the physical and psychological consequences for the surviving inmates, and the legal disputes over reparations.

Recommendations for the Reorganization of the Memorial

Organization

a. The Mauthausen Concentration Camp Memorial should enjoy a legal status which guarantees its viability and independence as well as insuring its financing in the long term. Its present legal status as an immediate component of a ministerial department is not appropriate to this purpose.
b. In order to sustain its numerous missions in education, scholarship and historic preservation, the memorial

requires finances and personnel proportionate to the endowment of comparable Austrian museums and of other camp memorials of this significance.

c. The directorate and staff of the memorial should be located on the site. The director must possess the qualifications, above all scholarly and educational, which are necessary for the supervision of the memorial's numerous activities.
d. An academic advisory committee should be established, which would advise the directorate of memorial in all important questions of scholarship, historic preservation, and education. To reflect the composition of the inmate population at Mauthausen, this committee should be composed of experts from Austria and other countries.

Treatment of the Historical Remains

a. A prerequisite for responsible treatment of the historical remains is a systematic and comprehensive survey of the present condition of the Mauthausen historic site, a study of the construction history of the Mauthausen camp, and an analysis and documentation of modifications to the structure since 1945, including renovations, remodeling, additions and demolitions. The above also applies particularly to the gas chamber, the Gusen camp and the subsidiary camps.
b. A far-reaching effort should be made to disentangle the various superimposed levels, functions, and phases of activity on the site. The archaeological substratum and historical remains, the information services, and the administrative offices should be clearly separated from one another. The former headquarters of the camp, for example, should not house the administration of the memorial, but instead, if possible, house displays containing information on the guards and the SS camp command.
c. The indoor areas currently available cannot accommodate additional teaching space for schoolchildren and other visiting groups. It would be advisable to construct new buildings, or to use existing ones outside the present

memorial, and to transfer these functions to them, along with other facilities such as the information desk, seminar rooms, the document collection, the archive, the library, the administration, a cafeteria etc.

d. A special problem of overlapping functions is presented by the Catholic chapel in the former laundry hut, where at least three areas intersect. The space is an original remnant of the camp's infrastructure, but since the establishment of the memorial it has fulfilled religious functions, and today it also serves as a venue for introductory explanations during school class visits. The building should bear a sign explaining that there was never a chapel in the camp and that this is the former laundry hut. In future the sanctuary is not to be used as a staging area for school groups. The entire laundry hut should be reconfigured to honor the memory of the different religions and denominations whose adherents were victims in the camp.
e. Disengagement also entails the designation and visually uniform labeling of the structures and artifacts belonging to the concentration camp and its infrastructure, as well as the establishment of clear distinctions between original constructions, reconstructions, and remodelings.
f. For the preservation of architectural remains in the main camp, the Gusen camp, and the subsidiary camps, legal steps should be taken for historic preservation and for the protection of the entire complex, as well as for the purchase of additional real estate where necessary. It is particularly important to prevent further construction on the terrain around the former camp of Mauthausen. The prompt securing of structural remains is urgent at the former concentration camp of Gusen, in order to forestall further destruction of central elements of the so-called *Jourhaus* or of the gravel crusher, which is a central landmark of the Gusen memorial.
g. The preservation of the buildings must be ensured as far as possible, and further encroachment upon the original architectural fabric is to cease. A bookstore, for example, is not to be installed as planned in the historic camp gate-

house. Renovations are to be undertaken only following appropriate scholarly consultation. Elements added later to protect the original material are to be clearly distinguished as such.

h. Any changes to the installations as they exist today should be kept as limited as possible. Careful dismantling of additions made after 1945 may only be undertaken where an approximation of the original condition can be attained by such removals, and where the additions do not themselves have a central significance for the history of the memorial. When anything is to be taken down, the period to which this is intended to restore the building's condition must be clarified in each individual case. Generally speaking, reconstructions must not go so far that they become mere replicas.

Monuments

Monuments shape and preserve the memory of historical events. They do not, however, serve only as milestones to the past. Upon them also hinge interpretations of history, which monuments as tangible objects further confirm and strengthen during public commemoration events. They are sources of learning as much as of emotions. But even they are not immutable, as their effects undergo a process of historical development. Consequently any interference with the monument structure of the Mauthausen Concentration Camp Memorial, and the erection of new monuments, is to be undertaken with considered deliberation and very cautiously.

a. In general no changes should be made to the existing monuments and memorial inscriptions. Corrections should be added in cases where inscriptions no longer correspond to established historical facts. In particular the statistics given on the large memorial tablet at the entrance to the former prison camp should be brought up to date by means of a commentary incorporating the results of subsequent research.
b. All monuments and all memorial plaques to groups and individuals, especially those at the former subsidiary camps, are to be inventoried. Any change to them must be documented. The history of the artifacts should be

kept up to date in a separate card catalog of monuments and memorial plaques.

c. The existing local efforts by schools and other institutions to preserve and maintain the monuments and memorial plaques should be supported and expanded, especially where new monuments are created, such as those along the deportation routes to Mauthausen.

d. The monument park at the memorial site is a part of the history of perceptions *(Rezeptionsgeschichte)* of the Mauthausen camp. It should be separated carefully, but with clearer architectonic definition, from the existing remains of the concentration camp, as a distinct entity and a museum precinct.

   The monument park should be designed by artists and architects. A public competition is to be held, and the principal criteria of content and form for such a contest are to be guided by the foregoing recommendations as well as by the stipulation that the memory of the victims of Mauthausen and its subsidiary camps should not be differentiated solely by nationality.

e. The history of the monuments and of the private memorial plaques should be separately treated and represented in the site museum. A map showing an overview of the monument area would be an appropriate means of explaining the monuments' situation and history. The history of the individual monuments should also be set out in a brochure.

f. The private memorial plaques and artifacts could also be used for the purposes of the memorial, since the life histories which are represented in them afford cognitive and emotional access to the history of the concentration camp. For this reason, the erection of monuments and memorial plaques by private persons to the memory of inmates at designated places should continue to be permitted and promoted in the future.

g. The signs and information placards installed by the memorial's administration are to be made as uniform as possible, so that they can be clearly distinguished from the memorial plaques even on a purely visual level.

Guidelines for the Content and Form of the Reconfigured Museum

The museum is of central importance in the transmission of knowledge about the history of the concentration camp. In accordance with the foregoing principles, the exhibition area should be reconceived and remodeled.

A. The principles of internationalization, updating, and scholarly accuracy hold true for the museum, which is to be reconfigured:
   a. Multilingual labeling is necessary in the exhibits. As far as possible, all linguistic groups involved must be offered access through their own languages.
   b. The displays should express the current state of research. They should therefore be designed to be easily adapted to incorporate new discoveries.
   c. Within the exhibition area, as outside, originals, reconstructions and copies must be clearly distinguished.

B. Configuration of the museum:
   a. The museum must be so conceived that it caters to audiences with differing time constraints, such as schoolchildren, adults with varying levels of prior knowledge, and specialists.
   b. The exhibition area inside the camp should be kept small and appropriate to a place of memory, and consequently should chiefly display relics, including, for example, the works of art produced in the camp. The larger exhibition area, designed for educational and informational purposes, should be located outside the camp itself. If possible, space is also to be provided there for temporary and traveling exhibitions.

C. Recommendations on the content of the museum:

   Without repeating in detail the interpretive emphases set out above, the museum should stress more strongly than in the past:
   a. the situation and changing function of the Mauthausen concentration camp in the Nazi camp system and regime;
   b. the subsidiary camps, the immediate surroundings of the main camp which provided for its maintenance, and the camp and production system which developed over the wider area;

c. the political and economic context, with representation of the various interests;
d. the inmate groups in the course of the concentration camp's changing function;
e. The SS guards, including the Austrian participation;
f. the site's postwar history, taking account of the differing symbolic value of the Mauthausen camp in the collective memory of the various nationalities.

Provision for Education and Visitors

a. Methodologically differentiated tours for schoolchildren and adults according to the prior knowledge of the visitors are to be instituted and maintained.
b. Provision is to be made for tours in various languages. In particular, visitors should have the opportunity to hear the testimony of former inmates on videotape in their own language, in the form of the original with subtitles. For the same reason, as many more former inmates as possible should be interviewed in collaboration with the camp associations abroad.
c. Special efforts must be undertaken to provide better qualified guides, since in the foreseeable future ever fewer former inmates will be able to work at the memorial. Even though "self-guided tours" must remain an option, a number of qualified docents sufficient for the volume of visitors must be available at the memorial to escort group tours, not only as guides, but also giving an accompanying educational commentary.
d. The memorial should seek close collaboration with schools and universities in order to expand the tour offerings to accommodate the differing prior knowledge of visitors, their various time constraints, and the particular interests of different groups, as well as to insure the continuous and systematic gathering and incorporation of new research for the benefit of the various categories of visitors.
e. The international character of the memorial should be underlined for visitors by the inclusion of foreign exchange teachers in the guiding of tours, and by the

convening of international seminars of continuing education for teachers, in order to improve the level of preparation for visits and to obtain new trained personnel.

Publicity

The memorial requires a systematic publicity effort. Publications and publicity work can be permanently taken over, supervised and coordinated only by a functioning administration and staff at the memorial. To this end the following in particular ought to be provided:

a. regular public events, also in collaboration with other institutions;
b. notices in the press of activities at the Mauthausen Concentration Camp Memorial;
c. the correction of false assertions, defamations and trivializations regarding the history of the Mauthausen concentration camp;
d. the institution of a publication program, the publication and sale of brochures, books and audiovisual materials on various aspects of the history of the concentration camp and on educational questions raised by the interests of various groups and by the latest research. All works on the Mauthausen camp and its subsidiary camps must be available at the memorial;
e. a regularly published bulletin should support the publicity effort. To this end, the inmates' organizations should collaborate with scholars in a joint editorial office.

Research, Documentation, the Archive and the Library

As already laid down in the general guidelines, scholarly research is a requirement for the future purposes of the memorial. The administration and staff of the memorial should themselves be in a position to carry out their own research on the history of the camp or to commission such work. The memorial should include a library and an archive alongside its facilities for education and information. Beyond this, the following functions should be carried on at the site itself:

a. the collection of relevant scholarly and memorial literature;

b. the collection and preservation of artifacts and of all relevant sources concerning the Mauthausen camp in the original or in the form of copies (objects, documents, pictures, photographs, film etc.), and their cataloging and use;
c. the instigation and collection of biographical interviews with former inmates and other contemporary witnesses;
d. the furnishing of information to the public and to private persons, especially the descendants of inmates, on particular questions concerning the history of the camp;
e. the further development of the exhibition areas;
f. the training and continuing instruction of educational guides and teachers from Austria and from abroad;
g. the convening of conferences for scholars and for the further education of teachers;
h. the fostering of relevant publications;

For these purposes the necessary resources and personnel are to be provided.

The Commission is fully aware of the cost which such a reconfiguration of the Mauthausen Concentration Camp Memorial entails. It nevertheless considers this absolutely appropriate and necessary in view of the significance which the Mauthausen concentration camp should continue to hold for the collective memory in the future.

Vienna, March 1995

FORUM

TOWARD A HISTORY OF AUSTRIAN INTELLIGENCE STUDIES

Creating the Myth of the *Alpenfestung*: Allied Intelligence and the Collapse of the Nazi Police-State

Timothy Naftali

In the final weeks of the Second World War, though Germany's armed forces seemed on the verge of general collapse, top Allied intelligence officers became pessimistic about the costs of final victory over Naziism. On 23 March 1945 General William Donovan, the director of the U.S. Office of Strategic Services (OSS), forwarded to President Roosevelt a report written by his counterespionage service on the Nazi Party's preparations for guerrilla warfare following the collapse of the German military command.[1] In his cover letter, Donovan emphasized evidence of extensive training of officers for a guerrilla army of 35,000-40,000 men. The last six months had brought the eclipse of the *Wehrmacht*'s own secret service, the *Abwehr*, by a more centralized and efficient intelligence apparatus answering only to Heinrich Himmler and the SS. It was assumed that this political service, the *Reichssicherheitshauptamt* (RSHA), would lead the expected German underground after the military defeat. A week later General George C. Marshall, the Chief of Staff of the U.S. Army, cabled General Dwight Eisenhower, the Supreme Commander, Allied Expeditionary Force, requesting a statement on this anticipated guerrilla war that could be released to the public "with a view to conditioning its members for this possibility."[2] The same day Eisenhower responded gloomily:

> VE Day will come about only by a proclamation on our part rather than by any definite and decisive collapse or surrender of German resistance. ...eventually all the areas in which fragments of the German Army, particularly paratrooper,

> Panzer and SS elements, may be located will have to be taken by the application of or threat of force. This will lead into a form of guerrilla warfare which would require for its suppression a very large number of troops.[3]

As the three army groups under Eisenhower's command, seven armies in all from four countries, closed to the Rhine, the assumption that the European war would end in costly operations against fanatical partisans in difficult terrain began to influence military strategy. Eisenhower's two fundamental decisions about ending the war were made with this possibility in mind. On 21 March with the Rhineland campaign a success and plans for the envelopment of the Ruhr industrial area moving apace, Eisenhower looked to the next phase of the Allied invasion of Germany and instructed his planners to draft orders for a body blow across the German midriff to cut the country in two.[4] He wished to make impossible a southern movement of more troops and officials into the Bavarian and Austrian alpine region, the most suitable area for a guerrilla war. Three weeks later, having lost confidence in the erstwhile Allied assumption that the capture of the Ruhr and Berlin would compel a German surrender, Eisenhower decided to invade as much of Germany as possible with maximum force to deter resistance. On 14 April with two of his army groups on the Elbe and one in Bavaria, Eisenhower ordered the bulk of his military force south to pacify the alpine region of Upper Bavaria and Austria.[5]

The consequences of Eisenhower's two strategic decisions in the spring are well known. Marshall Zhukov became the liberator of Berlin, Field Marshall Bernard Law Montgomery the liberator of Lübeck. The three U.S. armies and the First French Army sent south found thousands of Germans who were prepared to surrender, some incomplete defenses in the Vorarlberg, and a few fanatical SS holdouts, but no guerrilla army. After the war, when the arguments that Churchill had made to Eisenhower about the political utility of taking Berlin seemed vindicated by Soviet international behavior, a narrowly focused debate, largely pitting British commentators against Americans, arose over the wisdom of having passed up Berlin for a non-existent southern fortress. The controversy endures. In the late 1980s the volume of the British official intelligence history specifically treating this period stressed the responsibility of U.S. intelligence for having created the delusion of a Nazi *Alpenfestung*, alpine fortress or redoubt, thus denying the British army group the chance to spearhead the final push into Germany.[6]

The postwar focus on the myth of the *Alpenfestung* has ignored the central consideration motivating Eisenhower in the last six weeks of the war. Intelligence information about preparations in Southern Germany and Austria for a last stand only gave a geographical dimension to a conclusion already reached by U.S. and British intelligence officers about how the Nazi police state would die. Far more important to the analyses submitted to Eisenhower, Roosevelt, and even Churchill were assumptions about the implications of the strength of Heinrich Himmler's SS and of the ideology of the entire Nazi movement. A comment in February 1945 by the principal organizer of the Allied counterespionage system, a British officer at the Supreme Headquarters, Allied Expeditionary Force (SHAEF), Colonel Dick G. White, represents how these strands were drawn together:

> The Nazi myth, which is important when you are dealing with men like Hitler, requires a Götterdämmerung at least of all present public figures in the Party, SS and extreme Wehrmacht elements. Granted that the Bavarian redoubt could maintain itself from six months to a year, it could in that time direct and nourish underground resistance among the young and unpublic figures in the Party in the rest of Germany.[7]

This essay will examine the role played by intelligence in the propagation of the threat of underground Nazi resistance or guerrilla warfare in the last year of the Second World War. At issue is not why Ike did not take Berlin. Stephen Ambrose has already persuasively explained in *Eisenhower and Berlin 1945* the many factors that shaped that decision. In fact, he is one of the very few historians who has placed the fear of guerrilla warfare above that of the redoubt in the hierarchy of Eisenhower's concerns.[8] Nor is there a need to refute Rodney Minott's book on the myth of the redoubt, which some twenty years ago effectively proved that the Germans never intended to build the fortress feared by White and Eisenhower.[9] But the nature and consequences in 1945 of Allied assumptions over how a totalitarian regime would collapse—an issue that still bedevils us (witness our surprise in 1989)—have yet to find their full description.

What would become conventional wisdom by April 1945 started as the U.S. position in a debate between U.S. and British intelligence in August 1944 over how the war would end. Two events had sparked this debate. The first was the achievement of a major breakthrough on the Normandy Front. Starting at the end of July, using the town of St. Lo on the Vire as a pivot, General Omar Bradley of the U.S. First Army went around two German armies and outflanked them. The balance of fortunes on the second front had turned decisively: the liberation of Paris was only a few weeks away. The other event was an internal crisis in Germany that dispelled any hope that the evident tensions between the traditional military establishment and the Nazi Party would produce a surrender before the Siegfried Line was breached. The immediate consequence of the failed Generals' coup of 20 July 1944 was a brutal purge that seemed to put the Nazi Party and especially the *Reichsführer-SS* Heinrich Himmler, in absolute control of the German state. The day after the purge, Hitler appointed Himmler the Commander-in-Chief of the Home Reserves, further blurring the line between party and army.

The U.S. position, as stated by the Joint Intelligence Committee (JIC) of the Joint Chiefs of Staff, was that the Nazi Party, now supreme in Germany, intended to go underground after the military defeat that now seemed inevitable.[10] In the first months of occupation, the Allies would face the resistance of what were called "semi-autonomous" local units that would ultimately be centrally directed.[11] The JIC admitted that intelligence support for concluding a Nazi resistance plan was problematical. Relevant evidence in Washington was "confined to the inconclusive," though the committee was confident that "sufficient evidence has been collected in London to convince those familiar with it that such is the Nazi intention."[12] But the JIC argued that such evidentiary support was not essential because any other course on the part of the Hitlerite regime was improbable: "It would be completely inconsistent with what we know of the nature of the Nazi Party," the JIC reported, " not to do so [go underground]."[13]

The conclusion reached by the intelligence professionals of the U.S. Armed Services, the State Department, and the OSS, therefore, was less the product of induction than of deduction from a set of assumptions about the Nazi state. In positing a Nazi underground, the JIC relied heavily on historical lessons to predict the final phases of the war against National Socialism. The future actions of the Hitlerite regime were in part prefigured in the tactics employed by Nazis in the early 1930s to come to power. The penchant for clandestineness implicit in these tactics and the gift for social and political infiltration also shown at that time suggested that in defeat the Nazis would return to these old patterns of behavior to regain control. It was not assumed that the German masses would initially support this underground. The movement's leadership, as well as its rank and file, would come from the most ideological in Hitler's Germany, the SS, and the *Volksdeutsch* refugees from the rest of Europe, together with those hurt by the occupation—about a quarter of the German population. The JIC expected a vanguard of 500,000 Germans to direct this movement.[14]

It was the OSS that submitted the draft that became this pronouncement by the U.S. JIC. The OSS was convinced that the Nazi police state would create a formidable resistance organization. The German emigré scholars in the Central European Division of the Research and Analysis Branch, who wrote the August statement for the JIC, had largely inspired this view in the entire organization. Their historian, Barry Katz, has written that the goal of their writings was to deliver "an explicit rebuke" to those who cast the Second World War in terms of another war against "the Teutonic urge for domination."[15] In their eyes, victory over Nazi Germany entailed more than the defeat of the *Wehrmacht*. In their analyses, the emigré scholars stressed the need to eradicate the structures supporting totalitarianism in Germany. One of these scholars, Franz Neumann, supplied the "bible" for the entire division. His book *Behemoth* stressed the antidemocratic nature of Nazi Germany and the interdependence within the German ruling class that undergirded that system. Neumann's Marxist interpretation of German business' responsibility for Hitler did not gain as much currency as his emphasis on the inner strength of the Nazi Regime and his concomitant warning that a military victory alone would not destroy National Socialism.[16]

In its analyses of the bases for anticipating a German underground, the OSS argued that the Nazis had tapped into the aggressive nationalism of many Germans. Recalling the private military organization used by the Ebert Government in 1919 to put down communist revolutionaries in Bavaria, the OSS traced a direct line between the members of the *Freikorps* and the Nazis. Several Nazi leaders, Martin Bormann, the SS Panzer leader Sepp Dietrich, and Heinrich Himmler's chief of staff, *Obergruppenführer* Karl Wolff, for example, had started as members of the *Freikorps*.

The OSS believed that the experience of defeat would feed German political nationalism and spawn paramilitary groups in 1944 as it had in 1919. This time, however, the movement could draw on a society that had institutionalized violent nationalism. Members of the *Freikorps* in 1919 had not been as well trained in subversion as those belonging to the Nazi movement in 1944. In much the same way as analysts anticipated the socialization of the Czechs and the East Germans after four decades of communist rule, the OSS commented in 1944 about Nazi Germany:

> The thorough training and indoctrination of reliable formations during more than ten years of Nazi domination make the prospective Nazi Underground a most dangerous and effective weapon. By virtue of their totalitarian control over all spheres of public and private life, the Nazis have numerous and varied facilities for camouflage and a large fanatical following. The possibilities for underground activities are therefore almost limitless and will be exceedingly difficult to suppress.[17]

The British intelligence agencies, who formed a Joint Intelligence Committee of their own, disagreed with their U.S. colleagues.[18] They assumed that the Nazi regime would prove a paper tiger once Germany was invaded. The German people would acknowledge defeat as soon as some German soil was under enemy occupation. The British relied less on an ideological description of Nazi Germany than on a psychological rule-of-thumb about the German character. The chaos attendant to the invasion—the waves of refugees, foreign workers, and returning soldiers—would destroy any remaining allegiance to Hitler, for above all, it was argued by the British, the Germans hated upheaval and would "respect orders from any authority."[19]

An emphasis on ideology as a determining factor distinguished U.S. from British assessments of future German actions in mid-1944. A similar disagreement in the fall of 1943 over the consequences of Italy leaving the Axis had foreshadowed this later debate over the Nazi underground. Following the establishment of the pro-Allied Badoglio government, the British JIC sent a report to Washington that outlined the reasons why the war would be over by Christmas 1943.[20] A direct parallel was drawn between the effect of the loss of its Austro-Hungarian ally on Wilhemine Germany and Hitler's probable reaction to Badoglio. Implicit in this analysis was the assumption that in terms of international behavior, little separated Nazi Germany from the German state that had fought the First World War. The factors that had compelled General Erich Ludendorff to decide to sue for peace in

October 1918 existed once more and would produce the same result, although it was a Nazi who now led Germany.

As they would a year later, the U.S. intelligence agencies stressed the strategic importance of ideology as they rejected the parallel between the Germanies that underlay British optimism.[21] The U.S. JIC criticized the British paper for ignoring fundamental differences between Wilhemine Germany and Hitler's totalitarian state. By the fall of 1918, the Junkers had lost control of the country; this was not the case for the Nazis who, with their efficient organs of repression, were unlikely to face any internal pressures to end the war.

Between 1943 and 1944, the U.S. predisposition to expect stubborn resistance from the Nazis had dramatically metamorphosed into the conviction that the Nazis were capable of mounting as efficient a resistance as had the French. Perhaps the contribution of the French resistance to the success of the Normandy and Riviera landings had most abetted this transformation. There is little reason to believe that newly acquired intelligence itself played a significant role. The U.S. JIC stated, after all, that though sufficient evidence had been received in London to support a prediction of a German resistance, such information was not necessary to its own conclusions. Its overarching prediction followed logically from the emphasis on the ideological nature of the regime.[22]

The intelligence readily available in Washington at the time merely provided a "foreshadowing" of clandestine preparations.[23] Examples of this foreshadowing were indications that instruction in guerrilla warfare had been introduced at SS training schools in Sonthofen and Bad Tölz, both in Bavaria. Also mentioned in intelligence was the formation of a special unit in the Gestapo (*Amt IV* of the RSHA) to coordinate the future resistance campaign. This foreshadowing was very weak. None of these hints were to survive the scrutiny that the guerrilla problem received in later months. The reviews of information on the German underground produced for the entire Allied intelligence community in the winter and spring of 1945 never included them, though they reproduced other reports from 1944.

Despite the lack of any substantive proof of measures taken by Berlin to prepare an underground, the Director of the OSS, William Donovan, decided to act on the picture drawn by his analysts. On 2 September in the first of his messages to the White House about German resistance, Donovan forwarded to Roosevelt and the Joint

Chiefs of Staff a memorandum that premised future OSS missions in Central Europe on the existence of a German underground. At the same time, Donovan instructed all of the branches of the OSS to survey their manpower and other resources and direct their policy on the hypothesis that the Third Reich would go underground at the end of the military phase of the war.

Donovan stated that the OSS was "inclined to accept the manner of the last war's ending as the pattern for the finish of the present war," by which he meant he expected the chaos of the German revolution of 1918-19. He did not foresee an armistice: those most likely to have concluded a cease-fire had been removed by the Nazis after the failed coup attempt of 20 July. Donovan had no hope that Hitler or his followers would surrender: "the Nazi leaders appear to believe there is no way out except to fight it through." Donovan summarized the view earlier accepted by the JIC:

> If my assumption is correct, the ultimate struggle whether there is a surrender or not, could well be a continuing war against a Nazi government gone underground and offering resistance not so much by a people's army or partisan groups, but by a highly specialized and skilled clandestine army of the SS type extracting support from the people by fear and intimidation and exploitation of a deep-seated patriotism.[24]

Responsibility within OSS for studying any evidence of a German underground fell to X-2, Donovan's counterespionage branch. Consistent with the program he outlined to the President, in September Donovan ordered the German section of X-2's European headquarters in London to collate all its information about the German resistance. Although they had no direct evidence of German planning, the X-2 officers in London found "full information to confirm the fact of lively underground activity as well as stay-behind agent networks in areas liberated by the Allies."[25]

It can be assumed that X-2's most reliable information in September 1944 came from the British. X-2 had been established in March 1943 at the suggestion of the British, who wanted an opposite number with whom to share ultra-class signals intelligence on the German intelligence services. Although X-2 had come into its own by the summer of 1944 as a distinct U.S. counterespionage organization in Europe, its activities were largely influenced by this original mission. X-2 officers were and would remain until the end of the war entirely dependent upon the British for the bulk of their reliable information. When Donovan asked for resistance information from X-2, to a great extent it was Britain's MI6 and MI5 that answered. Knowing this, he put his question to X-2's London office, which maintained a joint German desk with Section V, the counterespionage service within MI6.

Donovan's inquiries came at a difficult time for Allied counterespionage. The fall of the *Abwehr*, the intelligence service of the German high command, jeopardized Allied understanding of the inner workings of German intelligence. The *Abwehr* had been thoroughly penetrated by the Allies. Several important anti-Nazis in the *Abwehr* had come to the Allies with information about the Regime and their own organization.[26] Other significant information about the *Abwehr* came through the operation of the Double-Cross System in Britain, a network of thirty German agents turned against the *Abwehr* by British counterespionage.[27] But the most important means of penetrating the *Abwehr* came from the successful British assault of the hand and machine-ciphers used by this organization—the source of the ultra-class signals intelligence. In the summer of 1944, British cryptanalysts sent over 250 deciphered German intelligence messages a day to the X-2 Branch of the OSS and its British mentor, Section V of MI6. The vast majority of these were communications by *Abwehr* officers and agents in the field.[28]

The RSHA was impermeable in comparison with the *Abwehr*. The Allies had no high-ranking penetration agents in its corridors. More importantly, the means of communications used by the RSHA were not as insecure and were becoming even more difficult to crack. Early in 1944, the RSHA had introduced a new machine-cipher that eluded Allied cryptanalysts to the end of the war. Throughout the war, the hand-ciphers used by RSHA agents in the field were more complicated that those used by the *Abwehr* and so the yield in these particular messages also fell far short of what could be attained from working on the messages of *Abwehr* field agents.

The takeover did not initially curtail the Allies' ability to peer into the German intelligence services. The RSHA kept the *Abwehr* networks intact and maintained the established communications routine, as neither the RSHA nor the *Abwehr* ever suspected that the enigma cipher had been compromised. Consequently, for a period of eight months from March through October 1944, the weakness of the *Abwehr* ciphers allowed some penetration of the SS. Thus, London and

Washington learned of the RSHA's determination to improve the efficiency of the old military service. The head of the *Abwehr*, Admiral Wilhelm Canaris, was removed, and Himmler received veto power over major appointments in the now almost defunct *Abwehr*.[29] Signals intelligence also outlined measures taken to lay a carpet of agents in soon-to-be-occupied areas that could report from behind enemy lines once the Germans retreated. The Germans first undertook the building of these networks in anticipation of a second front in France. To assure control of these stay-behind agents in a fluid military theater, the directing stations turned themselves into mobile commando units to keep ahead of the battlefield. By September 1944, the Germans had expanded stay-behind preparations to all of northwestern and southeastern Europe. The Allies knew of efforts to equip stay-behind agents in Albania, Belgium, Bulgaria, Greece, northern Italy, Yugoslavia, and even of a group in Turkey, whence the Germans expected a declaration of war. Most of these agents received radio sets and some were provisioned for six months.[30] It was to these stay-behind agents that X-2 referred in its assessment for Donovan of underground activity in the early fall.

The situation of the Allied counterespionage services would get worse before improving. Unfortunately, as concern over the future purpose of this German clandestine system mounted, the ability of counterespionage officers to monitor German intelligence decreased sharply. Little more than a month after Donovan called for extensive study of the prospective German underground, the RSHA changed its cipher system and that of the rump-*Abwehr*, now incorporated into the RSHA as the *Militärisches Amt*. With the exception of messages between Berlin and stations in Spain and Portugal, all German intelligence messages became unreadable. The capacity to decipher the messages of the *Militärisches Amt* would be recovered in mid-December, but the rest was lost for good.

This handicap must be taken into consideration when assessing the role played by the Allied intelligence community in the creation of the threat of guerrilla warfare. From October 1944 the community's counterespionage services, who were most responsible for monitoring the likely organizers of this underground, lacked what had been the lifeblood of their activities against the German military intelligence services. Through the capture of some agents and the defections of others, a clear picture would develop of German operations in occupied

Europe, yet the OSS and MI6 had to rely on fragmentary information to divine RSHA capabilities and intentions in Germany and Austria.[31] Not until well into the spring of 1945 would signals intelligence play a significant role in shaping perceptions of the German underground. Before then, the door was left open to far less reliable sources.

In October 1944, the British JIC issued two reports on the prospect of a German underground. The concerns raised by Americans such as William Donovan prompted the first reply on 2 October, and its tone was generally dismissive.[32] As could already have been inferred from X-2's response to Donovan, the British were convinced that the RSHA was building an underground. They even went so far as to argue that there was "sufficient evidence" to conclude that Himmler was planning an underground organization against the day of German defeat. Little stock need be placed in the sufficiency of this information. As late as the third week in April 1945, Anglo-American counterespionage officers would report that "whether we like it or not, the information at present available on German plans of this sort is too disjointed and unreliable to enable us to make a general statement."[33] The threshold of sufficiency for concluding a link between Himmler and a German underground was as low for the British as it was for the Americans.

The implications of assuming Himmler's intention to create an underground, however, were not nearly so dire for the British in early October as for the Americans. Given their skepticism about Nazi Germany, the British foresaw a significant gap between what Himmler might wish to do and what he could actually accomplish. Consequently, in spite of an acknowledgment of the RSHA's belief in immortality, the British rejected any notion that this organization could postpone the collapse of the German state.[34] It was felt that the Nazis feared their fellow Germans more than they did the Allies, and would therefore delay the start of any underground activities until after the military occupation, which would give Germans another target for their discontent. The British made clear they were not ignoring the totalitarian nature of Hitlerite Germany; however, it was averred that a total occupation of Germany was not required for this police regime to collapse. In sum, it was argued that whatever underground there might be, it would pose more of a long-term than a short-term threat.

The second report, which came only two weeks after the first, signaled a subtle change in those assumptions. The British suddenly accepted that the Allies would very soon face a determined Nazi subversive movement in Germany. New intelligence had reached the British that seemed to confirm the U.S. position on the threat of guerrilla warfare. On 16 October the British JIC reported:

> There have been many reports of German plans for guerrilla warfare and underground resistance. We believe that in the period before the complete collapse of German military resistance there will be a certain amount of guerrilla activity behind the Allied lines; preparations for such guerrilla activity have already been made and are likely to be implemented at least in part so long as German military resistance continues.[35]

The likely cause of this shift was the receipt by MI6, the British foreign intelligence service, of three sets of information between 2 October and 16 October that effectively gave structure to a hitherto amorphous fear. In early October the British gained access to a copy of a manual entitled "*Anweisungen Für Klein-und Partisanenkrieg*" ("Directions for Small-Scale, Partisan Warfare") that MI6 described as "Himmler's Underground Army Field Service Regulation Book."[36] According to this book, the underground would be organized on a territorial basis throughout Germany. The operating units were to be five-man teams, *Fünfergruppen*, that acted independently of each other under a "supreme central command." Although primarily envisioned as intelligence gathering units, each team was subdivided into intelligence, sabotage, and security sections. The sabotage and intelligence sections drew upon the *Waffen*-SS, the military wing of the SS, for their recruits. The RSHA was supposed to provide the security officers. Also coming into British intelligence at this time were reports that "Partisan warfare academies" were operating at seven locations throughout Germany.[37] MI6 considered the first two reports reliable as they did a third stating that the "Central Controlling Staff" of the underground movement was "rumored to include" Martin Bormann, Himmler, and seven other SS leaders, including Ernst Kaltenbrunner, the chief of the RSHA.[38]

A summary of the October revelations that was produced by MI6 formed the basis for all future general statements by British or U.S. intelligence on the German underground. The OSS forwarded a copy of this summary to the White House in November 1944 and X-2 later included it in its entirety in the report sent to Roosevelt in March 1945. At the time this summary appeared, British counterespionage had not yet produced a general statement on German short-term underground plans.[39] As is clear from the 2 October JIC report, up to that time the British had considered the German underground to be a long-term, possibly political threat rather than one with immediate military significance. In other words, it would be the concern of the security organizations of the occupying powers and not of the Allied forces themselves.

From October, therefore, the Joint Intelligence Committee in Washington was no longer alone in its anxiety about German resistance. Motivated both by the recent intelligence, including the announcement of a *Volkssturm* (people's army) by Himmler (which seemed to presage significant resistance in Germany), and the recent occupation of some German soil, the counterintelligence subdivision of the G-2 (intelligence) Division of Eisenhower's Supreme Headquarters (SHAEF) formed a small committee to centralize all Allied information about the German underground.[40] Meanwhile, the U.S. Theater Command began preparing a counter-sabotage corps in the U.S. Army in France. The U.S. Army organized five teams of two officers and fifteen enlisted men to give advice down to the company level on German sabotage. To assist them, counter-sabotage training manuals were compiled.[41]

SHAEF employed the analogy of the French resistance to prepare itself for Himmler's organization. Not only was the underground nicknamed the "German *Maquis*" by Allied specialists, but to counter this organization, SHAEF called for studies on the vulnerabilities in the German system of control exploited successfully by the French and Belgian resistance.[42] Aware of the contribution made by the French resistance to the Battle of France, the Allied military was particularly sensitive to the slightest hint of organized resistance as it would soon be in occupation of all of Germany. Pressures, therefore, mounted within the Allied counterespionage community to centralize all activity to facilitate a common approach to the problem.[43]

As field commands started to pay attention to German guerrilla preparations, the name Otto Skorzeny began to appear in descriptions of the German underground.[44] The stabilization of the Western Front in October brought an increase in German intelligence activity.[45] The Allies caught many of the agents sent over the lines by the RSHA, and these POWs proved good sources of information about Skorzeny's sabotage program.[46] In November 1944, Skorzeny, notorious as the liberator of Mussolini in 1943, established seven sabotage battalions called *Jagd Verbände* from the personnel of the sabotage division of the *Abwehr*.[47] He already controlled the sabotage service of the RSHA, the *Amt VI S*. The *Jagd Verbände* were envisioned as terrorist units to divert and inconvenience the enemy. Although their knowledge of the *Jagd Verbände* was limited, MI6 and the OSS assumed from the fall of 1944 that Skorzeny was Himmler's principal assistant in the formation of the guerrilla movement. All information received on sabotage by the RSHA confirmed that he was Himmler's principal saboteur. Assuming that the RSHA would avoid the *Abwehr*'s mistake of having overlapping jurisdictions, the Allied counterespionage community was confident that Skorzeny would also organize the guerrilla units.

It is useful at this point to compare Allied assumptions with German realities. Although the Allies were correct in their assumption that by the fall of 1944 the RSHA had begun planning subversive activities for behind Allied lines in occupied Germany, their thesis regarding guerrilla warfare rested on three other assumptions that were inaccurate. The first was that Skorzeny was in charge of planning a resistance that would take root in areas overrun by the Allies. In September 1944, Himmler had ordered *Obergruppenführer* Otto Prützmann to establish commando units in the areas of Germany soon to be occupied. Pruetzmann appropriated the name werewolf from Hermann Löns's romantic novel of the Thirty Year's War. By November 1944, Prützmann had five or six groups active in East Prussia and was training forty group leaders for sabotage in the Rhineland.[48]

The second false assumption was that Himmler's RSHA would coordinate the recruiting of this underground. Even after the defeat of the *Abwehr*, Nazi Germany was a far less centralized state than Allied analysts assumed. The Prützmann organization worked through the territorial representatives of the general SS organization, the senior police, and SS leaders in the Reich's military districts (*Wehrkreis*). Skorzeny viewed Prützmann as a rival and forbade his subordinates to provide the werewolves with as much sabotage materials as Prützmann wanted. Skorzeny did not want to jeopardize the expansion of his *Jagd Verbände*, which he viewed as more efficient saboteurs, for the sake of the werewolf organization.[49]

The most important misjudgment concerned the purposes that Himmler intended for this underground. He did not order Prützmann to prepare a movement that would supersede the state once the present regime had fallen. Nor did the Reichsführer-SS intend that this group would ever operate independently of the *Wehrmacht*. Prützmann was to train his werewolves to harass the invading armies in support of the *Wehrmacht*'s defensive operations.[50]

One misjudgment that Allied intelligence did not make in the fall was to assume that Skorzeny's, or as it turned out Prützmann's, underground army would be concentrated at any given point in Germany. The groups studying the problem of the German guerrilla movement only began to emphasize preparations in the southern portion of the Reich in December 1944. Until then, reference was only made to the South as being the place most geographically suited to partisan warfare. The matter of where resistance would occur seemed less important than whether it would occur at all. The building of defensive installations in southern Germany was considered unremarkable if associated with a German fear of an Allied invasion. Only when these preparations seemed harbingers of careful planning for a new phase in the war did they attract attention across the Allied intelligence world.

The first SHAEF counterespionage weekly summary to mention German underground preparations did so cautiously. In December, SHAEF whispered, "So far there are pointers only, but these may in time help to indicate the nature of the problem."[51] No mention was made of a south German or Austrian headquarters. Instead SHAEF suggested that the central command might have located itself in Switzerland from which it could direct the *Fünfergruppen*. Again the central assumption was that there would not be a popular resistance in Germany but that the underground structure would be the handiwork of the RSHA.

The weekly SHAEF G-2 intelligence summary published only a week later did refer to evidence of unusual activity surrounding the old defense lines in southern Germany. Photoreconnaissance sorties by Allied aircraft had not confirmed any of the reports, but SHAEF nevertheless thought that they might have "some basis in fact."[52] Since September 1944, the Americans, British, and French had received information about the building of fortifications in southern Germany and Austria. The British intelligence agency charged with studying enemy order of battle, MI 14, reported the first signs of unusual activity as early as late 1943 in the area surrounding Hitler's Alpine retreat near Berchtesgaden. In April and again in September 1944, MI 14 reported the building of numerous underground tunnels in Berchtesgaden.[53] Then in October it described an underground retreat in the same area that covered 600 square miles. Meanwhile, the Bern office of the OSS began picking up information from the Upper Rhine valley separating the Austrian Vorarlberg from Switzerland. These reports indicated fortifications in the towns of Feldkirch and Hohenems.[54]

The earliest of these reports on southern preparations drew the interest of the British JIC, which at the beginning of October 1944 had stated that the prospect of a last stand in the south, as suggested by some reports, was consistent with Nazi psychology. It would not be militarily significant, however, unless the SS had the support of some army and air force divisions. The SS alone, it was argued, could not match Allied military power.[55]

The Combined Chiefs of Staff, the Anglo-American military council that reported to both governments, made no mention of the possibility of southern resistance in its last pronouncement before the Ardennes offensive of December 1944. In a paper on the likelihood of a German collapse, dated 22 November, the Chiefs accepted the premise that the Nazi Party had so successfully penetrated the *Wehrmacht* that a surrender was unlikely. Events were pushing these military strategists away from the British contention that Hitler would respond to certain strategic imperatives. The Chiefs minuted to their governments, "German resistance has continued beyond the time dictated by any normal considerations."[56] The invasion of German soil in October 1944 had already invalidated the sanguine opinion held by the British. Yet the Combined Chiefs resisted the worst case scenario put forward by their U.S. subdivision the previous summer. A full invasion of Germany was still not considered necessary for a collapse of the Nazi regime. In all probability all that was needed was a "major breakthrough with sufficient means for exploitation." The combined weight of expectations and the new information received in October convinced the Chiefs, however, that there could be stubborn resistance in "some isolated pockets."[57]

Two events in December shifted the debate in the direction of accepting the worst case scenario. On 16 December, two German Panzer divisions smashed through the Ardennes forest in a surprise counteroffensive that left two U.S. divisions disrupted and one surrounded. The German maneuver created more alarm among the Allies than strategic advantage for Berlin. Hitler overextended the

Wehrmacht in a desperate attempt to take Antwerp and cut off the northwesternmost Allied armies from their supplies. His armies, however, never reached Namur. But the fact that he tried, when all Allied intelligence officers discounted the possibility of any additional German offensives, chastened those who had argued that Hitler could see the proverbial writing on the wall.[58] General Kenneth Strong, Eisenhower's G-2, was to describe what one might call the Ardennes effect as the sudden belief throughout the Allied intelligence community that thenceforth Hitler was capable of anything.[59] Eisenhower later put it in these terms: "many times in this war I have been wrong in trying to evaluate that German mind [Hitler's], if it is a mind. When it looks logical for him to do something, he does something else."[60]

Just as a new reality on the battlefield disrupted some old assumptions, new information landed on the desks of Allied intelligence officers that gave a geographical focus to Himmler's guerrilla preparations. The first intelligence report mentioning a redoubt, or mountain fortress, that received wide circulation stemmed from an interview with a Bavarian police chief who had fought the Nazis during the Weimar period and then fled to Switzerland. He was a joint U.S.-British source and his comments on the likelihood of a "*kernreduit*" got the widest possible circulation. He suggested that the heart of German resistance to Allied occupation would be the mountains of the Vorarlberg, the Tyrol, Salzburg, and Bavaria. There the Nazis would wait until a falling out between the Soviet Union and the Anglo-Americans made resurrection possible. The informant believed the underground movement consisted of 200,000 men and women between the ages of twenty and forty. For the past five months, he asserted, Himmler had tested its security by detailing the Gestapo to track down its members.[61] A second report coming from French intelligence served to confirm the police chief's views. It quoted a reliable agent in saying that the SS was building up a redoubt in the Austrian alps. Since October this had gone on without the assistance of the *Wehrmacht*. A *Waffen*-SS Lieutenant General was said to be in charge of the fortifications.[62]

These hints of an Alpine home for the resistance dovetailed so well with U.S. and, increasingly, British assumptions that in no time the redoubt, one or more, was accepted as a working hypothesis by the Allied counterespionage community. By January 1945, it would not be bold to aver, the operative assumption among counterespionage officers at SHAEF, the OSS, MI5, and MI6 had become that resistance would most likely be offered in a few areas rather than throughout what was left of the Third Reich. What little reliable information had been received regarding the location of the underground seemed to confirm the hypothesis that it would be centralized. One report in particular from December or January satisfied assumptions in the OSS, MI6, and SHAEF about Himmler's underground units. It came from Sweden and was never confirmed, but like the *Fünfergruppen* memorandum this intelligence would be included in every subsequent survey of reliable evidence.[63] Most importantly, despite its suspect veracity, it was the source of the numerical estimate of the size of the Nazi underground movement later sent to Eisenhower and Roosevelt in the spring of 1945. The Allies' Swedish informant reported that Himmler was planning an underground army of two to three thousand "*Stoßtruppen*" with a total strength of 35,000-40,000. These *Stoßtruppen* were intended to terrorize the civilian population and perform acts of sabotage from headquarters in the inaccessible areas of the Thuringian forest and the Bavarian alps. The joint MI6.V-OSS/X-2 German desk commented on the report: " [it] sorts out well with the theory that the Germans may prefer to offer all-out resistance from some such fastnesses rather than to expend their energy in fruitless subversion over the total occupied area of the Reich."[64]

The Ardennes surprise, the other important intelligence event of December, affected Allied assumptions about who would lead this resistance. Skorzeny had renewed his claim on notoriety in organizing English-speaking units to cause confusion behind Allied lines during the Ardennes offensive. In response SHAEF had instituted a policy of asking trivia questions of uniformed individuals seeking to penetrate the command area. At one point General Omar Bradley found himself arguing with a sentry who refused to believe that Chicago was not the capital of Illinois.[65] The audacity of Skorzeny's plan left Allied intelligence officers uncertain as to the limits of his capabilities. When a group of captured linecrossers "admitted" to having been sent by Skorzeny on a mission to kill Eisenhower, the Supreme Commander found himself under protective house arrest in Versailles for two days.[66] A French intelligence report widely disseminated on 12 December, a week before Eisenhower was to enjoy protective custody, stated what increasingly seemed obvious, that Skorzeny would lead the putative

German underground. His battalion-size *Jagd Verbände* were expected to be the nucleus of the partisan army.[67]

Once the shock of the Ardennes offensive had subsided and the new information about redoubts was assimilated, the matter of whether the anticipated German resistance would be militarily significant still had to be settled. The British position in the fall had been that such a resistance would not pose a military problem unless the SS obtained the support of the army or air force. The *Fünfergruppen* or even the *Stoßtruppen* might garner the support of some civilians and perhaps a few SS divisions, but there was no expectation that they would number more than 100,000. By March, however, Allied intelligence officers were impressed with the military threat of this underground and were able to successfully convey that alarm to Eisenhower.

The leap between the hypotheses of January and the apparent certainties of March actually happened as two steps. The first brought the accumulation of largely second-rate intelligence about preparations for guerrilla warfare and the subsequent drift into agreement by British and U.S. analysts. The second was briefer and served only to confirm hunches borne of the first period. Here better information played a part, though its fragmentary nature could never induce critical thinking about the validity of community-wide assumptions.

The winter of 1945 brought a flood of information to the intelligence agencies from a variety of different sources that depicted preparations for guerrilla activity in the south. To those who endowed the RSHA with better survival skills than it actually had, it seemed logical that a well-fortified base would be used because it enabled a small guerrilla organization to keep a much larger military force at bay for some time. After the war, students of this intelligence failure assumed that the OSS office in Bern, Switzerland, had provided most of this flawed information to the Allied intelligence community. It was also assumed that Allen Dulles, the OSS representative in Bern, was the victim of an RSHA deception. One must await the opening of French and British intelligence archives to be certain of this, but on the basis of available OSS material there can be no doubt that the OSS received a great deal of its intelligence on the redoubt from its Allies. A review of the relevant files at SHAEF and the Counter Intelligence Corps of the U.S. Army confirms that the military commands ate a varied diet of intelligence. All of the principal Allied intelligence agencies received information about a redoubt (*reduit*), or *Alpenfestung,* in the fall and spring of 1945, and no one service received more than any other.[68]

Because the question of the redoubt was slow to achieve the importance for intelligence officers that the general problem of guerrilla warfare had, it was not until mid-February 1945 that concern over the probability of a southern base for the guerrilla movement prompted the OSS to gather all available intelligence in its files, including French, British, and press materials, with a view to evaluating this threat.[69] Ernst Kitzinger, a Byzantine scholar, whose skills no doubt came in particularly handy for this task, wrote skeptically of any general assumption that the Nazis had planned a last stand in the mountains.[70] In outlining the intelligence reports he received, Kitzinger identified clusters of reports where a variety of intelligence agencies stressed a single development in a particular part of Bavaria or Austria. It seemed as if some fortifications had been built in Vorarlberg, and agreement existed in various reports with regard to the building of underground tunnels near Hitler's mountain retreat in the Obersalzburg. The OSS scholar refused, however, to link these regional events together into a grand redoubt scheme. He believed that the pattern of the intelligence belied such an interpretation. Only the vaguest, and often least reliable, reports mentioned the redoubt; the most precise information rarely, if ever, referred to a larger purpose.

From mid-December, Dulles forwarded nearly five reports a week about extraordinary preparations in the area along the Swiss-Austrian border to higher commands.[71] In that time he received nearly 100 reports suggesting defensive preparations, SS training, and the movement of high German officials and headquarters into the Alpine region. The majority of them referred to the Vorarlberg and the Lake Constance area. At the end of February, Dulles appended to a particularly lurid description of SS plans for the Vorarlberg— which placed Himmler's guerrilla base in the region—the following comment: "Am somewhat skeptical of above. High Lichtenstein official [*sic*] advises me no serious preparations as yet in Vorarlberg."[72]

Those who criticize Dulles for contaminating the Allied "food chain" ignore the interdependence of the intelligence agencies servicing the Allied command. Dulles' often-quoted piece of information on prospects for resistance in the redoubt came from a source who was jointly controlled by the British and who was probably a Swedish intelligence officer.[73] What is known about the background of this report is convoluted, but given the importance that this report would bear in future statements on German resistance, it should be mentioned. On 20 February, the OSS disseminated a report from an agent of the Office of War Information (OWI), the U.S. propaganda service (which was not supposed to run agents). This was a "k" agent: the "k" denoted an Anglo-American operation.[74] The OWI agent reported that the Swedish military attaché had learned from the Swedish military mission in Berlin that the "Nazis [were] undoubtedly preparing a bitter fight from the mountain reduit" and had been doing so since the summer of 1944. In conveying this information, Dulles cautioned that not much was known about the OWI source that acted as the conduit for this information. Nevertheless, the report introduced the figure of eighty units, each varying in size from 1,000 to 4,000 men, as an estimate of the size of Himmler's army. And this number joined the canon of information about the resistance.[75]

Early in the new year, signals intelligence began to play a role in softening London and Washington's skepticism regarding the reliability of the agent reports from Austria. It did so by apparently confirming that the Germans were selecting particular areas from which to launch guerrilla attacks.[76] In early February, decrypts showed that the German Navy had moved its Operations Department and Intelligence Division to Wilhelmshafen, perhaps in preparation for relocation to Norway.[77] A few days later it was learned, again from signals intelligence, that the German High Command's less operational staffs were moving to central and southwestern Germany.[78]

There is reason to believe that this signals intelligence was responsible for causing the British intelligence community to finally accept the full implications of the Nazi guerrilla scenario. On 18 February, in a major revision of British assumptions about the end of the war, the Joint Intelligence Committee announced that the "capture of Berlin in itself" would "not lead to a general collapse of the Nazi regime within a short space of time."[79] The British held to their belief that the SS alone could not keep the regime alive. The tenacity of the German army since October, however, had convinced the British that the line between party and army no longer existed. A military surrender after the loss of the Ruhr and Berlin was considered "increasingly improbable in view of the extensive penetration of the SS of the military hierarchy, and fear of retaliation against the families of the officers concerned."[80]

As a result of this turn-around, British intelligence officers were the first to state explicitly that a thorough invasion of Germany was necessary to destroy the regime. It was now assumed that German forces would maintain discipline until they experienced firsthand the Allied attack. The JIC also believed that though there was only "slight evidence" of a determination to hold an inner fortress in the Vorarlberg, the Tyrol, and Salzburg, the "most recent reports" made it seem "probable" that "Hitler and the Nazi leaders intended to establish their headquarters in the Salzburg and Berchtesgaden region."[81] Although the British did not anticipate that clearing out southern Germany would be too daunting a task, they suggested that "the possibility of the Nazi leaders attempting to hold a Southern Defense Zone...should be taken into account and Allied operations to clear it will probably be necessary in the event of either Hitler or Himmler remaining a free agent."[82]

The change of heart in the British JIC is puzzling. With the exception of the decrypts describing the movement of German administrative offices, no new intelligence of any particular value had come to the British since late 1944. The lone reports of *Stoßtruppen* and *Fünfergruppen* had not been confirmed by any other sources. An argument could even be made that these constituents of the canon of guerrilla warfare were mutually exclusive. Why then had the JIC abandoned its position that the resistance of the Nazi Party, if it happened, would be of no military significance? After all, the JIC statement of 18 February implied that all of Germany had to be occupied in force and was a green light to Eisenhower to dismiss Berlin as a principal military target.

A look at what the experts were saying about German underground plans on the eve of Eisenhower's Rhineland campaign suggests some answers. At that time the counterespionage officers in the joint OSS-MI6 Counterespionage German Desk were of the opinion that very little information of high quality had reached them on Nazi resistance plans.[83] Yet they did not challenge the picture formed by those reports. The areas of general agreement were that the main bastion of the resistance would be in South Germany and Austria, with Berchtesgaden as the controlling point. The SS and not the *Wehrmacht* would direct all aspects of resistance. Within the SS, the *Waffen*-SS would control the military side of the resistance, and *Amt VI*, the foreign intelligence department of the RSHA under Walter Schellenberg, would manage all other aspects. There was some confusion as to how Skorzeny would fit into this picture. It was still assumed that Skorzeny, whose *Jagd Verbände* were the only serious guerrilla units known to the Allies, would be responsible for all sabotage operations in the post-hostilities period. The Allies did not fear the *Volkssturm* as the experience in the Rhineland had shown that Nazi attempts to launch a people's war were unsuccessful.

Like the scholars in Washington who had produced the August statement on the threat of a new *Freikorps-SS* period, the members of the joint MI6-OSS counterespionage desk in London were more confident of their conclusions than of the facts that they relied on to make them. "Even aside from the accumulation of fairly good evidence," it was stated in one report, "the concept of a war to the end, and the area chosen for it, are both completely in line with the attitude of the Nazi Party leaders—though the former is presumably not in line with the ideas of the Wehrmacht."[84] If any difference remained between Washington and the Anglo-American analysts in London, it was the emphasis placed by the latter on a psychological interpretation for the "war to the end." The psychological interpretation was derived in part from the renewed interest in Hitler's personality following the Ardennes surprise. His character seemed to hold the key to the regime: "The combination of military defensibility, homeland love, and melodramatic setting that appears in the fight from a reduit in the Bavarian-Austrian Alps is exactly what would appeal to the Wagnerian sense of Hitler and his closest devotees."[85]

A debate within SHAEF between empiricists and idealists postponed the achievement of a similar consensus. Those battling the empiricists in the counterespionage subdivision of SHAEF also called on Richard Wagner to explain why the redoubt was such a certainty. One empiricist had complained in early February about having to write the general SHAEF report on German resistance: "The fact of the matter is, of course, that we really know extraordinarily little about the subject and so far as I am aware no one knows much more."[86] When Colonel White, the chief idealist of the counterspies at SHAEF, saw a draft of the finished report, he complained that it ignored the three stays of the idealist position: (1) the *Freikorp* analogy had not been adequately presented; (2) the parallel with the French resistance was missing; and most importantly, (3) not enough emphasis was given to the redoubt. White rejected arguments that dismissed a southern fortress as impossible because it could not be properly supplied. Why should the Germans bother with supply lines, he wondered. He expected this to be a last stand to create a legend for future Nazis. As quoted above, White believed that the Nazis needed a *Götterdämmerung*. "It may be significant," he added in a final bow to Teutonic lore, "that Berchtesgaden itself, which would be the headquarters of such a stand, is built on the site of the tomb of Barberosa [*sic*], who is believed in German mythology to be likely to return from the dead."[87]

The Allied counterespionage community, therefore, had effectively made up its mind before the receipt of reliable information about German resistance. When harder evidence was finally available it was fit into the structure built by ironclad assumptions and questionable intelligence. Three forms of hard intelligence reached the intelligence community in late February and March: photographic intelligence, a spurt of signals intelligence, and penetration information from highly placed members of the RSHA.

On the strength of photographic intelligence from reconnaissance planes sent to the areas singled out by the OSS in its February report on the redoubt, SHAEF issued its own redoubt summary on 11 March. Called by some one of the worst intelligence reports ever, the SHAEF statement outlined the information available on the southern region and then accepted the accuracy of this general picture on the basis of ambiguous indications of underground activity at twenty sites photographed by Allied airmen.[88]

Useful signals intelligence about the structure of the underground also appeared in mid-March.[89] Since December, some decrypts, presumably from the still readable mobile *Abwehr* lines, had referred to a *Dienststelle Prützmann*."[90] They spoke of the administration of radio schools in northern and northeastern Germany. No figures were given from which to extrapolate the number of trainees. Nor was it clear which organization directed this effort. Allies knew little about Prützmann as he had spent most of the war on the Eastern front. A breakthrough, however, came on 16 March when a message was deciphered revealing that this group was also known by the name of werewolf and as such was founded to use guerrilla tactics to resist the occupying forces.[91] There was also evidence that Prützmann worked with the local SS-chiefs in the various *Wehrkreise* and not with the regional representatives of Himmler's intelligence service as had been reported from the Nazi underground. For the rest of the war, the Allies would unsuccessfully try to puzzle out Skorzeny's relationship to Prützmann. At the very least, this reliable signals intelligence proved that at minimum one guerrilla force was forming.

Finally, an extraordinary group of informants approached the Allied intelligence community at this time with information that had to be taken seriously. Starting in late February three representatives of the RSHA contacted Allen Dulles in Switzerland. They joined a fourth who had been in contact since the end of 1944.[92] Himmler's former Chief of Staff, *Obergruppenführer* Karl Wolff, was one of those who signaled to Bern his desire to discuss ending the war. The three who established contact in February evinced distaste for a final stand in the Alps. One, an ambitious *Amt VI* officer who had hopes of working for U.S. intelligence after the war, Wilhelm Höttl, exaggerated the state of defensive works and provisioning in the redoubt. Intending to build himself up as a potential asset, he reported in March that the redoubt was only three months from completion, and he offered to penetrate its high command for the OSS.[93] The Wolff case was even more influential in terms of confirming everyone's worst case scenario. After demonstrating his earnest desire to remove the possibility of a redoubt, on subsequent visits to Bern, Wolff reported his actual difficulties in obtaining the support of the military commander in Italy. From 19 March to 1 April the OSS and the British, who were monitoring these discussions, heard nothing from him, feeding fears his mission had been cut short by Himmler.[94] After he restored contact, the channel remained open until the surrender of the German Army Group in northern Italy on 2 May. This channel provided accurate information on the uncertainty of purpose afflicting German officials in Italy and southern Germany.[95]

Thus as the progress of the Allied military campaign forced a decision regarding what final military measures would be used to defeat Nazi Germany, General Eisenhower was presented with a consensual view as to the significance of the German underground. The weight of accumulated reports from the south pointed to unusual preparations for a longer war. However, with the exception of the 11 March report by his own G-2, no one presented the redoubt information without qualifications. What was accepted unquestionably were the analyses of the Nazi regime provided by expert counterespionage officers who argued that it had become an SS-state. Thus, a motive for the crime seemed clear even if there was lingering doubt about the extent to which there was an opportunity for the German to commit it.

It did not seem to matter that the intelligence picture regarding the redoubt was not in focus. Agent reports contradicted each other over the extent of the southern defense zone, and the intelligence professionals were reluctant to put their stock in one report or single agent. But with the breaching of the Rhine in all but the Northern sector accomplished by March 1945, Eisenhower realized that ignoring this information was too great a risk to take. Before the Ardennes offensive there had been warnings that the Germans were building a reserve of Panzer tanks for an offensive in the fall of 1944, and Eisenhower had not listened.[96] This time he would heed the call for prudence.

On 10 March SHAEF's mini-Joint Intelligence Committee advised Eisenhower that "although it [was] unlikely that large-scale preparations for organized military resistance [were] being made, it [was] possible that military and administrative headquarters would be moved to the Salzburg area."[97] Repeating the argument of those who believed the Nazis would seek to provide for a future rebirth through the staging of a mythical end, they added, "Such a stand would be designed to prove to the younger generation that National Socialism and Germany never surrendered." It followed that the prudent course was to foreclose an option that seemed increasingly likely: "If this area is not rapidly occupied by the Allies, guerrilla or dissident movements will gain ground and the Nazis may be able to put into effect some of their plans for establishing subversive organizations in Germany and other countries." By that point in the discussion of the end of the war, this stance seemed anything but controversial.[98]

As we all know, the great German underground never materialized. The Allies had misperceived the objectives of Prützmann's werewolves. Once it was accepted that the werewolves were indeed the awaited German resistance, the movement was endowed with all of the characteristics earlier associated with the German *Maquis*.[99] It was thought that they would number into the tens of thousands and had been picked for operations after a surrender. In fact, like Skorzeny's *Jagd Verbände*, they were only intended to complement the *Wehrmacht*'s defensive actions by harassing the invading armies. Unlike the underground movement as it was envisioned by the Allies, Prützmann's werewolves were not organized around a system of impregnable fortresses. The first werewolves were trained for East Prussia and the

Rhineland because those areas were threatened with invasion in October when the program got started. Prützmann only began planning the werewolves in Bavaria and Austria in March 1945.[100]

The Nazis, especially Himmler and the RSHA, had not acted as had been expected. The RSHA waited until the Allies had almost cut Germany in half to begin preparing organizations that could go underground.[101] When they did so their organization lacked the central coherence assumed by the Allies. Once the Allies were across the Rhine, two branches and a leading official of the RSHA each tried to set up their own stay-behind organizations.[102] The Gestapo ordered its representatives in Augsburg, Munich, and Salzburg to establish *Sigrune*, an intelligence network that would collect intelligence on the Allies. Ernst Kaltenbrunner, the head of the RSHA, directed the establishment of what appeared to be his own personal stay-behind network in March. This was to be called either *Unternehmen Dessau* or the *R-Netz*. Finally, the administrative branch of the RSHA, *Amt I*, sent representatives out to regional offices to lay the foundation for a third clandestine force, the *Bundschuh*. Not surprisingly, the highest SS officials in the military districts were confused by the seeming redundance of the four stay-behind groups: *Sigrune*, *Bundschuh*, Kaltenbrunnner's group, and werewolf.[103]

As a spirit of *sauve qui peut* was pulling apart the RSHA, the Chancellery in Berlin began to request the creation of an Alpine redoubt. This idea had been floated earlier by the *Gauleiter* of Tyrol-Vorarlberg (Western Austria), Franz Hofer.[104] After the war Hofer astonished his U.S. captors by relating that he had picked up the idea of a redoubt from reading an intercepted OSS report that had highlighted this problem in September 1944.[105] On 24 April 1945, Hitler ordered the construction of this fortress.[106] It was too late for such an order to be implemented. Yet those who did fit the Allied conception of the Nazi fanatic did believe in it. All of the stay-behind organizations appearing at this last moment were premised upon the continued existence of the Nazi state. A *Sigrune* member was to relate to the Allies after his capture that his group of thirty decided to give up once they realized that there was no central redoubt under Nazi control to direct their activities.[107]

On the surface, the necessity of the redoubt for the stay-behind organizations seemed to vindicate one of the Allies' principal assumption. Had the Nazis begun to prepare sooner for military defeat, then all Allied predictions of guerrilla warfare would have come true. But the notion that Hitler's officials would have anticipated defeat in time to manage its consequences defied the reality of Nazi Germany. The Allies's failure to appreciate that the Nazis could not prepare for the defeat was one of the flaws in their understanding of the regime. Men like the *Gauleiter* Hofer were suggesting a redoubt long before it was militarily necessary. But in the distorted world of Hitler and his circle such ideas were heretical. Similarly, when Himmler himself heard of discussions about a German resistance like the French *Maquis*, he exclaimed: "This is complete nonsense, if I should discuss this plan...I am the first defeatist of the Third Reich."[108]

In emphasizing the apparent bureaucratic efficiency of a police state, the Allies had missed its internal weaknesses. Using Hugh Trevor-Roper's (Lord Dacre's) metaphor of the court to describe the highest level of the Nazi state, it can be said that no trust existed among the barons arrayed around the kings.[109] A structure founded in suspicion of outsiders eventually drives out trust, even among the founding revolutionary generation. A perfect illustration of the mistrust in the corridors of the Chancellery comes from the explanation that Himmler once gave to Walter Schellenberg as to why the RSHA was not responsible for tapping telephones in the Reich. *Reichsmarschall* Göring held that responsibility and was unlikely to give it up for fear of allowing the SS to grow too strong. Himmler admitted he did not mind, however, as his fear was that some day Hitler would think his telephone was being tapped and, in that case, he would rather the shadow of suspicion fall on Göring than himself.[110]

The picture of Himmler that developed in the course of the Allied investigations at the end of the war was not at all that of the man who had been expected to lead a fanatical resistance. Schellenberg's testimony, which came to be regarded as a benchmark against which to compare other statements by intelligence personalities, revealed an indecisive *Reichsführer* who childishly wrapped Adolf Hitler in an exaggerated aura. In the last year of the war, especially after the failed coup of 20 July 1944, the Allies had assumed that Himmler had become more powerful than Hitler and could draw the regime to himself were the *Führer* to leave the scene.[111] But Himmler, in fact, spent the last half-year of the war vacillating between feeling that the war was lost and believing in Hitler. The result was a series of pointless half-measures.[112]

The misperception of Himmler was a symptom of the Allies' ignorance of the leading personalities of the RSHA. The lack of signals intelligence was telling in that the Allies often knew very little about the careers of top RSHA officials.[113] Not surprisingly there had been less contact before the war between these individuals and the western business and academic elite that dominated the wartime Allied intelligence community than between officers of Admiral Canaris's *Abwehr* and the western Allies.[114] Consequently it was easy to fill in the blanks with assumptions of ideological purity and blind fanaticism. Thus the Allies missed that Schellenberg had considered the war lost as early as September 1944 and had instituted at that time a special research and analysis program to produce reports that would turn Himmler against Hitler.[115] The Allies were also unaware that Prützmann was indolent and proved incapable of administering the werewolf program. It was in part due to Prützmann's inadequacies that Hitler's chief propagandist, Joseph Goebbels, had indeed tried to wrest the entire program from him in April 1945.[116]

In addition to their individual blind spots, the Allies shared a general ignorance of the fact that in most cases they were dealing with human beings, however evil their deeds. Therefore, they failed to account for the instinct of self-preservation that would compel dedicated Nazis like Wilhelm Höttl, Karl Wolff, and Otto Skorzeny to recognize the futility of continuing the struggle when it meant certain death. Skorzeny as always became an important symbol, but this time he was one of pragmatic surrender. After he recognized the impossibility of securing any part of the Austrian alpine region—he was one of those who believed in a redoubt in April—Skorzeny gave himself up and turned over the 400 *Jagd Verbände* that he still had under his command.[117] In sum, the Allies never anticipated that the blind loyalty of the fanatics would ultimately make it impossible for the RSHA to defend itself; the only intelligence officials who recognized the war was lost were pragmatists too busy saving themselves to build a base for their institutions in the postwar environment. Ironically, in contrast to the notions of self-interest imputed to the Nazis by the Allies, few Nazi officials had perceived postwar planning as in their interest until it was too late to create the kind of guerrilla movement that William Donovan of the OSS and others had expected.

Most importantly, the Allies erred in assuming that the socialization caused by over a decade of Nazi propaganda would have endowed the state with a pool of men and women willing to join an underground. Instead it was the experience of six hard years of war that was a more important factor in determining which way the German and Austrian people decided to go once they had a chance to make their own decisions. Only the Hitler *Jugend* (Youth) organization found it easy to recruit for the werewolves.[118] Prützmann discovered that pressure was necessary to get older citizens to join. These conscripts hid their weapons as quickly as they could and once the regime fell, they melted into occupied Germany.

At the end of the war, the most fervent Nazis were likely to be men in their early twenties, who were in the Hitler *Jugend*.[119] But even these young men and their leaders could not provide a foundation for a successful guerrilla army, regardless of the amount of time they might have had. They were too young and the state had no means of supplying them over the medium-term.

In defense of Allied analysts in the Second World War, it must be stated that they had no modern historical precedent to call upon to predict how a police state would die. In their lifetimes, they had seen the rise of Soviet Russia and Nazi Germany, but they had not yet seen their demise. They were to discover in 1945 that when the authority holding an intrusive dictatorship together dissolves, the state collapses rapidly, with little residue. This lesson, of course, would be relearned less than fifty years later when the Soviet bloc in Central Europe dissolved in 1989. Also important for the historian to keep in mind was that the Nazis themselves were even more convinced than Allied analysts about the capacity of the Hitler myth to survive in some organized fashion. One of the gasps from the Nazi regime that was heard by Allied intelligence was a message to Heinrich Himmler, dated 1 May 1945, from an official in Austria:

> In the defense of the Fortress Tyrol-Vorarlberg the political attitude of the local population acquires great importance. Everything that helps to prolong the war is rejected. Slogans of the Viennese opposition government and of the clergy are being followed. However nowhere else do the terrain as well as the political atmosphere provide more favorable prerequisites for a continuation of a lasting resistance than in the Tyrol.... Unspecified measures must be promoted by political skill.[120]

Himmler never received this message.

This essay has attempted to show how conceptual mistakes in the form of flawed assumptions led to a prediction that was at odds with reality. All that is left to ask is whether there were any institutional causes. On paper, there was model coordination of all forms of intelligence by the Allies in 1945. As has been shown, military and civilian intelligence analysts from Britain, France, and the United States pooled their information about the German resistance. But their experience with centralization did betray some of its downfalls.

Nowhere was the essential flaw of Allied intelligence coordination better illustrated than in the refrain that accompanied the grumbling over the lack of high-grade source on the redoubt: "Unfortunately," an OSS analysis in March 1945 affirmed, "much of this information is not of high quality; but the variety of sources and the high confirmatory value of some of them, make it possible to present material...as having some substantial evidence behind it."[121] One of the reasons most often given for accepting the possibility of an Alpine redoubt was that so many reports, from so many sources had mentioned it. Pooling like this, without regard to source, proved in this instance to be more harmful than helpful.

When bad reports can chase out or swamp the good, the most likely outcome is exaggeration. If several intelligence agencies produce many accounts of the same event then it is possible that analysts will misinterpret the importance of that particular phenomenon. In this case, an example was the misinterpretation of preparations in the Vorarlberg that were reported by various sources who were controlled by different national services countries. Indeed the *Gauleiter* Hofer had initiated some fortifications work in January 1945 around Feldkirch and Hohenems because he feared an invasion through Switzerland.[122] But this small event grew large in the minds of students of the redoubt because it was repeated in many reports and refracted through many lenses. It came to represent part of a redoubt.

Finally, all of the intelligence and counterintelligence services lacked the capacity or inclination to question their basic assumptions about the course the Nazi movement would take. At no time did anyone ask whether the police in a police state could plan for life after the collapse of the state. Furthermore, no one attempted to predict the effect of Hitler's disappearance on institutional coherence in Germany. Although some of the British agencies played devil's advocate at various times in this process, by March 1945, when the decision had to be made as to how to bring the war to a close, the entire Allied intelligence community spoke with one voice: the Nazi Party had the capacity to save itself in the mountains.

After the war one member of the Allied counterespionage community complained of the assumptions that had distorted the study of the Third Reich. Hugh Trevor-Roper wrote, "How many people, in the past years, were unconsciously seduced by Nazi propaganda into believing that Nazi Germany was organized as a 'totalitarian' state—totally integrated, totally mobilized, centrally controlled!"[123] The answer was "many." It was the assumptions of those people that in 1945 trapped Eisenhower and the entire Allied intelligence system in a guerrilla redoubt of their own design.

NOTES

1. Memorandum For the President, 23 March 1945, Record Group 226, OSS Records, National Archives. The report itself is in the PS File, Box 171, FDR Library, Hyde Park, NY.

2. George C. Marshall to SHAEF Fwd., personal for Eisenhower, 31 March 1945, Eisenhower Mss., Cable File, *The Papers of Dwight David Eisenhower, The War Years: IV.*, ed. Alfred D. Chandler, Jr. (Baltimore: Johns Hopkins Press, 1970), no. 2377.

3. Eisenhower to George C. Marshall for FDR, 31 March 1945, *The Papers of DDE, The War Years: IV*, no. 2377.

4. Stephen E. Ambrose, *The Supreme Commander: The War Years of General Dwight D. Eisenhower* (New York: Doubleday 1970), 625.

5. Eisenhower to the Combined Chiefs of Staff, 14 April 1945, *The Papers of DDE, The War Years: IV*, no. 2413.

6. F.H. Hinsley, *British Intelligence in the Second World War: Its Influence on Strategy and Operations*, vol. III, part 2 (London: HMSO, 1988), 711-18, 733-7.

7. Col. D.G. White, Asst. Chief, SHAEF, G-2, CI to Lt. Col. Macleod, SHAEF, 2 February 1945. Record Group 331, Box 109, GBI/CI/CS/091.4-1 (Germany), National Archives. After the war, Colonel (later Sir) Dick White became the only man in history to head MI6, Britain's foreign intelligence service, and MI5, the domestic security service.

8. Stephen E. Ambrose, *Eisenhower and Berlin 1945: The Decision to Halt at the Elbe* (New York: W.W. Norton, 1986), 79.

9. Rodney G. Minott, *The Fortress That Never Was: The Myth of Hitler's Bavarian Stronghold* (New York: Holt, Rinehart and Winston, 1964). Thomas Albrich and Arno Gisinger have since written an essential companion piece, *Im Bombenkrieg: Tirol und Vorarlberg, 1943-1945* (Innsbruck: Haymon Verlag, 1992), that details the nature of actual preparations in the Redoubt area and the role of Swiss intelligence in giving some local Nazi officials ideas about ways to stave off the final reckoning.

10. The Joint Intelligence Committee was theoretically the first central intelligence bureau in U.S. history. On it sat the directors of the Military Intelligence Division of the Army, the Office of Naval Intelligence, an Assistant or Under-Secretary of State, the Director of the Federal Bureau of Investigation, and the Director of the Office of Strategic Services. In fact, the committee usually did little more than put its imprimatur on drafts written for its working group, the Joint Intelligence Staff, by one of the member organizations. The report of 9 August was entirely the work of the Office of Strategic Services. See also the short history of U.S. intelligence in Beer's essay in this volume.

11. Joint Intelligence Committee (U.S.), 9 August 1944, *The Records of the R&S Branch and the IRIS of the State Department* (Maryland: University Publications of America, 1977, text-fiche).

12. Ibid.

13. Ibid.

14. Ibid.

15. Barry Katz, *Foreign Intelligence: Research and Analysis in the Office of Strategic Services, 1942-45* (Cambridge: Harvard University Press, 1989), 40. Churchill uttered the phrase "the Teutonic urge for domination." (quoted in Katz, *Foreign Intelligence*, 40).

16. Ibid., 40, 67-8.

17. 9 August 1944, R&A Branch, Film A-215.

18. The British Joint Intelligence Committee served as the model for the U.S. JIC. It was established in 1936, with membership extended to all of the directors of the three armed services (British air force had already gained its independence), and to MI5, the British domestic and imperial security service

and MI6, the foreign intelligence organization, to assist the Joint Planning Staff of the British Chiefs of Staff. In 1939, a Foreign Office representative was added to chair the meetings. *Patrick Howarth, Intelligence Chief Extraordinary: The Life of the Ninth Duke of Portland* (London: The Bodley Head, 1986), 111-112.

19. Joint Intelligence Committee (U.K.), 10 August 1944, *Records of the Joint Chiefs of Staff* (Washington, DC: University Publications of America, 1979, text-fiche).

20. Joint Intelligence Committee (U.K.), 23 September 1943, *Records of the Joint Chiefs of Staff* (Washington, DC: University Publications of America, 1979, text-fiche).

21. Joint Intelligence Committee (U.S.), 2 October 1943. *Records of the Joint Chiefs of Staff* (Washington, DC: University Publications of America, 1977, text-fiche).

22. Ibid.

23. Ibid.

24. William J. Donovan to President Roosevelt, 2 September 1944, Record Group 226, Entry 162, Box 8, National Archives.

25. X-2 London War Diary, Record Group 229, Entry 91, National Archives.

26. For information about contacts between the *Abwehr* and Allied intelligence see Allen Dulles, *Germany's Underground* (New York: Macmillan Company, 1947). Dulles's principal informant was Hans Bernd Gisevius, an assistant to Major General Hans Oster, Canaris's deputy and the head of the *Abwehr*'s administrative section.

27. F.H. Hinsley and C.A.G. Simkins, *Security and Counter-Intelligence*, vol. 4 of *British Intelligence in the Second World War* (London: HMSO, 1990); J.C. Masterman, *The Double-Cross System in the War of 1939 to 1945* (New Haven: Yale University Press, 1972).

28. British cryptanalysts at Bletchley Park issued 268,000 German Intelligence decrypts during the Second World War, of which 52 percent were from the *Abwehr* Enigma-machine cipher, 36 percent from hand-ciphers used by *Abwehr* officers and agents and only 5 percent from RSHA ciphers. F.H. Hinsley and C.A.G. Simkins, *Security and Counter-Intelligence*, vol. 4 of *British Intelligence in the Second World War* (London: HMSO, 1990), 182.

29. See Circle Summary numbers 1 and 2, 14 & 21 March 1944. Record Group 226, Entry 138, Box 1, National Archives. "Circle" was the code name for signals intelligence that had been processed to disguise that the source was cryptanalysis.

30. Some Circle information on stay-behinds can be found in Record Group 226, Entry 138, Box 1, National Archives, Washington, DC

31. Hinsley and Simkins, *Security and Counter-Intelligence*, 266.

32. Joint Intelligence Committee (U.K.), *Records of the US Joint Chiefs of Staff*, Record Group 218.

33. *German Resistance Plans*, X-2 London (German Section) to X-2 Caserta, 20 April 1945. Record Group 226, Entry 109, Box 20, National Archives. Classified "Top Secret Control," this document was not to be shown to any foreign intelligence organization without prior approval.

34. Ibid.

35. Joint Intelligence Committee (U.K.), 16 October 1944, *Records of the Joint Chiefs of Staff*, (Washington, DC: University Publications of America, text-fiche).

36. The original British report as used by the Joint X-2/MI6.V German desk is in Record Group 226, Entry 128, Box 13, National Archives. On 8 November 1944, it was sent to the White House. Map Room collection, Box 73, MR 203(12), Sect. 1. FDR Library, Hyde Park, NY. This report is referred to in "Revision Notes No. 4 and No. 5 on the Handbook entitled 'The German Intelligence Services,'" which was prepared by the Joint German Desk and then sent to X-2 Washington on 27 January 1945. See Record Group 226, Entry 109, Box 1. References to it are also in the two reviews of underground information produced by X-2 London for use by the Austrian X-2 team training in Caserta, Italy. The 10 March 1945 review is in Record Group 226, Entry 109, Box 5; the 20 April review is in Box 20 of the same Entry and Record group. Finally, it is reproduced in the X-2 report sent by Donovan to FDR on 23 March 1944. This document is in Box 171 of the PS file at the FDR Library.

37. The schools were reported to be at Gablonz and Reichenberg in the Sudentenland, Spandau near Berlin, Linz and Innsbruck in Austria, and Hagen and Dortmund in Westphalia. Record Group 226, Entry 128, Box 13, National Archives.

38. The entire list was Himmler, Bormann and Kaltenbrunner plus 6 SS Generals (*Obergruppenführer*): Kurt Daluge, former chief of the Ordnungs-Polizei; Erich von dem Bach-Zelewski, head of Himmler's anti-partisan forces on Eastern front; Wilhelm Rediess, senior police and SS leader in Norway; Gunter Pancke, senior police and SS leader in Denmark; Otto Hofmann, commander of *Wehrkreis V* in Germany, and Karl Hermann Frank, senior police and SS leader in the Bohemian and Moravian Protectorate.

39. Record Group 226, Entry 128, Box 13. The Joint MI6.V/X-2 German Desk's version of the summary ends with "(i)t is hoped...that it may be possible to prepare a general statement on German short-term underground plans in the near future."

40. General H.R. Bull, G-3, to the Deputy Chief of Staff, 8 November 1944, "German Guerrilla Warfare Tactics and Underground Activity," Record Group 331, Box 109, SHAEF G-2, CI papers, National Archives.

41. Ibid.

42. 5 November 1944: Colonel Sheen, the head of SHAEF G-2, CI instructed a Major Beaumont at the SHAEF mission in Belgium to meet with leaders of the Belgian resistance, Record Group 331, Box 109 GBI/CI/CS/091.4-1 (Germany), National Archives.

43. X-2 Paris to X-2 London, 16 November 1944, Record Group 226, Entry 121, Box 16. As the specter of a German underground inspired a centralization of the Allied effort against the SS intelligence service, an Anglo-American dispute over who would control this work threatened to make coordination difficult. In an effort to promote Anglo-American harmony in the intelligence departments of SHAEF, U.S. division chiefs had British deputies, or vice versa. The chief of the counterespionage subdivision was an U.S. Col. H.G. Sheen, whose deputy was a pre-war MI5 officer, Col. Dick White. In early November, White called for the establishment of a central counterintelligence organization to meet the challenge of Himmler's underground. He suggested that it be composed of representatives from MI6, MI5, and the OSS and that SHAEF control it. General T.J. Betts, the G-2 of the U.S. Army theater headquarters in Europe, reacted violently to this proposal, which he interpreted as a British maneuver to control operations against the German *Macquis*. Apparently, Colonel Sheen, nominally White's superior, did not learn of this proposal until told about it by the OSS. Betts was so upset that he flew to Washington to suggest the formation of a separate integrated U.S. counterespionage command for operations in Germany. Sheen, who disliked having been circumvented, and Betts were eventually persuaded to accept White's plan, which seemed a sensible approach to a problem that loomed large, despite the lack of reliable

information about it. The SHAEF G-2, CI War Room did not begin its operations until March 1945.

44. The SHAEF X-2 CI summary No. 5 on 17 November 1944, said of Skorzeny that "this foremost of Himmler's thugs has police experience and his rising power may be chief reason for increasing sabotage preparations on all fronts," Record Group 226, Entry 138, Box 1, National Archives.

45. See SHAEF X-2 CI summaries for November 1944. Record Group 226, Entry 138, Box 1.

46. Hugo La Haye, a Dutch SS member was caught on 31 October 1944 trying to cross Allied lines in Belgium. His mission was to take over command of a stay-behind sabotage network, "Henriette," in Belgium. He provided information on VI-S, the sabotage service of the RSHA that controlled the Belgium network. Zeller, a French line crosser and another more senior but unnamed agent, provided information about Skorzeny's French sabotage group, "Jeanne," which operated into France from Swabia. X-2 London to Washington, 27 January 1945, "Revision Notes No. 4 and No. 5," Record Group 226, Entry 109, Box 1, National Archives.

47. SHAEF G-2, CI War Room, "*Amt VI S*," 28 November 1945. Record Group 226, Entry 190, Box 392.

48. SHAEF Counterintelligence War Room, 27 July 1945, "Resistance Movements in Germany," Record Group 226, Entry 109, Box 35, National Archives.

49. 12th Army Group, CI report on "Werewolf," Source: Obersturmbannfüher Otto Skorzeny, 31 May 1945, Record Group 226, Entry 109, Box 28, National Archives.

50. Ibid.

51. SHAEF G-2, CI Weekly Summary, 1 December 1944. Record Group 226, Entry 138, Box 1, National Archives.

52. Hinsley, Volume 3, Part II, 712.

53. R&A Branch, OSS, 22 February 1945 "The Alpine Reduit: An Interim Survey of Available Intelligence (Summer 1944 to Mid-February 1945)," Record Group 226, Entry 109. p. 18, National Archives.

54. Ibid., 7-8.

55. Joint Intelligence Committee (U.K.), 2 October 1944, *Records of the Joint Chiefs of Staff* (Washington, DC: University Publishers of America, 1979, text-fiche).

56. 22 November 1944, "Prospects of a German Collapse or Surrender," *Records of the Joint Chiefs of Staff* (Washington, DC: University Publishers of America, 1979, text-fiche).

57. Ibid.

58. See Forrest Pogue, *The United States Army in World War II, The European Theater of Operations: The Supreme Command* (Washington, DC: Office of Chief of Military History, 1954), 361-372.

59. Kenneth Strong, *Intelligence at the Top*, (London: Cassell, 1968), 187-8.

60. Ambrose, *Supreme Commander*, 610.

61. "Measures for Post-Hostility Designs of the Nazi Party," reported as a Unison source by OSS Bern on 12 December 1944. Record Group 331, Box 109, SHAEF Records, GBI/CI/CS/091.4-1 (Germany). National Archives. This report received the grade of B-0: the source was considered reliable, though the veracity of this particular report could not be judged. As a Unison source it was shared with the British. Record Group 226, Entry 190, Box 127, National Archives.

62. Report disseminated by OSS Paris, 27 December 1944. Record Group 331, Box 109, National Archives. The source for this report was French intelligence and its value was classified as B-3.

63. It is possible that this report was the product of signals intelligence. Only 7 percent of the intercepts sent to Allied counterespionage officers is unaccounted for in the British official history. It would not be surprising if the British monitored Swedish as well as German intelligence messages. In fact, there is one hint in a later X-2 document that the U.S. could read Swedish secret communications. The circumstantial evidence regarding the *Stoßtruppen* report is that it appeared in three Allied intelligence reports classified top-secret, a much rarer classification in the wartime intelligence community than later.

64. "Revision Notes No. 4 and No. 5 on the Handbook entitled "The German Intelligence Services," 27 January 1945, Record Group 226, Entry 109, Box 1, National Archives.

65. Omar Bradley, *A Soldier's Story* (New York: 1951), 467-469.

66. Ambrose, *The Supreme Commander*, 561.

67. 12 December 1944, Record Group 331, Box 109, National Archives. The source for this report was Haam, and its value was classified as B-3.

68. See SHAEF G-2, CI records, Record Group 331, Box 109. The Counter Intelligence Corp's werewolf file is in the IRR records, XE 049 888, National Archives.

69. R&A, OSS, 22 February 1945, "The Alpine Reduit: An Interim Survey of Available Intelligence (Summer 1944 to Mid-February 1945)," Record Group 226, Entry 109, Box 6, National Archives.

70. Kitzinger's study was sent to OSS and SHAEF G-2, CI in Paris on 26 February 1945. Record Group 226, Entry 190, Box 314, National Archives.

71. For Bern cables, see Record Group 226, Entry 108; and Record Group 226, Entry 134, Box 162, National Archives.

72. Bern SI cable File, 27 February, Record Group 226, Entry 134, Box 162, National Archives.

73. In his report to Washington, Dulles described this as an Office of War Information (OWI) source that was reporting from a "well-informed neutral source in Berlin," Record Group 226/191, National Archives. SHAEF's copy of the report carries the annotation that the source is the Swedish military attaché in Bern, who is reporting information from his colleagues in Berlin, SHAEF G-2, CI records, Record Group 331, Box 109, National Archives.

74. "K" sources, like Unison sources, were shared with the British. It is not known how or whether the actual running of the agent was shared. "History of Swiss Desk, SI Branch, MEDTO," Record Group 226, Entry 109, Box 127, National Archives.

75. This figure turned up in the well-known 25 March report by Colonel William Quinn, G-2 of the U.S. Seventh Army. Minott, *The Fortress That Never Was*, 54. Hugh Wilson, an OSS official in Paris, became so agitated over the Swedish report that he suggested on 26 February that the Allies consider

using the *Wehrmacht* against the Nazi guerrillas. While dismissing this suggestion because, among other reasons, it would have serious repercussions in the USSR and France, Major A.J.P. Crick of SHAEF did not find the threat in question at all fantastic. The correspondence is in Crick to Brigadier E. J. Foord, 14 March 1945, Record Group 226, Entry 190, Box 282, National Archives.

76. On 4 February 1945, MI 14 criticized MI6 for circulated a "dubious" report on "continued preparations" for a stronghold in the south. Hinsley, *British Intelligence*, III/2 (London: HMSO, 1988), 712-713.

77. Hinsley, *British Intelligence*, III/2, 713.

78. Ibid., 713-714.

79. Joint Intelligence Committee (U.K.), 18 February 1945, *Records of the Joint Chiefs of Staff* (Washington: University Publications of America, 1979, text-fiche).

80. Ibid.

81. Ibid.

82. Ibid.

83. X-2 London to X-2 Caserta, 10 March 1945 Record Group 226, Entry 109, National Archives.

84. X-2 London to X-2 Caserta, 10 March 1945, Record Group 226, Entry 109, Box 5, National Archives. This report was sent to Lt. Col. T.R. Bruskin, G-2, Seventh Army. It formed the backbone of Bruskin's infamous intelligence report of 25 March described in Minott, *Fortress That Never Was*, 54-55.

85. X-2 London to X-2 Caserta, 10 March 1945, Record Group 226, Entry 109, Box 5, National Archives.

86. Major E.M. Furnival Jones to Col. D.G. White, 3 February 1945, Record Group 331, Box 109, SHAEF G-2, CI papers. National Archives.

87. D.G. White to Colonel Macleod. 12 February 1945, Record Group 331, Box 109, SHAEF G-2, CI papers, National Archives.

88. Ambrose, *Eisenhower and Berlin*, 75. For the report itself see Major L. F. Ellis, *The Defeat of Germany*, vol. 2 of *Victory in the West* (London: HMSO, 1968), 302-304. For the number of sites found see Hinsley, *British Intelligence*, II/2, 716.

89. Record Group 226, Entry 190, Box 365, National Archives.

90. Ibid.

91. Ibid.

92. The men were Eggen, a representative of Walter Schellenberg, Franz Xaver Ritter von Epp, *Reichsstatthalter* of Bavaria, Wilhelm Höttl, the head of the Balkans division of *Amt VI*, RSHA, and Karl Wolff, the chief SS and police official in northern Italy. Information about all save the contact with Eggen are fully explained in the OSS archives. For some unknown reason reports about the Dulles-Eggen meetings, other than the fact that they took place, remain classified.

93. 20 March 1945, Report on Höttl, Bern SI. Record Group 226, Entry 108, Box 3, National Archives; SCI, 12 AG, report on Hoettl, 31 May 1945. Record Group 226, Entry 109, Box 28, National Archives.

94. "Memoranda For the President: Sunrise," *Studies in Intelligence* 7: 88. This article from the CIA's in-house journal was declassified in March 1990. It may be that the Wolff case (Operation Sunrise) convinced Dulles that the Germans were planning a reduit. On 29 March 1945, in one of his regular messages to Roosevelt about the Sunrise operation, Donovan wrote, "The OSS representative [Dulles] comments that it is becoming increasingly apparent that Hitler intends to use the bulk of the German forces in Italy for the defense of the German 'redoubt.'"

95. See Allen Dulles, *The Secret Surrender* (New York: Harper and Row, 1966).

96. Pogue, *The Supreme Command*, 368-69.

97. Joint Intelligence Committee SHAEF (45) 3 (Final), 10 March 1945, *Records of the Joint Chiefs of Staff*, Record Group 218, National Archives.

98. The British JIC wrote on 28 March: "Though Germany will then [after the Allies had thrust past Berlin] no longer have the men or the means to re-establish an 'Eastern' or a 'Western' front, Hitler will probably attempt to carry on resistance from Thuringia and ultimately in the South, as we forecast in a

previous paper [18 February]. Joint Intelligence Committee, *Records of the Joint Chiefs of Staff*, Record Group 115, National Archives.

99. SHAEF G-2, CI War Room, 9 April 1945, "The SS Guerrilla Movement," Record Group 226, Entry 190, Box 365, National Archives.

100. On werewolves in Salzburg areas, see War Room Cable to 7th Army, 22 June 1945, Record Group 226, Entry 109, Box 30, National Archives.

101. SHAEF CI War Room, 27 July 1945, "Resistance Movements in Germany," Record Group 226, Entry 109, Box 35, National Archives.

102. Intermediate Interrogation Report #12, Military Intelligence Service (G-2) Center: Obersturmbannführer Hans Helmut Wolff, 14 August 1945. Record Group 226, Entry 109. Box, National Archives. Wolff was temporary chief of the Gestapo office in Dresden in the spring of 1945 before moving to Weimar. SCI Unit A, "Stay Behind Units in the Salzburg Area," 2 June 1945. Record Group 226, Entry 109, Box 31, National Archives. This report was based on the interrogation of Erwin Schulz, SS Brigadeführer and General Major of the Police and Commander of the SIPO and SD in Gau Salzburg. Interrogation Report, CIC 7th Army, Joseph Brandl, Chief of Investigations, Gestapo at Augsburg, 24 June 1945, Record Group 226, Entry 109, Box 63, National Archives.

103. Interrogation Report, Obersturmbannführer Hans Wolff, 14 August 1945, Record Group 226, Entry 109, Box 40, National Archives.

104. Minott, *Fortress That Never Was*, 14-18.

105. Ibid.

106. Ellis, *Defeat of Germany*, Appendix 10, 429-430.

107. Interrogation Report, Joseph Brandl, Chief Investigator, Gestapo at Augsburg, 2 June 1945, Record Group 226, Entry 109, Box 63, National Archives.

108. Walter Schellenberg related this story to his Allied interrogators. He added that the names of three general staff officers shot for defeatism was circulated in February 1945. Record Group 226, Entry 125A, Box 2, National Archives.

109. H.R. Trevor-Roper, *The Last Days of Hitler* (London: Macmillan, 1978), 1-2.

110. Interrogation Report, Walter Schellenberg, Record Group 226, Entry 125A, Box 2, National Archives.

111. X-2 London, "The Career of Heinrich Himmler," 11 September 1945, Record Group 226, Entry 109. Box 41, National Archives.

112. IR, Schellenberg, Record Group 226, Entry 125A, Box 2, National Archives.

113. On 20 April, X-2 London wrote to the team that was in Caserta to prepare to enter Austria: "Austrian material... largely concerns operational details of the *Abwehr*." Record Group 226, Entry 109, Box 17, National Archives.

114. Anthony Cave Brown, *"C": The Secret Life of Sir Stewart Graham Menzies, Spymaster to Winston Churchill* (New York: Macmillan, 1987). On page 310 Cave Brown states that Churchill met with an emissary of Canaris, Fabian von Schlabrendorff at Chartwell in 1938; William Donovan had business dealings with Paul Leverkuehn in the inter-war period. It is alleged that Leverkuehn, who would become the wartime head of the *Abwehr* office in Istanbul, acted as Canaris' emissary in meetings with Donovan in New York City in 1938-39. Anthony Cave Brown, *The Last Hero: Wild Bill Donovan*, (New York: Times Books, 1982), 127-129. For more on Leverkuehn see Barry Rubin, *Istanbul Intrigues* (New York: McGraw-Hill, 1989), 53-54.

115. This involved a historian, G. Wirsing, who from September 1944 through March 1945 had full access to Schellenberg's political reports so that he could present an unvarnished view to Himmler. His analyses were called "Egmont" reports. Record Group 226, Entry 109, Box 35, National Archives.

116. The propaganda campaign of April 1945 usually associated with the werewolf program was launched by Goebbels without Prützmann's authorization. See Goebbels's diary entry for 31 March 1945, in *Final Entries, 1945: The Diaries of Joseph Goebbels*, ed. by Hugh Trevor-Roper (New York: G.P. Putnam's Sons, 1978), 289.

117. Glenn B. Infield, *Skorzeny: Hitler's Commando* (New York: Military Heritage Press, 1981), 121-4. Just after the Allies crossed the Rhine in March, Skorzeny considered going to the mountains with five or six groups of 400 to 500 to reinforce the *Wehrmacht* at important passes. This plan came to nothing. CI War Room, 28 November 1945, Liquidation Report #13, "VI S," Record Group 226, Entry 190, Box 392, National Archives.

118. See IR, O/Gruf. Jürgen Stroop, Chief SS and Police Official in Wiesbaden area, 10 October 1945, Record Group 226, Entry 109, Box 46, National Archives.

119. SHAEF G-2, CI War Room, 27 July 1945, "The Resistance Movements in Germany," Record Group 226, Entry 109, Box 35, National Archives.

120. HW1/3747/7549, Public Record Office, Kew, UK.

121. X-2 London to X-2 Caserta, 10 March 1945, Record Group 226, Entry 109, Box 5., National Archives.

122. Manfred Rauchensteiner, *Der Krieg in Österreich, 1945* (Vienna: Österreichischer Bundesverlag, 1984) 288-289, 306-307.

123. Trevor-Roper, *Last Days of Hitler*, 1-2.

Early CIA Reports on Austria, 1947-1949

Siegfried Beer

Over the last decade we have learned a lot about the impact of intelligence, defined broadly as the collection of information, the organization and implementation of covert operations, and systematic analysis of intentions and capabilities of potential and actual enemies. We have also learned a lot about its application, continuity, and quality in the context of international relations in this century, particularly since the outbreak of World War II.[1] Specialists of a newly developed historical sub-discipline termed intelligence studies have even spoken of an intelligence revolution. They have concentrated their research on intelligence and its relationship to major aspects of political, economic, and military strategy and behavior during the last global conflict from 1941 to 1945.[2] Furthermore, a number of serious attempts have been made to assess the role of this intelligence revolution in the emergence and subsequent evolution of the First Cold War.[3] However, while relatively liberal access to wartime archival sources has greatly benefitted research into the role of intelligence during World War II, lack of documentary evidence for the roughly forty-five year period of the Cold War has equally diminished the quality if not the quantity of intelligence-related analyses of international politics since 1947.[4]

Gorbachev's structural policies of perestroika and glasnost and the subsequent break-up of the Soviet empire as well as the total demise of the super-power Soviet Union have created conditions favorable to the partial opening of Soviet/Russian archives, including those of the KGB, and have thereby exerted new and necessary pressure on both London and Washington to follow suit in the policy of relaxing access to Cold War intelligence records.[5]

Studies on Austria during the early phase of the first Cold War have become possible only because of the recent declassification of CIA documents pertaining to the 1940s and 1950s. These reports originated in the Office of Reports and Estimates and were widely distributed among the highest echelons of the U.S. foreign policy establishment. Even if they hardly contain dramatic new insights into the U.S. perception of the Austrian problem during the thirty-month period covered by them, they provide concrete evidence of the analytical contribution made by U.S. central intelligence as re-established less than two years after the termination of the wartime Office of Strategic Services (OSS).

The Evolution of U.S. Intelligence from 1941 to 1949

During the interwar period, U.S. intelligence had been kept at traditionally low levels. It relied mainly on the work of military attachés and the usual political reporting from diplomatic outposts. Army intelligence continued to be organized within the Military Intelligence Division (MID), while naval intelligence, collected and implemented through the Office of Naval Intelligence (ONI), was considered of higher importance and prestige. Until June 1939 there was no real effort to coordinate intelligence centrally.[6]

President Roosevelt moved to create a national intelligence organization only as late as July 1941 when he appointed William J. Donovan as Coordinator of Information (COI). The latter's probably most important and long term accomplishment was the systematic build-up of a research and analysis branch, known as R&A, in which established and promising young scholars from various fields and backgrounds were asked to produce three general categories of intelligence: (1) the comprehensive regional study, (2) specialized studies of particular factors in a region or country, and (3) foreign policy studies to support the development of U.S. foreign policy in a given area. Eventually R&A also produced the Daily Intelligence Summary and the Political Intelligence Weekly. When the COI was transformed into the OSS in June 1942 and placed under the control of the Joint Chiefs of Staff (JCS), R&A became one of eight major branches. Other branches of the OSS were responsible for training (S&T), research and development (R&D), surveillance of exiles and immigrants (Foreign Nationalities), clandestine collection (SI), propaganda (MO), subversion and sabotage (SO), and counterespionage (X-2). By 1944 the OSS operated worldwide and on the whole successfully, but it had to accept throughout the war that it was only one of seven major intelligence producers.

Even though it became an early victim of postwar demobilization in the fall of 1945, the OSS was soon and generally recognized as a creator of important traditions for the future of U.S. intelligence.[7] Already in October 1945 R&A was taken over by the State Department and was combined with other analytical units to form the Interim Research and Intelligence Service (IRIS). The War Department took over the Secret Intelligence (SI) and the counter-espionage (X-2) branches which as the Strategic Services Unit (SSU) continued to perform their previous activities and functions in selected areas of strategic interest to the U.S., among them Germany and Austria.

On 22 January 1946 President Truman issued a presidential direction creating a National Intelligence Authority (NIA) under which a Central Intelligence Group (CIG) was established, headed by a Director of Intelligence (DCI) who became responsible for the coordination, planning, evaluation, and dissemination of intelligence.

When the apparatus for intelligence analysis at the State Department, first in IRIS, then in the Office of Intelligence Research (OIR), and finally in the Office of Coordination and Liaison (OCL) started to gradually disintegrate, CIG's role as producer of intelligence expanded almost analogously. By mid-1946 a new Office of Research and Evaluation (ORE) was formed within the CIG. By the end of 1946 it was renamed the Office of Reports and Estimates under the same acronym, ORE.[8]

The National Security Act of July 1947 totally restructured national defense and national intelligence in the United States. It created a National Security Council (NSC), a Central Intelligence Agency (CIA) under a DCI, and a national military establishment with three distinct services: Army, Navy, and Air Force under a Secretary of Defense. The CIA was at first only envisioned as a central coordinator and evaluator of intelligence, not necessarily as a new producer of it. The explicit role as separate collector and independent producer of intelligence, short term as well as broad estimates, fell upon the CIA only at the end of 1947 when the State Department, under George C. Marshall, finally and officially withdrew from covert intelligence gathering. ORE remained the office tasked with producing current intelligence as well as national estimates until the reorganization of the CIA in 1950 when ORE was replaced by the Office of National Estimates (ONE) and the Office of Research and Reports (ORR).

U.S. Intelligence and Austria, 1941-1949

An early example of U.S. intelligence activity on the territory of Republican Austria can be detected in the so-called Coolidge Mission of January to May 1919 when the Wilson Administration sent a team of observers and experts to Vienna to report on developments in the various countries of the collapsed Habsburg Empire. One of these militarily trained field agents was Lt. Col. Sherman Miles who was sent to Zagreb, Belgrade, and Sarajevo and played an important role in the settling of the border question between (German) Austria and the newly created Kingdom of the Slovenes, Croats, and Serbs.[9] Twenty years later, Sherman Miles was to become the Director of the Military Intelligence Division where he became one of the prominent victims of the intelligence disaster that was Pearl Harbor.[10]

It is also noteworthy that some of the higher echelon diplomats in Vienna during the last years of the First Austrian Republic later figured among the key players in the arena of U.S. intelligence during World War II. Outstanding examples of this are George V. Earle III, U.S. minister to Austria in 1933-34, who was stationed in Sofia and Istanbul during the war and John C. Wiley, U.S. *charge d'affaires* in Vienna in 1937/38 who was to occupy a leading position in the Foreign Nationalities Branch of the COI/OSS.[11]

The Final Report of the U.S. General Consulate in Vienna, written at the occasion of the closing of its office in the summer of 1941, was one of the first substantive reports analyzed and distributed by the newly established Office of the Coordinator of Information.[12] From the very beginning of its existence, the OSS started to produce situation reports on developments in Austria, relying on information from exiles, emigrants, deserters, POWs, and other informants. By 1943 the first contacts were made with Austrian resistance sources, mainly through OSS-stations in Algiers, Berne, and Istanbul, and by mid-1944 planning and preparations for the penetration of enemy territory within the borders of the former Republic of Austria were undertaken.[13] Most of these operations were organized through the

German-Austrian section of the 2677th Regt. OSS (Prov.) in the Mediterranean Theatre of Operations (MedTO), centered at Bari/Caserta, some of them also via OSS-London. At least seventy-six OSS agents infiltrated into Austrian enemy territory. Many of these agents were deserter volunteers (DVs), that is, deserted Austrian patriots willing to contribute to the Allied cause.[14]

As soon as hostilities ended in Central Europe, OSS field stations were erected first in Salzburg, Innsbruck, Klagenfurt, and Linz and later in Zell am See and Vienna.[15] The OSS in Austria was under the command of Lt. Col. Charles W. Thayer and by August 1945 employed close to 200 full-time officers and agents in Austria.[16] Its main functions lay in gathering intelligence on major political, economic, and social developments in the rebuilding of liberated Austria. A number of studies done by the Central European Section of the R&A during the war as well as later field studies by historians and economists stationed at Salzburg, Linz, and Vienna after the war were of outstanding analytical quality. Among the R&A specialists and military/civil administrators responsible for Austrian matters the following academics deserve mention: Franz Neumann, Carl A. Schorske, Hajo Holborn, Eugene N. Anderson, Frederick Burkhardt, Edgar N. Johnson, Robert Neumann, Paul R. Sweet, David F. Strong, Walter C. Langsam and Lorenz Eitner.[17] The OSS also contributed to the systematic pursuit of National Socialist functionaries, a task which was, however, apportioned primarily to the army's Counter-Intelligence Corps (CIC).[18] Its 430th Detachment in Austria was to develop into a major tool in the intelligence rivalry between the Western occupiers and their former Soviet ally. CIC and NKVD became direct opponents in the emerging Cold War as evidenced most dramatically in a series of political and economic kidnappings in Vienna or at demarcation points.[19]

With the take-over of the OSS branches SI and X-2, SSU-Austria continued to perform essential intelligence tasks which soon shifted from purely Austrian matters to monitoring developments and events in neighboring countries to the north, east, and south. SSU-Austria was under the leadership of Lt. Comdr. Alfred C. Ulmer and quickly turned into a major instrument of the emerging Cold War in Austria.[20] By the end of 1946, SSU-Austria was liquidated in name but simultaneously set up as a CIG operation and as such certainly became the nucleus of CIA operations in Austria by 1948.

It is quite evident that Vienna and the occupation zones in Austria as crossroads of Allied interaction became centers of information-gathering in the crucial early phase of the Cold War period. Moreover, they became an arena in which U.S. covert operational activism of the kind practiced during the OSS years in the various military theaters flourished. However, now it was directed *against* the Soviet Union and its communist satellites in Central and Eastern Europe.[21]

The Structure of ORE

In February 1946 the NIA created a Central Reports Staff within the newly founded CIG and gave it the task of correlating and evaluating intelligence relevant to national security. By March it produced the first daily intelligence summary for President Truman. In the summer of 1946 this Central Reports Staff expanded into an Office of Research and Evaluation. Soon thereafter its Assistant Director, Ludwell L. Montague, a veteran of the wartime Joint Intelligence Committee of the JCS, produced its first estimate of Soviet intentions and capabilities, now famed as ORE 1, which basically claimed that the Soviet Union anticipated an inevitable conflict with the capitalist west and would try to extend its domination of Eastern Europe to include Germany and Austria. [22]

By 1948 ORE came under criticism for its focus on short term problems and for performing a number of functions not really related to the production of national intelligence estimates. In the summer of 1949 another study of ORE production was undertaken. This eventually led to the replacement of ORE by an Office of National Estimates (ONE) in November 1950.

ORE originally consisted of a staff of analysts provided by the Departments of State, War, and the Navy and was organized by geographical area. Its Global Survey Division, headed by L.C. Montague, soon produced a monthly report for the NSC entitled "Estimate of the World Situation." It also prepared national intelligence estimates which proved quite difficult and slow to produce. It was often criticized for being too non-committal or too diluting in the substance of its finished intelligence. Its undisputedly academic approach to intelligence was due to the fact that pursuant to OSS legacy, the CIA already had close ties to the academic community, particularly to the historical profession.[23]

NOTES

1. A few outstanding contributions include Christopher Andrew and David Dilks, eds., *The Missing Dimension: Governments and Intelligence Communities in the Twentieth Century* (London: MacMillan, 1984); Ernest R. May, ed., *Knowing One's Enemies: Intelligence Assessment Before the Two World Wars* (Princeton, N.J.: Princeton University Press, 1984), and Walter T. Hitchcock, ed., *The Intelligence Revolution: A Historical Perspective* (Washington D.C.: U.S. Air Force Academy, 1991).

2. Their most spectacular findings probably relate to the availability of "Ultra" and "Magic" for the Allies, but the scope of secret warfare went far beyond signals intelligence. A few examples of this type of literature include Richard Langhorne, ed., *Diplomacy and Intelligence during the Second World War* (Cambridge: Cambridge University Press, 1985); Robin W. Winks, *Cloak and Gown: Scholars in the Secret War, 1939-1961* (New York: William Morrow, 1991); Bradley F. Smith, *The Ultra-Magic Deals and the Most Secret Relationship, 1940-46* (Novato, CA: Presidio Press, 1993), and Ralph Bennett, *Behind the Battle: Intelligence in the War with Germany 1939-1945* (London: Sinclair-Stevenson, 1994).

3. Cf. Trevor Barnes, ed., "The Secret Cold War: The CIA and American Foreign Policy in Europe, 1946-1956, Part I," *The Historical Journal* 24 (1981): 399-415, and by the same author, "The Secret Cold War: The CIA and American Foreign Policy in Europe, 1946-1956, Part II," *The Historical Journal* 25 (1982): 649-670, and John L. Gaddis, "Intelligence, Espionage and Cold War Origins, *Diplomatic History* 13 (1989): 191-212.

4. Cf. Lawrence H. MacDonald, "OSS Records at the National Archives," *Newsletter. American Committee on the History of the Second World War* 39 (Spring 1988):14-49, and Wesley K. Wark, "In Never-Never Land: The British Archives on Intelligence," *The Historical Journal* 35 (1992):195-203.

5. Just two examples of books based on newly accessible intelligence sources would be Stefan Karner, ed., *Geheime Akten des KGB. "Margarita Ottilinger"* (Graz: Leykam, 1992) and John Costello and Oleg Tsarev, *Deadly Illusions* (New York: Crown, 1993).

6. Surveys of the history of U.S. intelligence in the twentieth century are numerous. Three reliable studies are: Charles D. Ameringer, *U.S. Foreign Intelligence: The Secret Side of American History* (Lexington, MA: Lexington Books, 1990); G.J.A. O'Toole, *Honorable Treachery: A History of U.S. Intelligence, Espionage, and Covert Action from the American Revolution to the*

CIA (New York: Atlantic Monthly Press, 1991), and Mark M. Lowenthal, *U.S. Intelligence: Evolution and Anatomy* (Westport, CT: Praeger, 1992).

7. Among several comprehensive works on the COI and OSS the following stand out as authoritative: Bradley F. Smith, *The Shadow Warriors: OSS and the Origins of the CIA* (New York: Basic Books, 1983); Barry M. Katz, *Foreign Intelligence: Research and Analysis in the Office of Strategic Services, 1942-1945* (Cambridge, MA: Harvard University Press, 1989) and George C. Chalou, ed., *The Secrets War: The Office of Strategic Services in World War II* (Washington, D.C.: National Archives and Records Administration, 1992).

8. Cf. Thomas F. Troy, *Donovan and the CIA: A History of the Establishment of the Central Intelligence Agency* (Frederick, MD: Aletheia Books, 1981), and Arthur B. Darling, *The Central Intelligence Agency: An Instrument of Government to 1950* (London: Pennsylvania State University Press, 1990).

9. Cf. Georg Schmid, "Die Coolidge-Mission in Österreich 1919: Zur Österreichpolitik der USA während der Pariser Friedenskonferenz," *MOESTA* 24 (1971): 433-467; see also Siegfried Beer and Eduard G. Staudinger, "Grenzziehung per Analogie. Die Miles-Mission in der Steiermark im Jänner 1919, Eine Dokumentation," in *Als Mitteleuropa zerbrach*, ed. Stefan Karner and Gerald Schöpfer (Graz: Leykam, 1990), 133-152.

10. Cf. G.J.A. O'Toole, *The Encyclopedia of American Intelligence and Espionage* (New York: Facts on File, 1988), 301.

11. On Earle cf. Barry Rubin, *Istanbul Intrigues: A True-Life Casablanca* (New York: McGraw-Hill, 1989), and on Wiley cf. Siegfried Beer, "Exil und Emigration als Information. Zur Tätigkeit der Foreign Nationalities Branch innerhalb des amerikanischen Kriegsgeheimdienstes COI bzw. OSS, 1941-1945," in *Jahrbuch 1989. Dokumentationsarchiv des österreichischen Widerstandes* (Vienna, 1989), 132-143.

12. Final report of U.S. consul Harry E. Carlson and vice-consuls Theodore J. Hohenthal and Joseph M. Roland, 16 August 1941, "Conditions in the Vienna Consular District," COI Report 6040, Record Group (RG) 226, Entry 16, National Archives, Washington, D.C. On the role of Austria and Austrians within the intelligence community between the wars cf. Siegfried Beer, "Von Alfred Redl zum 'Dritten Mann': Österreich und ÖsterreicherInnen im internationalen Geheimdienstwesen 1918-1947," *Geschichte und Gegenwart* 15 (1996) (in print).

13. Cf. Siegfried Beer, "Die Widerstandsgruppe Maier-Messner und der amerikanische Kriegsgeheimdienst OSS in Bern, Istanbul und Algier 1943/44," in *Jahrbuch 1993. Dokumentationsarchiv des österreichischen Widerstandes* (Vienna: 1993), 75-100.

14. Most of these secret missions are mentioned by code name and date of operation in Siegfried Beer and Stefan Karner, *Der Krieg aus der Luft: Kärnten und Steiermark 1941-1945* (Graz: Weishaupt, 1992), 76. Some of the more spectacular successes and failures on Austrian territory are described in Joseph E. Persico, *Piercing the Reich: The Penetration of Nazi Germany by American Secret Agents During World War II* (New York: Viking, 1979).

15. On the OSS in Austria generally cf. Siegfried Beer, "Alliierte Planung, Propaganda und Penetration 1943-1945," in *Burgenland 1945*, ed. Stefan Karner (Eisenstadt: Burgenländisches Landesarchiv, 1985) 82-88.

16. Cf. the memoirs of its chief: Charles W. Thayer, *Hands Across the Caviar* (Philadelphia: J.B. Lippincott, 1952), 177-224.

17. Some of the more relevant SI and R&A reports and analyses of the early occupation period have already been published in Oliver Rathkolb, ed., *Gesellschaft und Politik am Beginn der Zweiten Republik: Vertrauliche Berichte der US-Militäradministration aus Österreich 1945 in englischer Originalfassung* (Wien: Böhlau, 1985), and Siegfried Beer, "Oberösterreich nach dem Krieg: Vertrauliche Berichte des amerikanischen Geheimdienstes OSS aus dem Jahre 1945, Eine exemplarische Dokumentation," in *Oberösterreich April bis Dezember 1945. Ein Dokumentarbericht* (Linz: O.Ö. Landesarchiv, 1991) 177-232. On major aspects of R&A work during the war cf. Oliver Rathkolb, "Professorenpläne für Österreichs Zukunft. Nachkriegsfragen im Diskurs der Forschungsabteilung Research and Analysis," in *Geheimdienstkrieg gegen Deutschland*, ed. Jürgen Heideking and Christof Mauch (Göttingen: A. Francke, 1993) 166-181. I am presently editing a selective collection of R&A and other studies in a documentary volume to be entitled: Evaluating, Penetrating and Administering Austria. Reports and Analyses of the American Intelligence Services on the Austrian Condition 1941-1946.

18. On the record of the CIC in Austria cf. *Occupation of Austria and Italy* (History of the Counter Intelligence Corps XXV, Baltimore, MD: U.S. Army Intelligence Center, 1959).

19. Cf. Siegfried Beer, "Monitoring Helmer: Zur Tätigkeit des amerikanischen Armeegeheimdienstes CIC in Österreich 1945-1950, Eine exemplarische Dokumentation," in *Geschichte zwischen Freiheit und Ordnung: Gerald Stourzh*

zum 60.Geburtstag, ed. Emil Brix et al. (Graz: Böhlau, 1991), 229-259, and Karner, *Geheime Akten des KGB*, 9-21.

20. Grateful acknowledgment is made for a memorable interview which the author was given by Mr. Ulmer on 9 August 1993 in Washington D.C.

21. Cf. Bradley F. Smith, "An Idiosyncratic View of Where We Stand on the History of American Intelligence in the Early Post-1945 Era," *Intelligence and National Security* 3 (1988): 111-123, and Siegfried Beer, "Die Geheimdienste im besetzten Österreich 1945-1955," in *Menschen nach dem Krieg Schicksale 1945-1955*, ed. Gerhard Jagschitz and Stefan Karner (Sankt Pölten: Niederösterreichische Landesregierung, Kulturabteilung, 1995), 40-44.

22. Cf. Darling, *The CIA*, 130f.

23. Cf. Sumner Benson, "The Historian as Foreign Policy Analyst: The Challenge of the CIA," *The Public Historian* 3 (1981): 15-17.

DOCUMENTATION

Editorial Comments

The following four ORE-reports have been located in Record Group 263 (Records of the CIA), Boxes 1-3 at the National Archives in Washington D.C. They are given here verbatim and in their entirety.

The first document, ORE 13/1 on "The Situation in Austria" of 20 February 1947 is still a CIG-report. It does not provide a distribution list.

The second document, ORE 13-48 of 28 April 1948 on the "Current Situation in Austria" lists twenty-five upper echelon recipients, from the President downwards to the Director of Security and Intelligence in the Atomic Energy Commission.

The last two documents, ORE 28-49 and ORE 56-49 include the standard warning, dissemination notice, and distribution list of twelve departmental recipients. The information provided reads as follows:

> Warning:
> This document contains information affecting the national defense of the United States within the meaning of the Espionage Act, 50 U.S.C., 31 and 32, as amended. Its transmission or the revelation of itscontents in any manner to an unauthorized person is prohibited by law.
>
> Dissemination Notice:
> 1. This copy of this publication is for the information and use of the recipient designated on the front cover and of individuals under the jurisdiction of the recipient's office who require the information for the performance of their official duties. Further dissemination elsewhere in the department to other offices which require the information for the performance of official duties may be authorized by the following:
>   a. Special Assistant to the Secretary of State for Research and Intelligence, for the Department of State
>   b. Director of Intelligence GS, USA, for the Department of the Army
>   c. Chief, Naval Intelligence, for the Department of the Navy
>   d. Director of Intelligence, USAF, for the Department of the Air Force
>   e. Director of Security and Intelligence, AEC, for the Atomic Energy Commission
>   f. Deputy Director for Collection and Dissemination, CIA, for any other Department or Agency
> 2. This copy may be either retained to destroyed by burning in accordance with applicable security regulations, or returned to the

Central Intelligence Agency by arrangement with the Office of Collection and Dissemination, CIA.

Distribution:

Office of the President
National Security Council
National Security Resources Board
Department of State
Office of Secretary of Defense
Department of the Army
Department of the Navy
Department of the Air Force
State-Army-Navy-Air Force Coordinating Committee
Joint Chiefs of Staff
Atomic Energy Commission
Research and Development Board

The editor has intentionally refrained from cross-referencing the views and findings of the ORE-analysts in order to let the reader judge their arguments and perceptions independently and uninfluenced.

Among the standard documentary and secondary literature pertaining to the Austrian problem during the period from 1947 to 1949 the following could be consulted for reference:

FURTHER LITERATURE

Rudolf Ardelt and Hanns Haas "Die Westintegration Österreichs nach 1945," *Österreichische Zeitschrift für Politikwissenschaft* 4 (1975): 379-399.

Günter Bischof, "Between Responsibility and Rehabilitation: Austria in International Politics 1940-1950," (Ph.D. diss., Harvard University, 1989).

Günter Bischof and Josef Leidenfrot, eds., *Die Bevormundete Nation: Österreich und die Alliierten 1945-1949* (Innsbruck: Haymon, 1988).

Audrey Kurth Cronin, *Great Power Politics and the Struggle over Austria, 1945-1955* (Ithaca, NY: Cornell University Press, 1986).

John Prados, *The Soviet Estimate: U.S. Intelligence Analysis and Russian Military Strength* (New York: Dial, 1982).

Gerald Stourzh, *Geschichte des Staatsvertrages 1945-1955: Österreichs Weg zur Neutralität. Studienausgabe* (Graz: Styria, 1985).

U.S. Department of State, *Foreign Relations of the United States*, vol. II, 1947 (Washington: Government Printing Office, 1973).

________, *Foreign Relations of the United States*, vol. II, 1948 (Washington: Government Printing Office, 1975).

________, *Foreign Relations of the United States*, vol. III, 1949 (Washington: Government Printing Office, 1974).

________, *Participation of the United States Government in International Conferences: 1 July 1946 to 30 June 1947* (Washington, Government Printing Office, 1948).

The Situation in Austria, February 1947*

Document 1 (Source: NA, RG 263, ORE Report 13/1,
20 February 1947, Box 1)
SECRET

Summary

The four occupying powers have recognized a coalition government in Austria which was formed after the national elections of November 1945. The authority of the government is still limited by the conditions of four-power occupation and particularly by the hostile attitude of the USSR. The three-party coalition, however, is genuinely representative of a population which, except for an extremely small Communist minority, is almost evenly divided into an agrarian Catholic party and a trade union socialist party. Both of these parties are united in their opposition to the demands of the USSR and are anxious to begin the reconstruction of the country under their own direction. The Communist Party has almost no indigenous support and is able to influence government policy only through Soviet assistance.

The USSR desires an Austrian regime subservient to Soviet policy. Unsuccessful in its attempts to influence the Austrian Government by infiltration and intimidation, the USSR has concentrated on establishing control over the Austrian economy. The USSR has implemented its policy in Austria by propaganda aimed at discrediting the government and by actions designed to disrupt its political and economic authority. In order to further their economic aims, the Soviets have removed industrial machinery on a large scale, seized industrial assets, and forced factories to produce for the USSR. The Soviets are now attempting to induce the Austrians to agree to a settlement of Soviet claims to alleged German assets in eastern Austria which will give the USSR permanent control over important industrial properties in this area. The Soviets want a treaty which imposes maximum restrictions on the sovereignty of the Austrian Government and legalizes future Soviet interference in Austrian affairs. Confronted by political difficulties and Anglo-American support for the present government, the USSR would probably accept as a temporary expedient a government under Soviet influence through dependency upon economic ties with Eastern Europe. The Soviets, however, are unlikely to make any major concessions for the sake of early agreement, since the best interests of the USSR may be served by a protracted military occupation of Austria, whose government is considered fundamentally anti-Communist.

The UK and France wish to terminate the present quadrilateral occupation, which they regard as a hindrance to Austria's economic recovery and to the establishment of stability in Western Europe. They wish to insure, however, that

* Only limited coordination of this report with departmental intelligence agencies has been attained. Substantial dissent, if any, will be submitted at a later date.

Austria will not be driven by either domestic or foreign pressure into a Soviet or German bloc. The British, therefore, have extended to the Austrian Government a credit of 10,000,000 pounds. The French, while agreeing with US and UK policy, have stated that they are unable to extend any credits. Furthermore, the French have made arbitrary requisitions of food and industrial products in their relatively unproductive zone of occupation. On a national policy level, however, they have combined with the US and UK in an attempt to conclude the treaty and terminate the occupation.

The Austrian people are primarily interested in putting an end to the occupation, which they regard as an intolerable burden on the nation's depleted resources. They realize that it is necessary "to make peace" with the Soviets, yet they do not desire to come under Soviet domination in order to accomplish this. The Austrian Government therefore wants to steer a middle course between Eastern and Western Europe. This policy is most difficult to effect in view of the fact that Austria requires close economic relations with the central European and Danubian states now under Soviet domination. The future of Austria as an independent state will rest upon such support from the West as will enable her not only to recover economically but also to bargain with her Soviet-dominated neighbors on a footing of equality. Lacking this support, Austria will inevitably be forced to yield to the influence exerted by the USSR.

Further discussion of the situation in Austria is contained in the Enclosure hereto.

Enclosure

Important Factors in the Austrian Situation

Government: The present Austrian Government, which was formed after the national elections of November 25, 1945, was recognized by the four powers represented in the Allied Commission "with due regard" to the supreme authority of the Allied Commission. The government operates with relative freedom but is still economically at the mercy of the occupying powers. The new control agreement adopted by the Allied Commission on June 28, 1946, gave the Austrian Government greater power; however, the Soviets have prevented the government from exercising its additional authority in eastern Austria and therefore this agreement has not materially altered the relationship between the Allied Commission and the Austrian Government.

The Austrian Constitution is essentially based on the constitution of 1920 as amended in 1929, supplemented by constitutional laws which grant the Federal Government certain transitional emergency powers.

Political Parties: The national and provincial elections of November 1945 resulted in a victory of the liberal pro-western parties, the Catholic People's Party and the Socialist Party. The Communist Party, despite a lavish propaganda campaign, was thoroughly defeated, securing only four out of 165 seats in the lower house of Parliament. The Soviet Command was clearly surprised by the elections, particularly in the ability of the Socialist leaders to retain their hold over the pauperized industrial workers of eastern Austria. Backed by the three Western Powers, Socialist and People's Party leaders have worked together and have prevented the Communists from infiltrating their ranks. With rare exceptions, the Soviets have refrained from acts of violence against the two liberal organizations, even though they regard them as hostile to the USSR.

The US, UK and France have not discriminated against any of the political parties, although they prefer the two liberal groups.

Pan-Germanism no longer exists as a political program. All political parties are now opposed to a union with Germany.

Denazification: Denazification, which for the past year has been substantially in the hands of the government, is difficult because more than 500,000 persons are involved. The two major liberal parties are opposed to a strict denazification. The Soviets, on the other hand, favor a program that would disrupt Austria's political and social order if it were applied. The Soviets recently agreed, however, in the Allied Commission, to certain modifications of a proposed Austrian law which provides for a program that is strict rather than punitive. Parliament, although generally opposed to the severity of the Allied Amendments, incorporated them in a law which was recently passed.

Displaced Persons: According to official Austrian figures, there are more than 500,000 displaced persons in Austria, concentrated in the US, British and French zones. Many of these are non-repatriable nationals of Eastern European and Balkan origin. They constitute an Allied rather than an Austrian responsibility. Both the USSR and the Austrian Government are vitally interested in disposing of these persons. The Soviets want them forcibly repatriated as being hostile to the USSR as well as to nations under Soviet influence. The Austrians, on the other hand, are anxious merely to get rid of them because they constitute a grave social menace as well as a future economic liability.

Although the US, UK and France desire to solve this problem, they have been unwilling to force these displaced persons to return to their nations of origin, since persons surrendered to the Soviets have frequently been shot.

Reparations: The Soviets are construing the Potsdam Agreement with respect to German assets in Eastern Austria in the broadest imaginable sense in order to serve immediate Soviet needs and to gain permanent control over a large proportion of Austria's economy. It is evident that they will drive a hard bargain, because it is the only clear means remaining to them by which they can influence the anti-Communist Austrian Government.

The official Soviet definition of German assets as stated in July 1946 includes (1) German property in Austria before March 15, 1938; (2) German property transfers to and capital investments in Austria after that date; and (3) Austrian property acquired by the Germans after 1936 at a fair price. The last proviso is interpreted by the Soviets in a manner wholly favorable to themselves.

In the Allied Commission, the US has opposed the Soviet interpretation of Potsdam, and, therefore, the mass Soviet seizure of industry in eastern Austria. The US has given wide publicity to its return to the Austrian Government of German properties in the provinces of Salzburg and Upper Austria as a means of arousing public opinion against the Soviet policy. The British also oppose the USSR position, and have endeavored consistently to place the discussion of German assets on a quadripartite basis. Although the French have generally supported the US-UK position in the Allied Commission, they have arbitrarily removed certain factories in their zone and have requisitioned badly needed foodstuffs.

Agricultural and Industrial Production: In addition to suffering from ravages of war, the Austrian economy has suffered from the isolation until recently of eastern Austria, arbitrary Soviet activities in that area, and from French zonal requisitions. The agriculturally rich zone of eastern Austria has not only been forced to feed a relatively large Soviet army of occupation, but has also been drained by Soviet removals of livestock and farm machinery as well as by seizures of agricultural estates. Austrian industry, also concentrated in the Soviet zone, was first crippled by mass Soviet removals of machines. Later production, sorely needed in the reconstruction of Austria's economy, has been in part diverted to the Soviet Army and the USSR itself. The Soviets have insisted that factories producing for the USSR receive preferential treatment in raw materials and workers' food rations. This discrimination serves to disrupt the national economy and further embarrass the Austrian Government. The Austrian Government has attempted, by measures such as the Nationalization Decree, to minimize Soviet control over the economy of eastern Austria, but the USSR, in violation of the control agreement of June 1946, has consistently refused to allow any such measures to be enforced in its zone.

Military occupation of the three Western zones in Austria has delayed economic recovery without basically weakening its industrial potential. Although the level of agricultural production is satisfactory, the food situation has remained desperate since, unlike Soviet-occupied eastern Austria, these areas are not self-supporting. Vorarlberg and the Tirol in particular have suffered as a consequence of French military requisitions. Austria's industrial potential was expanded between 50 and 100 percent after 1938. In contrast to eastern Austria, the western areas occupied by the US, UK and France retain the bulk of this expanded capacity. Industrial recovery here has nevertheless been slow to date because of shortages of raw materials and skilled workers, and because the importation from Germany of essential spare parts has been stopped.

International Trade: Up to the present, international trade has been largely limited to interim barter arrangement. The long-term credit agreement already reached with the UK, as well as similar agreements about to be negotiated with the US, Sweden and Switzerland, will serve to increase trade with the Western Powers, as well as to improve Austria's bargaining position in future trade negotiations with Soviet dominated states.

The French for their part propose to negotiate a barter-type agreement with the Austrian Government for products produced primarily in the French zone, including electric power generated in the province of Vorarlberg.

Result of the Programs Followed in the Various Zones of Austria

The most outstanding event of the occupation period was the resounding defeat of the Communist Party at the last election. The refusal of the pauperized common people to forsake the standards of liberal government marks a defeat for the Soviet program in this country.

For the rest, it is difficult to distinguish between the damage done by the war and the occupation. The economic situation has been greatly aggravated in eastern Austria by the Soviets, and, to a lesser extent, in the Tirol and Vorarlberg by the arbitrary requisitions and seizures of the French. This in turn has adversely affected the economy of the zones presently occupied by the US and UK.

Current Immediate and Long-Range Objectives

Soviet. Political: The immediate USSR aims are to discredit the present government by disrupting its authority in eastern Austria. The Soviet-influenced press demands a new election, while the Austrian Communists have made efforts to win over dissatisfied elements from both the People's Party and the Socialist Party. As a long-term objective, the USSR desires a regime subservient to Soviet policy. The Soviets, therefore, want a treaty which imposes maximum restrictions on the sovereignty of the Austrian Government and legalizes future Soviet interference in Austrian affairs. Pending accomplishment of this objective, they will probably accept as a temporary expedient a government influenced by the USSR through dependency upon economic ties with Eastern Europe. The Soviets, however, are unlikely to make any major concessions for the sake of early agreement, since the best interests of the USSR may be served by a protracted military occupation of Austria, whose government is considered fundamentally anti-Communist.

Economic: The USSR desires to weaken the Austrian economy. This has so far been achieved by the mass, indiscriminate removals of industrial machinery, and by forcing a large proportion of the industry remaining under Soviet control to produce for the USSR. The amount of food available for the local population has been reduced by the requirements of the relatively large Soviet army of occupation.

The Soviets doubtless hope to exert a long-term influence over Austrian economy by forcing a settlement of the German assets question which will leave them in control of important industrial assets. They have already indicated an unwillingness to relinquish their economic position in a cash settlement. The Soviets probably expect to extract further concessions before they will permit Austria to establish necessary commercial relations with Soviet-oriented states in the Danube basin. With respect to trade with Germany, the Soviets have taken the position in the Allied Commission that Austrian purchases in Germany should be limited to items which cannot be obtained from the United Nations.

British and French. Political: The British and French are anxious to conclude an Austrian treaty in order to terminate the burden of quadripartite occupation and complete the restoration of Austrian sovereignty. They are also interested in reaching a solution to the problems of denazification and displaced persons which will promote the political stability of the present regime. Both the British and French desire to insure the long-term independence of the Austrian Government and prevent it from either joining a regenerated Germany or being compelled to serve Soviet aims.

Economic: The British have an immediate concern in the problem of German foreign assets in eastern Austria because they have interests in some of the properties under negotiation; for this reason as well as for reasons of national policy, the British and French are anxious to prevent the Soviets from consolidating their present position in Lower Austria and the Burgenland.

As in the rest of Western Europe, the British want to resuscitate the Austrian economy as quickly as possible in order to promote stability. To this end, the British have extended a credit to the Austrian Government. While the French have indicated that they are unable to extend credits to Austria, they have shown an interest in barter-type agreements. Both the UK and France want to prevent Austria from becoming economically dependent on either the USSR and its satellites or Germany.

The Current Situation in Austria, April 1948*

Document 2 (Source: NA, RG 263, ORE Report 13-48, 28 April 1948, Box 2)

SECRET

Summary

Though the importance of Austria to the US is largely negative, US commitments and interests there require maintenance of a Western-oriented government which can be given eventual full independence. Despite its position on the fringes of the Soviet sphere of influence, virtually surrounded by Satellite countries, and partially occupied by the Soviet Army, Austria remains one of the most politically stable and anti-Communist countries in Europe. The people are apparently determined to maintain their identity with the West. The USSR could absorb Austria only by military force, or by a combination of economic and political pressures supplemented by Satellite interference following quadripartite troop withdrawal.

The present Austrian Government, which represents the overwhelmingly anti-Soviet sentiment of the people, is stable and is fundamentally cooperative with the West. The Communist Party is too small to exert any influence and has little chance of growing without direct outside support, because the well disciplined Socialists retain control of the elements through which the Communists would have to work.

Should the Communists gain control of Austria despite these obstacles, the immediate results would be: (a) a serious demoralization of pro-Western elements throughout Europe; (b) facilitated Communist penetration of Italy and exposure of that country to easier aggression; (c) loss of a most important current source of information on the USSR.

The major difficulties which the present government must overcome before it can attain its goal of real independence are economic. While in the western zones are located some major industrial installations and the hydroelectric power to run them, the USSR has control of the agricultural region, of the oil, and of industries in Eastern Austria claimed as German assets. By manipulation of these resources, the USSR has delayed economic recovery, thus weakening the Government.

If Austria should survive quadripartite occupation intact and if its political and economic autonomy could be re-established, its economic prospects would be good and thus also its chances of eventually becoming an economic asset to

* The information in this report is as of 22 March 1948. The intelligence organizations of the Departments of State, Navy, and the Air Force have concurred in this report; the Intelligence Division, Department of the Army, concurs with those sections having military implications.

the economy of Western Europe. Under present conditions, however, it is unlikely that Austria can achieve full economic stability within the next four years.

The Importance of Austria to the US

Austria, from a US point of view, is of considerable importance but almost entirely in a negative sense. The country contains little of intrinsic value to the US: it is economically weak to such an extent that it must remain an economic liability for some years to come, and its military capacity is negligible. Austria is, however, to be numbered among those European nations which are of great intrinsic importance to the US because they truly wish to attain the status of free and independent democracies. The United States has, moreover, firmly committed itself to a policy directed toward the early establishment of an independent Austrian state. The defeat of this policy by the USSR would have a far-reaching and deleterious effect on the US. European position as a whole, disproportionately magnified by the fact that a part of Austria is presently occupied by US troops The early establishment of Soviet control over Austria would have a seriously adverse psychological effect throughout Western Europe and would have the immediate concrete result of greatly facilitating Communist penetration of Italy. Possibly of minor importance but still of some consequence to the US would be the loss of one of the few remaining valuable US sources of information concerning the USSR.

The Political Situation

The most important single political circumstance relating to Austria, and one which overshadows and conditions all other problems is the fact that Austria is under the military occupation of the United States, Great Britain, France, and the USSR, with the country divided into four zones each occupied by the armed forces of a single power.

Functioning under the supervision of an Allied Commission, the present government is a stable coalition of the two major parties—the People's Party and the Socialist Party. The stability of this coalition, representing 95 percent of the voters in the 1945 election, is based on the determination of the Austrian people to recover their independence and to resist absorption into the Soviet sphere. Although the Austrian Communists are a negligible factor in Austrian politics and are not now represented in the Austrian Government, the Communist coup in Czechoslovakia and evidences of Communist strength in Italy, have considerably dampened the eagerness of both major parties for a withdrawal of the occupation troops as a first step toward actual independence. Although Austrian leaders are confident that no similar coup is possible in Austria, the prospect of a virtual encirclement by aggressive Soviet Satellite states is now particularly disturbing to them. These leaders consider it necessary that the Austrian police force be expanded and that an Austrian Army properly armed and trained, be created as soon as the treaty* is put into effect.

Austria's sovereignty is still greatly limited by conditions of the occupation, and the treaty which would terminate the occupation remains stalled by the conflict between the East and the West. Unanimous approval by the four occupying powers (US, UK, France, USSR) is required only for matters involving constitutional changes. The number of important matters left to the jurisdiction of the zonal commanders has, however, enabled the USSR unilaterally to nullify decisions of the Austrian Government by countermanding them in its zone. This has been done, for example, by the Soviet seizure of key firms as German assets, by nonrecognition of Austrian nationalization of industries, and by Soviet interference in the distribution of food supplies and petroleum,

Through employment of delaying tactics in negotiations on the treaty, and concurrently through economic penetration of Austria, the USSR has sought to force changes in the composition and orientation of the pro-Western coalition government, intensifying these tactics since the 1945 elections revealed the extreme weakness of the Austrian Communist Party. The few prominent members of the conservative People's Party who once felt that concessions to the USSR might procure Soviet agreement to a treaty now join in supporting the coalition government's opposition to any treaty which would violate Austrian sovereignty, or prejudice Austria's economic recovery. Austrians in general understand clearly, moreover, that firm resistance to Soviet pressure is prerequisite to continuation of US economic aid and that they are bound to the US by economic necessity.

The majority People's Party is a reservoir of all right-of-center political forces. Its instability is the result of a variety of sectional and class interests. This one-party bloc on the right is a novel development in Austrian politics. Because the former pan-German and Nazi parties obviously could not be revived, a vote for the rightist People's Party was the only means of expressing an anti-Marxist sentiment in 1945. This Party currently represents the middle class, and the industrial and peasant interests; its platform aims primarily at a capitalist democracy acceptable to the Catholic Church. The Party looks to the US for support.

The Austrian Socialist Party is highly disciplined. Its traditional policy of theoretical extremism and practical moderation has enabled it to retain left-wing elements and to extend party influence over some of the peasants and the lower middle classes, in addition to having the overwhelming support of the trade unions. Currently, its policy of gaining objectives by democratic, evolutionary means is expressed through active participation in the coalition government.

* Treaty for the Re-establishment of an Independent and Democratic Austria, presently under negotiation by the US, UK, France, and the USSR.

While its strong, conservative leadership has gained it enough prestige to win a narrow majority in a new national election, it would, however, probably not gain sufficient votes to give it a practical working majority in the lower house. The Socialist Party platform aims chiefly at the establishment of a Socialist democracy, in general corresponding to that espoused by the British Labor Party. This Party supports US objectives in Austria.

The Austrian Communist Party has been prevented from making any great gains, even during the hardships following each World War, by the strong Socialist hold over the working classes. The Communists withdrew from the government in 1947. The fact that Austrian communism is regarded as a tool of the USSR continues to stigmatize the movement.

The Economic Situation

Shortly before the Anschluss with Germany in 1938, Austria was dependent on imports for 25 percent of its foodstuffs, much of its industrial raw material, and about 90 percent of its hard coal. Given general European recovery, relaxation of Soviet economic controls, financial assistance for capital equipment, and favorable trade policy agreements with foreign nations, Austria could achieve within a few years an economic balance which would provide higher standards of living than it had before the war, by exporting electric power, timber, magnesite, and industrial products. At present Austria's economy, even though bolstered by large subsidies from the US, is little above the subsistence level.

Agricultural recovery lags behind that in all other European countries, and Austrians have one of the lowest food rations in Europe. The present basic calorie ration is 1,700 per day as compared with a prewar food consumption level of 2,900. Currently 60 percent of Austria's basic food ration comes from the US. Any delay or interruption in receipt of food from abroad would reduce the ration to approximately 820 calories per day.

Austria's industrial production stands between 50 and 60 percent of the 1937 level, but Soviet withdrawals from current production reduce still further the output available to the Austrian people. Revival of industry has been retarded primarily by the difficulty Austria has encountered in obtaining minimum hard coal requirements, although the supply has increased markedly during the past six months Most of such anthracite as has been obtained has come from the Ruhr and Poland and could be bought only because it was subsidized by the US. (Substantial quantities of brown coal, produced in the western zones, cannot substitute for hard coal.)

Although the crippling effect of zonal partition has diminished in the past year, Austria's potential for economic recovery is severely handicapped by the Soviet monopoly in key industries, its appropriation of current industrial production for shipment to the USSR, and its removal of industrial facilities from the eastern zone. Although current oil extraction is at a highly excessive rate, increasingly smaller amounts are being made available for Austria.

The eastern zone includes all of the Austrian oil fields and refineries, the industries manufacturing railroad equipment, heavy and light electrical equipment, machine tools, as well as important chemical factories, and automotive and related industries. The rich farming land that formerly produced 60 percent of all agricultural commodities produced in Austria also lies in the Soviet Zone.

In the three western zones are located the forests and the iron deposits, all the hydroelectric potential, pig iron and crude steel production capacity, the nitrogen, staple fiber, and aluminum plants, and the largest antifriction bearing factory in Central Europe, outside Germany.

The USSR not only has a monopolistic position in oil, heavy electrotechnical equipment, Danube shipping, heavy cables and dyestuffs, but it operates these key industries, seized in the eastern zone as German assets, as an effective instrument of economic penetration in the western zones. These industries, which are largely exempt from any form of control by the Austrian Government, have been systematically used by the USSR to influence the parts of the Austrian economy it cannot control directly: by means of forcing delivery of raw materials and finished products from the western zones to the Soviet Zone through carefully placed orders, and by tying up Austrian production capacity. This latter is accomplished, on a presently reduced scale, by keeping industrial facilities busy processing raw materials furnished by the Soviet Administration which in turn collects the finished goods.

Although the Administration of Soviet Assets in Austria (USIA), which operates these industries, has made large profits primarily through black market operations, the Soviet economic position in Austria is reportedly now less strong than it has been at any previous time. This decreased activity in Soviet-controlled plants is attributed to Soviet inability to operate the firms in a competitive economy, to reluctance to make capital investments for replacement of obsolete equipment, and to general shortages of raw materials. Soviet moves to integrate USIA enterprises with the economies of the Satellite bloc have apparently been abandoned. The loss of these enterprises, however, is highly detrimental to the Austrian economy, which receives no compensation for the products and raw materials shipped to the USSR or for the finished goods, critically needed at home, bartered by USIA to get raw materials from Czechoslovakia and Yugoslavia.

The actual potential of Austrian industry cannot be gauged by pre-Anschluss characteristics, and, until the future relationship of the USSR to the Austrian economy has been established, cannot be assessed with accuracy. Austria's industrial capacity, especially because of developments in petroleum and hydroelectric power, was expanded and diversified during the Anschluss, but exploitation of this potential has not yet been possible. The new industrial capabilities will require development abroad of new markets and supplies of raw materials; at the same time, Austria could produce important new industrial wares for home consumption and sale abroad in exchange for the needed raw materials.

By means of bilateral agreements with both western and eastern European countries, Austria has revived some international trade. Since 1946 the country's leading trade partners have been Switzerland, Czechoslovakia, and Italy, followed by other Western countries. Arrangements were completed recently for limited trade with the US-UK Zones of Germany. Although the immediate foreign trade outlook is poor, Austria's natural resources and increased industrial potential are sufficient to support foreign trade above the 1937 level, given rehabilitation and restored control of industrial capacity. Under improved conditions in general European trade, there is a reasonable prospect that Austria could balance its exports against its imports within a few years, meanwhile contributing exports of electric power, timber, and magnesite to the European Recovery Program.

Present meager foreign trade does not reflect Austria's expanded industrial capacity. While in 1947 Austria imported approximately $138 million worth of food and other relief supplies and $152 million in agricultural and industrial goods, it exported raw materials and industrial products totaling about $83 million. Serious deficits are expected to continue at least four years.

In the fiscal year 1948/49, Austria will require approximately 5 317 million in assistance to cover an anticipated balance-of-payments deficit. Under ERP it is probable that Austria as a whole will require assistance in excess of $1 billion during the next four years. Even with outside aid and a reasonable solution of its occupation difficulties, it is unlikely that Austria can expect any great improvement in its basic economy within the next four years. Agricultural recovery will be especially slow. Industrial replacement parts, machinery, and tools must be imported, as well as raw materials. The solution of all these problems depends on the extent to which Austria is successfully absorbed into the economy of Western Europe, or forced into subordination to the USSR, or is able to integrate its economy independently with Europe as a whole.

Military Situation

Currently, Austria has no military forces, and its 26,000 police are inadequately equipped and armed. Terms of the Austrian treaty will condition the eventual pattern of Austria's national defense policy. In the meantime, the four occupying powers have agreed on a ceiling of 53,000 men for the future Austrian Army, and 5,000 for the Austrian Air Force, with a top limitation of 90 planes. While Austrian leaders wish to have an adequate defense force available when the treaty becomes effective, they recognize that, as in the past, only international guarantees, backed by active support of major foreign powers, can assure Austrian territorial integrity and political independence.

At the end of March 1948, the occupation forces had the following strengths:

The USSR had 46,000 men broken down as follows: ground forces, 33,000 (2 divisions); air forces, 9,000 (100 fighters, 300 bombers, 50 other types); navy, 1,500; security (MVD), 2,500. All Soviet units in Austria are considered battle worthy because of rigorous combat training.

France maintained 5,000 ground force troops. There are no French Air Force units in Austria.

British occupational forces numbered 10,000 men, 5,000 being combat troops. Their occupational duties all but preclude military training. There are no operational Royal Air Force units in Austria.

Probable Future Developments

No drastic changes in the current situation in Austria are expected in the near future. It is unlikely that the USSR will sacrifice its present hold over the economy of Austria in order to reach a treaty settlement with the Western Allies, until the USSR decides that quadripartite occupation is blocking the communization of Austria.

The enthusiasm of both major parties in Austria for an early treaty settlement has been considerably reduced by the Communist coup in Czechoslovakia and by other external evidences of Communist strength, particularly in Italy. Moreover, the problems raised by virtual encirclement of Austria by aggressive Soviet satellite nations are beginning to take precedence in the minds of Austrian leaders over their concern with obtaining withdrawal of the occupation troops. In order, however, to counter Communist propaganda, it is likely that both Parties will continue to agitate publicly for a treaty, although on a reduced scale and with reservations. Under present conditions, the present coalition government will continue unchanged. Although the Socialists are now believed to have sufficient support to win a narrow majority in a new national election, they could not gain a practical working majority in the lower house, and hence are most unlikely in the near future to precipitate a collapse of the government which would call for elections. The negligible role of the Austrian Communists is expected to continue unchanged.

While the USSR would be capable of communizing its zone of occupation by violence or by a forced partition of the country, such moves are unlikely in the near future. From the Soviet point of view a *putsch* would seem undesirable because it would forfeit western Austria to the US, UK, and France. On the other hand, it is probable that a breakdown of the present treaty negotiations would cause the USSR to increase substantially its economic and political pressure on the government.

Under the circumstances, no drastic change in the Austrian economic situation is anticipated, although in the event that shipments of food are interrupted, a major crisis will arise in the food supply position in late May. The slow rise in the level of industry is expected to continue, but Austrian industry cannot be expected to become stable in less than four years.

Possible Developments in Soviet Policy Toward Austria, February 1949*

Document 3 (Source: NA, RG 263, ORE Report 28-49,
10 February 1949, Box 3)
SECRET

The major points of Soviet-Western disagreement concerning an Austrian treaty include: (a) Yugoslav territorial and reparation claims, (b) the lump sum to be paid by the Austrian Government to the USSR for German external assets returned to Austria, and (c) the amount and type of properties to be transferred to the USSR as German external assets.

While no specific supporting evidence is available, it is believed that a more conciliatory Soviet attitude might develop when Austrian treaty discussions are renewed in February. The following factors may prompt the Kremlin to adopt such an approach:

1. In view of Marshal Tito's break with the Cominform, the USSR may, in effect, withdraw Soviet support of the Yugoslav claims at the Big Four level, possibly by proposing that this problem be left to bilateral settlement between Austria and Yugoslavia.
2. In view of past Soviet exploitation of eastern Austria and the fact that further gains under present conditions are unlikely, the USSR may now be willing to compromise on a smaller lump sum for German assets than was originally demanded.
3. In spite of the grave risk involved, the Kremlin may consider that quadripartite withdrawal might improve chances of Communist infiltration into Austria, leading to the establishment of a new regime with greater Communist representation and power.
4. Achievement of an Austrian treaty could be used as the basis for a renewed "peace campaign" by Soviet propagandists.

Even if the forthcoming discussions fail to produce an Austrian treaty, it is doubtful that the USSR will resort to a blockade of Vienna similar to that of Berlin. Such action, while it would probably succeed in forcing the Western Powers and the Austrian Government from Vienna, would entail a risk of war which the Kremlin is not believed willing to assume at the present time. Furthermore, the resulting partition of Austria would be disadvantageous to Soviet economic interests.

Regardless of any tactical moves the Soviets may make with or without a treaty, their ultimate objective will continue to be the establishment of a Soviet-dominated government in Austria, and the integration of that country into the satellite political and economic bloc.

* The intelligence organizations of State, Army, Navy, and the Air Force have concurred in this report. The information herein is as of 13 January 1949.

It is believed that since the suspension of negotiations on the Austrian treaty in May 1948 conditions have changed sufficiently to make a conciliatory attitude on the part of the Soviet Union a distinct likelihood. From a Soviet view it may now appear that advantages to be gained from continued occupation are outweighed by those that would accrue from the conclusion of a treaty.

When the discussions on the Austrian treaty were last suspended, the delegates of the Four Powers had reached tentative agreement on a number of articles of the draft treaty. The major points of disagreement were: (a) Yugoslav territorial and reparation claims, (b) the lump sum to be paid by the Austrian Government to the USSR for German external assets restored to Austria, and (c) the amount and type of properties to be turned over to the USSR as German external assets and the conditions under which they will be exploited. It is believed that a more conciliatory attitude by the Kremlin may now develop, chiefly for the following reasons:

1. In view of the Tito-Cominform rift, the USSR may now be willing to drop support of the Yugoslav claims. In order to strengthen its bargaining and propaganda position, the Soviet Union will probably support the Yugoslav claims initially, but it may be expected to modify its position as negotiations progress, possibly by proposing that this problem be left to bilateral settlement between Austria and Yugoslavia. (The situation may, of course, be complicated by Soviet suspicions of a US-Yugoslav "deal," involving economic concessions to Yugoslavia, and Soviet reluctance to give added impetus to Tito's pro-Western trend.)
2. With regard to the problem of German assets, inasmuch as the Soviet Government has already intensively exploited eastern Austrian economy and can expect little further gain under present conditions, it now may be willing to compromise upon a smaller lump sum for German assets than that originally demanded. It may calculate, furthermore, that the economic rehabilitation of an independent Austria would serve as a bridge over which Western trade would pass to the East, thereby strengthening the potential of Soviet economy.
3. In spite of the grave risk involved of losing Austria completely, the Kremlin may consider that a quadripartite withdrawal might improve chances of Communist infiltration into Austria and eventually lead to the establishment of a new regime in which the Communists would have greater representation and power.
4. The achievement of a compromise on Austria would enable the Kremlin to start a new propaganda campaign in which it would try to prove its "peace intentions," again emphasizing responsibility of the Western Allies for the German impasse.

The USSR, however. will continue to press for restrictions on Austrian armament limitations on the Austrian economy. It will also attempt to prevent the establishment of an independent Austrian Government capable of dealing effectively with internal disorder and to press for extraterritorial status for which would accrue to the USSR in the treaty terms.

Regardless of any tactical moves the Soviets may make with or without a treaty, their ultimate objective will continue to be the establishment of a Soviet-dominated government in Austria, and the integration of that country into the satellite political and economic bloc. The real problem is the means of achieving this end, preferably, in this case, without resort to force.

Thus, as long as the possibility of achieving a settlement on the Austrian treaty exists, the Kremlin will probably avoid any strong action which would disrupt the present quadripartite administration or the basic authority of the Austrian Government. Even though no agreement were reached, however, it is doubtful that the USSR would decide upon partition of Austria, but would rather confine its activities to consolidation of its hold on eastern Austria, increasing interference in internal affairs preferential to Soviet interests, delaying Austrian economic recovery, and more actively supporting the Austrian Communists.

A blockade of Vienna, similar to that of Berlin, is a Soviet capability and may not be entirely discounted. It is, however, considered unlikely. Such a blockade would mean partition of Austria, withdrawal of the Austrian Government to the western zones, and probable withdrawal of the US, UK, and France from Vienna; it would imply denunciation of the Moscow Declaration of November 1943; it would split Austria economically, probably to the benefit of the West, and would open the USSR to more severe UN censure than did the Berlin blockade. To offset such disadvantages, the USSR could hope for little more than somewhat diminished confidence among Western European nations in US protection with the possible consequent growth of unilateralism rather than cooperation in US defense plans; and slightly enhanced Soviet prestige among the Satellites. Finally, the Kremlin would be reluctant at this time to take the risk of war entailed in a blockade of Vienna.

The Current Situation in Austria, August 1949*
Document 4 (Source: NA, RG 263, ORE Report 56-49,
31 August 1949, Box 3)
SECRET

Summary

Austria's strategic importance to the US lies in its contiguity to the Soviet-satellite area, and its status as an occupied country where US and Soviet forces are in direct contact. It is a natural center of east-west and north-south trade. Under present conditions the USSR controls the Danube Valley and uses Austria as a door to trade with the west and as a source of economic gain.

The power of the Austrian Federal Republic is limited by the four-power Allied Commission. The present government, elected in 1945, is a coalition of the People's Party (Catholic and conservative) which has a majority and holds the chancellorship; and the moderate Socialist Party. National elections, scheduled for October, are expected to result in a continuation of the coalition, which is stable and pro-Western. The Communist Party, the only other group to have parliamentary representation, is a negligible influence with virtually no chance of gaining legal power.

The USSR has not seized complete control of the eastern zone, and the general mildness of the occupation has encouraged the Austrians to be outspoken and self-reliant. While a desire for a treaty is paramount, Austrians are concerned over the economic burden they must bear by terms of the treaty, which they are not yet fully convinced will actually be signed.

That Austrian economic recovery since 1945 has been considerable, despite many adverse factors, is a consequence in the first instance, of foreign financial assistance, chiefly from the US-Soviet economic policy still exerts a drag on Austrian recovery. Despite Soviet removal of output from Soviet-seized firms and of two-thirds of oil production, the index over-all industrial production, was 113 in June 1949 (1937=100). Agricultural recovery has been slow, with Austria supplying only about half its rationed food needs. Austria's dependence on foreign assistance is indicated by its 1948-49 dollar area deficits of $229 million, and deficits with other areas totaling $49 million.

Austria's foreign policy revolves around the attempt to obtain a treaty which will assure the country economic independence and restoration of sovereignty. The government must balance its pro-Western leanings against fears of the USSR, and its hope of convincing the USSR of the advantage of an independent Austria. Consequently, although the US exerts the most important

* The intelligence organizations of the Departments of State, Army, Nave, and the Air Force have concurred in this report. It is based on information available to the CIA as of 1 August 1949.

influence on governmental policies, Austria, with calculated self-interest, "cooperates" with the Soviet element in the country.

Internal security rests with the police and gendarmerie (about 26,000 men) in addition to the occupation forces. Under present conditions, internal security appears contingent upon the occupation policies of the USSR. The agreed portion of the treaty provides for an Austrian army of 53,000 and an air force of 5,000. Austria plans to seek authority to begin organization of the army as soon as the treaty is signed. Western authorities are currently developing a gendarmerie regiment as a nucleus for an army, capable of maintaining internal security and safeguarding Austria against all but major encroachments.

Strategic Importance of Austria

Austria is important to US security because of its geographic location and its present occupied status wherein US and Soviet forces are in immediate contact. As the easternmost area of Western influence and the westernmost area of Soviet influence in Europe, Austria is a pivotal point in the East-West struggle. Supported and protected by the Western occupation forces, the pro-Western Austrian Government has cooperated with the United States in the face of Soviet occupation of eastern Austria and Soviet influence in adjacent areas. The fate of Austria, and US policies in regard to it, assume special importance to US security in connection with Western European consolidation, both political and economic, and with strengthening the determination of Western European people to resist Soviet aggression.

Military Aspects

From a military point of view, the strategic importance of Austria lies in its central geographic location, and in its present relationship with the Soviet-satellite area. Austria's own military role, negligible at present, must be limited to that of a defensive force or a component of allied armies. Despite natural barriers to the south and the defensive topography of the western part of the country, Austria's vulnerability to attack over the Hungarian plain in the east and the Bavarian plain in the north makes impracticable any defense against strong invasions from those directions. At the same time, the Danubian valley represents the natural gateway to south-central Europe as well as the natural entrance to the Balkan peninsula. The current predominance of Soviet occupation forces in Austria, and the Soviet position in the Danubian valley, results in effective Soviet control of Austria's natural gateway at the present time.

Economic Aspects

From an economic point of view, Austria's strategic importance to the US lies largely in its position as a transit center for east-west as well as north-south transit. Despite present limitations on over-all international trade, and the prohibitions on east-west Danube shipping in Austria, Austria's position as an important transportation artery is revealed by the extent of shipments—particularly east-west shipments—presently crossing the country. In addition, Austria is not only an important producer of hydroelectric power but also one of the most important potential sources of such power in Western Europe. Existing power facilities make it impossible for Austria to produce more than 20 percent of its potential annual output of 25 billion kwh; further development of this resource will enable Austria to increase greatly its power exports. Of other natural resources, magnesite and timber furnish considerable exportable surpluses. Austrian oil production, now under complete Soviet control, must be supplemented by imports because Soviet allocations have fallen far short of Austrian needs. Even under optimum conditions, however, Austrian oil resources, although substantial, are of limited strategic value. Other natural resources, the most important of which is high quality iron ore, are largely consumed by domestic industries.

Importance to USSR

The importance of Austria to the USSR is primarily a matter of geographic location. In extending its influence beyond the present satellite perimeter, the Soviet Union can exert considerable influence within Austria through the Soviet occupation forces. Either by continuing the occupation, or by specific treaty terms, the USSR can maintain that influence or, at least, neutralize Austria as a potentially active and integral part of Western European economic, political, and defensive planning. Currently, Austria has an additional importance to the USSR as a source of economic gain and as a door to east-west trade which is denied the Soviet areas from other sources. While the course of action which the USSR will follow toward Austria is still uncertain, at present it is unlikely that the Soviet Union intends to partition the country. Soviet decision in this respect would presumably be determined largely by its over-all European strategy which is presently directed toward avoiding a risk of war and increasing east-west trade rather than by the negligible factors involved in the local Austrian situation.

Political Situation

The power of the Austrian Government is subject to the limitations imposed by the Allied Commission (AC) composed of the four occupying powers. A Control Agreement in 1946 defined the position of the government and permitted its authority to extend throughout the country, subject to certain reservations. The most important provision of the Agreement stipulates that only constitutional laws require unanimous AC approval and that other legislation may go into effect automatically if the AC fails to act upon it unanimously within 31 days. Other provisions leave certain important matters subject to the jurisdiction of each zonal commander. Despite several noteworthy exceptions, the USSR has, in general, lived up to the specific stipulations of the Agreement. Soviet officials have, however, interpreted some clauses to authorize the Soviet zone commander to extend his control to cover phases of the Austrian economy not contemplated by other parties to the Agreement.

The Constitution

The validity of the Austrian Constitution, essentially that of 1929, rests solely on the authority of a law passed by the Provisional Government in 1945 and later approved by the AC. No permanent legislation enacted by the elected parliament exists. Despite an AC request (pushed through by the Soviet element) that the parliament submit a new permanent Constitution, the government, instead, announced its adherence to the 1929 Constitution. Sporadic Soviet reminders that the AC directive has not been complied with have so far failed to influence the Austrian Government. While the USSR could challenge the constitutional validity of the government, the Soviet legal position would be weak. Such a challenge is likely only should the USSR decide to take unilateral action outside the AC. Such action would extend far beyond constitutional considerations.

The Government

Within the framework of the Control Agreement and its Constitution, Austria functions as a federal republic of nine provinces. Provision is made for a federal president, a national government headed by a federal chancellor, a national parliament consisting of two houses, and provincial governors and governments. The provinces reserve far-reaching prerogatives and members of the Upper House (largely a rubber-stamp body) of the national parliament are elected by the provincial assemblies. The 165 members of the Lower House are elected by popular vote for four-year terms. Candidates, however, are elected only as names on lists drawn up by political parties, thus the voters choose a party, not an individual, and the primacy of political parties leads to voting on strict party lines, in both national elections and parliamentary debate. Indeed, before taking their seats in parliament, elected representatives submit undated letters of resignation to their party secretariat.

The present government, elected in 1945, is in the hands of the two large parties working as a coalition. The conservative People's Party, which is under the influence of the Catholic Church, has 85 deputies in the Lower House and 7 cabinet ministries; the moderate Socialist Party controls 76 deputies and 6 cabinet posts. (As the majority party, the People's Party fills the position of Chancellor.) Because almost all issues are decided between these parties before any measure is presented to parliament, parliamentary debate and criticism are rare and the voting is easily predicted. The far-reaching polarization of political life in Austria results in a virtual absence of independent pressure groups; these are represented within the parties and such interests rarely cross party lines. For example, the People's Party represents primarily the interests of the Chambers of Commerce and Agriculture, while the Socialists represent chiefly the Chamber of Labor and the Trade Union Federation (about 69 percent of all wage and salary earners). The Communist Party, the only other party able to gain parliamentary seats in 1945, received 5.4 percent of the vote and 4 seats in parliament.

Austrian Communists

The Austrian Communist Party is a negligible influence in the government, has virtually no chance of assuming legal control, and functions solely as a tool of Soviet policy. Popular recognition of the Communists' subservience to Moscow has contributed greatly to the continuing strong control of labor by the Socialists. On the other hand, the Communist Party has an importance out of proportion to its actual strength because Soviet backing gives it an influence in business and labor, and to some extent in lesser political positions, which would not otherwise exist. While there is scant possibility that the Communists, without Soviet assistance, could execute a successful *putsch* in eastern Austria and in Vienna situated within the Soviet Zone the chances of sustaining a coup in the Soviet Zone are considerably better than in Vienna. In Vienna, which is subject to quadripartite occupation, intervention by the Western Powers could probably negate such an attempt unless the USSR determined upon active assistance in attempt to overthrow the government. At present, as in the past four years, the USSR has the capability to seize complete control of the eastern zone and partition the country.

Political Aspects of Occupation

Quadripartite occupation, which is entering its fifth year, remains the most important consideration of the Austrian political scene. Stemming from this factor are the present stability of the federal government, the pro-Western attitude of the government and the people, the general distrust of the Communist Party, and the limitations on economic recovery. Some 90 percent of the population support the policies of the coalition government in its limited cooperation with the Soviet element within the country, in its considerable cooperation with, and reliance on, the US, and in its efforts to obtain a reasonable treaty. At the same time, the relative mildness of the occupation has encouraged outspokenness by the Austrians and has engendered a feeling of self-reliance which otherwise might not be so pronounced. In addition, the difficulties resulting from the occupation and from Austria's struggle to recover from Anschluss with Germany and the economic set-backs suffered during the war have created a spirit of nationalism which had been missing from the Austrian Republic from its inception in 1919. Both the unpopular policies of the Soviet Union and Austria's own economic ills serve to weld the coalition parties and the population into a stable front.

Coming Elections

The same coalition is expected to continue governing Austria after the national elections, scheduled for October. Although the addition of over 800,000 new voters, largely ex-Nazis who have received amnesty, will undoubtedly strengthen the Right, participation of new political parties (an issue on which legal confusion exists) would tend to splinter Rightist strength. The conservative People's Party is a heterogeneous organization, and the Socialists, more tightly organized, would, therefore, gain in overall political power by a splintering of Rightist strength. Should no new parties participate, the People's Party appears likely to retain its lead. Even with new parties it might hold a slim majority, because only one new group appears to be of any importance and it is still an uncertain organization which may yet be effectively countered by the People's Party. The Communist Party, even joined by a small group of left-wing Socialists, appears unlikely to develop new strength proportionate to the increased electorate, and its present representation in parliament may prove difficult to maintain. The present lack of official and definitive clarification regarding the participation of new parties (the confusion stems from a 1945 AC decision which reserved to the AC the right to recognize new parties) may present the Soviet element with an opportunity to challenge the elections or the legitimacy of the next government. Despite a Soviet desire to disrupt present coalition cooperation and strength, however, there are no present indications that the Soviet element will attempt to prevent the elections or intends to challenge their legality.

Treaty Considerations

Austrian reaction to the recent CFM agreements has been one of cautious optimism. Initial enthusiasm over the definitive separation of the Austrian from the German problem, and over the instructions to the deputies writing the treaty, has diminished somewhat with the realization of the economic burden which Austria must assume and the prolonged technical discussions which must precede treaty agreement. Previous disappointments over failure to write a pact, moreover, discourage complete belief that a treaty will actually be signed. Austrians are agreed, nevertheless, that the present efforts to effect a treaty give greater promise of success than any previous attempts.

Economic Situation

The Austrian economy is based equally on industry and agriculture and is greatly dependent upon foreign trade because, for example, about one-half of the food and most of the industrial coal must be imported. While the country's prewar economic characteristics were altered by developments during the Anschluss with Nazi Germany, these changes have not been entirely disadvantageous. Agricultural production suffered heavily during German domination, but it can be returned to previous levels of output; and German-built industrial and power installations are already contributing to the economy. On balance the country appears to have no less capability of becoming self-sustaining now than before the war.

Economic Recovery

Economic recovery since 1945 in the fields of both production and consumption has been considerable despite such adverse factors as over-exploitation of resources, war-damage, and dislocations resulting from war; unusual foreign and domestic marketing problems; the loss of foreign credits formerly derived from shipping, tourism, and foreign investments; and Soviet removals of equipment and current output. The primary positive factors in this recovery have been (in order of importance): the financial assistance extended to the country (through UNRRA and the ECA) chiefly by the US; the four powers' agreement to restore Austria as an independent state; and the flexibility and determination evidenced in Austrian recovery efforts.

The danger existed in the early days of the occupation that the Soviet authorities, through control of important industries and certain agricultural areas in the Soviet Zone, would be able to manipulate the production facilities of the entire economy for their own purposes. Although this threat has greatly diminished, Soviet economic policy continues to exert a drag on the Austrian economy and delays economic recovery.

Industrial Production

The index of industrial production rose from 44 in March 1947 (1937=100) to about 113 in June 1949. Electric power output reached 4.2 billion kilowatt-hours in 1948, as compared with 3.2 billion kilowatt-hours in 1947. Four main branches of industry—mining, metallurgy, machinery and equipment, and chemicals have recently been producing well above 1937 levels. Consumer goods industries, on the other hand, are operating at much lower rates.

A large amount of the production of about 300 firms seized by the Soviet authorities in the spring of 1946 as German external assets is taken out of Austria without compensation. These firms are producers primarily of electrical and mechanical goods and generally operate independently of Austrian laws on prices, wages, foreign trade and other economic matters. The government has obtained, however, a portion of the output of the seized plants for distribution throughout Austria in return for allocations of government-controlled raw and semi-finished materials. About two-thirds of the oil produced (total production in 1948 was estimated at around 900,000 MT) is removed from the Austrian economy by Soviet authorities.

The ECA program for 1949-50, calling for US assistance totaling $197 million (plus the equivalent of approximately $41 million from other countries), should make possible further increases, though modest, in industrial production. ECA-financed capital goods, scheduled for import during the next twelve months, make it physically possible eventually to increase the emphasis on the processing of indigenous resources and imported semi-finished materials, and thus permit a reduction in expenditures for imported finished goods without impairing the Austrian economy.

Agricultural Production

Agricultural recovery has been retarded by lack of seeds, fertilizers, fodder, and equipment as well as by the necessity to return to cultivation land which was allowed to remain unproductive during the war. Only about 50 percent of the present daily ration of 2,100 calories is being met from indigenous production; prewar Austrian production supplied 75 percent of a much higher caloric intake, but for a somewhat smaller population. As a result of this slow agricultural recovery, a disproportionate amount of ECA assistance has been spent for foodstuffs. (Food imports in 1948-49 are estimated at $149 million; ECA assistance at $215 million.) Because the Soviet Zone is the "breadbasket" of Austria, the question of equitable distribution of food throughout Austria arose early in the occupation period. It was solved by four-power agreement requiring all food, both domestic and imported, to be pooled for distribution by the Austrian Government. While the people are better fed now than at any other time since the war, governmental reliance on relief imports has tended to retard vigorous prosecution of agricultural development programs and collection of food quotas from the farmers since the majority People's Party, relying on rural support, has been careful to avoid antagonizing these voters. Increasing faith in the schilling has helped improve deliveries of farm products in recent months, and with the best crop since the end of the war in prospect, the ECA has scaled down the government's estimate of required food imports for 1949-50.

Transportation

The railroads are the primary facility in Austrians transportation system; road and water transport are currently unimportant. For Austrian purposes, Danube shipping is at standstill since no craft—Austrian or otherwise—moves east or west beyond the Soviet zonal demarcation line below Linz. With this exception, zonal restrictions do not seriously curtail inland transportation. Soviet authorities have imposed some restrictions on interzonal trade. For the most part these restrictions have served only to delay shipments. The Austrian railroads have greatly improved their operating efficiency since 1937, as indicated by about a 40 percent increase in tonkilometers of freight in 1948 compared to the earlier period. Nevertheless rail facilities include some obsolete and worn-out equipment and makeshift structures. Recent increases in rail rates and in tons carried will about cover operating deficits, but most capital replacements and improvements can only be effected through ECA funds. Soviet removals of rolling stock have not seriously affected operations to date, but further removals of Soviet-marked equipment would reduce Austrian transit capacity.

Unemployment

Unemployment in Austria today is a relatively unimportant problem and the largest laboring force since 1919 is at work. Unemployment over the past year, however, rose from about 51,000 persons in June 1948 to around 100,000 persons in April 1949 or to about 4 percent of the total working population.

There is, nevertheless, still a shortage of skilled workmen as well as a need for approximately 35,000 workers in agriculture. As a result of the increased unemployment, Austrian labor unions have recently sought to tighten labor laws in order to protect themselves from the 231,000 aliens in the Austrian labor force. These alien workers in Austria, however, are contributing greatly to Austrian reconstruction in every field, particularly agriculture. Unemployment can be expected to remain at about 4 percent of the total working population during the next twelve months.

Foreign Exchange

Austria's foreign balance of payments shows clearly the country's dependence on foreign assistance. The total foreign deficit on current account is estimated at the equivalent of $78 million for 1948-49 and at $230 million in 1949-50 (ECA estimates). The largest part of these deficits is with the dollar area: in 1948-49 the dollar area deficit was about $229 million, as against $49 million deficit with all other areas; estimated deficit for 1949-50 is $197 million, as against $41 million. Before the Anschluss invisibles netted considerable foreign credits (in 1937 about 15 percent of total credits on current account); now there is a small invisibles deficit. Merchandise trade, however, shows a heavy deficit estimated at $267 million in 1948-49, imports totaling $466 million and exports 5199 million. The merchandise trade deficit for 1949-50 is expected to decline to $220 million. Although there has been some growth in volume of commercial trade (which excludes imports financed by foreign assistance), commercial imports are not yet covered by commercial exports. Consequently it seems clear that even if the government's planned rate of economic improvement is attained, substantial foreign assistance will continue to be necessary for sometime unless current standards of living are reduced.

Foreign Trade

The revival of foreign trade has been retarded by the demands of the reconstruction program, the loss of German markets, political conditions in the satellite area, and changes in Austria's industrial structure and capacity. These factors have forced Austria to seek a different and more diversified trade pattern than that which prevailed before the war. About 70 percent of the currently expanding trade is with Western Europe and overseas countries; official trade with Eastern Europe has not attained its prewar relative importance and appears unlikely to do so in the near future. (The Soviet element, however, through its industrial properties seized in Austria, directs a flow of extralegal trade to the satellite areas and, in return, receives products which are frequently placed on the Austrian black market.) Compensation or barter transactions resulting from the acute postwar shortage of foreign exchange, are only slowly giving way to more flexible bilateral trade treaties and clearing arrangements.

The Fiscal Situation

Inflationary pressure has continued to be an important problem in spite of the two currency reforms since the liberation of the country. Budgetary deficits (amounting to 1,300 million schillings in 1948) caused mainly by payments to defray the costs of occupation and other extra-budgetary expenditures, and the release of blocked bank accounts, counteracted the reduction in the money supply resulting from the currency reforms. On the other hand, ECA counterpart funds in the amount of 1,450 million schillings were used in 1948 to cancel an equal amount of government debt held by the Austrian National Bank, thus contributing to a further stability of the currency.

A deficit of approximately two billion schillings was originally budgeted for 1949 as a result of: shrinking of revenues from the state tobacco monopoly (about $450 million) and additional expenditures such as a thirteenth month's payment to all federal employees, totaling about $300 million; increased social insurance payments, estimated at $300 million; and the need to finance extraordinary expenditures amounting to about $400 million owing to the smaller amounts available from ECA counterpart funds than originally expected. Furthermore, a payment of about $600 million occupation cost will be required in 1949 which the Austrian Government expected would be eliminated. Partly in an effort to bring the budget into balance, a far-reaching wage-price fiscal agreement was enacted into law in June 1949 and is now being implemented,

The new measures provide for a stoppage of all Federal government subsidies on such items as coal, public utilities, transportation, and food as well as an increase in taxation, customs duties, and public utilities and transportation tariffs. A 5 percent internal loan was authorized to cover the remaining deficit estimated at 400 to 700 million schillings. In partial compensation for the expected increase in the cost of living (official index) a general wage and salary increase was ordered, amounting to about 8.5 percent. Despite this increase, real wages have declined, although the set-back has been mitigated by increased variety of consumer goods.

It is hoped that a sound fiscal policy and the general tendency of world prices to decline will put a brake on further price rises. In this connection it is to be noted that the black market exchange rate of the schilling continues to show strength. As a result of these measures a considerable improvement in the over-all budgetary situation is now in prospect, although a deficit still seems probable.

The cost-of-living index rose about 20 percent between July 1948 and June 1949. Derationing of many items, a sharp drop in black market prices, and increased supplies of consumer goods, however, tended to cushion the effects of the cost rise. These factors are not reflected in the cost-of-living index. The standard of living, nevertheless, is still low. The new wage-price-tax program, as suggested above, will tend to raise the cost-of-living index from present levels, by an estimated 7 percent. On balance, however, it does not appear that this will put workers in a worse position than last fall.

Foreign Policy

Austria's foreign policy is irrevocably bound up with its efforts to obtain a treaty which will assure its economic independence and restore its sovereignty. In these efforts, the government must balance its pro-Western leanings and reliance on US economic aid and political support against fears of Soviet intentions and the necessity of convincing the USSR that a neutral and independent Austria can be a beneficial factor in the East-West struggle. Within the confines of this policy, Austria remains largely concerned with its own problems and the prevention of any deterioration in the present *status quo* within the country. To this end, it subjugates both its desire for closer economic and political integration with Western Europe and its antipathy to the USSR; Austria will continue to pursue this policy as long as any hope remains for obtaining a treaty or as long as such a policy promises to prevent the Iron Curtain from coming down on the eastern zone of the country.

Relations with US and USSR

Because of the limitations, both self-imposed and created by the Control Agreement, Austrian relations with the US and the USSR constitute the most important aspects of Austrian foreign policy. Whereas the US has endeavored to strengthen the position of the government and has contributed greatly to Austria's economic recovery, the USSR has sought to curtail the authority of the government and deprive Austria of economic resources. Austrians sometimes take US aid for granted and are not above playing one group against the other for some immediate benefit; nevertheless, the US continues to be the most important influence in government policies. With the USSR, Austria follows a careful, calculated policy of self-interest ln "cooperating" with the Soviet element within the country, and attempts on the international scene to maintain a neutral position. Above all, Austrians are displaying an increasing impatience with the occupation, with "liberation," and with their own inability to improve their position.

Relations with UK and France

Because the British and French have been unable to make the financial contributions that the US has made, and do not represent the military threat that the USSR presents, their present influence is small. Austria's relations with both countries and with their occupation forces are satisfactory, however. Relations between the British Labor Party and the Austrian Socialist Party, in particular, are fairly close. Sensitive over their country's position as a pawn in the East-West conflict, Austrians are envious of Italy's status and the improving status of Western Germany but are eager to achieve even limited security in cooperation with the Western European nations. Any appreciable shift in Austria's foreign policy and in its relations with other nations is dependent upon changes in its occupied status and in definitive changes in the East-West struggle.

Internal Security

Internal security within Austria rests not only upon the police and gendarmerie (some 200,000 men) but also upon the presence of the occupation forces who have, to date, exerted a restraining influence upon any disturbing elements. The Communists enjoy an artificial importance by virtue of the Soviet occupation forces but the USSR has given no evidence of desiring an overt attempt to disrupt internal security--possibly because active Soviet support of the Communists would threaten partition of the country and because the Western Powers could effectively control any such attempt in the Western zones. On the other hand, the coalition parties, united in opposition to the Communist-Soviet threat, have sub-merged the old enmities which caused the democratic regime to collapse and are working together. Should the occupation end and the present importance of the Communists dwindle, the possibility of strife between the People's Party and the Socialists might well represent the greatest danger to internal security. Under present conditions, however, the continuation of the stable internal situation appears contingent upon the occupation policies of the USSR. Communist para-military organizations and Soviet-controlled *Werkschutz* (factory guards) do not constitute a serious threat to internal security, either now or following quadripartite troop withdrawal, provided that no large-scale aggression is launched from Soviet-controlled areas.

The Armed Forces

Austria has been demilitarized and demobilized by quadripartite action. At present, it has no armed forces.

The agreed terms of the draft treaty provide for an army of 53,000, including gendarmerie, and an air force of 5,000. Although the government is officially prohibited from planning for this future army, the two major political parties have recently reached agreement on its essential features and the government plans to seek Allied permission to begin organization of the army on the date the treaty is signed. Should this be agreed, Austria would have more than the 90 days, the period between ratification of the treaty and the withdrawal of occupation forces, to get at least an army of 20 to 30,000 into being. In order to facilitate a more rapid army organization, and mitigate any possibility that an Austrian force capable of maintaining internal security would not be immediately available following quadripartite troop withdrawal, western occupation authorities are currently engaged in training and equipping a gendarmerie regiment in the Western zones. This force could form the nucleus for the future army.

Despite the possibility of some political differences over the composition and organization of the future army, it will be capable of maintaining internal security and of safeguarding Austria's frontier against all but major encroachments. Because Austria would be incapable of resisting major aggression, long-term national security can be found only in collective arrangements or guarantees by the great powers. Such guarantees will probably be sought from the Western Powers; Austrian participation in collective arrangements is unlikely so long as the country is immediately exposed to retaliation by the USSR.

Research Note: My Files at the Czech Ministry of the Interior Archives, Prague, May 1995

Radomír Luža

Since the collapse of the communist regime in Eastern Europe, I have been eager to consult the communist security files from the period of 1948-90, a period called the era of the Third Resistance in the Czech Republic (the first having begun in 1914 and the second in 1939 against Nazi Germany). My request for a permit to consult the files deposited in the archives was approved on 4-5 October 1994, by the Deputy Minister of the Interior, Martin Fendrych, and the Minister of the Interior, Jan Ruml. The Director of the Archives, Jan Frolík, informed me about the decision on 15 February 1995. At that time he indicated that there were *three* groups of files concerning my post-1948 activities in the communist era:

1. Files covering the period from 1948 to about 1954 that were not completely destroyed.
2. A special "Action Meadow" (*Louka*) run against me by the Czechoslovak Foreign Intelligence (CFI) since the end of the 1950s. Unfortunately, only brief lists remain. They give dates and summaries of internal memos and reports with cover names for reporting informers.
3. A third file, under the cover name "Radomír," was opened by the Czechoslovak Counterintelligence on 3 January 1985 and destroyed by them on 6 December 1989.

The first set of files are incomplete, and contain reports regarding my background, my role in the anti-Nazi Resistance, and depositions by some of my friends regarding their contact and relationship with me prior to my leaving the country in March 1948. There are police reports on my activities in Austria, Switzerland, and France during the years 1948-50. I had already consulted some of the CFI reports on my activities in Paris in 1949-51, which had been reported to the CFI by Josef Damián, then a state security agent in Paris and now a retired Colonel of State Security. Dr. Václav Kvasnička, former press attaché of the Czechoslovak Embassy and Deputy Resident of the CFI in Vienna from 1960-64, in 1994 published a book entitled *A Drug Called Espionage*.[1] In it, he reports that the Prague CFI devoted special attention to two social democratic leaders:

> Bohumil Laušman (who had been kidnapped from Austria in December 1953) and Radomír Luža. (CFI) had complete knowledge about their whereabouts....Luža had been expelled on February 29th, 1948 in Prague from all public functions by the Central Action Committee (of the National Front)...he left for Vienna...and settled in the USA in 1953 where he completed his studies of history at New York University. The topic of his dissertation was the transfer of the Sudeten Germans. Luža drew the attention of the Czechoslovak Intelligence by his unorthodox approach to the postwar development. He was known to have preserved his warm feelings toward his fatherland and to have been disturbed by the political development in West Germany. The Czechoslovak Intelligence had for several years good knowledge of his activities as well as of his views. It never succeeded in coming close to him. And one kidnapping was already enough.[2]

The last chairman of the Social Democratic Party, B. Laušman, had been drugged and kidnapped from Salzburg by the CFI in December 1953.

The second set of files, despite their fragmentation and the complete absence of some documents, present a detailed picture of the CFI's surveillance. Even the meager lists of report summaries and memos provide insight into the workings of the CFI. "Action Meadow" was a vast CFI operation conducted against me in Vienna. It had begun in New York at the end of the 1950s. My trip to Vienna was reported to Prague by the CFI Resident in the United States, Miloš Vejvoda, who was working at the Czechoslovak UNO Mission in New York. I lived in Vienna from 1960 to 1966 and was politically active at the International Union of the Socialist Youth (IUSY), a social democratic youth international, with its headquarters in Vienna. I discussed our activities in the *History of the International Socialist Youth Movement*, published in Holland under the auspices of the European Council in 1970.

Because of my work in Vienna, Prague apparently considered me to be one of the centerpieces of anti-communist political warfare. I was stunned to learn that "Action Meadow" lists alone contained 538 reports concerning my activities and views. By 1965, the CFI had put me under surveillance, duplicated my house keys, entered my apartment at Sonnenweg 113, Vienna XIV, installed listening devices (*Grundig*), rented a small flat nearby to service its operation, and made strenuous efforts to learn as much as possible about me and my work. The CFI regularly used twenty-five informers. Almost all my Czech and Austrian acquaintances who spoke Czech were working for the CFI while they pretended to be my friends. This large-scale CFI operation was run jointly with the Hungarian security organs since 1964. In 1965 I called on an expert to check for listening devices in my Vienna home. After an inspection that lasted ninety minutes, he assured me that my apartment was clean. Luckily, my Czech social life was only marginally political, and the CFI could not learn anything valuable since my activity was public and I had nothing much to hide. Moreover, my previous underground resistance experiences had made me aware that any friend or associate could be a potential CFI agent. I never suspected, however, the vastness of the "Action Meadow" which had a network of twenty-five informers (all with cover names) in addition to Jiří Stárek, the Czechoslovak cultural attaché in Vienna, and a few other operators who allegedly worked under their real names.

The CFI operation was aggressive, well-concealed, and professional. It was an ambitious commitment of human and material resources. Late in 1967, the Communist regime had set up mobile exhibits which featured hostile activities undertaken against the regime. Two special displays focused on two of its main adversaries. One exhibited the publication *Svědectví* which was edited in Paris by Pavel Tigrid. The other displayed copies of the Czech *IUSY Bulletin* and information about me and the Vienna IUSY secretariat. By setting "Action Meadow" apart as a "particularly refined kind of ideological diversion," the regime gave it special attention. The purpose of our activities was to destabilize the communist regime in Czechoslovakia while lending support to its internal liberalization through reforms. Our targets were reform-minded members of the Communist Party (CP). Through numerous contacts and publications we succeeded in bringing about dialogue with CP liberal elements. This was political and psychological warfare at its best. In 1961 we started publishing an *IUSY Bulletin* in Czech and clandestinely distributed some 2-3,000 copies in Czechoslovakia.

The third file about me, "Radomír," was concerned with my efforts to legalize the existence of the Czechoslovak Social Democratic Party. In the 1970s, we had contacts in Czechoslovakia; by 1985, with the help of Prěmysl Janýr, we launched, in Vienna, a social democratic bulletin, *Korespondence*, which was distributed illegally throughout Czechoslovakia. This was a deliberate continuation of IUSY activities, but under the new conditions of the era of normalization. "Radomír" also dealt with an array of contacts I had with reform-minded and not-so-reform-minded CP members who had been given materials about the international situation and the activities of other European socialist parties.

I am still surprised and saddened by the realization that I had been betrayed for so many years by twenty-five so-called friends who still live in Vienna. After I am able to obtain additional relevant files, both "Action Meadow" and "Radomír" should develop into a fascinating story.

NOTES

1. Václav Kvasnička, *Droga zvaná špionáž* (Prague: 1994).

2. Ibid.

Research Note:
German and Austrian Losses in World War II

Rüdiger Overmans

Why did the Austrians cope better with World War II? At a glance this question may seem amazing because it causes one to wonder in what way the Austrians coped better. The answer is simple: the death rate of Austrian soldiers in the *Wehrmacht* was significantly lower than the death rate of their German comrades. This finding is the result of a project designed to calculate German military losses in World War II.[1] To understand the problem completely it is necessary to describe the origin and development of this project that started with a simple question: how many German soldiers died in World War II?

By researching the literature regarding German military losses, I learned that the estimates ranged from three to seven million deaths—a discrepancy that led me to wonder whether there is any precise figure. Astonishingly there had never been an attempt to establish correct numbers, which suggested that the figures in German publications are not statements describing reality but metaphors for "many uncounted dead."[2] Realizing this, I began the search for unknown statistics or databases that were still unpublished or unexamined.

Since almost no literature existed, it first was necessary to research the methods of documenting and clearing up the fate of soldiers in World War II.[3] In the *Wehrmacht* there were several different ways of reporting casualties. The first group were numbers reported by military units or medical personnel, but they never agreed with each other. This way of reporting stopped in December 1944/January 1945 because of the collapse of the *Wehrmacht*. Because these statistics do not cover the last, bloodiest phase of the war and the fate of the prisoners of war, or the missing in action, the *Wehrmacht* statistics can never be accepted as correct figures.[4]

The second but rather little known method of reporting casualties was reporting by name. Each soldier owned a dog tag, and all these were registered. Every change of personal data, every promotion, transfer, injury, disease, or decoration had to be reported by name through different channels to several authorities. In the worst case the company commander had to inform the next of kin about the death of their relative. Especially in the last years of the war many soldiers seemed to have disappeared without such reporting to next of kin. But there was an organization, the *Wehrmachtauskunftstelle* (WAST), which collected all information concerning the fate of all soldiers during and after the war, especially the dead.[5]

Additionally there were other organizations, like the *DRK-Suchdienst* (German Red Cross Tracing Service), that looked for the missing in action, and the *Volksbund Deutsche Kriegsgräberfürsorge* (German Graves Commission), taking care of the graves. The *Wehrmachtauskunftstelle*, founded in 1939, today still has about 700 employees and the assumption seems to be satisfied, that more than 100,000 work years have been spent to build the card files of the *DRK-Suchdienst* in Munich (22 million cards), the WAST (18 million cards), and *DRK-Suchdienst Ost* (in the the former GDR) (15 million cards).

The aim of the project, on which the following analysis is based was to numerically analyze these huge databases. With the end of this project reliable figures concerning German military losses in World War II finally become available. The most important result is that the real losses were not 3-3.5 million deaths as the numerical statistics of the *Wehrmacht* indicate, but about 5.3 million deaths, much more than had been previously estimated.

Within the project not only the absolute number of deaths was examined, but also demographic variables, like region of origin, age, years of entry and death, and circumstances of death, especially theater of operations. Obviously it was impossible to analyze completely the huge databases mentioned above. Therefore two spot check were made from the card files of the *Deutsche Dienststelle* (former WAST). Both samples, the draftees and the deaths, each comprised at least 4,000 cases. This size ensured that a portion of 1 percent was represented in the sample with a confidence interval of

+/- .4 percent points on a 99 percent significance level. The analysis of these data forms the basis of this research note.

In the card files of the *Deutsche Dienststelle* about 17 million German soldiers are documented.

Table 1: Origin of Soldiers (in thousands) by Military Service[6]

	Army	Air Force	Navy	Total
Germany No. Soldiers % of Germans % of Total	 11,083 79 82	 2,029 14 85	 999 7 84	 14,111 100
Austria No. Soldiers % of Austrians % of Total	 1,075 85 8	 165 13 7	 45 4 4	 1,286 100 8
Others No. Soldiers % of Others % of Total	 1,299 80 11	 183 11 8	 149 9 12	 1,631 100 10
Total % Service % of Total	13,457 79 100	2,378 14 100	1,194 7 100	17,029 100

About 17 million men became soldiers of the *Wehrmacht* in the territory of the Deutsches Reich (within its borders of 1937), while only 8 percent were born in Austria. Some differences are worth mentioning. For example, there was a certain concentration of Austrians in the army, but the Austrians were underrepresented in the navy.

Table 2: Death Rates of Soldiers by Regions of Origin[7]

Region of Origin	Male Population	Soldiers		Deaths		
		Absolute	% of population	Absolute	% of number of soldiers	
Germany	33,981	14,111	42	4.080	12	29
Austria	3,378	1,286	38	0.242	7	19
Others	---	1,631		0.454		28
Total		17,029		4.775		28

About 34 million men lived in Germany of which about 14 million—42 percent—became soldiers. More than 4 million died, which is 12 percent of the male population or 29 percent of those who became soldiers. Table 2 also concerns the central question of this essay for it raises an important related question: why was the Austrian death rate lower than the German one? The difference is not marginal. If the Austrian death rate had been as high as the German death rate, then instead of 240,000 deaths there would have been 400,000 deaths, a difference of about 150,000 persons—the population of a city like Salzburg.

Do we have any convincing explanation for this unanticipated statistical finding? The following are some potential explanations:

Thesis 1: The results of the empirical inquiry are unreliable. This cannot be the case. In the 1950s the Austrian census bureau made its own study based on its own data, and its results by and large are in agreement with my inquiry.[8]

Thesis 2: Within the *Wehrmacht* there were concentrations of Austrians in certain units, which predominately were employed in theaters of operation where there was little fighting. First, there was no *Wehrmacht* policy to deploy soldiers from a specific region in certain theaters of operation.[9] But, as Table 1 indicated, there was a certain concentration of Austrians in the army.

Table 3: Death Rates by Region of Origin and Military Service

	Army	Air Force	Navy	Total
Germany % of death rate	11,083,000 32	2,029,000 19	999,000 12	14,111,000 29
Austria % of death rate	1,075,000 19	165,000 20	45,000 9[10]	1,286,000 19

While death rates in the air force and navy are the same for Germans and Austrians, a significant difference can be found in the army death rates. This is the branch where the portion of Austrians is slightly higher. Were there special Austrian units in the army? Originally the personnel replacement system was organized in such a way that every field unit had a replacement unit from which it received its troops. Each replacement unit had its recruiting area. Therefore, in the beginning of the war, "Austrian" units really existed—a situation that the military command fully intended. But this system broke down in the winter of 1941-42, and very soon the units were no longer regionally coherent and homogenous. Did this change have an effect on the death rates?

Table 4: Death Rates by Regions and Years of Entry

	1940 or earlier	1941	1942	1943	1944 or later	Total
Germany Death rate	28	28	34	27	30	29
Austria Death rate	19	16	20	19	24	19

There is a close relationship between the German and the Austrian death rates, but the Austrian ones are consistently almost 50 percent lower. If there had been a regional bias the difference between the German and Austrian death rates could not have been persistently the same. There is no reasonable argument that the different death rates can be explained by a regional bias deriving from personnel or unit deployment policies.

Thesis 3: Austrians were drafted later and/or different age groups were concerned than was the case with Reichs Germans.

Table 5: German and Austrian Soldiers by Age Groups and Years of Entry (in millions)

Age Groups				
Year Born	Germany		Austria	
	Absolute	In %	Absolute	In %
1905 or earlier	2,451	17	220	17
1906-10	2,686	19	187	15
1911-15	3,181	23	282	22
1916-20	2,503	18	216	17
1920 or later	3,290	23	381	30
Total	14,111	100	1,286	100
Years of Entry				
Year of Entry	Germany		Austria	
	Absolute	In %	Absolute	In %
1940 or earlier	7,632	54	541	42
1941	1,957	14	256	20
1942	1,867	13	226	18
1943	1,465	10	154	12
1944 or later	1,190	8	109	8
Total	14,111	100	1,286	100

There are certain differences concerning the years of entry. Generally speaking, within the first years of the war Austrians were drafted less often than Germans, but this deferment was compensated for within the next two years (1941-42). This corresponds with the findings of military historians. In the first years of the war the military recruitment organization did not yet function as well in Austria as it did in Germany; therefore the Austrian not drafted in 1939-40 were drafted in 1941-42.

But is this bias of great importance?

Table 6: *Wehrmacht* Losses by Years of Death

Year of death	Frequency	Percent	Cumulative Frequency	Cumulative Percent
1940 or earlier	97,000	2	97,000	2
1941	328,000	7	425,000	9
1942	543,000	11	969,000	20
1943	767,000	16	1,736,000	36
1944	1,645,000	35	3,382,000	71
1945 or later	1,393,000	29	4,775,000	100

Losses within the first years of the war were very low compared to the later phases of the war. Therefore the effect of the year-of-entry-bias can only be marginal.

The death rate of Austrians in the *Wehrmacht* was considerably lower than that of the Germans. This can be traced back to differentials in the Army where 84 percent of the Austrians served. There is no plausible explanation for this statistical variance from the statistician's perspective but historians surely will find these results of sufficient interest for further speculation.

NOTES

1. Rüdiger Overmans, *Deutsche militärische Verluste im Zweiten Weltkrieg*, in preparation.

2. See Rüdiger Overmans, "Die Toten des Zweiten Weltkriegs in Deutschland: Bilanz der Forschung unter besonderer Berücksichtigung der Wehrmacht - und Vertreibungsverluste," in *Der Zweite Weltkrieg: Analysen, Grundzüge, Forschungsbilanz*, ed. Wolfgang Michalka (Munich: Piper, 1989), 858-73.

3. Some remarks can be found in Rudolf Absolon's *Die Wehrmacht im Dritten Reich*, 5 vols. (Boppard: Harald Boldt, 1969-1989); Kurt W. Böhme, *Gesucht wird...Die dramatische Geschichte des Suchdienstes* (Munich, 1965); Burkhard Müller-Hillebrand, *Das Heer 1933-1945: Entwicklung des organisatorischen Aufbaues*, 3 vols. (Darmstadt: Mittler, 1954-1969).

4. See Müller-Hillebrand, *Das Heer*, vol. 3, 258-61; Overmans, "Bilanz," 861-65.

5. After the war the Americans renamed this organization the "German Agency for Notifications of War-Deaths in Former German Armed Forces to Next of Kin," which later was translated as "*Deutsche Dienststelle für die Benachrichtigung der nächsten Angehörigen von Gefallenen der ehemaligen deutschen Wehrmacht*," hereafter referred to as "*Deutsche Dienststelle*."

6. "Germany" in this table and in the following statements means Germany within its borders of 1937. *Wehrmacht* means soldiers in the army, air force, or navy; civilian employees (*Gefolge*), Waffen-SS, and paramilitary organizations are excluded. Numbers in this and all following tables are rounded to avoid the impression of an exactness that does not exist. All figures are the result of spot checks, only valid on a 99 percent significance level within a certain confidence interval. Because these figures are rounded they do not necessarily total 100 percent.

7. The male population numbers are result of the 1939 census. See Statistisches Reichsamt, ed., *Statistisches Jahrbuch für das Deutsche Reich*, vol. 58 (1939/40), (Berlin, 1940), 7. To give figures for the male population in regions other than Germany and Austria is not convenient, because only in these two regions was the whole male population required to perform military service. In all other regions only volunteers and ethnic Germans—ergo only a part of the male population—had to serve.

8. Minor differences between the inquiry at hand and the results of the Austrian studies can be traced back to differing definitions. The Austrian study included all military dead, while this inquiry only includes *Wehrmacht* losses. See Hansluwka, "Bevölkerungsbilanzen für die österreichischen Bundesländer 1869-1951," in *Statistische Nachrichten* 5 (1959): 194-95; and by the same author, "Totenverluste des zweiten Weltkrieges," in *Statistische Nachrichten* 4 (1955): 146-47. In one article Austrian death rates similar to the German ones are published, but these considerations are based on *Wehrmacht* losses of approximately 3.3 million, which is much too low. See "Die Bevölkerungsverluste Österreichs während des Zweiten Weltkrieges," in *Österreichische Militärische Zeitschrift* 3 (1974): 219-20.

9. Some exceptions are known for the last months of the war, but no Austrians were involved.

10. Frequency is less than 1 percent. This result should be regarded with caution.

Founding Myths and Compartmentalized Past: New Literature on the Construction, Hibernation, and Deconstruction of World War II Memory in Postwar Austria

*Günter Bischof**

"*Warum verhält sich das deutsche Volk angesichts all dieser scheußlichsten menschenunwürdigen Verbrechen so apathisch.*"
(Second Flyer of the "White Rose" Resistance Group, 1943)

"[M]emory privileges piety and consensus over freethinking and criticism. It tends to foreclose discussion rather than to free and encourage it."

Arno J. Mayer[1]

Meinrad Ziegler and Waltraud Kannonier-Finster, *Österreichisches Gedächtnis: Über Erinnern und Vergessen der NS-Vergangenheit* (Vienna: Böhlau, 1993).

Irene Etzersdorfer, *Arisiert: Eine Spurensicherung im gesellschaftlichen Untergrund der Republik* (Vienna: Kremayr & Scheriau, 1995)

Stefan Riesenfellner and Heidemarie Uhl, *Todeszeichen: Zeitgeschichtliche Denkmalkultur in der Steiermark vom Ende des 19. Jahrhunderts bis zur Gegenwart* (Vienna; Böhlau, 1994).

* I am indebted to Berndt Ostendorf, chair of American Studies at the University of Munich, whose suggestions improved this essay.

Reinhold Gärtner und Sieglinde Rosenberger, *Kriegerdenkmäler: Vergangenheit in der Gegenwart* (Innsbruck: Österreichischer Studienverlag, 1991)

Hannes Heer and Klaus Naumann, eds., *Vernichtungkrieg: Verbrechen der Wehrmacht 1941-1944* (Hamburg: Hamburger Edition, 1995).

Peter Bettelheim and Robert Streibel, eds., *Tabu und Geschichte: Zur Kultur des kollektiven Erinnerns* (Vienna: Picus, 1994).

Werner Bergmann, Rainer Erb and Albert Lichtblau, eds., *Schwieriges Erbe: Der Umgang mir dem Nationalsozialismus und Antisemitismus in Österreich, der DDR und der Bundesrepublik Deutschland* (Frankfurt: Campus, 1995).

Ian Buruma, *The Wages of Guilt: Memories of War in Germany and Japan* (New York: Farrar Straus Giroux, 1994).

Introduction

In 1941 the Nazi mayor of the Lower Austrian town Waidhofen an der Ybbs commissioned a large painting from a well-known *völkisch* painter. The task was to create a "*Heimat* apotheosis" for the town hall. The enthusiastic Nazi mayor in the Third Reich province *Niederdonau* wanted to bring a whiff of the monumental changes in Nazi-German culture home to his narrow-minded folk to inspire them towards working harder at the "tasks of a great new time." A Nazi careerist painted the quaint town with plenty of swastikas flying and full of proud citizens in the brown Nazi uniform. By 1943 the colorful historicist "symphony of genuine Germandom" was finished. Only two years later such dedication to the Nazi cause would be a huge embarrassment. On 12 May 1945, the local Soviet commander, who had arrived just three days earlier, ordered the painting to be *retouched*. Local painters quickly transformed brown flags into Austria's national colors: red-white-red. They turned Nazi uniforms into folksy local costumes. This successful *Übermalaktion* and "consciousness lifting"—an instant and mendacious reenvisioning of the past—going back to the first days after the end of World War II, stands as a metaphor for Austria's and Austrians' handling of World War II and its memory.[2]

In the culture of memory of World War II, Austria has been considered for some time to be among the postwar champions of forgetting this horrendous war, and Austrians have been considered the negative models of successful denial regarding their complicity in Nazi war crimes. When it came to amnesia about the war, Austria shared the honors of denying a dark chapter of their past with the Japanese and the French.[3] Waking up from a long hibernation of forgetfulness and seeming mastery over the past, the affair around the election of Kurt Waldheim to the Austrian presidency in 1986 shattered the comfortable **patriotic memory** of Austria's postwar **founding myth** of "nation of victims" (the *Opferdoktrin*) and some forty years of collective amnesia over war crimes committed by individual Austrian perpetrators (*Tätergeschichte*). The official "compartmentalization" of the past into "bright" spots such as the Austrian resistance and the myth of Austria as exclusive victim transformed Word War II into a chapter of history one could live with. The burdensome "dark" spots of Austrian complicity in the Nazi regime, which the "true" victims remembered, were purged.[4] Austrian government officials constructed this founding myth in the final days of the war, and started to enforce it as an official doctrine in the bureaucracy in the summer of 1945 and in the country at large and the international community during the course of 1946.

The historical memory of World War II features a specific generational pattern. In the second half of the 1980s Austria's World War II generation reluctantly found itself involved in a spirited debate over their roles in Hitler's criminal Nazi state, which most of them had relegated into the deep recesses of memory if not oblivion.[5] Prodded on by both public debates and a younger generation of more critical teachers, Austria's grandchildren started to ask the question, "What did you do in the war, granddaddy?" the famous question the West German children of the war generation often asked twenty years earlier. This revived an interest in a more complex vision of Austria's role in World War II, hitherto the preserve of a younger generation of historians and political scientists whom the accomplices of patriotic memory and a broader public usually preferred to dismiss as unpatriotic *Nestbeschmutzer*[6] (dirtying their own nest). The reappearance of dark shadows from the past threatened the postwar founding myth of collective "victimhood" of German National Socialism (that is, the "victim's doctrine"). The confrontation with such a complex past including victims and perpetrators, many feared, might even threaten Austria's identity of being an "island of the blessed." To allow the newly reconstituted Second Republic to prosper, the skeletons of the past had to be kept in the closet, otherwise they might unleash the civil strife that had shattered the first Republic (see Anton Pelinka's essay in this volume).

The 1980s underwent a paradigm shift in Austrian World War II historiography,[7] increasingly focussing research on Austrians' participation and complicity in Nazi war crimes. The complacent Austrian postwar consensus on the "victim's doctrine" was dissected and its opportunistic myths deconstructed and punctured. Along the lines of Arno J. Mayer's observation quoted above, a younger generation of freethinking and critical World War II specialists challenged the prevailing consensus of Austrian historical memory by developing a research agenda beyond the traditional interest in Austrian resistance, which had complimented the official Austrian victim's doctrine and been the principal focus of the historical profession for more than a generation (some of the best studies of the Austrian resistance were written by resistance fighters themselves[8]). This paradigm shift in World War II historiography—and the resulting construction of a less emotional and more objective and truthful memory—clearly was a generational matter. As the war grew more distant, the postwar collective memory of the victim's doctrine became less convincing and harder to "enforce" by the political leadership and the hagiographers. Mayer has explained the process: collective memories "do not remain raw and burning too long after the extinction of the members of the group which experienced the events firsthand, and their immediate progeny and 'heirs.'"[9]

The publication of two pathbreaking collections of essays on Austria's culture of memory and its World War II history, following the Waldheim fiasco, pointed the way. The first more essayistic one started to deconstruct the many taboos obscuring Austria's World War II past and thus helped initiate a more vigorous debate (at least among intellectuals) about Austria's failure of mastering its past. (The code word "*Vergangenheitsbewältigung*," bandied about with such abandon in the German *Historikerstreit* in 1985/86, also became fashionable in Austria.)[10] The second collection summarized the rich empirical work of a younger generation of scholars demonstrating the vast record of Austrian collaboration with the Nazi regime, and more specifically tackling hitherto largely off-limits topics such as the unsavory "aryanization" of Jewish property after the Anschluß, the Nazi terror regime in Austria, the sad fate of the Austrian Jewish community, the exploitation of forced foreign labor in the vast subcamp system of the Mauthausen concentration camp, and the dutiful role of Austrian soldiers in the German *Wehrmacht*.[11] The Austrian historical profession also needed some outside prodding. No one probably contributed more to minutely and mercilessly dissecting the Austrian victim's mythology and exploding the myth of Austrian innocence than the British historian Robert Knight.[12] Heidemarie Uhl's impressive documentation and shrewd analysis of the public debates about the Anschluß during its fiftieth anniversary year in 1988 (in the old Josephinian tradition the Austrian government controlled history and memory and ordered a year of commemoration and reflection—"*Bedenkjahr*"), however, demonstrated that most politicians and the public never abandoned their patriotic memory, and defended it more desperately than ever against the intellectuals' assault on it.[13]

The year 1988 may have been the highpoint of the old "patriotic memory" before its partial collapse and gradual decline. As suggested above, generational change played a crucial role here. The progressive demise of the wartime generation will take their patriotic memories (and undoubtedly their nightmares rarely confronted) to the grave. Less sanctimonious and more realistic *official* views of Austria's role in World War II, which among Austrians who embrace statism seem to hold particularly strong sway, may be another factor. At least some recent speeches by Chancellor Vranitzky suggest that numerous Austrian perpetrators of war crimes no longer can be excluded from history and mention Austrian *Täter* along with the *Opfer*.[14] The most crucial and heartening factor may well be that a younger generation of Austrian scholars is now accumulating a body of sophisticated research and exposing the processes of *construction* of public and private memories after the war. A vigorous new historiography about specific culture of Austrian memory of World War II analyzes Austria's denial of the past—*Vergangenheitsverdrängung* rather than *Vergangenheitsbewältigung*—as a complex interaction between official constructs of collective memory and local as well as private memories of individual Austrians. Public and private memories fed on each other and became the all-pervasive memory of postwar Austrian society (social memory).

Themes and Chronology

The works under review here may usher in something akin to a paradigm shift in the Austrian memory of World War II (and thus are part and parcel of the larger paradigm shift in World War II historiography suggested above). These works dissect the (1) private and social construction of memory, (2) the public cultural construction of memory in war memorials, and (3) the comparative construction of postwar memory in Central/Western Europe and Japan.

Particularly the Ziegler/Kannonier-Finster and Uhl works suggest a basic **chronology** in the postwar transmutations of Austrian World War II memory:

1) The **construction of the founding myth** (1945-1949):[15] After the end of the war and prodded by the Allied occupation powers Austrians were still eager to bring the Nazis and war criminals to justice and still showed some sympathy to what might be called the "true" victims[16] of the war such as Jews, gypsies, forced laborers and resistance fighters.[17] Even before the strict Allied control of 1945 changed into benign tutelage in 1946, the Viennese government seized the opportunity offered by the Moscow Declaration's "Austria as Hitler's first victim" clause and began to **insist** that the vast majority of Austrians were "victims" of the war. The official Austrian definition of "victim" now began to include the returning soldiers and the numerous "less implicated" Nazis and bystanders (*Mitläufer*) on the homefront. The official *Rot-Weiß-Rot* book published in 1946 laid out the consensual bipartisan party line for this new state sponsored and bureaucratically enforced victim's doctrine for both domestic and international audiences.[18] The Austrian government utilized the momentum of the incipient Cold War and began watering down the strict Allied denazification provisions, pursuing Austrian war criminals only half-heartedly.

With their abandonment of denazification the occupation powers became accomplices of Austria's *Vergangenheitsverdrängung*. The Austrian government wasted no time and issued a general amnesty for almost half a million "little Nazis" (*Mitläufer*, i.e. "fellow travelers").[19] With the general amnesty began the unsavory process of competing for the Nazis' votes by all parties during the 1949 election campaign.[20] This completed the construction of the great postwar consensus that the little Nazis were "victims" of the war and should not be held responsible for anything. Like the Southerners after the U.S. Civil War, the Austrians abandoned "radical reconstruction" of civil society as soon as the Allies ended their strict control over the purge of the Nazis. The withdrawal of the Allied soldiers in 1955 only completed the process.

By then the Austrians were waving their "bloody shirt." In 1949 some Austrian politicians loudly started to agitate for the notion of ten (by 1955 seventeen) years of "occupation;"[21] according to this view Austrians were both victims of Hitler and Nazi occupation and the Allies and denazification/four-power occupation. The equalization of Hitler's murderous totalitarian regime with the rather generous American "coca-colonization" regime is one of the most unsavory historical lies in the official postwar construction of memory.

2) The **petrification of the founding myth** and the **hibernation of the complex past** (Ziegler/Kannonier-Finster, p. 242) (1950/55-1980/86): Nazi war crimes were "externalized," (Ziegler/Kannonier Finster, p. 68)—both Austria and the German Democratic Republic shifted all responsibility and guilt onto the Federal Republic as *the* successor state of Hitler's Third Reich. Austria's growing oblivion to the complicity of the Austrian perpetrators set in, and individuals increasingly dwelled on their innocuous anecdotal memories of the war (see Ziegler and Kannonier-Finster, pp. 63ff). Austrian identity came to be built on the paradox of Austrian "victims only having done their duty." The suffering of the "real" victims was increasingly forgotten and willfully purged from Austrian memory. Unlike the German government, the Austrian government felt no moral compulsion to show reverence to some 65,000 murdered Austrian Jews (it is assumed that overeager Austrian Nazis may be responsible of as many as half of those who perished in the Holocaust[22]), or to pay restitution to the state of Israel, and procrastinated endlessly in paying restitution to surviving Austrian Jews, as Thomas Albrich and Brigitte Bailer have shown. Instead the Nazi small-fry-turned-"victim" increasingly started to benefit from war related government pensions (*Kriegsopferfürsorge*).[23]

Austria did not experience the revolution in the official construction of public memory that the Federal Republic did as a result of vigorous scholarship on National Socialism and comparative fascism going back to the 1950s and the 1968 upheavals. In the Federal Republic the Socialist Chancellor Willy Brandt showed profound personal contrition with his highly symbolic *Kniefall* in Warsaw. In West Germany the famous question of the self-righteous '68ers on the Left "What did you do in the war daddy?" shattered the private postwar amnesia of the *Wirtschaftswunder* generation.

Bruno Kreisky is rightly praised as a big modernizer in postwar Austria.[24] Yet he comforted the *Vergangenheitsverdränger.* Brandt's friend and socialist *Genosse* Kreisky, who came to power in Austria at roughly the same time, missed a great opportunity to question and reflect upon the postwar consensus centered around the victim's ideology. To the contrary, Kreisky put four former Nazis into his Cabinet and single-handedly helped the FPÖ (with its many unreconstructed Nazi voters) out of their isolation on the right fringes; Kreisky also helped make the former SA-officer from the killing fields of Eastern Europe, Friedrich Peter, turned-FPÖ-party-leader, acceptable ("*salonfähig*"). Kreisky's consensual politics with the right resulted in a veritable "pissing match" and long drawn out court battle with Austria's famed Nazi hunter Simon Wiesenthal. Instead of shattering Austria's pervasive amnesia about the country's "difficult legacies," Kreisky aided official complicity in keeping the past compartmentalized and purged; the long hibernation of the complex past continued into the early 1980s.[25]

We will need much more research into the paradoxes why the Austrian Jew and wartime *emigré* Kreisky, who lost family members in the Holocaust[26], did not challenge the compartmentalized Austrian historical memory. Was it mere political opportunism not to rock the boat and adhere to the bipartisan postwar consensus? Was it a shrewd Freudian approach where denial is a healthy and necessary instinct? Was it the traditional overcompensation of an assimilated Viennese Jew?

The 1979 Hollywood docudrama "Holocaust" seemed not to have the same profound effect in Austria that it had in the Federal Republic where it sparked renewed interest and debate in German war crimes and genocide.[27] Since Austrians were all "victims" they did not need to educate themselves about the holocaust or feel guilty for the Nazis' most egregious war crimes.

3) The **de-construction of the founding myth** and the **advent of a non-compartmentalized and complex past** (1980s to the present): This phase, sped up by the Waldheim debate, has already been discussed above.

Private and Social Construction of Memory

Österreichs Gedächtnis by the two sociologists Ziegler and Kannonier-Finster is a signal contribution to the understanding of postwar Austrian historical memory of World War II. The argument is balanced and, given some complex theoretical problems involved, the writing remarkably fresh and jargon-free. Their sophisticated interdisciplinary methodology successfully incorporates history, social psychology, and sociological approaches to their task as well as a superbly sensitive handling of oral history methods. Their empirical evidence is gathered from some twenty-five oral histories conducted by their students with World War II survivors. From these initial twenty-five life-stories the authors chose five narratives and went back to their subjects for second more in-depth "reflective" interviews. By both narrating these five quintessential Austrian lives and boiling down what is remembered and what is forgotten, they carefully construct something akin to a **structured** memory of history—the mentality (*Alltagsbewußtsein*) of Austrian society as it relates to World War II past (pp. 73-75).

This **private memory** (or "inner memory") they juxtapose with what they call Austria's institutionalized **social memory** (or "outer memory") (p. 40).[28] From a close reading of Upper Austrian newspapers the authors outline the official construction of Austrian World War II memory that became institutionalized by the early 1950s. Newspapers reflect the parameters of public discourse that is possible and not possible at a given time. The memory constructed by newspapermen—often only reflecting the official views—is manipulated and deformed. It willfully papers over the history of the perpetrators[29] and thus reinforces the official views of compartmentalized history. It aids the forgetting of the myriad instances of collaboration and complicity of innumerable Austrians in the inhumane Nazi system and war of expansion and extermination—the countless individual acts of collaboration and complicity, which collectively constitute Austria's deep involvement (*Verstrickung*) in the Nazi heart of darkness.[30]

By 1949 Austrian collective social and individual private memories had become a seamless web. The failure of Austria's postwar leaders to urge their people to work towards a more truthful memory (*Erinnerungsarbeit*), and instead aiding oblivion (*Nichterinnerung*) of the dark sides of the Nazi regime consequently became part of Austria's collective postwar memory (pp. 44f). The authors' reading of the newspapers shows how in 1945 people were still deeply afflicted (*betroffen*) by the horrors of war; by 1946 they began to forget and deny them (grabbing onto the official consensual party line emerging at the time). Indeed, as Mario Erdheim has observed in the introductory essay, the paradoxical process set in whereby the fascists and perpetrators insisted on forgetting rather than incessantly dwelling on the past whereas the "true" victims demanded the memory of a complex past (p. 10). By 1949 the Austrians were exclusively "victims" of the war and denied any responsibility and resisted guilt. Nazi crimes and denazification were "externalized" (the burden of genocide was exclusively shifted onto the shoulders of the Germans, and the Anschluß was unloaded on the Allies who had appeased Hitler and betrayed Austria). The widespread enthusiasm for the Anschluß in March 1938 was forgotten—only a small minority cheered the Nazis. Austria had become a nation of "victims" and the public increasingly shared this view. Postwar Austrian identity was built on this founding myth (p. 67). Austrian identity was built on externalization of war crimes and establishing a firm boundary vis-à-vis the Germans. The "*verschworene Schuldgemeinschaft*" (p. 66) of Austrians became the "*schicksalshafte Opfergemeinschaft*" (p. 80) of Austria. The core of what they call Austria's "patriotic memory" (pp. 238ff) became operative and a convenient construct for the individual as a cover for denial of personal responsibility.

This increasingly assertive compartmentalized "*Geschichtsbild*" of Austria as "a nation of victims" provided a potent "collective defense mechanism" for individuals to purge and cleanse their nightmarish personal memories from the criminal and dark sides of Nazi totalitarianism and their role in it. Individuals negated what had been ambivalent and threatening in their memory only yesterday. They increasingly refused to keep an open mind about the past or truthfully reflect upon it. The official consensus aided them. The founding fathers failed to construct a complex past for political reasons, even though some of them had personally experienced the Nazi chamber of horrors in concentration camps or "inner exile."

Roughly one million Austrian soldiers who survived the war[31] were included in the Austrian victims collective and initiated the long "hibernation" (p. 242) of the facts regarding their participation in Hitler's aggressive war of expansion and extermination. They "externalized" what might be individual responsibility in the Nazi war. According to this view, they had fought in a foreign army whose ideology of expansion and exterminating Slavic *Untermenschen* had been alien to their beliefs.[32] Many returned from the fighting fronts thinking that they had dedicated their life to a noble cause, but Chancellor Leopold Figl quickly told them differently and indoctrinated them with the victim mythology which gave them the cue for the emerging patriotic memory (pp. 242f). Surely such a collective memory helped them psychologically to master the horrors of war that individual memory carried and subsequent imprisonment caused (the Allied armies did not make a distinction between Austrian and German *Wehrmacht* soldiers when millions of men became prisoners of war in the final months and weeks of fighting).[33]

One alternative for a admitting to a less compartmentalized and more complex personal memory would have been to claim the age old defense of any raging *soldateska* in wartime—being *both* aggressors as well as victims: "aggressors because they killed innocent people, victims because they were forced to do so."[34] Of course, such ambiguity was not compatible with naive *Pflichterfüllung*.

The heart of Ziegler's and Kannonier-Finster's brilliant analysis are five highly representative case studies. In these, the swift construction of collective memory comes to light as does the manner in which such a social memory served and reinforced the construction of insular individual memories. This quintet—three soldiers and two women—remains anonymous. Yet in their anonymity they strike me as a national gallery of carefully selected quintessential *homines Austriaci*. These are not one-dimensional people but **archetypes** representing the complex and multi-dimensional Austrian experience of World War II. There is the bitter *Herr* Hausmann, a perpetrator who was a rabid anti-Semite and an illegal Nazi of the first hour who fought in Poland, North Africa, and Normandy who saw his ideals shattered after the Anschluß and psychologically never really recovered from it.[35] *Herr* Knittler, the archetypical Austrian perpetrator as "*Pflichterfüller*" who followed orders (what Christopher Browning calls the "grass-roots perpetrator"); he was a soldier in the *Ständestaat*, a member of the murderous German *Schutzpolizei*[36] which hunted anti-Nazi partisans from Norway to Greece, and again a policeman after the war. He sees himself as a "good man" who during the war experienced the "best time of his life" (he never faced any denazification proceedings). *Frau* Scherer, a pathetic and uneducated house servant who lived in the proximity of a concentration camp, whose husband was a camp guard in one of Mauthausen's subcamps, and who denied knowing what went on inside the camps[37] (she witnessed death marches and still refused to show empathy with the camp inmates during the interview);[38] her world collapsed not in 1938 when the Nazis came but in 1945 when the Soviets came to Upper Austria. *Frau* Angerer, the rare bird who had been socialized into a German nationalist Nazi family but who developed a "reflective memory" after the war, questioning the official version of history and working to construct her own highly critical of the Nazi party line ("she has to construct her memory against the pressure of her culture to forget" [p. 161]). The teacher *Herr* Lang, the supporter of the Dollfuß regime who fled into the *Wehrmacht* to express his displeasure with the Anschluß appears to be the quintessential Austrian *Mitläufer* who regrets having wasted six years in the German army; his worst memory is not the war but being a Canadian prisoner of war. What unites him with the two perpetrators is his solidarity with Kurt Waldheim in 1986 and *Pflichterfüllung* during the war. He is not as extreme as the unreconstructed old Nazi and anti-Semite Hausmann who castigates the 1986 attacks on Waldheim in the old discourse of the 1930s as "*jüdische Schweinerei*" (p. 111).

Österreichs Gedächtnis is so persuasive because it presents five **ordinary** Austrians who are representative of an unadulterated complex Austrian war experience of both the home and fighting fronts; these are not the overzealous Austrian "newcomers" to the Nazi cause such as Arthur Seyss-Inquart, Otto Wächter and Odilo Globocnic[39] that could be dismissed as "un-Austrian." The memory of these model Austrians fed on the officially constructed collective memory. This helps us understand the construction of individual memory after the war—insular memories that in turn again reinforced the pervasive social memory. My generation grew up hearing views like theirs on the *Stammtisch*. We were ignorant and suspicious and without the tools to dissect such memories. Now we do possess these tools thanks to a brilliant book that should help change the Austrian culture of memory, at least in the educational arena.

While Ziegler and Kannnonier-Finster lay open psychological strata of memory, Irene Etzersdofer's *Arisiert* unearths an archeology of memory. She traces the netherworld of forced transfers—euphemistically known as "aryanizations"—of Jewish property after the Anschluß and the attendant aryanizers' hyena instincts. The aryanizations of 1938 surely must be one of the bleakest chapters in Vienna's long history (the vast majority of the Jews lived in Vienna). Of 26,000 Jewish enterprises in Vienna, 5,000 were aryanized, the rest liquidated (7,000 had already been dissolved earlier). Of 190,000 Austrian Jews, 66,000 perished in the Holocaust, the rest scattered all over the world, many never to return. What happened to their factories, hotels, sanatoriums, palaces, villas, houses, apartments, paintings, pianos, furniture, furs, books, bedpans, etc.? Everything was aryanized. In one of the most unbelievable frenzies of *enrichez-vous* ever experienced in a civilized society at peace, the Jewish property was forcibly seized and transferred into the hands of reliable Nazi party members. (Leading among them were the cream of the crop of Austrian Nazis, the "illegals" of the pre-Anschluß era; some carpetbaggers came to look for "opportunities" from the *Altreich.*) (See particularly Etzersdorfer's introduction, pp. 11f, 24.)

This story, of course, has been told before.[40] But it has never been told as poignantly as in these gripping case studies. Etzersdorfer also uses the *pars pro toto* approach where individual lives illuminate the Austrian context and the practice of Nazi totalitarian rule. In seven examples she traces the life stories of real people with whom the reader can identify and sympathize. Her job is indeed the serendipitous investigation of the unrelenting historian as sleuthing detective (using both archival sources and conducting oral interviews on three continents). What comes to life are paradigmatic Jewish family histories. The Jews came in the great nineteenth century largely orthodox Jewish exodus from the Eastern provinces of the Habsburg Empire to the center in Vienna. They were looking for better opportunities very much like their brethren from the Polish Pale who went to New York and other U.S. cities. With hard work, endurance, shrewdness and great devotion to "Austria" (some of them even fought in the imperial army during World War I), they succeeded only to see their lives' work precipitously shattered by the Anschluß. Some of the instances of aryanization discussed here were among Vienna's best-known enterprises in the world. Many of these healthy and highly productive model businesses were ruined by the aryanizers in the course of the war; after all the aryanizers had distinguished themselves as reliable party hacks and not businessmen. In these haunting tales Etzersberger stresses that those who only lost their earthly possessions and saved their lives were the lucky ones.

Even though this is not her principal focus, *Arisiert* fits into the context of postwar construction of collective and private memory. Here is the proof of what a shameless construct the postwar "victim's mythology" was. Etzerberger unmasks the aryanizers' conniving ways of securing the valuable Jewish properties. "Wild aryanizations"—the brutal seizure of properties from the Jews without any official papers—for a while became part of Viennese daily life in 1938. Etzersberger's evidence suggests that much of the population of Vienna must have personally observed the aryanizations and thus became "bystanders." She concludes, "The 'aryanizers' [were] the prototypical collaborators of the totalitarian National Socialist system" (p. 14). These zealots were among the quintessential "grass-roots perpetrators" (Browning) of the Nazi regime. In 1938 they profited from the suspension of the rule of law; after the war, in their attempt to get off the hook, the same barbarians quickly claimed the protection of the very rule of law (*Rechtsstaat*) that they had helped bury in 1938. After the war, these classical Austrian perpetrators hid in the wide bosom of the victim's doctrine. Often they even succeeded in hanging on to their stolen property if no former owners came back to claim it (pp. 95-98). A staggering 66,000 among the former owners died in the Nazi death machine and did not return to Vienna. The Germans presumably were exclusively responsible for the failure of the Jews of Vienna to return.

What price did the aryanizers pay? Some languished in Allied internment camps for Nazis for a while; some went through denazification procedures, which never lasted long. Some returned their property, if the rightful owners returned to claim it. Many flats, and much unclaimed property remain in the families of the aryanizers and in depositories if the Austrian government to this day. Small wonder that aryanizations are not part of the collective or individual memories. If the aryanizers and their children are traced down, they usually feel no remorse for what happened and only rarely offer apologies (p. 64).

Hibernation and De-Construction: Public Memory in War Memorials

Just as the memory of aryanizations has been effectively suppressed in Austrian public memory with the help of the victim's doctrine, so the individual Austrian soldiers' memory of the war has been effectively purged of all the *Tätergeschichte* with the help of the same mythology.[41] This is most visible in Austrian war memorials and the transformation in the memorial culture along the lines of the chronology outlined above. Two fascinating studies allow us to understand the specific culture of Austrian war memorials and its curious euphemistic language much better. *Kriegerdenkmäler*[42] by the two political scientists Gärtner and Rosenberger is an extended essayistic think piece—a general introduction of sorts to the topic --, while the historian Uhl's empirically rich and methodologically sophisticated essay is a more specific case study on the Austrian province of Styria with important conclusions for the general Austrian culture of World War II memorials.

Based on an in-depth study of war memorials in Upper Austria, Gärtner and Rosenberger analyze more generally how the war memorials project a "fragmented and mendacious" (p. 12) historical portrait of the past. Along the lines of the official victim's doctrine the war memorials commemorate the soldiers' struggle "to defend their homeland" (*Heimat*) and betray forgetfulness about the "real" victims of the war. Their involvement in the war is portrayed as "patriotic 'duty'" pure and simple (p. 21). In this way the war and their participation in it is normalized and legitimized (if not glorified). The soldiers' memorials commemorate the "heroes of the fatherland" (*Helden der Heimat*) (p. 28). Most poignantly, the one million survivors of the 1,2 million Austrian soldiers (p. 27)[43] never have questioned what *Heimat* exactly they were defending. These war memorials are oblivious to the Nazis' abuse and instrumentalization of the notion of *Heimat*. National Socialism as an expansionist and exterminationist terror regime, the *Wehrmacht* "as a foreign military power that destroyed Austrian sovereignty," and the Austrian "heroes of the fatherland" swearing a personal oath to Hitler are not confronted in Austrian memorial culture. These war memorials' naively *völkisch* and uncritical notion of "*Heimat*" constitutes the **local** level of a popular culture of remembrance reflecting the cues of the **national** victim's version (the authors in fact call it "the consensus of victimhood ordered by the state" [p. 42]). They are designs of the official "externalization" doctrine, namely building a new Austrian identity purged of the negative past by separating it from Germany and its mental agonies of feeling responsible and guilty for the war. In the process they close the circle of reinforcement between the social public memory, the local public memory and the insular individual memory.

Gärtner and Rosenberger like Ziegler and Kannonier-Finster stress that the victim of this public memorial culture is a sensitive reflective memory (*Besinnlichkeit* [p. 24]) of war and National Socialism. Heroizing the soldiers and the collaborators on the home front, while ignoring and forgetting the crimes of National Socialism vis-à-vis the Jews, the Russian POWs, and all the other victims amounts to a horrendous distortion of history and a "defilement" (p. 37) of the tombs of the real victims (Jews etc.). One can go a step further than these authors do and call the founding fathers of the Second Republic and their denial of Austrians' participation in the criminal side of National Socialism "assassins of memory."[44] A bloody war survives in the sanctimonious euphemisms of "*Pflicht*" and "*Heimat*" in these war memorials, the "brutal Nazi past is reduced and mythologized into a simple-minded past" (p. 50). The echoes of this conspiracy of silence from Figl/Gruber to Kreisky/Waldheim, recurring in every village cemetery from Bruck an der Leitha to Bregenz, today ring in the ears.

In these war memorials Austria's bland undifferentiated victim's perspective became "petrified" (p. 96). Total war reduced to "following orders" and "*Pflichterfüllung*" constitutes a *reductio ad absurdum*. The soldiers were heroized and the location of the graveyards next to the village churches gave this pious memory a sacral aura. The veterans organizations (*Kameradschaftsbünde*) thus quietly reaffirmed and even celebrated the soldiers' heroic exploits in Hitler's army. The *Wehrmacht*'s murderous war in the East as shown in the volume *Vernichtungskrieg: Verbrechen der Wehrmacht 1941-1944* is one purged from such patriotic memory.[45] Such defiance of memory and denial of guilt went even further among the notorious "Glasenbacher"—a tight group of former Nazis (some of them SS war criminals) interned after the war in the U.S. Camp Marcus W. Orr outside of Salzburg. They considered themselves "victims" of the American internment and denazification procedures and demanded restitution from the Austrian government.[46] The role of the veterans' organizations in Austrian war memorial culture became a central factor in aiding and abetting the ongoing hibernation of a complex non-compartmentalized past, at least among the war generation.

Uhl's study generalizes less than the Gärtner and Rosenberger essay and chronologically differentiates more in defining the transmutations of the subjects of commemoration and the pictorial language in the postwar trajectory of memorial culture by taking an in-depth look at Styria. In fact, hers is a model study of an Austrian "regional landscape of memory/commemoration" (*regional Gedächtnislandschaft*) (p. 116). Uhl analyzes a paradigm shift after 1949 towards a commemoration of "all" the victims of the war, or a fragmentation of memorial culture between soldiers' memorials (*Kriegerdenkmäler*) and victims' memorials (concentration camp inmates, Jews etc.). (p. 139). In the "antifascist climate" (p. 114) of the immediate postwar era, Styrian memorials concentrated on the "true" victims of the Nazi regime—concentration camp inmates (of the Mauthausen subcamps in Styria), Jews, Yugoslav partisans (!), hostages and particularly victims of the grisly final weeks of the war when the fighting front impinged on the home front, namely the numerous victims of death marches and **dissident** soldiers who went AWOL as well as resisters to the NS regime.

Most of these memorials built in the first few years after the war commemorated **local events**. In 1945, some of them even posed the question of "Austrian responsibility and guilt" in Hitler's war (pp. 117ff). There was also memorials to French POWs and one to an Austrian who had been gassed in Auschwitz ("*Als Kämpfer für Österreichs Freiheit von den Hitlerfaschisten im KZ Auschwitz im Jahre 1942 vergast. Sein Opfer sei uns Mahnung*") (p. 121). While many of these memorials were locally sponsored by various groups of surviving concentration camp inmates (*KZ-Verbände*), who in 1945/46 were still the driving force in the short-lived sensitive culture of commemoration, by 1947 Styrian officials started to take a hold of the various annual memorial celebrations and prepared the paradigm shift towards a purged past highly insensitive to the "true" victims. After everything that has been said in this essay the result became predictable. The bipartisan, official victim's doctrine asserted itself on the local level with an attendant "parity among the dead" (*Gleichheit der Toten*)—the soldiers (the euphemistic *Gefallene* became the code word) and the victims of the air war and concentration camps (usually in this order!) (p. 119) were all remembered at the same time.

Surely, the emerging Cold War played a crucial role in the Western Allies abetting the official Austrian consensus and in allowing the government to isolate the *KZ-Verbände*—dominated by Communists who had constituted the majority in the Austrian resistance and among the *KZ*-inmates—and thus increasingly suppressing the memory of the "true" victims.

The Allies indeed were still in the land and they initiated the construction of their own war memorials in Austria. Most were Soviet memorials commemorating the Red Army soldiers who had died for the defeat of the Nazis and the liberation of Austria (not the indigenous victims of National Socialism). Usually massive heroic tombs in the Socialist realist style featured Cyrillic writing and red stars and remained alien to the indigenous Styrian culture of remembrance. They were considered symbols of a hostile foreign occupation power; numerous attacks and defacements of Soviet memorials were recorded (p. 126). Paradoxically the *Wehrmacht* soldiers who had invaded the Soviet Union were allowed to rest in peace but not the Red Army soldiers who had helped liberate Austria from the Nazi yoke!

There is also a lonely memorial in a suburb of the Styrian capital city of Graz that commemorated the cold-blooded murder of three downed U.S. pilots (the plaque reads: "At this place on [sic] March 1945 three defenseless American pilots became victims of cowardly Nazi-fascist murderers") (p. 129). Two of the alleged murderers in fact had to stand trial for war crimes in 1959/60. This modest memorial to U.S. flyers also had become subject to innumerable

This memorial stone in *Graz-Webling* was dedicated on 4 June 1945, to the memory of three American pilots murdered on 4 March 1945 by local Nazis after the downing of their plane. The city of Graz renovated this memorial in the course of the *Bedenkjahr* 1988 after numerous defacements. (Photo Heidemarie Uhl)

A rare exception to the Austrian postwar memorial culture of the "good comrade," is the memorial in the soldiers' cemetery of *Hieflau-Wandau* (1965). Here some 33 German soldiers, who tried to preserve their lives in the final weeks of a senseless war, deserted the frontlines and were executed by *Standgerichte* of the Wehrmacht or SS. (Branko Lenart Art Photographs, Graz)

defacements; such attacks resurfaced in the 1980s which led to the building of a new memorial by Styrian authorities. One can argue that Austria's founding myths confirmed the defacers in their belief that the U.S. pilots were perpetrators.

By 1949/50 the consensus view prevailed and profoundly transformed Styria's war memorial culture. Memorials built to (Communist) Austrian resistance fighters and "true" victims of the war were isolated from the larger bipartisan ÖVP/SPÖ culture of remembrance which now came to include **all** the dead of 1938-45 war, most prominently the patriotic soldiers (*gute Kameraden*) that had heroically defended the "fatherland" (namely the undefined *Heimat* noted by Gärtner and Rosenberger).

These soldiers' memorials were built in virtually every town and became symbols of a pervasive *Alltagskultur* of remembrance. Fully incorporating the official victim's doctrine they defined and enforced Austrian collective memory locally. Uhl notes that "in this version of World War II the war is separated from the origins, the goals and the conduct of the German Reich; instead this time is turned into one of common suffering of the entire population—both the soldiers on the fronts and the civil population at home threatened by the bombing war and the approach of the Red Army" (p. 147).

The veterans organizations take over the **local management** of public memory and insist on making heroes of the "fallen comrades" who only did their duty in defending the fatherland. The new code language in the various heroes' memorials and graveyards becomes one of sacrificing their lives for the "defense" of the homeland against the "attacking" Red Army (i.e,. the usual conspiracy of silence about the complex past of an expansionist and murderous *Wehrmacht*). In the local war memorial version the war is reduced to a minimum of *Pflichterfüllung*: "*unsere besten Söhne ihre Gesundheit und ihr Leben einsetzen mußten, um die Heimat von den ungestüm andrängenden Feinden zu schützen*" (p. 148). The *Kameradschaftsbund* makes sure that a "healthy" (p. 149) positive image of World War II soldiers prevails in the public against the "defamations" of "certain groups" ("*gewisse Kreise*"[47]) who dare to mention "war crimes" instead of speaking of simple "soldierly duty." In these memorials the fallen soldiers now became pious *Helden der Pflichterfüllung*. In Reinhold Gärtner has summed it up laconically:

the *Kameradschaften*'s job was "honoring the fallen comrades not their war crimes."[48]

The attendant speeches given by officials on the local and national level revived the World War I "cult of the fallen soldier."[49] The legacy is that a populist politician such as Jörg Haider honors these "heroes" from the *Wehrmacht* and SS to this day.[50] They honor these soldiers as virtuous men who did their manly duty in keeping the oath sworn to the *Führer* ("*die soldatische Pflichterfüllung zu den höchsten Mannestugenden gehört und die Einhaltung des beschworenen Eides heute endlich wieder die rechte Würdigung erfährt*" [p. 149]). Not enough, this pathos of honoring and glorifying the war heroes became a sacred patriotic duty for everyone (*heilige Verpflichtung*). The entire generation of World War II soldiers was thus rehabilitated, and the memory portrayed in the war memorials helped create social harmony and aided the shaping of a new national identity in postwar Austria by including a million men that returned to Austrian civil society after the war.

This unchallenged hibernation of selective memory and compartmentalized history lasted into the 1980s. Uhl shows how individuals and groups driven by the emergence of the more complex World War II history paradigm and memory (with the Waldheim fiasco and the *Bedenkjahr* 1988), defied the veterans' organizations hibernating memory. They deconstructed the official founding myth and initiated a new memorial culture that concentrated on the hitherto blind spots on the mental map of collective memory (p. 171). From a safe historical distance, a younger generation started to unearth Austria's hidden Nazi past. Such a changing historical consciousness influenced both collective and individual memory; the social memory of Austria began a transformation that is by no means completed (see the Mauthausen report in this volume). Making reference to violent crimes committed by Austrians and their latent anti-Semitism was designed to shatter "the silence that was shrouding Austrian history" (p. 173). In 1988 Graz in the commemoration of the *Reichskristallnacht* (a crucial stepping stone towards the Holocaust), held a number of activities which culminated in the unveiling of the *Synagogendenkmal*, a memorial reminding locals that the synagogue in Graz had also been burned. Local memorials to Jews and concentration camp inmates became a primary focus of these new initiatives. Forgotten local victims of political persecution and resistance ("the other Austria") (p. 176) now began to intrude on public memory. This new variety of what could also be called localized "micro memories" did not entirely alter the prevailing collective "macro memory" but presented alternatives of memorial culture and complex history.

Austria Is Not Unique: World War II Memory in a Comparative Perspective

After a more critical generation had shattered the Austrian silence about the dark side of Austrian World War II history, the question arose regarding the ways in which Austria's memory might differ from that of the two German successor states of the Third Reich and other European countries.[51]

Two new collections of essays suggest a comparative structure of memory; they examine the processes of construction of historical memory after the war from a larger European perspective.[52] *Schwieriges Erbe* presents the conference papers of a fall 1993 meeting in Salzburg comparing Austrian, East and West German mastering of their "difficult legacies."[53] *Tabu und Geschichte* are the published lectures delivered in the fall of 1992 in Vienna on the culture of collective memory in Europe.

Schwieriges Erbe is a very structured and focussed comparison divided into four sections, dealing respectively with the constructions of memory of the principal political parties, the memory "institutionalized" in national memorial culture as well as official days of remembrance, the particular roles Jewish organizations played in the construction of World War II memory, and the role intellectuals and public opinion played. Since the detailed studies of the parties and institutions reflect the specific "national" cultures of memory of Austria and the two German "succession states" of the Third Reich, it must suffice for the purposes of this review to summarize Agnes Blänsdorf's excellent introductory essay.[54] By now we are quite familiar with what Blänsdorf has to say about Austrian memory, namely how the victim's mythology was used to build a postwar identity with an unscientific history entirely devoid of the complexity surrounding World War II and Austrian *Verstrickung* in the Nazi war crimes. Apart from the very different ideological underpinnings, what comes as a great surprise is how much Austrian memory resembles East German memory.

The purge of the past by the German Democratic Republic was built on Marxist-Leninist ideology. The "anti-fascist" East German political leadership of the later GDR externalized responsibility and guilt of the Germans living in the Soviet occupation zone to the Germans living in the Western zones (the future FRG). The "*Irrweg*" of Hitler and the Nazis was a result of "monopoly capitalism." The West German "capitalists and imperialists" continued this dark strain of German history, and the workers and farmers of the Soviet zone (and later the GDR) had nothing to do with this. Like Austria, the GDR denied that National Socialism had taken root among their Germans and refused to share in any responsibility or guilt for Nazi genocide; any continuity of anti-Semitism was simply denied.[55] Among other things, this also meant, of course, that the East Germans were not liable to pay restitution to the Jews. This anti-fascist "founding myth" (p. 32) enforced and instrumentalized by the GDR is the counterpart to the Austrian "victim doctrine."

The totalitarian GDR did not have a generational revolt like West Germany challenging the verities of the past. Neither did the party hacks in the Academy face a revolt of a critical younger generation in the historical profession. Given that this myth was part of the strictly enforced East German official doctrine and political culture, it survived until the final years of the regime. Bländsdorf does not mention that the freely elected East German *Volkskammer* issued a highly self-critical resolution in the final days of the GDR on 13 April 1990 accepting responsibility for the Nazi genocide and apologizing to the Jews and other victims.[56] To this day the Austrian Parliament has not issued a comparable document that comes close to this last minute East German admission of responsibility and apology to the Jews, the victims and their succeeding generations, presumably because Austria was invaded and occupied and is not a successor state to the Third Reich.

The facts are well known that the Federal Republic of Germany admitted responsibility for the Nazi *Unrechtsstaat* from the very beginning of its existence and need not be discussed here. West Germans were liable for the Nazi holocaust and Nazi war crimes and billions of German marks were paid as restitution to Israel and the Jews. West Germany also paid billions of dollars in reparations as did East Germany and Austria.[57] A relatively open discussion of a non-compartmentalized World War II with many shades became a constituent part of postwar West German democratic political culture. Instead of repeating these facts in detail, Blänsdorf concentrates on postwar West German historiography and the role the historians played in exploring National Socialism and the "wrong paths" (*Irrwege*) the course of German history took in the twentieth century. Ever since its foundation in 1950 the Munich Institute of Contemporary History played a central role in the vigorous scientific research of the Nazi state and the deep complicity of all segments of the German population in it (the comparable Viennese Institute started the same task with the usual time lag of fifteen years). While the conservative government of Konrad Adenauer and the war generation at large tried to suppress the memory of the criminal wartime past, such a purge never succeeded in the FRG. In West Germany the vigorous resurgence of war crimes trials (particularly the Eichmann trial in Jerusalem and the Auschwitz trials in Frankfurt in the early to mid-Sixties) played a crucial role in reviving public interest and debate in the Nazi terror state and individual complicity. Such trials, of course, had the roles of poignant history lessons in West Germany (lessons that the East German and Austrian governments did not want to see taught). These events and the revolt of the self-righteous young idealists of the Left in 1968—who some fifteen years before the Austrians, were "on the side of the victims"[58] not the perpetrators—led to an open confrontation with the past unheard of in East Germany and Austria at this time.

While the 1980s saw the emergence of a new critical paradigm constructed by the young, a conservative resurgence in West German politics and the historical profession (led by historians from the older war generation like Ernst Nolte and Andreas Hillgruber) in the 1980s tried to reverse the course of West German memory and "normalize" and "historicize" National Socialism. Such an agenda with an inherently nationalist mission sparked the famous *Historikerstreit*[59] of the mid-1980s, which blocked this ill-conceived premeditated purge of West Germany's historical memory. While the conservatives did not succeed with their mission of "historicizing" the past, the passage of time will do it eventually.

The role of a rigorous prosecution of war criminals and the 68ers in West Germany in keeping the complex past alive has been noted above. We have already noted that the 68ers did not play such a role in Austria; neither did postwar Austrian justice. The journalist

Hellmuth Butterweck points this out in his essay on Austrian war crimes trials in *Tabu und Geschichte*. The special "people's courts" (*Volksgereichte*) tried 23,000 cases, found 13,607 persons guilty, and executed 30. But these numbers are deceiving because most of those found guilty were amnestied (p. 45). Butterweck's conclusion about the failure to vigorously prosecute the war criminals is that consensus history and the politicians' ill-conceived obsession with reconciliation produced the opportunism that equated the murderers with the *Mitläufer* which by 1955 got most all of them off the hook. Given that the Nazis executed 2,700 Austrian resisters and murdered 65,000 Austrian Jews as well as the 32,000 killed and murdered by the Gestapo in the Mauthausen concentration camp system (p. 54), surely Austrian complicity in the Nazi genocide was much deeper and broader than the measly judicial record of Austrian war criminals indicates.[60] With the return of many former Nazis into its ranks, the postwar Austrian judicial profession refused to threaten the postwar consensus with a vigorous persecution of war criminals. In Austria (and West Germany) there was continuity in the legal profession—it experienced only mild denazification.

It would be interesting to investigate what reactions the Eichmann trial caused among Austrians in the early 1960s and why it would not have led to the same kind of soul-searching the Germans went through. All the implications of the victim's doctrine, presumably that the Austrian Eichmann committed German crimes, permitted "externalization" which continued to soothe consciences, guilty or not.

The various essays in the small *Tabu und Geschichte* volume are too disparate to allow for any structured comparison. In a thoughtful essay Anton Pelinka analyzes the function of taboos in postwar Austrian political culture; he particularly stresses the importance of the circumvention of potential conflicts about the past for the reconciliation of the two principal parties. (See also Pelinka's essay in this volume.) The essays by Hartmut Mehringer on the French, by Drago Roksandic on the Yugoslav, and by Virgilio Ilari on the Italian postwar founding myths are valuable contributions to a postwar comparative history of historical memory. In all these countries the bloody past was purged and taboos about a rich pattern of complicity with the Nazi in all of Europe's occupied societies became the common ground of historical memory.[61] What emerges in a comparative history of postwar European historical memory is that those countries occupied by the Nazis with the longest record of collaboration during the war denied that collaboration most vigorously after the war.

But nowhere in postwar Europe was history as willfully constructed and the past as notoriously purged as in Japan. Ian Buruma makes a fascinating comparison of German *Vergangenheitsbewältung* and Japanese *Vergangenheitsverdrängung*. Buruma is a Dutch-born journalist who has immersed himself into both of these cultures to understand their specific cultures of World War II remembrance. While the Germans have a deep sense of guilt (even youngsters to this day are *betroffen*), the Japanese do not. Buruma explains that in Japanese culture shame (losing face), not guilt, defines the memory of World War II.[62] While there have been efforts to incorporate the Holocaust into German history, the Japanese have virtually purged from their history books and public memory notorious Japanese war crimes such as the "rape" of Nanking, the medical experiments (vivisection of prisoners of war etc.) of the infamous Unit 731,[63] or the barbarous warfare of their soldiers in the Pacific. While total defeat has not only humiliated the German military class but also effectively suffocated German nationalism, it has only humiliated the Japanese. While the Germans see 1945 as their "zero hour," the end of the war does not constitute a clear break with the past for the Japanese.

The Japanese, of course, also constructed their founding myth for a livable past. Here Buruma's analysis is particularly persuasive. He shows how the Japanese have instrumentalized Hiroshima and the dropping of the atomic bomb to construct their own "victim mythology" (pp. 92ff). Hiroshima is considered the Japanese "martyrdom." Hiroshima is completely isolated from the Japanese war of aggression prior to it. The memorial culture of Hiroshima has universalized their city's unique experience into a pacifist anti-war theme with broad popular appeal. While "the point of view of the victim is jealously guarded in Hiroshima" (p. 106), Japanese officials and the public to this day do not want to know what happened before.

Their barbarous war of aggression and expansion in the Far East is pooh-poohed as a war like any other war in which soldiers kill and get killed. In the collective memory of the soldiers and the broader public, the Japanese did not admit to any war crimes or accept guilt. U.S. propaganda and its harping on Japanese war guilt during the occupation was aimed at sapping Japanese virility and threatening Japanese identity (p. 97). Japanese nationalists still feel that the Americans wanted to wipe out the memory of Hiroshima to hide their own war guilt. Along the lines of wartime propaganda, Japanese nationalists still argue that the Pacific War was a **patriotic** war of national liberation against Western imperialism. When individual soldiers break the collective silence with their individual memory of how the war transformed them form normal men into savage killers, they usually encounter death threats since such personal admissions of guilt threaten the entire fragile edifice of postwar patriotic social memory (pp. 129ff). It seems that challenges to majority patriotic memory by a minority carry penalties of stigmatization and denunciation everywhere (the "*Nestbeschmutzer* syndrome"). The messengers of bad tidings are scapegoated.

To this day it still takes courage in Japan to speak the truth. Nationalist revisionists denounce and reject historical truth as it showed its ugly face in the Tokyo war crimes trials as "the Tokyo trial view of history" (p. 161). With regard to Japanese atrocities, only the Allies put the Japanese on trial; the Japanese never tried their own war criminals. The Japanese did not care for the lively history lessons that come from putting the past on trial. Patriotic history and patriotic memory demands that the skeletons be kept in the closet. Not even the doctors of Unit 731 were put on trial; instead they embarked on distinguished postwar careers. Buruma concludes "There never were any Japanese war crimes trials, nor is there a Japanese Ludwigsburg. This is partly because there was no exact equivalent of the Holocaust" (p. 162). Indeed, the Japanese never planned and premeditated genocide.

Historical memory often grows and prevails in isolation. The rest of the world knows about Japanese atrocities (p. 166), only the Japanese remain oblivious to it. From an Austrian perspective, Buruma's study is so striking because it suggests more parallels between the Austrian and Japanese constructions of World War II memory than between the Austrian and West German constructions. While Austria deceived itself with its founding myth, the rest of the world[64] was well aware of the Austrians' *Verstrickung* in Nazi war crimes. Buruma's stunning comparative essay on the construction and the psychology of historical memory among the two principal aggressors and losers of the war is both superb intellectual and cultural history. Steeped in Japanese culture, Buruma succeeds in opening a window into the Japanese mental map of historical memory hitherto largely closed to Westerners.

Conclusion

In 1943 the death-denying young "White Rose" student resisters at the University of Munich posited the question about German apathy in the face of horrendous crimes all around them. Given our increasingly detailed knowledge about Austrian *Verstrickung* in Nazi war crimes, one is tempted to ask why so many Austrians remain either apathetic towards or even defiant of a less compartmentalized and more complex vision of the past, including the darker sides of Austrian World War II history? Compartmentalization may have been a necessary evil for a fledgling democracy trying to paper over the deep rifts between its traditional political *Lager*. A mature democratic society ought to confront its multi-faceted past and value open discourse about it.

All of the books under review here either implicitly or explicitly conclude that only the presence of a complex past in historical memory allows a society to "learn from history" (see, for example, Ziegler and Kannonier-Finster, p. 85). Ultimately, *Vergangenheits-verdrängung* by forgetting or externalizing the shadows of the past only procrastinates confrontation and *Vergangenheitsbewältigung*. Every generation needs to internalize and rework the past truthfully and honestly. Historical remembrance demands an active and reflective discourse with a complex past and all its bright spots and darker hues. The burden of history also offers opportunities for a better future.[65] If the past remains a foreign terrain never fully explored it might more easily be repeated. Confronting the truth leaves hope for the future. In Austria, as elsewhere, the past cannot be suppressed it has a tendency to prevail over time.

The complex past has ways of intruding and reasserting itself as the people of Waidhofen an der Ybbs have learned in the course of the past fifty years. In their homage to Germandom mentioned at the beginning of this essay, the old colors—the contours of the swastikas and brown uniforms—had a disconcerting habit of resurfacing by shining through the new gloss despite a regular retouching of the patriotic red-white-red colors.[66]

NOTES

1. Arno J. Mayer, "Memory and History: On the Poverty of Remembering and Forgetting the Judeocide," *Radical History Review* (1993): 7.

2. This painting greeted the visitor at the entrance of the great 1994 Vienna exhibition on "art and dictatorship." In the very rich two volumes of essays accompanying the exhibit, see Gabriele Petricek, "Unter der blühenden Linde: Die patriotische Übermalung in Waidhofen an der Ybbs," in *Kunst und Diktatur: Architektur, Bildhauerei und Malerei in Österreich, Deutschland, Italien und der Sowjetunion 1922-1956*, vol. 2, ed. Jan Tabor (Baden: Grasl, 1994), 944-49.

3. Tony Judt, "The Past is Another Country: Myth and Memory in Postwar Europe," *Daedalus* 121 (1992): 83-118; Judith Miller, *One by One, by One: Facing the Holocaust* (New York: Touchstone, 1990), 61-92; on the French, see Henry Rousso, *The Vichy Syndrome: History and Memory in France Since 1944*, trans. Arthur Goldhammer (Cambridge, MA: Harvard University Press, 1991), and Hartmut Mehringer's essay in *Tabu und Geschichte*, 78-99; on the Japanese see Buruma's book reviewed in this essay.

4. In his 1989 "White Rose" memorial lecture given at the University of Munich, Peter Steinbach castigated such compartmentalization (*Aufteilung*) of a nation's past "*in einen dunken und in einen hellen Strang*" as "dishonest." See his "'Erinnerung - aktives Gedenken': Annäherung an den Widerstand," in *Die weiße Rose und das Erbe des deutschen Widerstandes: Münchner Gedächtnisvorlesungen* (Munich: C.H. Beck, 1993), 137.

5. See the cover story "Mein Vater, ein Nazi: Der schwierige Umgang mit der Kriegergeneration," *profil*, 15 January 1996, 56-62.

6. In the course of her investigative interviews, surviving widows of aryanizers have denounced Irene Etzersdorfer as an "impudent intruder" ("*frecher Eindringling*") in their private lives *Etzersdorfer, Arisiert*, 17). Critically questioning the Austrian patriotic and militaristic culture of memory in war memorials usually leads to severe attacks through the war generation, see Gärtner and Rosenberger, *Kriegerdenkmäler*, 40ff. For my deconstruction of Austria's "victim's mythology," a spokesman of a patriotic organization denounced me as "a gifted pupil of Stalin," see Günter Bischof, "Die

Instrumentalisierung der Moskauer Erklärung nach dem 2. Weltkrieg," *Zeitgeschichte* 20 (1993): 359, 366n86.

7. For the best introduction to World War II historiography, see Evan B. Bukey, "Nazi Rule in Austria," *Austrian History Yearbook* 23 (1992): 202-33. Heidemarie Uhl concentrates on these paradigm shifts in postwar historiography and historical memory of World War II in her essay in this volume.

8. Fritz Molden, *Der Ruf des Gewissens: Der österreichische Freiheitskampf, 1938-1945* (Vienna: Europaverlag, 1970); Radomir Luza, *The Resistance in Austria, 1938-1945* (Minneapolis: University of Minnesota Press, 1984).

9. Mayer, "Memory and History," 11.

10. Anton Pelika and Erika Weinzierl, eds., *Das große Tabu: Österreichs Umgang mit der Vergangenheit* (Vienna: Edition S, 1987); on the German *Historikerstreit*, see Charles S. Maier, *The Unmasterable Past: History, Holocaust, and German National Identity* (Cambridge, MA: Harvard University Press, 1988).

11. Emmerich Talos, Ernst Hanisch, and Wolfgang Neugebauer, eds., *NS-Herrschaft in Österreich 1938-1945* (Vienna: Verlag für Gesellschaftskritik, 1988).

12. Robert Knight, "The Waldheim Kontext: Austria and Nazism," *Times Literary Supplement*, 3 Oct. 1986, 1083f; idem, ed., *'Ich bin dafür die Sache in die Länge zu ziehen': Die Wortprotokolle der österreichischen Bundesregierung von 1945 bis 1952* (Frankfurt: Athenäum, 1988); idem, "Besiegt oder befreit? Eine völkerrechtliche Frage historisch betrachtet," in *Die bevormundete Nation: Österreich und die Alliierten 1945-1949,* ed. Günter Bischof and Josef Leidenfrost (Innsbruck: Haymon, 1988).

13. Heidemarie Uhl, *Zwischen Versöhung und Verstörung: Eine Kontroverse um Österreichs historische Identität fünfzig Jahre nach dem "Anschluß"* (Vienna: Böhlau, 1992).

14. For Vranitzky's speech at the Hebrew University on 8 June 1993, see *Salzburger Nachrichten*, 9 June 1993. For a critical view of this speech, see Thomas Albrich, "'Es gibt keine jüdische Frage'. Zur Aufrechterhaltung des österreichischen Opfermythos," in *Der Umgang mit dem Holocaust: Europa - USA - Israel*, ed. Rolf Steininger and Ingrid Böhler (Vienna: Böhlau, 1994), 165f.

15. With the outbreak of the Cold War, Judt sees the postwar European (including Austria) inventions of World War II memory in place and operative by 1948. In the Austrian chronology, 1949, however, seems to be the crucial turning point; see Judt, "The Past Is Another Country," 84-97.

16. "Unlike the perpetrators, the victims were perpetually exposed. They were identifiable and countable at every turn. To be defined as Jews, they only had to have had Jewish parents or grandparents." For an unmistakable definition of victims, see Raul Hilberg, *Perpetrators, Victims, Bystanders: the Jewish Catastrophe 1933-1945* (New York: Harper Collins, 1992). x, 105-91.

17. Like the picture in Waidhofen an der Ybbs for the local arena, the political infighting over the contents of the great anti-fascist propaganda show "*Niemals vergessen!*" (never forget) provides the metaphor for construction of public collective memory for the national arena. Instead of its initial artistic concept to show the netherworld of *Alltags*fascism in Austria during the war, the government forced the artists to accept the newly constructed consensual doctrine of Austria as victim. See the highly instructive analysis by Wolfgang Kos, "Die Schau mit dem Hammer: Zur antifaschistischen Ausstellung 'Niemals vergessen!' in Wien 1946," in *Kunst und Diktatur*, II: 950-64.

18. Günter Bischof, "Die Instrumentalisierung der Moskauer Erklärung nach dem 2. Weltkrieg," *Zeitgeschichte* 20 (1993): 345-66; for a critique of my "instrumentalization" thesis, see Gerald Stourzh, "Erschütterung und Konsolidierung des Österreichbewußtseins - vom Zusammenbruch der Monarchie zur Zweiten Republik," in *Was heißt Österreich? Inhalt und Umfang des Österreichbegriffs vom 10. Jahrhundert bis heute*, ed. Richard G. Plaschka, Gerald Stourzh, and Jan Paul Niederkorn (Vienna: Verlag der Österreichischen Akademie der Wisenschaften, 1995), 289-311; see also Thomas Albrich's essay "'Es gibt keine jüdische Frage': Zur Aufrecherhaltung des österreichischen Opfermythos," in *Der Umgang mit dem Holocaust*, 147-66.

19. Dieter Stiefel, *Entnazifizierung in Österreich* (Vienna: Europaverlag, 1981); Sebastian Meissl, Klaus-Dieter Mulley, and Oliver Rathkolb, eds., *Verdrängte Schuld, verfehlte Sühne: Entnazifierung in Österreich 1945-1955* (Vienna: Verlag für Geschichte und Politik, 1986).

20. Thomas Albrich, "Die Linken für die Rechten: Labour Party, SPÖ und die 'Vierte' Partei 1948/49," *Tel Aviver Jahrbuch für Geschichte* 19 (1990): 383-410.

21. Foreign Minister Karl Gruber was one of the most prominent spokesmen for this view; see, for example, his views on the Allied "*Befreierokkupation*" and on Allied troops as "*Usurpatoren*" in various 1949/50 speeches in Michael

Gehler, ed., *Karl Gruber: Reden und Dokumente 1945-1953* (Vienna: Böhlau, 1994), 247, 273, 298, 334. The legacy of such selective memory can be seen from the fact that Chancellor Vranitzky, as late as April 1945, spoke of "17 years of occupation," see Robert Streibel's column in *Der Standard*, 21 April 1995, 35.

22. Simon Wiesenthal's figures are cited in Gerhard Botz, "Eine deutsche Geschichte 1938 bis 1945? Österreichs Geschichte zwischen Exil, Widerstand und Verstrickung," *Zeitgeschichte* 13 (1986): 30.

23. On Austrian evasion of Jewish restitution claims on the national level, see the depressing study by Brigitte Bailer, *Wiedergutmachung kein Thema: Österreich und die Opfer des Nationalsozialismus* (Vienna: Löcker, 1993), and Bailer's essay in this volume; from an individual's perspective, see the memoirs by Albert Sternfeld, *Betrifft: Österreich* (Vienna: Löcker, 1990). On Austria's evasive diplomacy with Jewish organizations on the international level, see Thomas Albrich, "Jewish Interests and the Austrian State Treaty," vol. 1, *Contemporary Austrian Studies*, ed. Günter Bischof and Anton Pelinka (New Brunswick: Transaction, 1993), 137-64.

24. See, for example, the various essays in *The Kreisky Era in Austria*, in Günter Bischof and Anton Pelinka, eds., vol. 2, *Contemporary Austrian Studies* (New Brunswick, NJ: Transaction, 1994).

25. For the unsavory Kreisky-Wiesenthal affair, see Herbert Pierre Secher, "Kreisky and the Jews," *CAS* 2: 10-31; and his chapter "The Protector" in *Bruno Kreisky: Chancellor of Austria* (Pittsburgh, PA: Dorrance, 1993), 178-93; and Simon Wiesenthal's memoirs *Justice not Vengeance*, trans. Ewald Osers (New York: Weidenfeld, 1989), 289-304.

26. On Kreisky's wartime experiences, see the first volume of his splendid memoirs *Zwischen den Zeiten: Erinnerungen aus fünf Jahrzehnten* (Berlin: Siedler, 1986), 290-403.

27. Without giving any empirical evidence, Reinhold Gärtner does see a caesura in the 1979 "Holocaust" showing and debate, see "Der Umgang mit Gedenkstätten und Gedenktagen in Österreich," in *Schwieriges Erbe*, 270. The public debates over and the impact of the "Holocaust" series on Austrian memory is a topic demanding further research.

28. They rely heavily on Maurice Halbwachs' theory of collective memory [*La Mémoire Collective* (Paris 1968)] as does Arno Mayer who speaks of insular individual memory *vs.* shared collective memory, see "Memory and History," 9.

29. I rely on Raul Hilberg's useful working definition of "perpetrator": "The perpetrators were people who played a specific role in the formulation or implementation of anti-Jewish measures. In most cases, a participant understood his function, and he ascribed it to his position and *duties* [!]. What he did was *impersonal*. He had been empowered or instructed to carry out his mission. Moreover, no one man and no one organization was solely responsible for the destruction of the Jews. No single budget was allocated for this purpose. *The work was diffused in a widespread bureaucracy, and each man could feel that his contribution was a small part of an immense undertaking*. For these reasons, an administrator, clerk, or uniformed guard *never referred to himself as a perpetrator*. He realized, however, that the process of destruction was deliberate, and that once he had stepped into the maelstrom, his deed would be indelible. *In this sense he would always be what he had been, even if he remained reticent or silent about what he had done*" (emphasis added). See Hilberg, *Perpetrators, Victims, Bystanders*, ix, 3-102. Hilberg's bureaucratic definition, of course, is also applicable to the bureaucracies of Mauthausen and its subcamps, to euthanasia in Castle Hartheim, to the hunting down of partisans and treatment of POWs on the Eastern fronts.

30. What Daniel J. Goldhagen says in his powerful new book *Hitler's Willing Executioners: Ordinary Germans and the Holocaust* (New York: Knopf, 1996) about the Germans, surely also applies to the Austrians: the Germans participated in the slaughter of Jews by the tens of thousands because they were steeped in a historical culture of anti-Semitism. They eagerly tortured, massacred and starved Jews because of their birth.

31. For exact figures of Austrian *Wehrmacht* soldiers and dead, see the research note by Rüdiger Overmans in this volume.

32. That the leadership of the German *Wehrmacht* and millions of soldiers bought into the Nazi ideology of a war of extermination in the East against "Slavic *Untermenschen*" (and bolshevists to boot) and Jews has been exhaustively documented by a growing body of recent literature on the subject matter. See Omer Bartov, *Hitler's Army* (New York: Oxford University Press, 1992); Hannes Heer and Klaus Naumann, eds., *Vernichtungskrieg der Wehrmacht 1941-1944* (Hamburg: Hamburger Edition, 1995). While we can assume from this literature that what is true for German *Wehrmacht* soldiers on the Russian fronts may by and large also be applied to Austrian soldiers, Walter Manoschek has made the case more specifically for Austrian *Wehrmacht* soldiers in the Balkans, see his brilliant *'Serbien ist judenfrei': Militärische Besatzungspolitik und Judenvernichtung in Serbien 1941/42* (Munich: Oldenbourg, 1993).

33. Most normal human beings think that war is horrific, Anglo-American World War II soldiers particularly so. This emerges clearly when reading U.S. soldiers wartime memories. Representative of a vast literature is the incisive memoir of a regular infantry soldier, Leon C. Standifer, *Not in Vain: A Rifleman Remembers World War II* (Baton Rouge: Louisiana State University Press, 1992); see also the oral history collection by Ron Drez, *Voices of D-Day* (Baton Rouge: Louisiana University Press, 1994), and Chad Berry's essay in this volume. Some two dozen oral histories conducted with German and Austrian D-Day soldiers make me think that Austrian *Wehrmacht* soldiers have had a similar human response.

34. Japanese soldiers of the Pacific War did this and so did American soldiers in the Vietnam War, see Buruma, *Wages of Guilt*, 41.

35. From the location of Hausman's various engagements as a soldier, one cannot conclude that he was a perpetrator. But his prewar ideological commitments and his postwar construction of memory lead to this assumption; the authors mildly suggest it with their ironic categorization of one "*der Haltung bewahrt*" (p. 92). Hilberg suggests a framework for determining perpetrators of the Holocaust in the Nazi armed forces, namely those who were involved in "logistic support of killing operations in the occupied USSR; direct killings in Serbia and the occupied USSR; ghettoization in the occupied USSR; discriminatory measures and deportations from France, Belgium, and Greece; regulation of forced Jewish labor in armament plants; employment of forced Jewish labor by armed offices; transport questions." See his list in *Perpetrators, Victims, Bystanders*, 23. This list can be expanded to armed forces involvement in the killing of Soviet POWs, partisans all over occupied Europe and other victims.

36. For a highly revealing recent study on German police work in the occupied areas of the East that the authors did not consult, but which is very instructive about the Knittlers of this world, see Christopher R. Browning, *Ordinary Men: Reserve Police Battalion 101 and the Final Solution* (New York: Harper Collins, 1992). Browning's conclusion about routinized mass-murder as part of the "*Alltag*" of the Third Reich is chilling: "Ultimately, the Holocaust took place because of at the most basic level individual human beings killed other human beings in large numbers over an extended period of time. The grass-roots perpetrators became 'professional killers.'" (p. xvii, xix). For the categorization of order police in the various Nazi occupations as perpetrators, see also Hilberg, *Perpetrators, Victors, Bystanders*, 24 and passim.

37. As a KZ camp guard her husband surely was a perpetrator while with her almost certain passive knowledge she would qualify at least as a "bystander;" on bystanders, see Hilberg, *Perpetrators, Victims, Bystanders*, 195-286.

38. The authors do not cite Gordon J. Horwitz's study *In the Shadow of Death: Living Outside the Gates of Mauthausen* (New York: Free Press, 1990). Like the authors, Horwitz has reconstructed from oral history the knowledge of the *Frau* Scherers and their complicity of silence. They lived around Mauthausen and its subcamp empire and witnessed unspeakable crimes on a daily basis. Horwitz shows how Austrians have tried to wipe out the traces of Mauthausen and thus tear down the fabric of remembrance. By forgetting they shirk their responsibility as witnesses of history. He concludes: "muteness is the sign of complicity." (pp. 175-88).

39. Hilberg describes the type of zealous Austrian "newcomers" to the flock of Nazi perpetrators: "For the Austrians, there was continuity in the regional bureaucracy of Austria itself. Inasmuch as the small Austrian military was integrated into the German army, Austrians rose in rank and some of them obtained important commands. Austrian business expanded its influence in the Balkans. The Austrians also had territorial preserves in several parts of Germany's Europe. In the Netherlands, the Reichskommissar, Arthur Seyss-Inquart, and much of his entourage were Austrian. The military administration and garrison in Serbia contained many Austrians. In the Galician district of the Generalgourvernement, the Austrian Nazi Otto Wächter was Gouverneur. Later on, he was chief of the military administration in Italy. Another Austrian Nazi, Odilo Globonic, was the SS and Police Leader in the Lublin District. He was organizer of deportations in his district, and in the Warsaw and Bialystok ghettos. In addition, he ran death camps. Most of the principal officers were also Austrian. Finally, the Austrian Ernst Kaltebrunner was the last Chief of the Reich Security Main Office, which contained the Security Police (comprising Gestapo and Criminal Police and the Security Service." See Hilberg, *Perpetrators, Victims, Bystanders*, 37f. For a highly instructive case study of an archetypical Austrian perpetrator in the second rank, see Jonathan Petropoulos, "The Importance of the Second Rank: The Case of the Art Plunderer Kajetan Mühlmann," *Austro-Corporatism: Past, Present, Future*, vol. 4 of *Contemporary Austrian Studies*, ed. Günter Bischof and Anton Pelinka (New Brunswick: Transaction, 1996), 177-221.

40. The studies of Gerhard Botz come to mind, especially his *Wohnungspolitik und Judendeportation in Wien 1938-45* (Vienna, 1975), and Hans Witek's "'Arisierungen' in Wien: Aspekte nationalsozialistischer Enteignungspolitik 1938-1940," in *NS-Herrschaft in Österreich*, 199-216.

41. The generational dialogue about World War II in Austria has been a difficult one full of misunderstanding and distrust. The war generation usually kills any meaningful discourse about the memory of war with "You don't know, you have not been there!" This has reinforced the resounding Austrian silence about the war and helped maintain the postwar consensus. To prevent any

misunderstanding, I want to state clearly that obviously I do not consider **all** Austrian soldiers perpetrators. I am not operating with a blanket assumption of guilt (*pauschaler Schuldbegriff*) (see the introduction to Bergmann, Erb, and Lichtblau, *Schwieriges Erbe*, 12). I am well aware of the few choices of my father's generation's (he fought in a *Gebirgsjäger* division in Finland and was a POW in the U.S.) between being drafted into the *Wehrmacht* or going Franz Jägerstädter's courageous path of death defying resistance.

I am aware of the great variety of Austrians' emotional and ideological attachment or detachment to serving the Nazi cause in the German *Wehrmacht* (along the lines of the archetypical "Austrians" interviewed and dissected in *Österreichs Gedächtnis*). I also assume that in Austria, as in other countries occupied by the Nazis, numbers of volunteers for the *SS* tended to be higher than in Germany. See George L. Mosse, *Fallen Soldiers: Reshaping the Memory of the World Wars* (New York: Oxford University Press, 1990), 205-209. There is no question that the anti-Semitism of Austrians in general and in the SS in particular was more rabid; See Hans Safrian, *Die Eichmann-Männer* (Vienna: Europaverlag, 1993). One possible interpretation for Rüdiger Overmans' statistics on death rates in this volume may be that the Austrians were less eager soldiers than the Germans even though that is not the impression I have been getting in interviews with German and Austrian veterans. But based on the literature under review here the point is that they were not **all** "victims" either.

My task as a historian is to provide building blocks for a more critical understanding of the past. As an Austrian "*Spätgeborener*" I am well aware of the survivor's instincts of passivity in the face of totalitarianism (I stress, however, that I find Chancellor's Kohl's statement of the "*Gnade der späten Geburt*" singularly unfortunate). Few humans muster the courage of Jägerstädter's choice.

On the issue of the "children of the perpetrators" and their mastery, or more often denial of the past, see for a popular account by an Austrian journalist Peter Sichrosvsky, *Born Guilty: Children of Nazi Families*, trans. Jean Steinberg (New York: Basic Books, 1988); for a scholarly account based on extensive interviews in Germany by an Israeli psychologist, see Dan Bar-On, *Legacy of Silence: Encounters with Children of the Third Reich* (Cambridge, MA: Harvard University Press, 1989).

42. The literal translation of the term is "soldiers' memorials"; but since the these "*Kriegerdenkmäler*" became the principal vehicle of the highly selective **local remembrance of the entire war** they in fact mutate to "war memorials."

43. This figure needs to be revised to 1,286,000 soldiers according to Overmans' "research note" in this issue!

44. Of course, they were not Holocaust revisionists, denying the holocaust in Pierre Vidal-Naquet's stricter sense of "assassins," see his splendid essays in *Assassins of Memory: Essays on the Denial of the Holocaust*, trans. Jeffrey Mehlman (New York: Columbia University Press, 1992).

45. Gabriele Rosenthal has summarized it poignantly in her chapter "Vom Krieg erzählen, von den Verbrechen schweigen," in *Vernichtungskrieg*, 651-62. Hitler's generals were as instrumental in shaping this selective mendacious image of the past by writing memoirs purged of the *Tätergeschichte* as the official victim's doctrine was for the public at large, see Friedrich Gerstenberger, "Strategische Erinnerungen" in *Vernichtungskrieg*, 620-29, and Bartov's final chapter in *Hitler's Army.*

46. Wilhelm Swoboda, "'...vorbehaltlos meine Plicht erfüllt': Das Inernierungslager Glasenbach (Camp 'Marcus W. Orr')," *Zeitgeschichte* 22 (1995): 3-29. This is a model case study of a postwar veterans organization and its revisionist activities and culture of remembrance feeding into Austrian right-wing politics; we need many more of them. Swoboda's study is not complete, however, in as much as he failed to consult U.S. records on Glasenbach.

47. While in the early 1950s the code word "*gewisse Kreise*" probably denoted particularly Communist critics of this Austrian culture of memory, it resurfaced in the 1980s during the Waldheim affair and came to signify a Jewish world conspiracy (a notion that of course has deep roots in the Nazi world view).

48. Reinhold Gärtner, "Der Umgang mit Gedenkstätten und Gedenktagen in Österreich," in *Schwieriges Erbe*, 273.

49. It would be worthwhile to test the thesis of George Mosse's brilliant study of the "cult of the fallen soldier" in a detailed study of Austrian memorial culture. Mosse concentrates on Germany but also deals with France and Italy. He notes that the World War I myth of the "cult of the fallen soldier" was not revived in Germany after World War II after the devastating and total defeat of the German army (see Mosse, *Fallen Soldiers*, 211ff). It seems to me that Uhl's Styrian evidence (and Gärnter and Rosenberger's evidence from Upper Austria) point into the opposite direction: based on the "victim's mythology," which externalized the defeat in total war to Germany, the *Kameradschaftsbünde* in Austria managed to revive the making of soldiers into heroes and the "cult of the fallen soldier" and thereby unthinkingly also glorified the military tradition. In fact, many World War II memorials were simply added to the World War I memorials which usually dominated the local church graveyards. The Allies played along in Austria even as they did not in Germany.

50. Haider's speech before a *Waffen-SS Kameradschaft* in Krumpendorf recently scandalized Austria. On Haider and the historical memory of World War II, see the interview in *Die Presse*, 8 February 1996. On Haider's populism, see the Forum "The 'New Right' in Austria," in *CAS* 4, 280-368.

51. For an excellent introduction into the comparative European memory of war crimes and genocide, see Alfred Grosser, *Verbrechen und Erinnerung: Der Genozid im Gedächtnis der Völker*, trans. Ulrike Bokelmann (Munich: DTV, 1993).

52. These studies must be complemented with the comparative volume of European holocaust remembrance *Der Umgang mit dem Holocaust* reviewed separately by Daniel Rogers in this volume.

53. Michael Gehler's, Reinhold Gärtner's, Walter Manoschek's and Richard Mitten's essays from this volume were published in English in the FORUM "The 'New Right' in Austria," in *CAS* 4, 289-350.

54. Agnes Blänsdorf, of course, has penned the admirable pioneering essay of such a structured comparison, see "Zur Konfrontation mit der NS-Vergangenheit in der Bundesrepublik, der DDR und Österreich: Entnazifizierung und Wiedergutmachungsleistungen," *Aus Politik und Zeitgeschichte* B16-17 (1987).

55. For more detail on this issue, see Olaf Groehler's essay "Der Umgang mit dem Holocaust in der DDR," in *Der Umgang mit dem Holocaust*, 233-45.

56. In the epilogue to the German edition, Alfred Grosser has observed correctly that the world has ignored this East German apology, see *Verbrechen und Erinnerung*, 279f.

57. On the numbers, see Jörg Fisch, *Reparationen nach dem Zweiten Weltkrieg* (Munich: C.H. Beck, 1992).

58. This is Ian Buruma's phrase; he adds, "Many young Germans rejected everything their parents stood for. They sat in judgment over their past [and] hated them for their silence"; see *Wages of Guilt*, 19.

59. For the basic texts, see *'Historikerstreit': Die Dokumentation der Kontroverse um die Einzigartigkeit der nationalsozialistischen Judenvernichtung* (Munich: Piper, 1987); for the debate, see Dan Diner, ed., *Ist der Nationalsozialismus Geschichte? Zu Historisierung und Historikerstreit* (Frankfurt: Fischer, 1991); Richard J. Evans, *In Hitler's Shadow: West German Historians and the Attempt to Escape from the Nazi Past* (New York: Pantheon, 1989).

60. The *terra incognita* of the records of Austrian *Volksgerichte* reflecting the complicity of Austrians in the crimes of National Socialism is starting to get the deserved attention of professional historians, e.g. see Wolfgang Muchitsch, 'Das Volksgerichte Graz," in *Die 'britische' Steirmark 1945-1955*, ed. Siegfried Beer (Graz: Historische Landeskommission, 1995), 141-56; for a comparison see, Helge Grabitz, 'Die Verfolgung von NS-Verbrechen in der Bundesrepublik Deutschland, der DDR und Österreich," in *Der Umgang mit dem Holocaust*, 198-220.

61. On this, see also Judt's "The Past is Another Country," 86ff.

62. In his thoughtful review of Buruma's book, Gordon Craig finds this cultural model of German guilt vs. Japanese shame only of limited heuristic usefulness, see "An Inability to Mourn," *New York Review of Books*, 14 July 1994, 43.

63. See also "Japan Confronting Gruesome War Atrocity," *New York Times*, 17 March 1995, 1, 4.

64. For American perspectives in 1946, see Günter Bischof, "Between Responsibility and Rehabilitation: Austria in International Politics 1940-1950" (Ph.D. diss., Harvard University, 1989), 413-20.

65. Steinbach, "Erinnerung - aktives Gedenken," in *Die weiße Rose*, 132-36.

66. Petricek, "Unter der blühenden Linde," 946.

Austria-Hungary and World War I

Günther Kronenbitter

In his reflections on the outbreak of the First World War, written in the winter of 1918-19, Leopold Baron von Andrian-Werburg, Hugo von Hoffmannsthal's friend and in 1914 Austria-Hungary's envoy to Warsaw, maintained that "we," the Austrians, "began the war, not the Germans and even less the Entente—that I know."[1] Despite the fact that it was Austria-Hungary that triggered the Third Balkan War and thereby provoked the outbreak of the Great War, historians interested in the origins of World War I have tended to focus on the system of international relations or on Germany's role before and during the July crisis. Even today, it seems to be received wisdom among scholars in Germany and elsewhere to consider the Habsburg Monarchy as the weak-willed appendix of the powerful German Reich. It is highly probable that the Cold War experience of superpowers favored such an approach, but even more important has been the controversy over Fritz Fischer's theses which stimulated numerous studies on all aspects of German history before and during the Great War. In 1976, Fritz Fellner published a still unsurpassed analysis of the so-called "Hoyos mission" intended to encourage research on Austria-Hungary's part in the July crisis.[2] Roughly two decades later, a number of studies have shed new light on the domestic and foreign policy of the Habsburg Monarchy in the last decade of its existence. Unfortunately, the results of these scholarly efforts have not yet reached a broader audience outside the Central European academy and small circles of specialists elsewhere; neither the public nor the international scholarly community are aware of them.[3] But now there is hope because there are books and articles that will bridge the gap between research and reception, quite a few of them in English.[4]

Together with Fellner and other Central European scholars, British and North American historians like Francis Roy Bridge, István Deák, Norman Stone, Solomon Wank, and Samuel R. Williamson have paved the way to what recently has evolved as a flourishing field of late Habsburg Monarchy studies. Particularly outstanding examples of thorough and comprehensive scholarship are two articles by John Leslie, whose work was tragically cut short by his death in 1993. In the words of Fellner, Leslie's

> broad concept of an account of Austro-Hungarian war aims and the history of the Polish question in the First World War was not completed, but...in the fragments he has left behind, and in the many suggestions he made in innumerable private and public historical discussions, [he] has made such a rich contribution to our knowledge of the history of these years.[5]

In the 1980s Leslie published Andrian's memorandum quoted above. Then, just before his death, his article "The Antecedents of Austria-Hungary's War Aims: Policies and Policy-Makers in Vienna and Budapest Before and During 1914."[6] appeared. The subtitle indicates the scope of the study, which bears witness to the author's unequaled knowledge of relevant archival and published sources. The key decision-makers of 1914—Conrad von Hötzendorf, the Chief of the General Staff, bellicose by profession and by calling; István Tisza, the Hungarian prime minister, whose veto blocked Austria-Hungary's appeal to arms for two weeks in the July crisis, and his most important foreign affairs advisor Stephan Burián; Ludwig Thallóczy, scholar and Balkan expert; the Austrian prime minister, Karl Stürgkh; Leon Bilinski, the common finance minister; and of course Leopold Berchtold and his staff at the foreign ministry—are considered as are their opinions on war and peace. The Balkans and the South Slav question, the relationship between domestic and foreign policy, and Austria-Hungary's status as a Great Power in decline are analyzed with impressive scrutiny. Leslie shows how these highly divergent views could meet in July 1914. Joined by Fellner's and Wank's contributions, his articles demonstrate that the Austro-Hungarian leadership opted for a war against Serbia, regardless of a probable—and widely expected—Russian intervention. In particular, among the *Ballhausplatz* staff the admirers of Berchtold's predecessor in office, Aehrenthal, considered activism and an expansionist foreign policy as the only way to cope with Austria-Hungary's perennial political crisis.

Whereas Leslie and Wank[7] lay the stress on the domestic background and the internal coordination—or lack thereof—in the Habsburg Monarchy's foreign policy, Williamson[8] and especially Bridge, who gives a brief account of Austria-Hungary's foreign policy from 1908 to 1914,[9] are more interested in the international context. Williamson's *Austria-Hungary and the Origins of the First World War*, written for the Macmillan series *The Making of the Twentieth Century*, concentrates on the last years before the war. But what distinguishes this book as such a remarkable achievement is the masterful selection and arrangement of pieces of information on the bewildering complexity of the Dual Monarchy's internal structure as well as its foreign relations. The author has coped with the problem of providing the necessary background which makes his account intelligible to the reader who is unfamiliar with the oddities of *Kakania* without boring the already initiated. The chapters on the domestic context and the instruments of Habsburg foreign policy, and on the Monarchy's allies and enemies are concise and focused and give an idea of the difficulties Austria-Hungary's governing elite had to face. According to Williamson, "the story of the coming of the war of 1914 is in part a story of how this government came to convince itself that only force would resolve the problem of the South Slavs."[10]

To explain this process, Williamson describes the reaction of the Habsburg Monarchy's political elite to Austria-Hungary's deteriorating position in the system of international relations since 1911. He makes the reader understand how and why Berchtold, who initially had advocated a peaceful solution to the Dual Monarchy's problems with Serbia and Montenegro, came to rely more and more on what Williamson calls "militant diplomacy," military measures short of war as means of an otherwise unenforceable foreign policy. After the three war/peace crises of 1912-13, Berchtold and others among the civilian leaders—not including some in the Habsburg Monarchy—were more willing than ever to view "war and force as necessary elements of the international system."[11] Even worse,

> by making every facet of the Albanian problem a test case, Berchtold managed to confront Serbia, Montenegro *and* Austria-Hungary with situations that demanded success for

> the latter. By converting issues into prestige matters on which compromise was impossible, the minister necessarily had to escalate his pressures if the other party balked.[12]

The emergence of Austria-Hungary's militant diplomacy and prestige politics in the course of the First and Second Balkan War and the manner in which the experience of 1912-13 shaped the Habsburg Monarchy's foreign policy in 1914 are at the core of Williamson's analysis. Therefore, Vienna's decision for war in July 1914 is seen as the result of a process of learning, even if Berchtold and the other decision-makers jumped to the wrong conclusions. All in all, it will be a long time before this book is overtaken by a more comprehensive and readable account of Austria-Hungary's way into the July crisis, when "a set of leaders experienced in statecraft, power and crisis management consciously risked a general war to fight a local war."[13]

Thanks to the research done in the last two decades, the internal and external factors that made Austria-Hungary go on the warpath seem to be quite clear. But there is still enough room for debate, even about apparently well-known issues like the significance of the Dual Alliance in 1914. Bridge, for example, considers the built-in tensions between Vienna and Berlin as the driving force in the Dual Alliance policy at the beginning of the July crisis:

> Ironically enough, one of Berchtold's arguments for taking a strong line was that otherwise Germany might despair of Austria-Hungary and abandon her for lost. In the final crisis, the solidarity of the Dual Alliance Powers was more the product of their mutual mistrust than of *deutsche Treue*.[14]

The point, on which both partners "were for once agreed, was that there must be no retreat; and that this particular Near Eastern crisis must be resolved in favour of the Central Powers, whether at the cost of a European war or not."[15]

Fellner holds a totally different view of Germany's policy in 1914. To him, the Germans played foul, pretending to support Austria-Hungary's goal of a localized war against Serbia but at the same time plotting for something quite different:

> While people in Vienna were preparing—with unintelligible dilatoriness and lack of consistency—to wage the 'third Balkan War' to subdue Serbia, people in Berlin were not only thinking about a great war, but also, from the very

> start, carrying out a well-deliberated and well-prepared concept."[16]

According to Fellner, the political and military preparations for carrying out the Schlieffen Plan undertaken in July, and in particular the German pressure on Vienna to mobilize against Russia at the end of the month, indicate that Berlin purposely misled the ally. Little wonder that he comments as follows on Wilhelm II's telegram to Franz Joseph of 31 July, asking for Austria-Hungary to abandon the campaign against Serbia and mobilize as many troops as possible against Russia:

> I do not understand why in the discussion about the outbreak of the First World War so little weight has been attached to this document, so monstrous in its wording, in its total disregard for the interests of the alliance partner, and its complete misrepresentation of the situation...Betrayal of an ally's interests has never been more crassly formulated than in this telegram.[17]

To be sure, the messages wired from Berlin to Vienna and vice versa in the last days of July mark the first major crisis in German-Austro-Hungarian relations in the summer of 1914. But there are basically two possible explanations for this strain on the Dual Alliance: first, a well-hidden conspiracy of German politicians and military people sought to use Austro-Hungarian aggression against Serbia as a pretext for a Great Power war—dating from the first half, not from the last days, of July—culminated in the enforcement of Germany's strategic needs; second, the divergent political goals of both Dual Alliance partners and mutual distrust made the military agendas incompatible. The conspiracy approach can only be dealt with in a detailed examination of the German decision-making process, if at all. To stress Germany's betrayal of Vienna's interests, *deutsche Tücke* instead of *deutsche Treue*, might be a modified way of falling back into the superpower-centered portrait of the Dual Alliance, the homemade nature of Austria-Hungary's willingness to launch the war against Serbia and to risk a Great Power war notwithstanding. Less thrilling, but demonstrating the by no means negligible influence of the junior partner in an asymmetrical alliance, the second of the two possible approaches mentioned above fits the line of interpretation favored not only by international historians like Williamson and Bridge but also by military historians.

As Norman Stone[18] and Holger Herwig[19] have suggested, the cooperation between the general staffs in Berlin and Vienna from 1909 onwards was based on quite different strategic needs and priorities. To make the Schlieffen Plan applicable to a strategic situation that was permanently getting worse, the Germans demanded an Austro-Hungarian offensive against Russia at the beginning of a war in order to pin down Russian troops and cover the eastern parts of Germany in the first weeks of the campaign. Given Austria-Hungary's need for German support to back up a more active Balkan policy, and with the Germans being the stronger military power by far, Franz Conrad von Hötzendorf had to accept the German plan as the basis of his own calculations, whereas Helmuth Moltke, German chief of staff, promised to distract Russian troops by a small scale operation from East Prussia southward.

Germany's growing isolation among the Great Powers—accelerated by the naval race with Britain and the Second Moroccan Crisis in 1911, and the build-up of the Russian army and navy, which was accompanied by new strategic railways that would speed up mobilization—nourished German fears. To reduce the strategic vulnerability, Moltke promoted closer military cooperation not only with Vienna, but also with Italy, the somewhat unreliable Triple Alliance partner, which had never really renounced the irredentist goal, the liberation of the Italian minority living in the Habsburg Monarchy. Conrad, who had pleaded for preventive war against Italy, Vienna's allied foe, was persuaded that Rome had to be considered a more or less trustworthy ally. This was miscalculation that proved to be fateful in 1914.

Germany's security policy was shaped by the diplomatic and—eventually—military confrontation between the Entente and the Triple Alliance plus Rumania, attached to the alliance by a secret treaty of dubious value. Austria-Hungary, facing Italian and Rumanian irredentist movements, had a different agenda: seen from Vienna and Budapest, the Balkan wars in 1912 and 1913 not only strengthened Serbia, but left the Habsburg Monarchy isolated, with Rumania, Greece and Serbia on the road to an anti-Austrian Balkan league, backed by Russia. The limited success of Austria's militant diplomacy in 1912 and 1913 offered no real compensation. Even more threatening, Germany still trusted Romania and Italy, favored Greece, and did nothing to support Austria-Hungary's belated imperialistic aspirations in Asia Minor. Once again, Austria-Hungary had to realize that the Dual Alliance, as Bridge states, "could only prove its worth if the war it was designed to deter actually broke out. In normal times of peace it was, for diplomatic purposes, useless."[20]

Habsburg military planning had to take into consideration different political scenarios: War Case B (Balkan: against Serbia and Montenegro), War Case R (against Russia), or War Case R+B, apart from a war against Italy. But only Case R and Case R+B had to be conceived in the context of coalition warfare. The strategically most awkward and at the same time politically most probable scenario would be if War Case B developed into War Case R+B while the deployment of troops according to Case B was already in progress. By shifting the Second Army from the Balkans to Galicia at an early stage of the mobilization timetable, Conrad seemed to be able to cope with such a situation. The evolution of Austria-Hungary's planning for war and the military understandings between Berlin and Vienna have been analyzed by Gerhard Ritter, Stone, Herwig, Lothar Höbelt[21] and Dieter Degreif.[22] In his recently published book, Graydon A. Tunstall[23] also deals with these policies from 1871 to 1914 in what is so far the most comprehensive study on the topic, discussing also the "interaction between the military and diplomatic leadership within and between Germany and Austria-Hungary"[24] and finally the "battlefield reality of the First World War in order to assess the adequacy of Central Power...military strategy and preparation on the eastern front."[25]

Needless to say, Tunstall cannot cover all these dimensions in an equally convincing way, but his account of the mismanaged mobilization of Austria-Hungary's troops in 1914, the subsequent military debacle in Galicia and in Serbia, and the attempts by Conrad, his admirers, and the general staff's railway bureau officials to cover up the general staff's lapse is fascinating and illuminating. Tunstall's statement that the "dispatch of an enlarged Second Army to the Balkan front was one of the most tragic decisions the Austro-Hungarians made during the early stages of the First World War"[26] is absolutely correct, and in the very end it is Conrad who is to blame for the disaster.[27] However, Conrad's slip has to be explained not so much as the result of "cognitive dissonance"[28] but as the consequence of Austria-Hungary's specific political priorities: as Fellner has stressed, it was for a war against Serbia, not against

Russia that Hoyos had to secure German backing.[29] But Conrad, Berchtold, and the Emperor had little doubt that Russia would intervene in case of an Austro-Hungarian-Serbian war.

Austria-Hungary's freedom of action had depended on German support; Germany's blank check provided Vienna with a opportunity to turn the tables. At the end of July, when the German Kaiser and his chancellor, too late, too wavering, maybe insincerely, tried—or at least pretended to try—to prevent a great Power War, Berchtold and Conrad had to face a possible restriction on their new Balkan policy, because Russian partial mobilization and troop deployment at the Galician border might have forced the *k.u.k.* (imperial and royal) army to give up the campaign against Serbia for an extremely expensive stand-off in the northeast. But, with Russia's general mobilization underway, Germany's security depended on Austro-Hungarian support. By mobilizing against Serbia as if there were no Russian threat, Conrad gained time for a campaign against Serbia and forced Germany to call Russia's bluff. With the experience of Germany's conduct in 1912-13 in mind, and in view of signs indicating that Berlin might stop the blank check, Conrad had reason to cash it; "after all, for Conrad, Germany was as much a threat to the Monarchy's position in the Near East as Russia was."[30] Therefore, when Russia and Germany actually went to war, Conrad had to shift troops from the Balkans to the north. They left the southern border too early to be of any use for the offensive operations against Serbia and reached the northern theater of war too late to prevent Russian victories there. The military diplomacy of the Dual Alliance contributed to the sloppy calculation of chances and risks in 1914, and divergent political priorities, mutual mistrust, and the mishandled strategic cooperation paved the way to Austria-Hungary's military disasters in Serbia and Galicia.

Tunstall's most interesting chapter, on the "historiography of mobilization" and the "Habsburg command conspiracy," casts light on the efforts of Austro-Hungarian officers to deceive the public and posterity by handing down a highly distorted image of the war.[31] The publication of certain works in the interwar period—Conrad's *Aus meiner Dienstzeit*; the Carnegie Foundation series on the economic and social history of the war; and a multi-volume official history of Austria-Hungary's three-front war, written by former high-ranking officers and officials—made it relatively easy to whitewash the army command and preserve retrospectively at least a bit of *k.u.k.* glory. In his short but very instructive article on Austria's historiography of the First World War, Rudolf Jeřábek points out that in interwar Austria there was "an astonishing identity of those who made and those who wrote history."[32] The military history of Austria-Hungary was still dominated by an apologetic tendency until the late 1960s.

Studies such as (to mention only two examples of works recently published in English) István Deák's book on the social history of the officer corps[33] or Lawrence Sondhaus' book on the *k.u.k.* navy[34] have changed this unpleasant situation. And it is Jeřábek 's biography of Oskar Potiorek, the Governor-General of Bosnia and Herzegovina from 1911 to 1914, that has epitomized an informative modern form of military biography.[35] Meticulous in his attention to detail, Jeřábek portrays the career of Conrad's greatest rival, his rise to one of the top positions available to an officer in the Monarchy, and his fall in the wake of Franz Ferdinand's assassination, when Potiorek commanded the unsuccessful offensives against Serbia in the summer and fall of 1914. Following Potiorek's career step by step, the reader can see how social networking and political plotting worked in the *k.u.k.* army. Potiorek's failed attempts to solve the extremely difficult task of reforming and pacifying Bosnia and Herzegovina depict the problems the Monarchy's men had to face and raise questions regarding the extent to which their reports and correspondence influenced the decision-making process in Vienna. Finally, Potiorek's performance as commander of the punitive campaigns against Serbia, and his reckless pressing ahead with the offensive regardless of the enormous casualty figures foreshadows the kind of warfare so typical of the following years of the First World War.

A reliable overall account of Austria-Hungary's share in the Great War was missing until 1993, when Manfred Rauchensteiner, now the director of Vienna's *Heeresgeschichtliches Museum* and an extraordinarily prolific writer of numerous books and articles on Austria's contemporary and military history, published *Der Tod des Doppeladlers*.[36] The book is obviously written not only for students and scholars but for a broader audience as well. It tries to sum up and to arrange in an intelligible and meaningful way the available historical knowledge, "to compile and to generalize."[37] The maps are helpful, the pictures impressive, and the straightforward narration, now and then interspersed with vivid primary source material, make for a good read. But Rauchensteiner also utilizes a great number of unpublished archival sources, enriches historical controversies by his conclusions, and even offers some new interpretations. This is a serious and in many respects masterful work, well-written and interesting throughout, for both the general reader and the serious student of Austro-Hungarian history.

The opening pages deal with what Rauchensteiner sees as the growing militancy—not to be confused with militarization *à la Prusse*—that pervaded the social and political life in the Monarchy in the last years before the war. This is followed by an account of the military apparatus, the war planning, and the state of the Dual Alliance at the time. The July crisis is discussed at length, and Rauchensteiner's interpretation of the events is innovative. Putting the primary sources under scrutiny, he points out that the reports on the so-called *Gefecht bei Temes Kubin* (fight at Temes Kubin) were not only made up but deliberately used by Berchtold to get the Emperor's signature on the declaration of war against Serbia as soon as possible in order to avoid any interference by other Great Powers. In the light of some new evidence, Rauchensteiner argues, it would be more accurate to say that the war was *entfesselt* (unleashed) than that it broke out.

Beginning with the mobilization, the miscarried offensives against Serbia and disastrous battles in Galicia in 1914, and the subsequent Austro-Hungarian winter of discontent, the author gives a roughly chronological narration of the military and political history of the war until the bitter end in 1918. But very prominent in his work are the other aspects of the war, for example the social and economic development of the Habsburg Monarchy between 1914 and 1918, and the impact on domestic politics of everything from the army's attempts to get political control of the hinterland to the final collapse of the empire. The experiences of war, the suffering and death, the daily routine of the soldiers, and the everyday life of civilians are also examined. The author does not skirt by the nasty oddities of Austria-Hungary's war, for example the harshness of the martial law regime in Galicia and Serbia or the measures taken against suspect nationalities or political activists. The overall picture is broad in scope and quite rich in color, but the account is most interesting where Rauchensteiner can base it on archival studies.

Enlivened by bits of diaries, papers, and correspondence of high-ranking army command officers, the sections on Conrad's headquarters give a vivid impression of the highly developed culture of intrigue in the *k.u.k.* military elite and the permanent quarrel between the Austro-Hungarians and their German allies. The diaries of the general staff officers Rudolf Kundmann and Karl Schneller, the memoirs of Archduke Friedrich's adjutant Herbert Herberstein, and Conrad's correspondence with Artur Bolfras, the head of Franz Joseph's military chancellory, are among the most enthralling unpublished sources quoted by Rauchensteiner. The fierce struggle of Conrad, the army command, and others to preserve at least some freedom of action for the Habsburg Monarchy and to contain German encroachment on Austria-Hungary's strategy, chain of command, and foreign policy (something that has already been analyzed by Gary W. Shanafelt[38]) is one if not *the* recurring theme of the book. It is closely related to the frequently very poor performance of the army command and a number of commanders of army units that made Austria-Hungary ever more dependent on German assistance.[39]

The Austro-Hungarian troops, on the other hand, did fairly well, and Rauchensteiner makes every effort to stress this. It was not the occasional problems with unreliable Czech or other Slav units that shattered military discipline. It was the sheer exhaustion, the repercussions of the revolutions in Russia and the U.S. entry into the war, and the failed attempts to make peace which discredited even the monarch in the eyes of soldiers and civilians that did it. The military operations and the discussion of war aims and peace terms demonstrated the mounting dependence on Germany, and in the very end, as Bridge notes, "even in the event of a German victory, the Monarchy would be hard pressed to make good its aims as an independent Great Power."[40] Rauchensteiner shows how the Entente, after the ill-fated Sixtus Affair, lost all interest in preserving Austria-Hungary. Facing the imminent military and political collapse and the policy of dismemberment finally adopted by the Entente, the army command mishandled the last act of the drama, the Villa Guisti armistice, just as it had done at the beginning of the war.

All in all, the study's range is not likely to be matched. To be sure, some aspects could be presented in even more detail. The account of domestic political developments in Austria, for example, is much more detailed than that on the situation in Hungary.[41] To a great extent, the emphasis on the upper strata of military and political decision-makers is a reflection of a historiographic trend that was dominant until a few years ago.

The impact of the war on Austria-Hungary's economy, society, culture and mentality still needs to be scrutinized, and this can only be done on a regional basis. What is still missing are more studies like those on the Tyrol, now underway thanks to the initiative of the *Tiroler Landesarchiv* and Innsbruck University's *Institut für Zeitgeschichte.* A new anthology, initially a series of lectures at the University of Innsbruck, gives an idea of the scope of possible fields of study.[42] Not only did the war change life in the Tyrol profoundly, but it also gave birth to powerful mythological topoi of the Tyrolese collective memory, like the *Standschützen* and the *Kaiserjäger*. More studies of this kind have to be done. In the meantime, and as long as the volume on the First World War of the handbook *Die Habsburgermonarchie*[43] has not been published—which is to say, for the next couple of years—Rauchensteiner's book has to be the point of departure for anyone interested in the final flapping of the double eagle's wings.

NOTES

1. John Leslie, "Österreich-Ungarn vor dem Kriegsausbruch: Der Ballhausplatz in Wien in July 1914 aus der Sicht eines österreichisch-ungarischen Diplomaten," in *Deutschland und Europa in der Neuzeit: Festschrift für Karl Othmar von Aretin zum 65. Geburtstag*, ed. Ralph Melville, Claus Scharf, Martin Vogt, Ulrich Wengenroth (Stuttgart: F. Steiner Verlag, 1988), 675.

2. Fritz Fellner, "Die Mission Hoyos," in *Recueil des travaux aus assies scientifiques internationales: Les grandes puissances et la Serbie à la veille de la première guerre mondiale*, ed. V. Čubrilović (Belgrade, 1976), 387-419.

3. Fritz Fellner, "Austria-Hungary," in *Decisions for War 1914*, ed. Keith Wilson (London: UCL Press, 1995), 9-25.

4. For a general survey of Austria-Hungary 1908-1918, based on recent research, see Mark Cornwall, ed., *The Last Years of Austria-Hungary: Essays in Political and Military History 1908-1918* (Exeter: Exeter University Press, 1990).

5. Fellner, "Austria-Hungary," 10-11.

6. John Leslie, "The Antecedents of Austria-Hungary's War Aims: Policies and Policy-Makers in Vienna and Budapest Before and During 1914," in *Archiv und Forschung. Das Haus-, Hof- und Staatsarchiv in seiner Bedeutung für die Geschichte Österreichs und Europas*, ed. Elisabeth Springer and Leopold Kammerhofer (Vienna: Verlag für Geschichte und Politik-München: R. Oldenbourg Verlag, 1993), 307-94.

7. Solomon Wank, "Desperate Counsel in Vienna in July 1914: Berthold Molden's Unpublished Memorandum," *Central European History* 26 (1993): 281-310.

8. Samuel R. Williamson, Jr., *Austria-Hungary and the Origins of the First World War* (Houndsmills: Macmillan, 1991).

9. Francis Roy Bridge, *The Habsburg Monarchy among the Great Powers, 1815-1918* (New York: Berg, 1990), 288-344. See also Francis Roy Bridge, "The Foreign Policy of the Monarchy, 1908-1918," in *The Last Years of Austria-Hungary. Essays in Political and Military History 1908-1918*, ed. Mark Cornwall (Exeter: Exeter University Press, 1990), 7-30.

10. Williamson, *Origins*, 15.

11. Ibid., 155.

12. Ibid., 155.

13. Ibid., 215. For the reasons for Austria-Hungary's slow proceeding in July 1914, see Samuel R. Williamson, Jr., "Confrontation with Serbia: The Consequences of Vienna's Failure to Achieve Surprise in July 1914," *Mitteilungen des Österreichischen Staatsarchivs* 44 (1993): 168-77.

14. Bridge, *Habsburg Monarchy*, 339.

15. Ibid., 340.

16. Fellner, "Austria-Hungary," 19.

17. Ibid., 22-23.

18. Norman Stone, "Moltke-Conrad: Relations between the Austro-Hungarian and German General Staffs, 1909-1914," *The Historical Journal* 9 (1966): 201-28.

19. Holger Herwig, "Disjointed Allies: Coalition Warfare in Berlin and Vienna, 1914," *Journal of Military History* 54 (1990): 265-80.

20. Bridge, *Habsburg Monarchy*, 379.

21. Lothar Höbelt, "Schlieffen, Beck, Potiorek und das Ende der gemeinsamen deutsch-österreichisch-ungarischen Aufmarschpläne im Osten," *Militärgeschichtliche Mitteilungen* 36 (1984): 7-30.

22. Dieter Degreif, "Operative Planungen des k.u.k. Generalstabes für einen Krieg in der Zeit vor 1914 (1880-1914)" (Ph.D. diss., Wiesbaden, 1983).

23. Graydon A. Tunstall, Jr., *Planning for War Against Russia and Serbia. Austro-Hungarian and German Military Strategies, 1871-1914* (New York: Columbia University Press, 1993).

24. Ibid., 3.

25. Ibid., 4.

26. Ibid., 220.

27. Norman Stone, "Die Mobilmachung der österreichisch-ungarischen Armee 1914," *Militärgeschichtliche Mitteilungen* 16 (1974): 67-95.

28. Tunstall, *Planning for War*, 222.

29. Fellner, "Austria-Hungary," 16-18.

30. Bridge, *Habsburg Monarchy*, 343.

31. Tunstall, *Planning for War*, 189-209.

32. Rudolf Jeřábek, "Die österreichische Weltkriegsforschung," in *Der Erste Weltkrieg. Wirkung, Wahrnehmung, Analyse*, ed. Wolfgang Michalka (München: Piper, 1994), 959: "*...eine verblüffende Einheit von Männern, die Geschichte machten, und Männern, die Geschichte schreiben....*"

33. István Deák, *Beyond Nationalism: A Social and Political History of the Habsburg Officer Corps, 1848-1918* (New York: Oxford University Press, 1990).

34. Lawrence Sondhaus, *The Naval Policy of Austria-Hungary, 1867-1918: Navalism, Industrial Development, and the Politics of Dualism* (West Lafayette, Indiana: Purdue University Press, 1994).

35. Rudolf Jeřábek: *Potiorek. General im Schatten von Sarajevo* (Graz: Styria Verlag, 1991).

36. Manfred Rauchensteiner, *Der Tod des Doppeladlers: Österreich-Ungarn und der Erste Weltkrieg* (Graz: Styria, 1993).

37. Ibid., 674.

38. Gary W. Shanafelt, *The Secret Enemy: Austria-Hungary and the German Alliance, 1914-1918* (New York: Columbia University Press, 1985).

39. See Rudolf Jeřábek, "Die Brussilowoffensive: Ein Wendepunkt der Koaltionskriegführung der Mittelmächte" (Ph.D. diss., Unversität Wien, 1982).

40. Bridge, *Habsburg Monarchy*, 369.

41. See József Galántai, *Hungary in the First World War* (Budapest: Akadémiai Kiadó, 1989).

42. Klaus Eisterer and Rolf Steininger, eds., *Tirol und der Erste Weltkrieg* (Innsbruck: Österreichischer Studien Verlag, 1995).

43. Adam Wandruszka and Peter Urbanitsch, eds., *Die Habsburgermonarchie*, vol. I-VI/2,(Vienna: Verlag der Österreichischen Akademie der Wissenschaften, 1973-1993).

Gertrude Enderle-Burcel, Rudolph Jeřábek, Leopold Kammerhofer, eds., *Protokolle des Kabinettsrates der Provisorischen Regierung Karl Renner 1945*, vol. 1: 29. April bis 10. Juli 1945 (Horn: Berger 1995).

Robert Knight

The importance of this collection for historians and political scientists of the Second Republic can hardly be exaggerated. Although it covers only the first sixteen cabinet meetings of the provisional government, two subsequent volumes covering the remaining five months of the Renner government are planned. They—and the minutes of succeeding cabinets—will make a fundamental rewriting of the history of postwar Austria not only possible but inevitable.

It is probably too early to say what form such a revision will take, but it should shift attention away from what might be called the trivia of high politics and increase our understanding of the pressures and complexities of political decision-making. Of course there will also be plenty of material here for debunkers and iconoclasts, while the gulf between public relations and political decision-making will often stretch wide. If this brings a less reverential attitude towards the Republic's founding fathers it will be no bad thing. But overall there is likely to be more pragmatism than shock, conspiracy, or scandal.

For the sake of simplicity five linked themes can be distinguished here: the establishment of the government's legitimacy; the overwhelming practical problems it was confronted with in the aftermath of the war; its dealings with the Soviet authorities; the internal dynamics of the three party "concentration government," including Karl Renner's leadership of it; and, finally, attitudes towards both the Nazi and Austrofascist past.

Western reactions to the Soviet *fait accompli* that set up the Renner government overshadowed it from the start. Renner moved from initial hopes for imminent recognition to increasing frustration. When the West finally sent a Military Mission to Vienna at the start of June, it was under strict instructions to ignore the government. The memoranda, detailing the actions, and above all the needs of the government, could not be presented, and the Mission itself was, as Renner complained, *"nicht fassbar, wir können zu ihr nicht sprechen"* (Session 12). Linked to this frustration was the fear of a revival of centrifugal, anti-Vienna forces in Western Austria, or, as Renner put it, the dangers *"wie seinerzeit Widerstandsbewegungen [sic] gegen die zentrale Staatsgewalt entstehen. Wichtig sei, daß die Einheit des Staatsgebietes auf jeden Fall gewahrt werde."* (Session 4). Renner described the frontier cordon (*Grenzkordon*) separating the government from the west as *"ganz unerträglich"* (Session 8), but in a way things got worse rather than better, and his visit to Graz on 20 May (reported to the Cabinet in some detail) was nullified shortly afterwards when Styria became part of the British zone.

The issue of legitimacy did not trouble Renner at all. His legendary self-assurance is evident on nearly every one of these pages, and it clearly never occurred to him that, seven years after he had publicly welcomed the Anschluß, he did not have the right to speak for the whole of Austria. His earlier position was reinterpreted as an honest lapse, cruelly misused and exploited by the Nazis. And he felt no embarrassment in asserting (on, of all issues, the importance of not giving any priority to Jewish redress) that *"alle Schichten der österreichischen Bevölkerung ein gewisses Vertrauen in meine Objektivität und Gerechtigkeit haben"* (Session 5).

It is stating the obvious to say that the practical problems of the postwar period were enormous, yet this volume brings this home with a fresh impact. Inflation, the black market, the influx of refugees from Czechoslovakia, the complexities of property, a mass of administrative details, and above all the food crisis took up long hours of discussion. It is more difficult to judge how well or badly the government coped with these problems or to assess the extent to which they were helped or hindered by the occupying authorities. What is clear is that in some key areas—notably the organization of the harvest and the regulation of food supplies to Vienna—the government could hardly assert its authority over the black market. As several ministerial comments show, they were operating in an administrative vacuum. Another major problem was the necessity but also the apparent impossibility of a currency reform; Finance Minister Georg Zimmermann warned that *"wir stehen volkswirtschaftlich vor einem Trümmerhaufen und müssen einen Ausweg finden"* (Session 10), but the issue was to dog the government for several years. Here and elsewhere some members of the government complained—more or less openly—about the damage (and lawlessness) of the Red Army. Yet when the latter did step in with food supplies this was gratefully acknowledged. The Soviet authorities for their part considered the government to be spending too much time drafting laws and not enough on practical work (Session 4).

Renner's domination of cabinet proceedings is evident and there is no hint of a challenge to it. The nearest approximation to it was the dispute over the restoration of the 1929 Constitution (*Verfassungsüberleitungsgesetz*) on 13 May. The position of Renner (and Schärf) was in line with the legal advice from Ludwig Adamovich, that the constitution had been *"demokratisch bis zur Lahmlegung des Parlamentes"* (i.e. 1933). The communists objected to pre-empting any later attempt to redraw the constitution, and the non-party Justice Minister Josef Gerö also had his doubts. In the sixth meeting the confrontation developed into an open dispute. The official minutes bear out the version later given by the SPÖ leader Adolph Schärf[1] (though not necessarily his interpretation of communist subversion). Far from letting the principle of unanimity be used against him, Renner put an ultimatum to his opponents (*"Unterwerfen Sie sich dieser Auffassung oder nicht?"*) and won his point. In short, Renner's lifetime experience of tactics and procedure made him a masterful chairman, who sensed when to force an issue, when to ignore it, when to refer it to a subcommittee, or when to hold a historico-philosophical lecture about it. To some like the diplomat Josef Schöner, whose fascinating diary is useful when read in conjunction with this volume,[2] his digressions appeared backward-looking and self-indulgent. Renner's admirers will doubtless see them as proof of his intellectual stature. Aside from Renner it is interesting to see some evidence of the start of a twenty year People's Party-

Socialist co-operation, but also points of convergence between the two "left-wing" parties (for example, in managing the economy) as well as points of divergence (like the treatment of Nazis).

For most of the Cold War the Renner government appeared as the "one which got away" in successfully confronting or evading a Soviet attempt to turn it into a puppet. This volume offers little support for this view, although it is clear that the relationship between the two was far from cozy. An interview with Marshal Tolbuchin on 12 May shows the gulf between the two sides; Tolbuchin stated with brutal clarity, *"Das Gesetz des Krieges ist: Wer die Beute macht, der nützt auch diese Beute aus."* The Soviet Union had lost *"ihre ganze Industrie bis an die Wolga."* A later discussion with Marshal Konev at the start of July produced a moment of optimism; Leopold Figl spoke of being treated as an equal partner for the first time (16th Session). But, in regard to Soviet economic claims, this was premature. Soviet dismantlement, which is discussed in this volume under the heading of "War Booty," was to continue after the Potsdam Conference in August under the title of German external assets.

As for the communist members, they come across in the discussions not so much as Trojans in a Soviet horse as spokesmen of passion, patriotism, and more than a little wishful thinking. One example of this came when Franz Honner reported improbably that returning soldiers of the Honner battalion, who had fought with the Yugoslav partisans, were *"lebhaft begrüß,"* on their entry into Vienna (7th Session).

Finally, what of the past, or pasts? For Renner it often seems to be a matter of resuming threads which had been lost in 1920; he and other socialist leaders saw the repression of 1934-38 as the central theme. As for the Nazis, Renner sometimes came close to the view that National Socialism was a "good idea badly executed" (as postwar U.S. opinion polls put it.) For example, in the 8th Session, he comments: *"man kann dem Nazi-regime [sic] alles Mögliche nachsagen, aber eine radikale gleichmäßige Verteilung haben sie tatsächlich in Angriff genommen."* On another occasion he argues the case for non-Nazi "civilized" eugenics since *"es ein berechtigtes Interesse jeder Volksgesamtheit [sic!] ist, einen erbkranken Nachwuchs zu verhindern"* (10th Session).

The difference from the perceptions of Catholic victims of the Nazis is often striking. One of the most dramatic moments of this whole collection comes in the 13th Session when Figl relates, with some emotion, that the man who arrested him on the eve of the Anschluß (one Alois Spitzer) is now asking for advancement as a victim of the Nazis. For Figl the end of the war was a *"seit Jahren [sic] ersehntes Ereignis"* (4th Session), which should be marked by a radio broadcast by the head of the government. Renner was more ambivalent, and from Schöner's diary we know that he had to be cajoled into making the speech marking V-E Day. To Schöner, and presumably Figl, Renner seemed too passive and defensive on the issue of Austria's status as a victim. For example, his response to Tolbuchin's comment, already cited, was, *"Wir sind weit entfernt von irgendwelchen Rechten unserer Seite zu reden—wir haben solche Rechte nicht."* Elsewhere he refers to Austria as a *"besiegten und...verelendeten Staat"* (14th Session).

Differences can also be seen in discussions about what to do with Nazis and war criminals. The communists urge radical measures, aware of a measure of Austrian complicity and suggest that if the government does not act, popular anti-Nazi resentment will spill over into vigilante justice. They find some support from Peoples Party figures like Figl and from Gerö. The latter argues from the position of an anti-Nazi, Austrian, patriotic jurist: *"Sie können sich nicht vorstellen, mit welcher Vehemenz sich die Nationalsozialisten auf Strafgesetz und Strafprozess geworfen und wie weit sie diese guten Gesetze durchlöchert haben...sodaß eine umfangreiche Arbeit notwendig war, diese Infiltration unseres österreichischen Rechtes zu beseitigen"* (12th Session). In contrast, socialist leaders are lukewarm. The result of these divergent positions for denazification was already clear two months after the formation of the government—bureaucracy mitigated by *Protektion.* The decision to register all Nazis but to allow even nominal members to appeal against registration soon led to an avalanche of applications for exemption; by June *"Die Gesuche...häufen sich zu Bergen"* (13th Session).

I would like to make two final points. First, the outstanding editorial quality of this edition compares favorably, not only with earlier editions of the cabinets of the First Republic, but also with the equivalent West German project (which has now reached 1954). Foreword, introduction, and apparatus are excellent, as are the biographical details of the *Personenregister* (even if George Kennan, though old, is not dead).

Second, I would like to answer the intemperate criticism directed several years ago by Thomas Albrich at my own publication of cabinet discussions regarding the restitution of Aryanized property and Jewish Displaced Persons.[3] Much of this attack can be safely dismissed as a product of *odium academicum* (e.g. on my permission to research in the Cabinet minutes: *"einem Dissertanten wurde gestattet, was Professoren weiterhin verwehrt wird!")*; some of it is just plain silly (Albrich's description of ministers as *"verbal Antisemiten"* for example). But two core points need to be addressed. First, he states that access to the Austrian Staatsarchiv became more difficult after the publication of my book (*"dank Knight und nicht nur wegen Waldheim"*!) because I had misused my research permission. I can only record that I have never received any official or unofficial objection or complaint, before or after publication, which would support such a view. If, however, my publication really had led the archival authorities to become more restrictive because it contained embarrassments, this obviously would be a matter of concern—though I could hardly consider myself to be responsible. In any case, the publication of this volume offers welcome counter-evidence for such an interpretation. Second, and more important, Albrich insinuates that I deliberately selected those cabinet discussions which showed the Austrian government in a bad light, and that this *"drastisches Bild"* would be revised if the whole discussions were known. I am happy to submit my selection to the test of comparison with the official and complete edition, but Albrich's prior assumption that I am biased in this sense is, to put it mildly, offensive. Since he states that his assumption is a *"berechtigte Annahme,"* I think I am entitled to ask what his *Berechtigung* is.

To return to the book under review, its value is that it provides access to a central source of political decision-makers not merely to historians but also to ordinary citizens, who can now find out what their political masters were up to. The drawback, of course, is that such editions often take an inordinate time to appear. For this reason, warm thanks to the editors of this volume should be mixed with the fervent hope that enough resources are made available to them to publish its sequels speedily.

NOTES

1. Adolf Schärf, *Österreich Erneuerung 1945-1955: Das erste Jahrzehnt der zweiten Republik* (Vienna: Wiener Volksbuchhandlung, 1955), 57.

2. Eva-Marie Csáky, Franz Matscher, and Gerald Stourzh, eds., *Josef Schöner: Wiener Tagebuch 1944/1945* (Vienna: Böhlau, 1992).

3. *"Ich bin dafür, die Sache in die Länge zu ziehen"; die Wortprototkolle der österreichischen Bundesregierung von 1945 bis 1952 über die Entschädigung der Juden*, ed. Robert Knight (Frankfurt a. Main: Athenäum, 1988); Thomas Albrich, ("Heiligt der Zweck die Mittel? Anmerkungen zu Robert Knights Auswahledition der Wortprotokolle der österreichischen Bundesregierung von 1945 bis 1952 über die Entschädigung der Juden,") *Innsbrucker Historische Studien* 10/11 (1988): 407-411.

Klaus Eisterer, *"Die Schweiz als Partner:" Zum eigenständigen Außenhandel der Bundesländer Vorarlberg und Tirol mit der Eidgenossenschaft 1945-1947*, in *Schriftenreihe des Instituts für Föderalismusforschung*, vol. 64 (Vienna: Braumüller, 1995).

Dieter Stiefel

Austria is a small country. Americans are often astonished to hear that cities like New York or Los Angeles have more inhabitants than the whole of Austria. In addition, Austria is divided into nine federal "states" (*Bundesländer*, *Länder*) of which some, like Carinthia or Vorarlberg, do not even hold the population of a middle-sized U.S. city. But such a political structure based on small units—irrational as it seems—has proven remarkably durable. This year we celebrate one thousand years of Austria, but it has been the *Länder* that gave this larger political unit its stability and continuity. The persistence of these small political and social units became especially clear in the three severe political ruptures Austria had to deal with in the twentieth century: the disintegration of the Habsburg empire in 1918, the Anschluß to the German Reich in 1938, and the rebirth of the nation in 1945.

At the end of the Habsburg monarchy the Republic of Austria did not exist as a political unit. But the *Länder* still existed and after some reluctance they joined the new state. The persistence of the *Länder* became even clearer after the Anschluß in 1938. The political structure of the German Reich was quite different from that of Austria. The large German state Bavaria, for example, alone had more inhabitants then than the whole of Austria. But in spite of some changes even the National Socialists never succeeded in adapting the

Austrian structure to that of the Reich. The importance of the *Länder* emerged most clearly after 1945.

At the end of the war Austria no longer had a central government. What remained functioning was the *Länder*. In the first year after the war these small units were ignored, left to struggle for survival on their own. Austria's occupation hindered the *Länder* as they tried to return to normalcy. The country was divided into four occupation zones; Vienna had a quadrapartite occupation—roughly analogous to the occupation of Germany. In the first months after the war, all traffic, communication, and economic cooperation were virtually non-existent between these occupation zones. The small country crumbled into even smaller political and economic units which had to find ways to survive independently.

Thus the year 1945 would be very hard to write about for an Austrian historian who is accustomed to living in contemporary Austria with its central government. It would be equally hard for that historian to write about the slow beginnings of foreign trade in postwar Austria which, apart from relief programs, consisted mainly of bartering on a very primitive level. Klaus Eisterer takes on this challenge and shows that Tyrol and Vorarlberg had much more complex economies than did other parts of Austria.

Vorarlberg in the very west of Austria was in quite a favorable position, as it was the only *Bundesland* with a neighboring country that had not been involved in World War II. Switzerland still had a well-functioning economy, a fact that gave Vorarlberg the chance to start the process of reconstruction earlier than all the other *Länder*. By its own initiative and despite the reluctance of the French occupying power, Vorarlberg succeeded in organizing a very efficient trade with Switzerland, which had been initially skeptical of this enterprise. The main obstacle to Vorarlberg's success had been the currency problem.

There was no official exchange rate between the Austrian schilling and the Swiss franc, as this lay within the powers of the non-existant central government. For valid reasons the French government did not want to arbitrate a solution to this problem, therefore the Vorarlberg business world had to find a more informal and provisional solution. Thus, Vorarlberg established an office in Switzerland so as to have control over the Swiss currency which resulted from Vorarlberg's export trade. Austrian businessmen were paid in schillings at domestic price levels, but they got the opportunity to import raw materials and investment goods through the Vorarlberg office in Switzerland. The difference, which resulted from divergent price levels and exchange rates, allowed the government of Vorarlberg to import additional food, raw materials, and investment goods for their own people. This was a very simple and efficient system which soon came to include the pay of the Austrian workforce living in Switzerland (*Grenzgänger*).

Tyrol, which was also part of the French occupation zone, operated a similar scheme. Thus the two *Länder* came to engage in more foreign trade in 1945 than the rest of Austria put together. This innovative system, born out of the immediate need of a destroyed postwar economy, functioned smoothly until the beginning of 1946, when the Austrian government finally established firm control over the whole country and a regular foreign trading regime and currency control was reestablished.

This is a model study of regional history. It integrates political and economic history at a very sophisticated level. In an appendix, the fascimiles of the most important files are included. The book shows that a political entity is not only more than the sum of its parts—in this case, that Austria is more than the sum of its *Länder*—but that the *Länder* are more than merely parts of Austria.

Rolf Steininger with Ingrid Böhler, eds., *Der Umgang mit dem Holocaust: Europa–USA–Israel* (Vienna: Böhlau, 1994).

Daniel E. Rogers

Dealing with the Holocaust—in German, the *Umgang* with it—has proven itself to be a repeatedly contentious issue in public life and historiography throughout the Western world. Nowhere is this more evident than in a classroom whose entire subject is the systematic murder of Europe's Jews during World War II. As many teachers could attest, it is not the students who wonder or even protest about an apparently morbid fixation on the details of millions of murders. Rather, as I myself have discovered, it is their friends, their relatives, their colleagues, and even strangers who wonder at their ghoulish fascination. In America, they are usually spared the "*schon wieder*" that Rolf Steininger encountered when requesting support for a lecture series in Innsbruck in 1992-1993 on the *Umgang mit dem Holocaust*. Students today are nonetheless asked why they would want to deal with a subject so gruesome and so far away, both in physical distance and in popular perceptions of time and history.

Their questioners stand on solid ground, although for reasons they may not be able to articulate. They have grasped intuitively what Omer Bartov recently explained as

> the unbearable sense of despair and helplessness regarding not only the past but also the present.... Indeed, it is precisely the meaninglessness of the event, made all the clearer now with the benefit of hindsight, the utter uselessness of it all, the total and complete emptiness in which this hell on earth unfolded, that leaves us breathless, bereft of the power of thought and imagination. And what is especially frightening is the impossibility of learning

> especially frightening is the impossibility of learning anything from the Holocaust, of drawing any lessons, of putting its facts to any use.[1]

Considering this point of view, so cogently expressed by a scholar of the Holocaust, how can we fault those who might think that purposefully "dealing with the Holocaust," that a conscious and deliberate *Umgang*, is at the very least a matter of serious intellectual confusion, masking a bizarre obsession with violent crimes? Why not adopt the *Schlußstrich* mentality that would grant the Nuremberg tribunal, other immediate postwar trials and the attendant contemporaneous publicity their validity, but would otherwise end popular confrontation with the subject?

Perhaps for no other reason than that to forget or ignore the Holocaust completely is to say that it was, in the long course of human history, *acceptable*, in the same manner that all minor acceptable facets of everyday life—from the color of a traffic light to the shapes of clouds—fade into comfortable oblivion. But if we believe that the Holocaust was unacceptable, then we still need to deal with it precisely *because* it is a morbid subject, but we must from time to time evaluate our success with our particular *Umgang*. Otherwise we will be willing to accept anything, including repeated bouts of mass murder.

All this is a roundabout way of saying why books like the collection of essays edited by Steininger are still necessary. The result of the lecture series he did manage to stage in Innsbruck, *Der Umgang mit dem Holocaust* is a splendidly well-rounded collection that serves as a broad introduction to both the Holocaust and reactions to it. Steininger is to be praised not only for his thorough and thoughtful introduction to the book and his own essay on anti-Semitism, but also for persevering in Austria against the "*schon wieder dieses Thema*" mentality that cannot cope with repeated inquiries into the Holocaust (p. 12).

The host for the lecture series, Austria, emerges clearly as the country the least successful in dealing with the Holocaust and in fact the most recalcitrantly anti-Semitic.[2] Relying on studies of the "victim myth," that Austria was Nazi Germany's first victim rather than a willing co-perpetrator in the war and the Holocaust,[3] Thomas Albrich, Frank Stern, Brigitte Bailer, and Helge Grabitz demonstrate how Austria proceeded to use its victim's status to circumvent meaningful reparations, an articulated national sense of shame, or anything remotely implying responsibility. And why should anyone be surprised? The Moscow Declaration of 1943, in which the Allies declared Austria to be Germany's first victim, combined after 1945 with the developing Cold War to make the United States and other Western powers cleanly separate Austria from Germany. The fledgling Austrian government and its successors after 1955 used the leverage of this separation to defend Austria from all sorts of reparations claims, both from Jewish groups and the Soviet Union. Moreover, as Albrich points out so clearly, denying material responsibility for Jews after 1945 was indispensable in Austria's foreign, domestic, and Jewish policies. Austria could fend off Soviet claims, please ex-Nazis who formed an important voting bloc, and save a lot of money to boot.

Open discourse became possible decades later in the 1980s when what Robert Wistrich has called "the Waldheim syndrome"[4] made the taboo subject of anti-Semitism widely mentionable again. A public dialogue could begin, even as it revealed how stubborn anti-Semitism could be in a country in which 0.1 percent of the population is Jewish. Chancellor Franz Vranitzky could inform the *Nationalrat* in 1991 that "*wir bekennen uns zu allen Daten unserer Geschichte und zu den Taten aller Teile unseres Volkes, zu den guten wie zu den bösen; und so wie wir die guten in Anspruch nehmen, haben wir uns für die bösen zu entschuldigen—bei den Überlebenden und bei den Nachkommen der Toten*" (p. 18). Similarly, he could visit Israel in 1993 and declare a collective responsibility to deal with the legacy of "some of its citizens" during the Holocaust (p. 166). But it was easier to be humble now that the ex-Nazi vote so assiduously courted by earlier Austrian politicians had become far less meaningful.

Not that the Federal Republic of Germany has fared much better. Especially during the last decade, a concerted effort has been made by members of the historical community in Germany to deal with or "master" the Nazi past and specifically the Holocaust by attempting to create a context for it in which the mass murders of Jews were like other genocides, therefore less inexplicable and shameful, and ultimately "masterable." This *Historikerstreit* has shown that even the far greater official steps taken by the West German government since 1949 and the slightly less anti-Semitic climate of Germany as compared to Austria cannot lead one any closer to the desired

Schlußstrich.[5] The German counterparts of Austria's Jörg Haider realize, as Wolfgang Benz demonstrates in his contribution on the "Auschwitz Lie," that decriminalization of one's history is the first necessary step towards a strong (and usable) national identity. So there is method in this crassness. But, as Dan Diner explains in his essay on National Socialism and Stalinism, we cannot throw out the good with the bad. Comparative history is a legitimate tool, and the fear that mentioning Stalin's murders in the same breath as Hitler's will minimize the Holocaust should not stop historians from wrestling with comparative methodologies. The Holocaust cannot be spared all the historiographical rigor we can muster.

The 1952 agreement on reparations that eventually led to $33 billion in transfers from the Federal Republic to Israel had long since provided some measure of "rehabilitation," but as Frank Stern demonstrates in his essay, it was less a rehabilitation of Jews in the German consciousness than one of West Germany within the Western common of nations. Further essays make this failure to accept Jews even more starkly evident. For example, Ernst Klee's nearly polemical article on the Protestant and Catholic churches during and since the Holocaust provides graphic evidence that both churches harbored and still harbor anti-Semitism within their clerical establishments (while the same article does not offer explanation of how the clergy defend themselves against such charges). Michael Phayer's more balanced piece on the Catholic Church in Germany gives some credit to reconciliation attempts since the papacy of John XXIII (1958-1963), but it still leaves one to wonder if there is any comfort for those who would seek an answer other than anti-Semitism to the puzzle of the Catholic Church's behavior during and after the Holocaust.

Communist East Germany was long infamous for pretending it bore no responsibility for the legacy of Nazi Germany's crimes against Jews. Leaders of the German Democratic Republic could take pride in the theoretical ability of any Jew who wished to abnegate Judaism and be fully assimilated into the socialist polity. On the other hand, as Olaf Groehler's essay demonstrates, Marxist ideology was incapable of explaining racial ideology and made it impossible for the GDR to deal with the Holocaust effectively. Only when Erich Honecker began entertaining the fantasy of improving relations with the United States by first seeking to strengthen ties with the World

Jewish Congress could there be a measure of true public commemoration of the Holocaust; in November 1988 there were even ceremonies marking the fiftieth anniversary of *Kristallnacht*. But as Angelika Timm shows with reference to newly opened archives, GDR celebrations of 9 November had long ignored 1938 in favor of 1918, and there could be no real attempt to deal with the Holocaust in eastern Germany under GDR socialism.

Other Communist states of Eastern Europe endured equally vexing problems in dealing with the Holocaust, for anti-Semitism was alive and well and politically useful. In Poland, as Israel Gutman's article makes plain, anti-Semitism shifted from a phenomenon of the far right during the violent, murderous years from 1945-1947 (the notorious Kielce pogrom killed 42 Jews in July 1946) to a more official phenomenon thereafter, when Jews were made scapegoats for the failure of the Communist regime. Livia Rothkirchen portrays Czechoslovakia's Communist leadership as using anti-Semitism "periodically, on a pragmatic level, for clearly defined both domestic and foreign policy purposes" (p. 280). Only in Hungary, where Jews were able to retain a double-identity as both Hungarians and Jews, was there not only a large Jewish presence after 1945, but also a reluctance to take part in anti-Semitism or the "anti-Zionism" of the 1970s that was the vogue in the Communist and Third Worlds. Maria Schmidt's essay on Hungary also shows that the Jews were actually over-represented in the party hierarchy and resented by non-Jewish Hungarians for this reason.

Formal justice against perpetrators had been the first way the world dealt with the Holocaust in the late 1940s, and it remains the linchpin of any truly successful *Umgang*. Murderers among us make us all feel party to the crime. Thus it is appropriate on one level that the only essay in the volume specifically targeting the U.S. response to the Holocaust was written by Neal Sher, the head of the U.S. Justice Department's Nazi-hunting Office of Special Investigations. Alas, however, Sher's essay reads much more like the cheerleading report of a corporate executive to his shareholders, or like a canned speech delivered to one too many Rotary Clubs. While Sher rightly stresses the vigor with which the U.S. government has been pursuing Nazis at home and abroad, a more balanced assessment is impossible. The most glaring weakness is the lack of a single word devoted to the most famous case the OSI ever prosecuted (and, in the end, its greatest failure), the denaturalization and deportation case against John Demjanjuk, later freed by Israel's Supreme Court for lack of convincing proof of his identity as the erstwhile camp guard Ivan the Terrible of Treblinka. He returned to live quietly in the United States, and the OSI director's silence about this most famous of cases leads one to conclude the OSI, and by extension America's *Umgang*, has not been as successful as all that.[6]

Sybil Milton takes on the issue of the U.S. reactions to the Holocaust in a broader sense when she looks at European and U.S. Holocaust memorials, fully in line with her earlier book-length study.[7] She sets an agenda for U.S. portrayal of the Holocaust as "an event of universal significance," but in her detailing of Germany's memorials demands much more than memory. It is as if nothing short of constant alertness will do, in ignorance of the psychological price such vigilance would entail. Arno Mayer, rescued by Steininger's lecture series from near historical disgrace (at least among the Holocaust establishment and Jewish students at Princeton University) due to his 1988 book *Why Did the Heavens Not Darken?*, provides a nice contrast to Milton's piece. He quotes Nietzsche as stating that "life was 'absolutely impossible' without unremembering. Indeed, he held that memory unalleviated by wise forgetting was a 'festering sore'.... Nietzsche was led to consider that '*to be redeemed from vengeance*—that is for me the highest hope, and a rainbow after long storms'" (p. 453). Now, Nietzsche might not have been the most apposite choice to quote in arguing that the time for using memory as a vehicle for vengeance has passed. But we do see in Mayer's essay some consideration, at least, of what U.S. politicians and military strategists, in trying to determine how the U.S. Army will leave Bosnia, call an "exit strategy"; remembering must have the clear and ultimate goal of reconciliation of the living. As that reconciliation has not yet been achieved, the *Umgang* must continue.

Ultimate reconciliation will come from the children of Germany, Austria, Israel, and other lands. Falk Pingel, in his essay on German schoolbooks and the Holocaust, notes the effect of the passage of half a century has already had on German youth: history since 1945 is now properly termed *Zeitgeschichte*, leaving World War II to the hoarier realm of true history. Perhaps this indicates that some Nietzschean deliberate unremembering is in fact occurring—not forgetting, but a decision not to use the past to inflict pain on anyone, oneself and one's society included. We may never know the precise moment when the waves of pain stirred up by the Holocaust have finally subsided. Until they have, books like Steininger's are vital for helping our progress in unremembering, but never forgetting or accepting the Holocaust.

NOTES

1. Omer Bartov, "An Idiot's Tale: Memories and Histories of the Holocaust," *Journal of Modern History* 67 (1995): 55. Bartov's masterpiece on the German army and the Holocaust is *Hitler's Army: Soldiers, Nazis, and War in the Third Reich* (New York: Oxford University Press, 1992).

2. Bruce J. Pauley, *From Prejudice to Persecution: A History of Austrian Semitism* (Chapel Hill, NC: University of North Carolina Press, 1992).

3. See especially the work of Günter Bischof, "Die Instrumentalisierung der Moskauer Erklärung nach dem 2. Weltkrieg," *Zeitgeschichte* 20 (1993): 345-66.

4. Robert S. Wistrich, *Antisemitism: The Longest Hatred* (New York: Pantheon, 1991), 88-97.

5. For the basic texts of the early part of the dispute, see Rudolf Augstein et al., *Historikerstreit: Die Dokumentation der Kontroverse um die Einzigartigkeit der nationalsozialistischen Judenvernichtung* (Munich: Piper, 1987); see also Charles S. Maier, *The Unmasterable Past: History, Holocaust, and German National Identity* (Cambridge, Mass.: Harvard University Press, 1988).

6. Stephen Labaton, "No Review of Court Ruling That Let Demjanjuk Return," *New York Times*, 4 October 1994.

7. Sybil Milton, *In Fitting Memory: The Art and Politics of Holocaust Memorials* (Detroit: Wayne State University Press, 1991).

Franz Olah, *Die Erinnerungen* (Wien-München-Berlin: Amalthea, 1995).

Matthew Paul Berg

A wide range of new sources on the history of social democracy during Austria's Second Republic has become available for primary research since the late 1980s, and for historians and political scientists engaged in such study they represent an important, indeed vital, addition to the documentary record. These materials include impressive collections of archival documentation, housed primarily in Vienna, but also the publication of memoirs by Socialist Party (SPÖ) leaders such as Bruno Kreisky and Karl Mark. Memoirs, of course, are a genre that must be approached with a degree of care when considered as primary sources. That being said, Franz Olah's *Erinnerungen* might later contribute to a critical rethinking of institutional histories of the SPÖ, and if this proves to be the case, Olah's memoirs will indeed have proven themselves a welcome addition to this literature. Often insightful, yet all too frequently self-righteous in tone and overly concerned with his vindication, Olah reflects upon his experiences as a convinced social democrat, attracted by the Party's calls for the realization of social justice, civil equality, and economic security from the very moment he became politically active as a fifteen-year-old *Vertauensmann* in the construction and wood workers' union in 1925. Olah recounts that these early experiences expressed themselves as a life-long dedication to the labor movement. realized in his readiness to suffer for his convictions under Austrofascist and National Socialist dictatorships, and his efforts to promote stability and security in postwar Austria. The result is an engaging reflection upon life in the upper reaches of the SPÖ during the years of reconstruction and the take-off of the *Wirtschaftswunder* from the perspective of the party's most prominent pariah.

Olah's thread of continuity throughout his reminiscences is his commitment to democratic pluralism and antipathy towards the intolerance and dehumanization of dictatorship in any form. Consequently, Olah's entire young adult life was spent in fighting for these convictions. Despite his profound Catholic faith, for example, Olah joined the underground Revolutionary Socialists (RS) organization during the years of the clerical-fascist *Vaterländische Front* (VF) in order to continue to press the social democratic agenda, and was imprisoned several times for conspiracy to commit high treason. Spared the ill-treatment suffered by other social democrats or communists, Olah's democratic sensibilities were heightened nevertheless by his incarceration, during which he was instrumental in organizing a hunger strike for better treatment for all political prisoners, whether RS, Austrian Communist Party members (KPÖ), or Austrian Nazis. Prison fraternization with individual communists notwithstanding, Olah was targeted by KPÖ officials as a bitter adversary. Arrested by the new National Socialist regime in March 1938, he soon found himself in Dachau, where, between the brutality of the SS camp regime and the seniority enjoyed by German and Austrian communist inmates, he was presented with far more trying challenges. Olah's account of his odyssey through Dachau, Buchenwald, and other camps between 1938-45 is sparing, but forceful nonetheless; it serves to underscore his abhorrence of dictatorship effectively, as well as to recount his personal rapprochement with Austrian Catholic Conservative inmates (including, among them, Leopold Figl, later the first elected Chancellor of the Second Republic) which presaged the inner Austrian détente that would be essential for postwar stability.

Olah's treatment of the postwar years chart his steady ascendance, during which he accumulated positions within the Party, the Austrian Trade Union Federation (ÖGB), and the government between 1945 and 1964: district chief of the SPÖ in Wien-Hernals and later member of the *Parteivertretung*, parliamentary deputy, chair of the construction and wood workers' union and eventually President of the ÖGB, and Interior Minister. But this ascendence ends with his fall in 1964. Thoughtful attention is directed towards the reconstruction of trade union activity, as well as to Austrian social and economic conditions during the period of the Wage-Price Agreements (1947-51) and in Soviet-occupied eastern Austria (1945-55). Olah's self-depiction is consistently that of the shrewd, dedicated, virtuous party soldier and democratically-minded ÖGB *pater familias*. There is undoubtedly some truth in this. In the autumn of 1950, Olah played an instrumental role in organizing socialist resistance against a wave of violent communist strikes. Along with several SPÖ leaders (including Bruno Kreisky and Bruno Pittermann), he helped steer the party toward a more reformist course, as evinced in the new 1958 party program and negotiations with the Catholic Church that yielded the Concordat of 1960. In these cases, the *Erinnerungen* offer the greatest promise as a supplement to current primary documentation. Not without coincidence, these were developments in which Olah participated while he continued to enjoy a position of strength within the Party. He is generous in his praise for the teamwork involved in such initiatives, and presents an absorbing account of generational change and the dynamic of theoretical and policy shifts.

Under the protection afforded by Adolf Schärf as *Parteivorsitzender*, Olah was able to withstand the challenges of personal enemies and rivals within the party and trade unions. After Schärf was elected federal president in 1957, and Olah's enemies had consolidated their hold on central party positions by the early 1960s, his days were numbered within the SPÖ leadership—despite his enduring popularity among union members organized by the social democrats. Conspicuous in its absence, though, is Olah's even-handed attempt to come to terms with the sources of the profound animus certain party rivals felt towards him. The *Erinnerungen* would have us conclude, for example, that Anton Proksch (long-time ÖGB General Secretary, later Minister for Social Affairs) was a self-interested, conniving man whose loss of composure before VF prosecution and failure to adhere to the aforementioned prison hunger strike were indications of a fundamentally flawed character, that Christian Broda (SPÖ legal expert and eventual Justice Minister), whom Olah alleges harbored deep-seated communist sympathies and had been strangely close to a series of political and mistaken-identity murders during the interwar years, shared the long-standing resentments towards Olah demonstrated by openly-declared communists on prior occasions, and that Bruno Pittermann, Schärf's successor as *Parteivorsitzender* was so insecure in his position that he availed himself of the assistance offered by many a cunning rascal. Olah does not reflect upon whether his brusque, brash manner (the result, perhaps, of his experience of personal sacrifice, or of his status as one of the very few people within the SPÖ leadership who had actually been a blue collar worker) might not have brought out the worst in some of his party colleagues—particularly if he considered himself, and not Pittermann, to be Schärf's rightful successor.

His strong support within sectors of the ÖGB and his allocation of trade union funds to create a nonparty working class newspaper, the *Kronen-Zeitung*, which took a markedly critical position vis-à-vis the SPÖ leadership, might have lent some credence to concerns that Olah had designs on the position of *Vorsitzender*. Diagnosed as a paranoid schizophrenic (the examining physicians had never had face-to-face interaction with their purported patient), dismissed from the party for disobedience, stripped of his ministerial position, Olah was charged with a series of crimes that included fraud and misappropriation of union funds in connection with the *Kronen-Zeitung* affair. Convicted on the latter count, he served eight months in prison. The reader is likely to conclude that Olah's outrage, intensified, perhaps, by the passage of time, is innocent enough, that he regards himself a faultless victim of hostile intriguing, and that he remains incapable of recognizing any share of culpability in his own downfall. Given the largely self-congratulatory nature of the ninety-eight pages of documents that comprise the appendix, such a conclusion may seem all the more plausible. Given the degree of controversy that surrounded Olah's career, though, perhaps this is the extent to which Olah will have vindicated himself in the eyes of his readers.

Heinz Fischer,
Die Kreisky-Jahre: 1967-1983, 3rd ed. (Vienna: Löcker Verlag, 1994).

Andrei S. Markovits

There can simply be no doubt in anybody's mind that the subject of this book, Bruno Kreisky, ranks among the few truly towering figures of postwar European politics. His position as the Second Austrian Republic's most important politician has become commonplace by now. Whereas the author of this book, Heinz Fischer, is not in Kreisky's league, he nevertheless has consistently been one of Austria's most innovative political minds, a fine lawyer, political scientist, professor, and writer who over the years developed into one of Austria's most significant public figures and "organic intellectuals" in the best sense of that Gramscian concept. One of Kreisky's closest disciples, Fischer, who at the time of this writing continues to hold the presidency of the Austrian parliament's National Chamber, has been at the fulcrum of Austrian and European social democracy for three decades by dint of his many positions of power (in state and party) as well as his consistent intellectual engagements on behalf of virtually all policies, strategies, and questions which defined the development of European social democracy in these fateful three decades. Given the prominence of subject and writer one would have expected a book of unsurpassable quality, a publication of unique distinction. Alas, this is not the case in this reviewer's opinion. While certainly informative, erudite, and in parts even brilliant, the book fails to live up to its potential as an authoritative, let alone critical, assessment of the Kreisky years in Austrian and European politics.

Before I turn to my criticisms, let me dwell on some of the many positive aspects which inform this interesting book. Even though serious in content, at times even complex, Fischer maintains a breezy style which—at certain junctures—renders the book into a real page turner, a rarity, to be sure, in most books of this genre. I also found Fischer's honesty regarding his inability to be objective about Kreisky refreshing and commendable. The author admits openly that his close political and emotional association with Kreisky resulted in a degree of affection for Kreisky on Fischer's part which eliminates the possibility of a detached "academic" objectivity by the author for his subject. This is good for two reasons: first, because it reflects the actual reality of the relationship which Fischer enjoyed with Kreisky for two decades, and second, because it allows for a lively and engaged writing style.

Indeed, to this reviewer, the most valuable passages of the whole book are those in which Fischer portrays Kreisky in intimate situations. For example, through Fischer's description of how Kreisky prepared some of his most important speeches, we learn a lot about Kreisky's work habits, ways of thinking, and intellectual brilliance, but we also glimpse Kreisky's hesitation, procrastination, and egomania. Fischer describes how he and a few other Kreisky confidants and party leaders would gather in Kreisky's Viennese home in the *Armbrustergasse* the evening before the major event. They would arrive at Kreisky's home armed with data and reports which they deemed necessary for the formulation of Kreisky's major speech that was to occur the next day. Kreisky would greet them in his dressing gown, putter around, take detailed telephone messages for his son, Peter, leave the room several times, then offer a good meal which the housekeeper, who was out for the evening, had prepared. Then, after all this procrastination, the meeting would finally start late in the evening and last well into the middle of the night. Fischer's account makes it amply clear that Kreisky, while listening to his advisers, was completely in charge of every aspect of these meetings, including their final product, that is, the epochal speeches delivered the next morning in parliament. I have read many accounts of Bruno Kreisky as a leader, an intellectual, and a politician. But nowhere was this man's quiet charisma, iron will, and total control better conveyed to me than in these few pages which Fischer offers us. It is precisely because of the normalcy of the described context (Kreisky's dressing gown, his procrastination) that the potency of this man's charisma becomes evident. At the same time, we also perceive a certain human frailty. Kreisky was obviously brilliant. He also knew what he wanted to say well before he actually got together with his friends and advisers who—in Fischer's description—appear to be more like Kreisky's sounding board than his peers. And yet, there is something very human, even endearing in all of this.

Fischer portrays a Kreisky who appears to have synthesized the best qualities of social democracy with those of a brilliant political strategist. Thus, we learn that Kreisky was a great believer in modernity. Indeed, in his acceptance speech as the SPÖ's new leader in early 1967, Kreisky marveled at the wonders of modern computers and extolled technological prowess as a necessary precondition for the building of a modern *as well as* equitable Austria. In this speech, it is obvious that Kreisky, a product of central European social democracy, not only believed in the beneficial value of technology as a societal modernizer and social equalizer, but also maintained a deep commitment to compassion, another key ingredient of European social democracy. It was this combination of a profound belief in modern technology and the advantages of modernization with a deep commitment to compassion for the less advantaged in society that yielded the many reforms that were initiated and implemented by the social democrats under Kreisky in the 1970s. Kreisky wanted Austria to have a modern economy in order to compete with its modernizing European neighbors, but he also believed that such an economy would be more able to help the poor. He tried to improve the country's woefully inadequate and unequal education system so that Austrians would have the necessary technical expertise to create and maintain a modern economy in an increasingly complex and interdependent world, but he also implemented educational reforms to enhance opportunities for the children of less privileged Austrian citizens. While modernity had value to Kreisky the social democrat, it also had value to Kreisky the political strategist. By portraying the SPÖ as Austria's modernizer, Kreisky hoped to change the perception that social democrats were poor managers of the economy. Modernization was used as the SPÖ's central profile, in order to give it a *Wirtschaftskompetenz* which attracted many managers and entrepreneurs who would otherwise have voted with their "natural" constituency, the bourgeois ÖVP. Kreisky's political *Fingerspitzengefühl* led him towards a rapprochement with social democracy's erstwhile enemies, the Catholic church and the country's farmers. To the careful reader, Fischer's book offers sufficient evidence that Kreisky's political innovations and strategic maneuvers proved partly responsible for the beginnings of the "depillarization" and secularization of Austrian politics which has reached proportions in the mid 1990s that were simply unimaginable at the end of the Kreisky era, barely thirteen years ago.

Unlike many other social democrats in Austria and elsewhere, Kreisky, according to Fischer, had a certain innate understanding of, if not a deep appreciation for, what was then the New Left and what was to become social democracy's most serious political threat in the form of the new social movements and later the Green parties. Kreisky's political sense, as well as his love of modernization, coincided with the necessity for a societal overhaul and cultural shift that would liberalize institutions and mores that Kreisky viewed as anachronistic and deeply unjust. His commitment to democracy, too, welcomed a certain *Aufbruch* that these young intellectuals—the so-called "68-ers"—embodied. Yet, as late as 1970, and probably well beyond, Kreisky had virtually no idea that this commitment would encourage a fundamental challenge to social democracy that still exists. It was not until the Zwentendorf incident that Kreisky and the social democrats awoke to a "modern" world which was neither of their own making nor to their liking.

Next to Fischer's passages describing Kreisky's work habits and private sphere, it is the author's account of Zwentendorf which I found most compelling. Correctly labeling this event a paradigm change, Fischer shows how the fundamental axes which defined social democracy since the 1880s had suddenly and surreptitiously shifted in less than eight years. When the social democratic minority government first introduced the Zwentendorf project to the public in February 1970, it was a virtual non-event. So was the actual construction of the plant. As late as the parliamentary elections in October 1975, Zwentendorf was a non-issue. By the late 1970s a majority of Austrians wanted the whole project scrapped. A change had occurred which altered the hitherto accepted paradigms of political discourse in most industrial democracies. Despite Kreisky's last—and most impressive—electoral victory in October 1979, for

Austrian social democrats the world would never be the same after Zwentendorf. Modernity was to turn out very differently from what Kreisky and his generation had expected.

Let me now briefly turn to what I believe to be the book's shortcomings. First, Fischer writes as an insider *for* insiders. In tone as well as content, the book assumes a sort of "inside the *Ringstrasse*" knowledge of Austrian politics. This is partly the result of poor editing. Thus, for example, Fischer never explains what exactly the NEWAG scandal was, nor does he list the complete names of people when first presented. Moreover, the book fails to have a proper subject index beyond the all-too-lengthy index of names, which further highlights its clubiness. This insider approach diminishes the book's importance and renders it far too parochially Austrian, actually Viennese, even though its subject and author could (and should) easily capture the attention of an international readership. Second, despite Fischer's commendable disclaimers in the preface regarding any objectivity on his part concerning Bruno Kreisky, a trait which I found admirable and sincere, the book should not have become the hagiography that it really is. For example, Fischer need not have engaged in an obvious cover up regarding Kreisky's less attractive traits, such as his obvious impatience with people whom he deemed uninteresting, irrelevant, or simply not quite to his liking. Yet Fischer hints at Kreisky's contempt for parliament, which he frequently viewed—especially in the later years of his chancellorship—as little more than window dressing for his personal rule. For someone so committed to democracy, so concerned with compassion as Kreisky obviously was, such undemocratic and dispassionate behavior was at least an interesting contradiction in his personality, if not an essential ingredient for the quality of his governance. I strongly believe that Fischer would not have compromised his obvious affection and gratitude for Kreisky had he offered the reader a less gingerly treatment of Kreisky as a person and politician. Kreisky's immense stature would not have been diminished by a more critical assessment of him.

My last criticism of Fischer's book emanates perhaps from my being an American Jew with continuously strong Austrian ties. It pertains to the virtual absence in Fischer's book of Kreisky's "Jewish problem." More irritating than this absence are Fischer's hints that being Jewish was—in whatever manner—an issue for Kreisky. For example, Fischer informs us obliquely that Kreisky—aware of the immense burden of being Jewish in Austria—articulated concerns to his friends in the party whether his impending leadership of the SPÖ might not be a handicap in light of his being of Jewish origin. I was eager to read more on this matter to which few, if any, are more privy and sensitive than Heinz Fischer. Silence. The "*causa* Wiesenthal" is amply discussed in the book, and Fischer makes it clear to the reader that this issue agitated Kreisky perhaps more than anything else discussed in nearly 300 pages of text. After all, here was a man full of deliberation, evenheadedness, rational thinking, and calculated strategizing, a statesman of stature who was ready to resign his parliamentary immunity to fight Simon Wiesenthal in court only to be saved from such folly by Fischer and other close associates. What was going on here? Clearly, the Jewish issue pushed some immensely popular buttons in Kreisky's psyche. Although Fischer was under no obligation to write a book analyzing Kreisky's psyche, one would have hoped that someone as knowledgeable of and comfortable with Kreisky as Fischer obviously was would offer some insights into this fascinating—while completely incongruous—aspect of Kreisky's persona. What bothers me most about this is my absolute conviction that Fischer knows a good deal more about this aspect of Kreisky's life than he was willing to put to paper.[1] Hagiographies, of course, are intolerant of any blemishes, even interesting ones. Thus, in a funny way, they actually diminish the hero whom they purport to extol because, by avoiding anything controversial and potentially negative, they ultimately present a much flatter though decidedly less flattering portrait of their subject than they could have. Heinz Fischer wrote a good book about Bruno Kreisky. I am convinced that he could have written a great one.

NOTES

1. On Kreisky and the Jews, see Herbert Pierre Secher, "Kreisky and the Jews," in *The Kreisky Era in Austria*, vol. 3 of *Contemporary Austrian Studies*, ed. Günter Bischof and Anton Pelinka (New Brunswick, NJ: Transaction, 1994), 10-31, and *idem, Bruno Kreisky - Chancellor of Austria: A Political Biography* (Pittsburgh, PA: Dorrance, 1993).

Wolfgang C. Müller, Fritz Plasser, Peter A. Ulram, eds., *Wählerverhalten und Parteienwettbewerb. Analysen zur Nationalratswahl 1994* (Vienna: Signum Verlag, 1995).

Kurt Richard Luther

The editors' stated aim is to examine, by means of a variety of primarily empirical political science approaches, recent trends in Austrian electoral behavior, to relate these to alterations in the structure, or context of party competition, and to tease out long term trends. Between them, the fifteen chapters contain approximately 100 tables and three dozen diagrams. In addition, an appendix details the results of all presidential elections, national referenda and popular petitions, as well as all federal and state elections since 1945. The volume's utility as a reference tool is enhanced by the inclusion of not only the parties' percentage shares of the vote, but also their absolute number of votes and seats.

Peter Ulram and Wolfgang Müller set the scene with great clarity in their chapter on "*Die Ausgangslage für die Nationalratswahl 1994.*" It discusses recent alterations in the internal dynamics and electoral forunes of each parliamentary party and argues their cumulative effect has been a qualitative change in the postwar party system. The growing salience of "new" issues such as the environment, immigration, and crime is documented, as is the growth of diffuse fear and declining political trust, which, it is argued, are related *inter alia* to the economic costs of modernization. Finally, Ulram and Müller emphasize the predicament of an increasingly defensive government confronted by an ever more polarized, bilateral opposition.

Karl Ucakar's useful essay on "*Wahlrecht und politische Legitimation: Nationalrats-Wahlordnung 1992*" reviews the background and provisions of the new, regionalized electoral system, the most important innovations of which include a reduced voting age and an electoral hurdle of 4 percent of the national vote, or one directly elected regional seat. Overall, Ucakar is skeptical about the capacity of the reforms (the declared aims of which included enhancing the links between electors and the elected, and greater personalization through enhanced opportunities for preference voting) to further democratize the political process.

Rainer Nick's chapter on "*Die Wahl vor der Wahl*" describes in considerable detail the 1994 candidate recruitment procedures of the five parliamentary parties, noting also how these differed from *Land* to *Land*. His conclusions provide a salutary lesson for all who equate democratization with the introduction of primaries. While regionalization of the electoral system did influence the nomination processes, it did not result in the greater local personalization many had predicted. Second, parties have not surrendered their monopoly of the recruitment process. Finally, Nick's evidence suggests a negative correlation between open recruitment procedures and vote maximization. The greatest gains were made by the FPÖ, where candidate recruitment was conducted via "*medialer Inszenierung*" and governed by considerations not of intra-party democracy, but of electoral advantage. Conversely, openness and competition were greatest in the ÖVP, which lost by far the most votes.

One of the volume's highlights is the excellent contribution by Wolfgang Müller, Wilfried Phillipp, and Marcelo Jenny on "*Ideologie und Strategie der österreichischen Parteien.*" It is predicated on the approach of the celebrated ECPR manifestos project, the theory and methods of which are succinctly introduced, before an examination of the parties' 1994 manifestos is undertaken. The core of the chapter lies in a quantitative analysis of all postwar manifestos. Using Sartori's typology, the authors divide the postwar party system into three periods and document both the frequency of the key manifesto themes in each period, as well as changes over time in individual party's priorities. Thereafter, a two-stage factor analysis is used to illustrate the interrelationship of the themes and their position in policy space. Though the insights this section offers are fascinating, a more detailed explanation of its complex methodology would have been welcome, not least for non-experts and those who may be surprised by, for example, the counter-intuitive positioning of the Liberal Forum's manifesto to the right of the FPÖ's on the socioeconomic dimension. Finally, the authors show how their analysis helps identify the limited coalition possibilities available to parties motivated primarily by policy objectives.

Three chapters relate broadly to the conduct of the election. Christian Schaller and Andreas Vretscha's informative and well-structured examination of the organization, conduct, and central issues of the parties' 1994 campaigns demonstrates how the wider spectrum of political competition has increased polarization, personalization, and the use of strategies seeking to reduce issue complexity. They conclude that "campaigns do matter": the FPÖ benefited by successfully imposing its preferred issue agenda, while the SPÖ and ÖVP campaigns succumbed to internal divisions or self-inflicted injuries. Fritz Plasser, Christian Scheucher, and Franz Sommer report the results of an interesting analysis of the 1994 campaign coverage in the main print and electronic media. They identify a trend to further personalization, "dethematization," and negativism, and assert not only that the increased "Americanization" of campaigns will lead to enduring change in the structure of party competition, but that "in future populist actors could be even more oriented towards determining the agenda, aggregating emotions and changing elections into protest filled anti-plebiscites."

Herbert Sickinger's short chapter on "*Partei- und Wahlkampffinanzierung*" offers an instructive, but predictably incomplete account of the size and structure of party income and expenditure. The inexorable rise of state financing is attributed to a de facto policy of "nationalization of the financial risks of the *staatstragende Parteien*." Though Sickinger succeeds in demonstrating how small a proportion of parties' overall turnover is devoted to campaign expenditure, the significance of his conclusion is considerably qualified by the fact that Austria is "very probably a serious contender for the leading position in the league of party and political financing in western democracies"

The remaining chapters deal with the outcome and or consequences of the 1994 election. A useful albeit purely descriptive chapter by Erich Neuwirth identifies gross voter flows. Wolfgang Müller and Christian Scheucher's compact consideration of "*Das verstärkte*

Vorzugsstimmenrecht" proves that while the new electoral system engendered the greatest number and distribution of preference votes, it resulted merely in the nominal election of candidates who had already won seats by virtue of their position on official party lists.

For their part, Fritz Plasser and Peter Ulram provide a masterly overview of "continuity and change in Austrian voting behavior," the bulk of which constitutes an extremely well-documented and convincing analysis of a variety of indicators of electoral dealignment. Drawing on exit polls from 1986, 1990, and 1994, it considers party identification, electoral mobility, the declining capacity of religiosity, union membership, and other sociostructural variables to predict party choice, and the consequent changes in both the political behavior of social groups and the social composition of parties' electorates. Thereafter, it utilizes a 1994 opinion poll to assess the extent of electoral re-alignment predicated upon value orientations. Using value dimensions such as statism versus self-help, egalitarianism versus individualism, reformism versus stability, and integration of foreigners versus ethnocentrism, Plasser and Ulram identify seven attitudinal clusters. Of these, the "moderate conservatives" and "liberal individualists" constitute the core of ÖVP voters, while the SPÖ's strength is amongst "traditional welfare statists," "insecure materialists," and (albeit less markedly) "welfare state chauvinists." Though the two large parties face stiff competition in many of these segments, the FPÖ's support is greatest from "authoritarian anti-system (*Systemverdrossene*), "welfare state chauvinists," and "insecure materialists," while the Liberal Forum and Greens recruit especially well from the "liberal individualists" and "liberal postmaterialists."

Similar techniques are used in two other contributions. Alfred Grausgruber's essay on "voter types and party competition " uses sociostructural, political-cultural, and sociological indicators to identify nine electoral segments. Though the statistical significance of his smallest segments (4 percent and 0.9 percent) is debatable, Grausgruber's analysis does highlight the extent and sociodemographic location of the recent change from two-party to multiparty competition. Franz Sommer's chapter on "Rural Peripheries - Urban Centers" first outlines variations in the impact of the 1994 "electoral earthquake" in the forty-three new regional constituencies. It then uses socioeconomic and political criteria to categorize electoral districts into six types, and shows with the assistance of helpful graphics how the parties' uneven and changing electoral fortunes are related *inter alia* to the degree of urbanization and changes in economic structure.

The multiplicity of variables *prima facie* related to voter choice and the inability of established models of voting behavior to combine them into a convincing explanation of Austria's increasingly unpredictable electorate causes Fritz Plasser and Gilg Seeber to venture "in search of a model." Their reflective expedition seeks to identify, on the basis of the 1986 to 1994 exit polls, relationships between a selection of the variables and concludes that expectations for an elegant explanatory model for the 1990s have not yet been realized.

In the last two chapters, Plasser and Ulram consider the implications of the 1994 elections for party competition. They devote the first to the FPÖ, Europe's electorally most successful example of radical right-wing populism. The Party's rise is explained by reference to both global socioeconomic and sociostructural change, as well as to specific national factors such as Austria's political culture, its high degree of politicization, and the available opportunity structures. Thereafter, there are sections on changes in the FPÖ's thematic focus and in Haider's image, as well as in the social profile and motivation of the FPÖ's electorate. The chapter ends with reflections on the Party's present competitive advantages and the likely long-term significance of its profound challenge to the traditional style of Austrian politics. In large measure because it eschews polemics in favor of objective analysis supported by empirical findings, this constitutes one of the best contributions on the FPÖ this reviewer has read.

The concluding chapter on "constellations and scenarios of party competition" outlines the three major parties' strategic options and then shows how the latter are constrained by popular preferences and perceptions of the ideological distance within Austria's more polarized party system. Finally, four possible future scenarios are identified: restabilization of the traditional parties; the creation of party blocks akin to those in France; a "Scandinavian format" characterized by one larger party competing with smaller parties; and system collapse. While the authors resist the temptation to opt for one of these scenarios, they do conclude that the Austrian party system has moved decisively from "hyperstability to instability," and that the latter is "very likely to remain on the political agenda of the coming years."

Soon after this volume appeared, a snap election was called and though the December 1995 poll resulted in a slight improvement of the position of the major parties, it neither reversed the profound changes analyzed in this volume, nor rendered any less useful this well-integrated and exceptionally interesting collection of essays. The editors are to be congratulated for having produced a first class volume that adds considerably to our understanding of Austrian politics. It will undoubtedly become essential reading for all serious students of Austrian parties and elections. Moreover, by its frequent and convincing use of "state of the art" political science analysis, this volume also makes a significant contribution to the wider community of comparative political scientists.

Survey of Austrian Politics: 1995

Reinhold Gärtner

These were the most conspicuous political events in Austria in 1995:

* Austria's membership in the European Union;
* letter bombs and the bomb attack in Oberwart, Burgenland;
* the cabinet reshuffle and the People's Party Conference;
* Cardinal Groer's past;
* the bankruptcy of *Konsum*;
* the *Kirchenvolks-Begehren* (Catholics' referendum);
* the trials of Austrian extreme rightists;
* New National Council elections on 17 December;
* Styrian State Diet elections on 17 December;
* the death of Hermann Langbein.

Austria and the European Union

Six months after the EU referendum in June 1994, Austria—along with Sweden and Finland—became a member of the European Union. While on 12 June almost two-thirds of voters opted in favor of EU membership, in 1995—according to polls—at least some of them woke up with a headache (or a slight hangover). Some might have expected too many goods reduced in price and no expenses.

Letter Bombs and Oberwart

The first series of letter bombs were sent to high-profile people who publically favored helping aliens and refugees. The most prominent among the victims was the then major of Vienna, Helmut Zilk, who lost some fingers when opening a letter addressed to him. After the bomb series of December 1994, in 1995 other letter bombs were sent, and some addressees were seriously injured. After the letter bombs, a mysterious *Bajuwarische Befreiungsarmee* (Bajuvarian Liberation Army) with supposed connections to the extreme right sent letters of confession. Until now, though, it is not clear who—or which group—is behind it.

In February 1995, a bomb explosion killed four gypsies—and startled Austria. A sign with the inscription "*Roma zurück nach Indien*" ("Gypsies go back to India") was placed on a small road leading to a settlement of houses near Oberwart where gypsies were living. The sign was a carefully constructed bomb which exploded when four gypsies tried to remove it.

A few aspects of this attack were remarkable. First—contrary to the letter bombs, which were mainly sent to persons helping refugees and aliens—the target of Oberwart was both clearly defined and arbitrary. It was clearly defined because it was an attack against a specific minority, the gypsies. It was arbitrary because the murderer(s) did not care about who would remove the bomb and be killed. Oberwart was not only the bloodiest such attack in the Second Republic, but it also made clear that prejudices against minorities remain a significant part of Austrian society.

Though not completely free of politically motivated assassinations in the past, this series of letter bombs and the ghastly bomb of Oberwart have involved Austria with violent, extreme, right wing terrorism.

One side is the tragedy among the victims of the bomb attacks. The lacksadaisical police investigations are another side. For more than two years the police have been astonishingly unsuccessful in the apprehension and prosecution of those who committed the crimes. Accusations that there might be indiscretions or rightist sympathizers within the official committee of inquiry have not yet been satisfactorily refuted.

The Cabinet Reshuffle

Only a few months after its formation at the end of 1994, the cabinet was reshuffled in the spring of 1995. Among the social democrats, Franz Löschnak, the Minister of the Interior, had been criticized both because of the government's policy towards refugees and aliens and because of his lack of success in the letter bomb investigations. Ferdinand Lacina, Minister of Finance, had been criticized by trade unions because of his efforts to cut the huge budget deficit and social spending. Among the People's Party, the reshuffle was connected with a change in leadership. At the party conference in April 1995, the party leadership was passed from Erhard Busek to Wolfgang Schüssel.

Table 1: Spring 1995 Cabinet Reshuffle

Office	Incumbent	New Cabinet Member
Chancellor	Franz Vranitzky (SPÖ)	Franz Vranitzky (SPÖ)
Vice-Chancellor	Erhard Busek (ÖVP)	Wolfgang Schüsse (ÖVP)
Foreign Affairs	Alois Mock (ÖVP)	Wolfgang Schüssel (ÖVP)
Economics	Wolfgang Schüssel (ÖVP)	Johannes Ditz (ÖVP)
Social Affairs	Josef Hesoun (SPÖ)	Franz Hums (SPÖ)
Finance	Ferdinand Lacina (SPÖ)	Andreas Staribacher (SPÖ)
Women's Questions	Johanna Dohnal (SPÖ)	Helga Konrad (SPÖ)
Health	Christa Krammer (SPÖ)	Christa Krammer (SPÖ)
Interior	Franz Löschnak (SPÖ)	Caspar Einem (SPÖ)
Environment	Maria Rauch-Kallat (ÖVP)	Martin Bartenstein (ÖVP)
Youth and Family		Sonja Moser (ÖVP)
Justice	Nikolaus Michalek (SPÖ)	Nikolaus Michalek (SPÖ)
Defense	Werner Fasslabend (ÖVP)	Werner Fasslabend (ÖVP)
Agriculture	Franz Fischler (ÖVP)	Wilhelm Molterer (ÖVP)
Education	Rudolf Scholten (SPÖ)	Elisabeth Gehrer (ÖVP)
Public Economy and Traffic	Viktor Klima (SPÖ)	Viktor Klima (SPÖ)
Science	Erhard Busek (ÖVP)	Rudolf Scholten (SPÖ)
State Secretaries		
Office of the Chancellor	Brigitte Ederer (SPÖ) Peter Kostelka (SPÖ)	Brigitte Ederer (SPÖ) Karl Schlögl (SPÖ) Gerhard Schäffer (ÖVP)
Foreign Affairs		Benita Ferrero-Waldner (ÖVP)
Economy	Maria Fekter	
Finance	Johannes Ditz (ÖVP)	

The Bankruptcy of *Konsum*

In the spring of 1995, *Konsum*, one of the great Austrian retail grocery store chains, declared bankruptcy.

In the late nineteenth century, this cooperative became one of three main pillars of socialism along with party organization and trade unions. Cooperatives such as *Konsum* were meant to provide the members of the working class with a wide range of cheap goods. In the course of time *Konsum* had become a regular chain of retail shops, but it still had symbolic meaning for many members of the Social Democratic Party. In 1995 the liability of *Konsum* amounted to some ös 26 billion ($2.6 billion), which was by far the biggest bankruptcy in the Second Republic.

The *Konsum* crash was by far the biggest, but only one of some 5,000 insolvencies with total liabilities amounting to some ös 62 billion ($6.2 billion), about twice the amount of 1994.

Cardinal Groer's Taciturnity

In the autumn of 1994, the magazine *profil* revealed accusations about Vienna cardinal Hermann Groer's alleged child abuse. A former student of a boarding school in which Groer had served for years as a priest and educator charged that the cardinal had sexually abused him. Groer—instead of replying to the accusations—never answered his accuser and critics and remained silent. He simply ignored the charges and public debate.

The Catholic Church reacted only slowly. At the beginning, church officials tried to show their solidarity with Groer. In April, however, Christoph Schönborn became archbishop designate, and in September he succeeded Groer as archbishop of Vienna.

Catholics' Referendum

In June, a group of activist liberal Catholics started a referendum for liberalizing the Roman Catholic Church. Ordinary Catholics—especially women—were campaigning for more participation in church matters and a moderate democratization of the institution.

Though some 500,000 people signed the referendum, the response from church officials—especially bishops—was less than enthusiastic. One could not expect support from fundamentalists in the Bishops Conference (Krenn, Küng, or Eder), but even moderate and liberal bishops such as Weber agreed only that a dialogue was necessary.

The widespread support for this referendum made clear that the issue of liberalization within the Catholic Church is a priority for many Catholics, and the support for fundamentalism arises from only some of the bishops and only a small part of their flock.

Meanwhile, both the German and Italian faithful in the Catholic Church will follow the Austrian model with referenda of their own (Germany in the autumn of 1995 and Italy in 1996).

The Extreme Right

While the extreme right continued its activities, trials against some of their representatives were held. Hans Jörg Schimanek, Jr., son of FPÖ politician Hans Jörg Schimanek, Sr., was sentenced to fifteen years in prison (reduced to eight years after appeal). Schimanek, Jr., had been active in the extreme right for years. Part of the evidence against Schimanek was a videotape showing him teaching his comrades to cut throats.

Herwig Nachtmann, editor of the extreme right paper *Aula* was fined ös 240,000 ($24,000) and received a suspended sentence with ten months probation. In the summer of 1994 the *Aula* wrote that mass murder by gas would be impossible, which Nachtmann wrote was a milestone towards "truth."

In December, the so-called "letter-bomb" trial ended with "not guilty" verdicts for both defendants, Franz Radl, Jr., and Peter Binder. Radl and Binder received prison sentences (three and five years respectively) for *NS-Wiederbetätigung*. The letter-bomb trial rested only on circumstantial evidence; Radl and Binder never made confessions.

The final word came—again—from Jörg Haider. In December, a German television station (ARD) revealed what Haider had told a meeting of former *Waffen SS* members in Carinthia in September 1995. Haider had praised the former *Waffen-SS* members as respectable strong-minded human beings who in times of adversity stuck with their convictions. Though not in the majority at the moment, "we're still mentally superior to the rest," Haider concluded.

The 1995 National Council Elections and Elections to the Styrian State Diet

In October, the grand coalition decided to hold new elections—only one year after the 1994 elections. The main reason was their inability to agree on a budget for 1996. Vice-Chancellor Wolfgang Schüssel (ÖVP) was the main initiator of these new elections; he thought his party might have a chance to overtake the SPÖ (after having been runner-up for twenty-five years).

The main issues in the campaign were budgetary questions and proposals for balancing the budget. Balancing the budget in Austria has entered the forefront of domestic politics as it did in Gingrich's United States.

In December, though, the ÖVP experienced a serious setback to its ambitions. Though the ÖVP scored small gains, the SPÖ again improved its standing among the voters.

Table 2: December 1995 National Council Election Results

Party	1995 National Election (% of total vote)	Margin of Change in %	Number of Seats in Parliament 1995	1994 National Election (% of total vote)
SPÖ	38.1	+ 3.2	71 (+ 6)	34.9
ÖVP	28.3	+ 0.6	53 (+ 1)	27.7
FPÖ	21.9	- 0.6	40 (- 2)	22.5
Greens	4.8	- 2.5	9 (- 4)	7.3
Liberals	5.5	- 0.5	10 (- 1)	6.0

Source: Complied from official data.

In this election both the SPÖ and ÖVP made modest gains for the first time since 1983. The SPÖ's success was due in part to the fact that during the campaign ÖVP chairman Wolfgang Schüssel had never made it clear that a middle-right ÖVP-FPÖ coalition was out of the question. Thus the SPÖ could successfully warn the voters of a possible black (ÖVP) and blue (FPÖ) coalition. For the first time since 1983 the FPÖ lost voters. After increasing their vote from 5 percent (1983) to 22.2 percent (1994), the FPÖ was one of the losers of these elections.

The other opposition parties, the Greens and the Liberals lost, too. The Greens hardly scored enough votes to stay in parliament.

On the same day, "an earthquake shattered the ÖVP-Styria" as *Die Presse* commented on these crucial state election results.

Table 3: December 1995 Styrian Elections

Party	1995 Election Results in %	Margin of Change in %	1995 Number of Seats	1991 Election Results in %
ÖVP	36.6	- 7.9	21 (- 5)	44.2
SPÖ	36.0	+ 1.1	21	34.9
FPÖ	17.2	+ 1.8	10 (+ 1)	15.4
GREENS	4.2	+ 1.3	2 (+ 2)	2.9
LIBERALS	3.8	+ 3.8	2 (+ 2)	n.p.*

Source: Official election data.
* n.p.—no participation in these elections.

The Styrian People's Party lost nearly 8 percent and the Social Democrats almost gained the majority of the votes.

Immediately after the elections, the long time Styrian governor Josef Krainer handed in his resignation. Krainer's successor is Waltraud Klasnic. Klasnic is the first female governor in Austria. A middle-right coalition of the People's Party and the Freedom Party brought her to power and in turn the People's Party supported the Freedom Party's candidate for the Third President of the National Assembly.

The Death of Hermann Langbein

Hermann Langbein died on 24 October 1995. Langbein was a former inmate in Auschwitz and one of the leading members of the camp resistance (*Widerstandsgruppe Auschwitz*). After his liberation, Langbein became one of the most important chroniclers of Auschwitz and of National Socialist extermination policies. Langbein was also one of the initiators of the Frankfurt Auschwitz trial in the 1960s.

In Austria, Langbein got the Ministry of Education to agree that victims of National Socialist terrorism could be invited to schools and talk to pupils about their experience. On the issues of moral conscience and Holocaust remembrance he played a similar role in Austria that Leon Wieseltier played in the international community.

Final Remarks

Looking back at 1995, there was one outstanding political affair: the bomb attack in Oberwart. The grisly murder of four gypsies signals a growing lack of political sensitivity and a deterioration of the political climate in Austria. Such political assassinations are only possible within a special political atmosphere. Open terror and violence have been encouraged by brutal and violent political discourse on the right of the political spectrum. Responsible for these murders are both those who committed the crimes and also those who have been preparing the political climate necessary for nourishing terrorism of this sort.

Despite this outstanding act of violence, there is reason for some optimism. The result of the general elections of December 1995 was not the beginning of Haider's "Third Republic"—but a possible beginning of the restoration of both the Social Democrats and the People's Party. The first loss of the Freedom Party in elections since Haider's takeover in 1986 can be seen as a sign for the people's demand for stability instead of crude emotionalism. Haider is the Pat Buchanan of Austrian politics. For the time being his crude populism has been contained.

FURTHER LITERATURE

Bundespressedienst des Bundeskanzleramtes, *Der Österreich-Bericht*, vol. 46 (Vienna: 1995).

Müller, Wolfgang C., Fritz Plasser, and Peter A. Ulram, eds., *Wählerverhalten und Parteienwettbewerb* (Vienna: Signum Verlag, 1995).

Nick, Rainer and Anton Pelinka, *Österreichs politische Landschaft* (Innsbruck: Haymon-Verlag, 1993).

Plasser, Fritz, Peter A. Ulram, Erich Neuwirth, Franz Sommer, *Analyse der Nationalratswahl vom 17. Dezember 1995* (Vienna: Fessel + GfK Institut für Marktforschung und Zentrum für angewandte Politikforschung, 1995).

Der Standard

Die Presse

News

profil

Salzburger Nachrichten

List of Authors

Brigitte Bailer is a research fellow at the *Dokumentationsarchiv des Österreichischen Widerstandes* in Vienna.

Gunda Barth-Scalmani is an assistant professor of Austrian history at the University of Innsbruck.

Siegfried Beer is an assistant professor of modern history at the University of Graz and in 1996/97 will be a Schumpeter fellow at Harvard University.

Chad Berry is an assistant professor of history at Maryville College in Maryville, Tennessee.

Matthew Paul Berg is an assistant professor of history at John Carroll University in Cleveland, Ohio.

Reinhold Gärtner is a research fellow at the Institute of Politics at the University of Innsbruck.

Robert E. Herzstein is a Carolina Research Professor in History at the University of South Carolina.

Wolfram Kaiser is a research fellow at the University of Essen and affiliated with the Institute of Contemporary History in Vienna.

Robert Knight is a lecturer in history at the Department of European Studies at Loughborough University.

Günther Kronenbitter is an assistant professor of history at Augsburg University and in the fall of 1995 was a visiting professor at the University of British Columbia in Vancouver.

Hermann J.W. Kuprian is an assistant professor of Austrian history at the University of Innsbruck.

Richard Luther is a lecturer in politics at the Department of Politics at Keele University.

Radomir Luža is professor emeritus of history at Tulane University and a frequent visiting professor at Brno University; he now lives in Pennsylvania.

Andrei S. Markovits is professor and chair, Board of Studies in Politics, at the University of California in Santa Cruz, and in the spring of 1996 was a visiting Fulbright professor at the Institute of Politics at the University of Innsbruck.

Franz Mathis is a professor of social and economic history at the University of Innsbruck.

Brigitte Mazohl-Wallnig is a professor of Austrian history at the University of Innsbruck.

Timothy Naftali is an assistant professor of history at the University of Hawaii at Manoa; in the fall of 1995 he was a research fellow at the Charles Warren Center for American History at Harvard University and in the spring of 1996 a research fellow at the Kennan Institute of Advanced Russian Studies at the Woodrow Wilson Center in Washington, D.C.

Rüdiger Overmans is a research scholar in Potsdam at the German *Militärgeschichtliches Forschungsamt*.

Daniel E. Rogers is an assistant professor of history at the University of South Alabama in Mobile, Alabama, and is an editor of H-German on the Internet.

Dieter Stiefel is professor of social and economic history at the University of Vienna and acts as the Austrian coordinator of the Schumpeter programs at Harvard University.

Heidemarie Uhl is a research fellow at the Institute of Contemporary History at the University of Graz.